Key Issues in Sustainable Development and Learning

A critical review

Edited by
**William Scott and
Stephen Gough**

**With a foreword by Sir Neil Chalmers
Director of the Natural History Museum**

 RoutledgeFalmer
Taylor & Francis Group

LONDON AND NEW YORK

First published 2004
by RoutledgeFalmer
11 New Fetter Lane, London EC4P 4EE

Simultaneously published in the USA and Canada
by RoutledgeFalmer
29 West 35th Street, New York, NY 10001

RoutledgeFalmer is an imprint of the Taylor & Francis Group

Typeset in Baskerville by
Florence Production Ltd, Stoodleigh, Devon
Printed and bound in Great Britain by
MPG Books Ltd, Bodmin, Cornwall

British Library Cataloguing in Publication Data
A catalogue record for this book is available from the British Library

Library of Congress Cataloging in Publication Data
A catalog record for this book has been requested

ISBN 0–415–27649–7 (hbk)
ISBN 0–415–27650–0 (pbk)

CONTENTS

With the consent of publishers, we have extracted these readings from books, journals and other published documentation, and though we have often taken the readings from much longer texts, we think that each makes a substantial argument as it stands. At the same time, however, we do recommend that if readers want to engage intensively with particular texts they should consult the originals. Please note that square brackets around an ellipsis [. . .] shows that some of the author's original text has been removed, and when there are square brackets around some text, e.g. [these], this is our addition or rewording to improve comprehension.

CONTRIBUTORS TO VIGNETTES

Chet A. Bowers is now retired, and serves as Adjunct Professor of Environmental Studies at the University of Oregon. He has authored fifteen books and has lectured at universities in South Africa, Australia, Hong Kong, Canada, Europe and South America. His most recent books include *Educating for an Ecologically Sustainable Culture* (1995), *The Culture of Denial* (1997), *Let Them Eat Data* (2000), *Educating for Eco-justice and Community* (2001), *Detras de la Apariencia* (2002), *The False Promises of Constructivist Theories of Learning* is now in press.
Email: chetbowers@earthlink.net

Judy Braus has been actively involved in national and international environmental education efforts for more than twenty-five years and is currently the Director of Education at World Wildlife Fund. She has written and edited a number of books and other publications for educators, the public and young people.
Email: judy.braus@wwfus.org

Bjarne Bruun Jensen is Professor and Director of the Research Program for Environmental and Health Education at the Danish University of Education. His main research areas are: action-oriented health and environmental education, ideologies in environmental and health education and promotion, pupils' concepts of health and action, children and schools as catalysts of social change, and action competence.
Email: bjbj@dpu.dk

Darlene E. Clover was Co-coordinator of the International Journal for Environmental Education at the 1992 Rio Earth Summit and Coordinator of a global programme on environmental adult education from 1995 to 2000. She is currently a Professor in Leadership Studies at the University of Victoria, British Columbia.
Email: clover@uvic.ca

Andrew Dobson is Professor of Politics at the Open University. He is an environmental political theorist and his publications in this area include: *Green Political Thought, Justice and the Environment* and *Fairness and Futurity* (ed.). His latest book is *Citizenship and the Environment*. He is now working on globalization and justice, and on 'nature' and the production of human identity.
Email: A.N.H.Dobson@open.ac.uk

John Fien is Professor of Environmental Education at Griffith University, Brisbane, Australia, where he is also Director of the EcoCentre, the university's community outreach and environmental training centre. His research spans formal and informal education and includes studies of youth environmentalism, teacher professional development in environmental education, the politics of education and sustainable development and issues of social learning, public participation and community change. He is the chief author of the UNESCO multimedia teacher education programme, *Teaching and Learning for a Sustainable Future*, www.unesco.org/education/tlsf. Email: J.Fien@mailbox.gu.edu.au

John Foster is Research Fellow in the Institute for Environment, Philosophy and Public Policy at Lancaster University. He has worked in school teaching and management as well as academia. When challenged, he describes himself as a philosopher. His interests include economics, ethics, literature and education in their environmental contexts.
Email: j.foster@lancaster.ac.uk

Bronwen Golder has worked for the WWF for the past ten years. Her work with WWF conservation programmes and partners around the world has focused on strategic planning, socio-economic/environment linkages, coalition building and learning. She is currently providing support to large-scale conservation initiatives across the Asia Pacific.
Email: bgolder@xtra.co.nz

Noel Gough is Associate Professor in the School of Social and Cultural Studies in Education at Deakin University. He teaches curriculum inquiry, postpositivist research methodologies and futures in education, and has reasearch interests in environmental education, cultural studies of science and the globalization of knowledge work.
Email: noelg@deakin.edu.au

Paul Hart is Professor of Science and Environmental Education in the University of Regina Faculty of Education where he currently teaches graduate courses in research methods and curriculum studies. His research, funded by the Social Sciences and Humanities Research Council, includes studies on teacher thinking and children's ideas in environmental education. He is an executive editor of the *Journal of Environmental Education*, and a member of the Board of the North American Association of Environmental Education.
Email: paul.hart@uregina.ca

Helen Haste is Professor of Psychology at the University of Bath. Her research publications include work on the psychological and cultural functions of metaphor, science and culture, gender issues and the development of social and moral values with particular reference to citizenship education, on which she is currently writing a book. She is the author or editor of six books including *The Sexual Metaphor*.
Email: helhaste@aol.com

Joe E. Heimlich works in teaching-learning exchange theory across the lifespan and has been engaged in the arena of environmental free-choice learning for 13 years. He is Professor of Environmental Education and Interpretation at the Ohio State University and Senior Research Associate with the Institute for Learning Innovation in Annapolis, Maryland.
Email: heimlich.1@osu.edu

Lesley Le Grange is Professor of Education at the University of Stellenbosch. He teaches and researches in the fields of environmental education, science education and research methodologies. He is Associate Editor of the *South African Journal of Higher Education* and is a rated social scientist in South Africa.
Email: llg@sun.ac.za

Gustavo López Ospina is the Director of the UNESCO regional office for the Andean countries and is based in Quito, Venezuela. Prior to this, he was the Director of UNESCO's Transdisciplinary Programme, Education for a Sustainable Future, where he was responsible for the development of innovative international programmes to facilitiate the reorientation of education towards sustainable development. He has also served as UNESCO's chief representative at the United Nations in New York.
Email: glopez@unesco.org.ec

Timothy W. Luke is University Distinguished Professor of Political Science at Virginia Polytechnic Institute and State University in Blacksburg, Virginia. His research interests are focused upon issues in political and social theory, international affairs and environmental politics.
Email: twluke@vt.edu

André Mottart studied Linguistics and Literature, worked as teacher and teacher-trainer, and wrote a Ph.D. on Education and Knowledge as Postmodern Constructions. He now works in the Education Department at Ghent University where his teaching and research focus on: language/literature teaching, teacher training, multiliteracies in general, qualitative research and academic literacies.
Email: Andre.Mottart@UGent.be

Richard D. North was (1986–1990) Environment Correspondent of *The Independent* and a columnist on green issues for the *Sunday Times* (1990–1992). His *Life On a Modern Planet, A Manifesto for Progress* (Manchester University Press, 1995) summed up that work and his www.richarddnorth.com develops the themes.
Email: rdn@richarddnorth.com

Tim O'Riordan is Professor of Environmental Sciences at the University of East Anglia in Norwich. He promotes the cause of interdisciplinarity and sustainability science. He is active in actual case work on inclusive public involvement in complex decision making over sustainability themes. He is a member of the UK Sustainable Development Commission, The Prince of Wales Business and Environment Programme and is a Fellow of the British Academy. His research covers the movement to governance for sustainability at all scales of governing, but especially at local government level. He plays the classical double bass to reflect life passing by graciously.
Email: t.oriordan@uea.ac.uk

Michael Peters is Research Professor of Education at the University of Glasgow (UK). He has research interests in educational theory and policy, and in contemporary philosophy. He has published many articles and books in these fields, including most recently: *Critical Theory and the Human Condition* (eds) (2003), *Heidegger, Education and Modernity* (ed.) (2002), and *Poststructuralism, Marxism and Neoliberalism: Between Politics and Theory* (2001).
Email: m.peters@educ.gla.ac.uk

John Quicke was formerly Professor of Education in the Department of Educational Studies at the University of Sheffield and now works part-time as an Educational Psychologist for Rotherham LEA. He has worked as a teacher in primary and secondary schools. As director of an ESRC-funded project, he developed a research programme which examined the social and cultural aspects of learning. He has written *A Curriculum for Life, The Cautious Expert, Disability in Modern Children's Fiction* and *Challenging Prejudice Through Education*, plus numerous journal articles.
Email: john@quicke.fslife.co.uk

Franz Rauch is Associate Professor at the Centre for Interdisciplinary Research and Continuing Education of Austrian Universities, Department of School and Societal Learning, and is Head of the Professional Development of Teachers Division. His interests include: education for sustainable development, school development and school leadership, continuing education for teachers, action research and networking. Email: franz.rauch@uni-klu.ac.at

Alan Reid is Lecturer in the Centre for Research in Education and the Environment at the University of Bath. His academic interests focus on the philosophy, policy and practice of environmental education and geography education in schools, within the wider context of deliberations and research on education, environment and sustainable development. Email: a.d.reid@bath.ac.uk

Michael Redclift is Professor of International Environmental Policy in the Geography Department of King's College, University of London. His principal interests include the environment and development, especially in Spain and Latin America. Currently he is working in the Yucatan peninsula and the Mexican Caribbean, where he is undertaking research into the history of chewing gum and the impacts of tourism on human security. Email: michael.r.redclift@kcl.ac.uk

Lucie Sauvé is Professor at the Faculty of Science Education of the University of Québec at Montréal and titular Research Chair of Canada in environmental education. She is Director of the UQAM postgraduate programme in environmental education and Co-director of the international research journal *Éducation relative à l'environnement*. Email: sauve.lucie@uqam.ca

Karsten Schnack is Professor in Educational Theory and Curriculum at the Danish University of Education; he is a core member of the Research Program for Environmental and Health Education, and his main research areas are: action competence as an educational ideal, education and democracy, ideologies in sustainable development, environmental and health education, comparative curriculum research and participation and action research. Email: schnack@dpu.dk

Michael Singh is Professor of Education at the University of Western Sydney where he is engaged in collaborative research into issues of social justice and socio-cultural diversity. His research on global/local education takes issues concerning eco-cultural sustainability as its integrating theme. Email: m.j.singh@uws.edu.au

John Smyth is an Emeritus Professor of Biology and was President of the Scottish Environment Education Council. Among other international activities he was rapporteur to the working group which advised the UNCED secretariat on the content of *Agenda 21*: *chapter 36*, on education, public awareness and training. Email: JOHNSMYTH@aol.com

Ronald Soetaert studied Linguistics and Literature. He worked in Teacher Education, received his Ph.D. in the Faculty of Arts and Philosophy (The Communicative Turn in Education), and now has a Chair in the Education Department at Ghent University. His research and teaching focus on: language/literature teaching, multi-literacies, cultural studies and new media. Email: Ronald.Soetaert@UGent.be

Stephen Sterling is a Consultant in Environmental and Sustainability Education working in the academic and NGO fields. He was an architect of the Education for Sustainability masters programme at South Bank University, London, where he is an academic tutor. Key publications include, *Education for Sustainability*, *Education for Sustainable Development in the Schools Sector* and *Sustainable Education – Re-visioning Learning and Change*.
Email: srsterling@compuserve.com

Michael Strain teaches at the University of Ulster, where he is Course Director for the Doctor of Education. His research interests are in lifelong learning and the social organization of learning. His recent publications explore alternative conceptions of a knowledge economy and their implications for social justice.
Email: dm.strain@ulster.ac.uk

Arjen E.J. Wals is Associate Professor within the Education and Competence Studies Group of the Wageningen University of the Netherlands. He specializes in sustainability education and social learning. His Ph.D., obtained from the University of Michigan under the guidance of the late William B. Stapp, focused on young adolescents' perceptions of nature and environmental issues.
Email: arjen.wals@wur.nl

FOREWORD

Few issues are so important but so elusive as sustainable development, and there can be very few such issues indeed where the role of learning is so crucially important to our future. To many people, sustainable development is a difficult and nebulous concept and yet its main themes are fundamental to the daily lives of everybody on our planet. People from all walks of life, whether they be politicians, business leaders, journalists, educators, working people, students, parents or people in retirement, readily appreciate and often have strong views about the main components of sustainable development. How we generate enough wealth to enjoy a good quality of life; how we organize our society so that this quality of life is available to all; how we do so in a way that protects our wonderfully rich but fragile natural world are all things that, to a greater or lesser degree, are understood to be important. But learning about sustainable development is more than learning about economic development, social policy or environmental protection. It is a question of learning about how these three fundamental areas are intimately related. It is a question of learning about the perspective of time.

There are hard issues to tackle. The resources of our natural world help us to create the wealth that, if wisely used, will enable people to enjoy a good standard of living. Yet we must not use such resources in a way that compromises the ability of future generations to create a good standard of living for themselves in turn. In particular, we must not allow our pursuit of wealth-generation in the short term to mutilate or destroy our natural environment, for not only can this undermine the important cultural and aesthetic contribution that the environment makes to our lives, but it can imperil the very survival of countless people.

Sustainable development presents a complex and challenging learning agenda and raises many questions. What skills are needed to learn effectively across all of the many components of sustainable development? How can learning experiences best be designed for all of the many stakeholders for whom such learning is, or should be, essential? How does one create learning programmes suited respectively to governments, to the world of work, to the formal education sector and to life-long learners? How do we measure the effectiveness of different vehicles for learning about sustainable development? And how do we measure the effectiveness, or otherwise, of the outcomes in the field of sustainable development itself?

It is this crucial interface between sustainable development and learning that is explored in the two books. In *Key Issues in Sustainable Development and Learning* William Scott and Stephen Gough draw upon key readings from the literature, each of which is accompanied by concise critical appraisals by leading authorities in the field of learning and sustainable development. The companion volume *Sustainable Development and Learning*, written by Scott and Gough, adopts the same framework, setting out an authoritative and searching analysis of the concepts underpinning sustainable development. They explore policy, then range across many important areas including learning, theory and practice, evaluation and future challenges.

The World Summit on Sustainable Development in 2002 in Johannesburg showed us the overwhelming need for effective learning in relation to sustainable development. These two books are therefore exceedingly timely and will be invaluable to all, whether they be professionals in the field, those undertaking academic programmes of study and research, or readers from a wide variety of other backgrounds who need to explore further this vitally important field.

Neil Chalmers
The Natural History Museum

ACKNOWLEDGEMENTS

In putting this book together, we have attempted to identify key literature from significant contexts across the world which has a bearing on the relationships between sustainable development and learning, and we are grateful for publishers' permissions to reproduce these texts here. We have also sought out a number of significant current writers and researchers to comment critically and succinctly on those extracts, and we are very grateful to all those who have contributed, not only for what they have done, but for their patience during the editorial process. In assembling this text and its companion book *Sustainable Development and Learning: Framing the Issues*, we owe a debt of gratitude to many people and institutions; to attempt to identify everyone individually runs the risk of inexplicable and unforgivable omission. However, it is very clear that the following networks and organizations need a special mention and a big on-going 'thank you':

- our close colleagues in the Centre for Research in Education and the Environment at Bath with whom it is a privilege to work;
- the wider network of colleagues in the Department of Education and the University's International Centre for the Environment who are a constant source of stimulus and opportunity;
- colleagues working in nearby universities, NGOs and local government whose work 'on the ground' is of continued interest and hope;
- members of the UK's FERN research network whose friendly stimulus and penetrating challenge to each other is an excellent example of effective collegiality;
- the director and staff of the UK's Council for Environmental Education whose keen interest in these issues is matched only by a dedicated professionalism which greatly benefits the field;
- editors within RoutledgeFalmer who not only put so much into this text and its companion publication, but who also, via Taylor & Francis, provide continuing world-class support for the development of *Environmental Education Research* as a vehicle for exploring the important ideas we are discussing here;
- colleagues within national and international NGOs and government ministries and agencies whose interest and stimulus are felt across sectors;

- colleagues who come together for regular international research development seminars which continue to prove so valuable in nurturing new researchers and stimulating cooperation;
- colleagues within the North American Association of Environmental Education who bring long-established and well-honed expertise and interest but who are not afraid to think outside the box;
- colleagues within the special interest group on ecological and environmental education in the American Educational Research Association whose annual meetings helpfully continue to provoke and inform in equal measure;
- colleagues within the Worldwide Fund for Nature for the continuing invaluable stimulus to our thinking, and the Director of Education and her colleagues within the US's World Wildlife Fund for the highest quality of partnership one could desire.

And finally (but in truth, firstly and uniquely), there are Jean, Pam, Ruth, Jim, Jonathan and Alex to whom this book is dedicated with love and gratitude.

William Scott and Stephen Gough
Bath, 2003

INTRODUCTION

These two companion books, *Key Issues in Sustainable Development and Learning: A Critical Review* and *Sustainable Development and Learning: Framing the Issues*, explore in complementary ways the relationships between learning and sustainable development. This book, *Key Issues in Sustainable Development and Learning: A Critical Review*, uses the same chapter headings as the companion book and explores differing perspectives by presenting seminal readings from existing literature alongside specially commissioned critical vignettes from leading practitioners with interests in sustainable development and learning.

The central thesis of both books is that there is a need to bring about constructive engagement between the diverse perspectives on both learning and sustainable development, and to explore their interrelationship. In order to do this, the books set out to communicate both the essentials and the complexities of a wide range of interrelated issues, raising important topics for discussion, reflection, and on-going consideration by readers. These books are written for all those with an interest in sustainable development and learning and for those who, irrespective of background and discipline, are seeking support for professional activities, and/or undertaking academic programmes of study.

A matter of definition

Definition is, of course crucial, and a major purpose of the books is to help readers to develop an understanding of both sustainable development and learning.

There exists considerable confusion in the popular usage of the phrases 'sustainable development' and 'sustainability', and often the terms are used interchangeably. The literature, however, shows a clear distinction in meanings. The Brundtland Commission (1987) saw sustainable development as a process of change with the future in mind: '... a process where the exploitation, the orientation of technological development and institutional change, are made consistent with future as well as present needs.' For Hamm and Muttagi (1998), the goal of sustainability is: '... a capacity of human beings to continuously adapt to their non-human environments by means of social organisation.'

The notion of sustainable development that informs both books is that of a process through which we shall need to learn to live more in tune with the environment. But it is not enough to say that sustainable development and learning need to go hand in hand. Rather, we need to recognize that there will be no sustainable development where learning is not happening. Thus, sustainable development is, for us, inherently a learning process through which we can, if we choose, learn to build capacity to live more sustainably.

Emphasizing learning

The emphasis on *learning* here (rather than on teaching, instruction, training or other input processes) is deliberate for two reasons. First, the learning that will need to be done transcends schools, colleges and universities; it will be learning in, by and between institutions, organizations and communities – where most of our learning goes on anyway. Thus, we begin with a view of learning which is as inclusive as possible in order to draw in all the learning that a person does (lifelong) between birth and death, including all that done in formal education and training. The second reason is that, as we do not yet know what we shall need to learn in relation to sustainable development, it is hard to be definitive about what needs to be taught, except perhaps that we need to be taught how to learn and how to be critical in order to build our collective capacity to live both sustainably and well.

Rationale

In relation to sustainable development, learning (or, more precisely, life-long learning) has been consistently seen by the United Nations and its agencies, national governments, the European Union, and NGOs as a key component of innovation and development because it is acknowledged as a prime vector of social change. The argument goes: through schooling, further and higher education, professional training and development, and more informal awareness-raising and capacity-building, people can be helped both to begin to understand emerging ideas about the need for change, and to engage in debate and critique of the issues, thus making meaning for themselves and developing personal and social action plans. In addition, it is now widely accepted by institutions and organizations of all kinds that, if change is to be facilitated, bringing the purpose and practice of learning into line with the process of sustainable development, there is a need for (1) new ways of conceiving and operationalizing learning with shifts in curriculum, pedagogy, and in institutional management practice; and (2) novel approaches to the professional development of teachers, trainers, and non-formal educators across the field.

The case relating learning to environmental issues has been advanced by the conservation and environmental education movements for many decades. However, the World Commission on Environment and Development (1987) influentially introduced the terminology of sustainable development, and this became a powerful focus for further work, such as that of the IUCN which, in 1990, produced *Caring for the Earth: A Strategy for Sustainability*. These ideas were further developed through Chapter 36 of *Agenda 21* following the Rio Earth Summit (1992), the UNESCO conference in Thessaloniki on educating for a sustainable future (1997), the UNESCO/World Bank conference on environmentally and socially sustainable development, and other United Nations and NGO initiatives since that time. Additionally, the concept of sustainable development is now subjected to searching scrutiny across the full range of academic disciplines.

Activity and development of these kinds which support the linkage of (lifelong) learning to the process of sustainable development can now be seen both nationally and internationally, and are partly the result of United Nations and other treaty obligations. The effectiveness of developments thus far was an important consideration at the World Summit on Sustainable Development (Rio + 10) in Johannesburg in 2002. Many issues, of course, remain. Though sustainable development is now actively pursued in many quarters, there exists a range of not necessarily compatible views about what exactly it is, how it might best be pursued, and the nature of the changes which will most appropriately support such developments. Because of this and other factors, progress is variable both in scale and scope from one place to another. It is, however, this very contentiousness which underlines the need for the sort of critical exploration of issues which these books set out to achieve as they explore and open up the issues for study. The main point, however, which is compatible with both the goals of learning and sustainable development, is to help people build personal and social capacity so that they, as learners and social actors, are enabled to grapple with the issues and relate them to their own lives and work, while at the same time appreciating and empathizing with the perspectives of other individuals and institutions whose social context and the issues they face may well be quite different.

This book, together with its companion volume, will enable readers to explore both the practical and theoretical consequences of the idea of sustainable development for learning, and help readers develop their own understandings. It will provide a means by which readers can explore the continuing development of their own and others' positions in relation to explicit and implicit theories of both learning and sustainable development, recognizing that different approaches to practice are likely to be grounded in, and defended on, particular ideological grounds, and contested by others. The book focuses on the joint development of curriculum and management in order to meet the demands of learners, and critiques programmes which have little or no regard for the management realities of effective curriculum and institutional development. Structural and pedagogical issues are explored in relation to curriculum design. A range of assessment and evaluation approaches which have been used in practice are critically appraised from a number of theoretical positions. Problems underlying the design and application of assessment and evaluation instruments are explored in relation to practical questions concerning how we can know whether learning is taking place, how we can know that sustainable development has been enhanced, and what indicators can sensibly be used to gain such information. The concept of social capacity building for sustainable development is explored. Readers are encouraged to develop informed views of how learning might best link to other key elements in capacity building. The relationship between environmentally beneficial behaviour and economically beneficial behaviour is explored. In particular, the book examines reasons for the apparent oppositions between these desired ends. Readers are encouraged to reflect on the implications for their own professional work of the insight that economics and ecology are inseparable and interdependent. The book examines how contemporary life can be characterized by two apparently contradictory trends: towards globalization (of language, meanings, symbols, economic structures, communications etc.) and towards fragmentation (of nation states, belief systems, cultures, families etc.). It involves readers in an exploration of the prospects for learning focused on sustainable development as a global process, but one which is targeted at what people and institutions do, each in their own time and place.

Each of the fourteen chapters has a distinctive focus, although the structure is broadly similar. Each chapter begins with two keynote readings which have been selected to exemplify the issues being discussed. Typically, these readings are brief extracts from more lengthy papers, chapters or documents. These readings are then followed by a number of specially commissioned vignettes which explore the issues raised by the readings. Vignette writers were asked to focus on the issues raised by the key readings, but were invited, where appropriate and sensible, to draw more widely on the full text from which the readings were taken and to refer to other published works, including their own. In doing this, we were looking for a focus on the issues, rather than seeking a particular approach. As a consequence, the vignettes vary considerably in a pleasing way regarding both style and format.

CHAPTER 1

FRAMING THE ISSUES: COMPLEXITY, UNCERTAINTY, RISK AND NECESSITY

READING 1.1 DIVIDED WE STAND: REDEFINING POLITICS, TECHNOLOGY AND SOCIAL CHOICE

M. Schwarz and M. Thompson

Source: University of Pennsylvania Press, Philadelphia, 1990: 4–13

Ecologists who study *managed* ecosystems, such as forests, fisheries and grasslands, encounter the managing institutions as sets of interventions in those systems. Time and time again they have found that different managing institutions, faced with exactly the same kinds of situation, adopt strategies based on one of four different interpretations of ecosystem stability (Holling 1979, 1986; Timmerman 1986). These four 'myths of nature' as they call them – each of which, the ecologists insist, captures *some* essence of experience and wisdom – can be graphically represented by a ball in a landscape (Figure 1).

Nature benign gives us global equilibrium. Such a world is wonderfully forgiving: no matter what knocks we deliver the ball will always return to the bottom of the basin. The managing institutions can therefore have a *laissez-faire* attitude. *Nature ephemeral* is almost the exact opposite. The world, it tells us, is a terribly unforgiving place and the least jolt may cause its catastrophic collapse. The managing institutions must treat the ecosystem with great care. This is the view of the German Greens. *Nature perverse/tolerant*, though it may look like a cross between the first two, is quite different. Its world is one that is forgiving of most events, but is vulnerable to an occasional knocking of the ball over the rim. The managing institutions must therefore regulate against unusual occurrences. Our multinational is to be found here. It accepts that the small risk of disaster necessitates government regulation, but believes that, once minimum standards

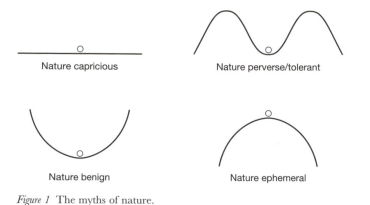

Nature capricious

Nature perverse/tolerant

Nature benign

Nature ephemeral

Figure 1 The myths of nature.

have been met, it should be free to make its own decisions. Finally, *nature capricious* is a random world; institutions with this view of nature do not really manage, nor do they learn. They just cope with erratic events.

Each of these views of nature appears irrational from the perspective of any other. For the Greens, the multinational is irrational because it fails to see that paradichloro-benzene could be the final insult that sends the ball rolling down the slope. For the multinational, the Greens' failure to recognize that nature is relatively stable creates an irrational concern with 'obviously' minor risks, like paradichlorobenzene and a neglect of apparently more serious ones, such as smoking or car-driving. As a result, society is deprived of the benefits of innovation.

Another way of putting it is that each actor is perfectly rational, given his or her convictions as to how the world is. The situation is one of *plural rationality*, and the question it prompts us to ask is: how is each actor given his or her convictions? This brings us to the social science.

The social science

The four myths of nature identified by ecologists map onto the typology of social relationships that has been developed by the anthropologist Mary Douglas and her co-workers (Douglas 1978, 1982; Thompson 1983a, b; Gross and Rayner 1985). This typology is based on the answers to two central and eternal questions of human existence: 'who am I?' and 'how should I behave?' Personal identity, it is argued, is determined by individuals' relationships to *groups*. Those who belong to a strong group – a collective that makes decisions binding on all members – will see themselves very differently to those who have weak ties with others and therefore make choices that bind only themselves. Behaviour is shaped by the extent of the social prescriptions (the *grid* dimension) that an individual is subject to: a spectrum which runs from the free spirit to the tightly constrained. These two 'dimensions of sociality', as they are called, generate four basic, and stabilizable, forms of social relationship. And, in each instance, just one of the plural rationalities can *do* the stabilizing (Figure 2).

Two of these 'archetypes' – individualists and hierarchists – are already familiar to social scientists. Indeed, the sociologist Max Weber (1958), the political scientist Charles Lindblom (1977) and the institutional economist Oliver Williamson (1975), are only three of the scholars who have based entire bodies of theory on this distinction between *markets* and *hierarchies*, and the accompanying observation that each promotes a distinctive form of rationality that legitimizes and enables its operation. Market cultures stress the autonomy of individuals and their resulting freedom to bid and bargain with each other: they have a *substantive rationality*. The 'bottom line' is what they care for, not the relational niceties of the people who happen to have come together to achieve that result. Hierarchies are made up of bounded social groups, each of which is in an orderly and ranked relationship with each other. Their attempts to coordinate these components, without violating status differentials, creates a *procedural rationality* that is more concerned with the proprieties of who does what than with trying to evaluate the outcome (if there is one).

But this is an inadequate taxonomy. Many people reject both the individualism of the market and the inequalities of the hierarchy: they prefer the *egalitarian groups* of our diagram. They have a communal and *critical rationality*, which stresses the importance of fraternal and sororal cooperation, and therefore strives for social relationships that are voluntaristic and egalitarian. But, since this desired state of affairs is always threatened by the encroachment of hierarchy (which brings status differences) or by excessive individualism (which all too easily introduces inequalities of wealth, power

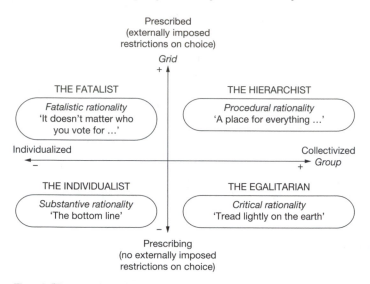

Figure 2 The two dimensions of sociality and the four rationalities.

and knowledge), collective identity has all the time to be sustained by a shared and strident criticism of what goes on outside the group. Historically, this rationality has been the driving force of socialism (but, as that movement has grown, it has been increasingly diluted by hierarchy and political entrepreneurialism) and today it is alive and well as the preferred organizational form of the Greens (and of many single-issue public interest groups in the United States).

It is also a cruel travesty to describe all those who are individualized as bustling and untrammelled entrepreneurs: as paid-up members of 'the enterprise culture'. Many have so many prescriptions on their behaviour that they have minimal freedom of choice: for example, the unemployed, trailing from one welfare centre to another *ad infinitum*. These are the marginal members of society – *the fatalists* – whose inability to influence events this way or that engenders a *fatalistic rationality* in which outcomes, good or bad, are simply to be enjoyed or endured, but never achieved.

Each of these rationalities, when acted upon, both sustains and justifies the particular organizational form that goes along with it. The high-rise, system-built tower block, for instance, is the hierarchist's solution to the housing problem; gentrification, the individualist's; cooperative self-build, the egalitarian's; homelessness, the fatalist's. Hierarchists trim and prune social transactions until they fit neatly into their orderly ambit, individualists pull them into the marketplace, egalitarians strive to capture them into a kind of voluntary minimalism (which, to those on the outside, often looks more like 'coercive utopianism'), and fatalists endure with more or less dignity whatever comes their way.

We can now see how each of the myths of nature (the ecologist's explanation for 'managerial heterogeneity') legitimates and reproduces certain kinds of institutional relationships (the anthropologist's cultural categories) (Figure 3).

This diagram, of course, is just the two earlier ones – the ecologist's and the anthropologist's – combined, and to back-track for a moment, this is what we meant about the study of contradictory certainties bringing natural and social scientists together in a new and interesting way.

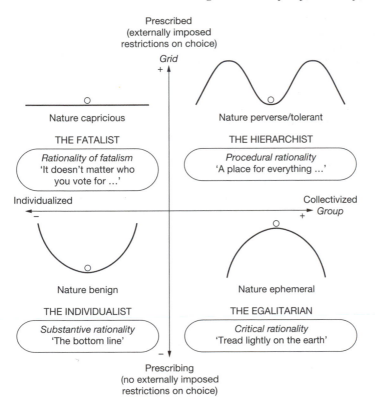

Figure 3 The myths of nature mapped onto the rationalities.

The new synthesis

The world of nature benign is most hospitable to individualists. As long as we all do our individualistic, exuberant things, a 'hidden hand' (the uniformly downward slope of the landscape) will lead us to the best possible outcome. Since restrictions on individual freedom, and therefore on experimentation, would impede the attainment of this outcome, the myth of a benign nature furnishes a powerful moral justification for these particular modes of acting and learning. If we take, for example, the topical issue of hazardous waste management, nature benign would indicate that a sharpening of market incentives (transferable 'rights to pollute', brokers to reduce the transaction and information costs of connecting some firms' waste streams into other firms' feedstocks, self-policing to increase consumer confidence, etc.) is the way to go.

By contrast, an ephemeral nature suits egalitarian groups very well. Their small-scale organizations tread lightly upon our fragile earth, and they are only too happy to re-educate those who, in persisting in stamping around wildly, threaten the destruction of the entire planet. Minimal perturbation becomes the overriding moral imperative, and small becomes beautiful. Trials can go ahead only if it is certain there will be no errors. By these criteria many of the products of our consumer society are not just unnecessary, they are actually destroying the one earth that should be our most sacred trust. The myth of nature ephemeral tells us that there will have to be radical change *now*, before it is too late. Since most hazardous wastes are discharged into the environment from the production systems that, directly or indirectly, give us all these products (rim-blocks, for instance) that we do not need and should not have, the solution is an outright ban (or, better still, a consumer rejection) on all unnecessary products: a solution that has the added advantage of bringing us much nearer to the desired future – harmony with nature.

Nature perverse/tolerant requires strong social controls to ensure that the ball never crosses the rim. And to apply those controls effectively you need precise knowledge of the line between equilibrium and disequilibrium. Neither the unbridled experimentation that goes with the zone of equilibrium, nor the timorous forbearance that accompanies the zone of disequilibrium can command much moral authority here. Rather, every-thing hinges upon mapping and managing the boundary line that separates these zones. Complete knowledge, certainty and predictability, generated by and for those whose pre-eminent task is to keep each mode of action – social sanctions and individual exper-iments – in its proper place, becomes the dominant moral concern. The situation cries out for hierarchy: sober, expert and, above all, enduring. Only then can we have an orderly solution matched to the time scales and complexities of the problem: standard-setting, cradle-to-grave materials accounting systems, trip tickets, site licences, spot checks and precisely detailed lists of hazardous wastes.

Nature capricious is the natural habitat for those with neither standing nor influ-ence in society. In the other three rationalities, learning is possible (though each is disposed to learn different things) but in the flatland of nature capricious there are no gradients to teach us the differences between hills and dales, up and down, better and worse. Life is, and remains, a lottery. The world does things to you while you do nothing to it. All you can do is try to cope, as best you can, with a situation over which you have no control. Though those who find themselves attached to this myth produce no policies for the management of hazardous wastes, they are by no means irrelevant to those policies that are produced. They are the great risk absorbers, enduring with more or less dignity, greater or lesser ignorance, whatever comes their way: a social sponge that the active policy makers, in their different ways, publicly wring their hands over and privately make good use of. Without the passive risk absorbers (and the contradictory claims that are always made on their behalf), the rest of us would not be able to get any of our preferred policies to work.

It is by teasing out these rationalities that we can begin to make sense of what is going on in all those policy debates that are characterized by contradictory certainties. Though this approach *is* saying that knowledge is socially constructed, it is *not* saying that the world can be any way we want it to be. It is *not* saying that we can know nothing; only that we cannot know everything and that within that uncertain and inchoate region, it is our institutions – our social involvements – that lead us to grant credibility to one possible state of affairs rather than another.

There are a great many predictions that follow from this 'new synthesis', but the most useful for our present purposes is that each rationality will generate its own distinc-tive engineering aesthetic: its own definition of the good, the beautiful and the socially desirable.

Modern hierarchies are biased towards large-scale, high-technology approaches that demand much specialized knowledge and centralized direction. The egalitarians' distaste for these requirements drives them towards small-scale, environmentally benign tech-nology (usually low-tech, but using microelectronics when this saves energy and reduces pollution). For many years their watchword has been 'appropriate technology' but in reality this is the motto of the individualists: it is they who are happy to operate at any size, to any technical specification, within their capabilities, providing it is cheap enough to make them a profit and cheerful enough to attract the punters.

Returning now to the lavatory rim-blocks, we can observe that large corporations face outwardly towards markets but, within themselves, tend to be strongly hierarchical. Their normal manner of progress is towards ever more specialized products, using ever more specialized processes and materials, and ultimately creating ever greater organizational differentiation and complexity. Their primary focus is the internal technology/skills package rather than the customer (the individualists' primary focus) or the human race and its biosphere (the egalitarians' primary focus). Nothing more natural, then, for a multinational to utilize a high-tech material such as paradichlorobenzene (and the moulding technology which goes with it) in one area of its business and then to extend it to others.

But the egalitarian engineering aesthetic is suspicious of lavatory rim-blocks. Are they, like deodorants, a corporate appropriation of hygiene: a conspiracy aimed at convincing us that what is natural is nasty: original sin slickly harnessed to company profits? But, since this critical aesthetic does not (and probably could not) exist within the company, it is initially manifested as *the enemy*, an homogeneous green *other* that threatens not only the company's business but also the entire way of life of its members and of its contented customers.

The individualists are less doctrinally committed. Being pragmatic materialists, they will try to align themselves with whichever development path offers them the best financial prospects. They do exist within our multinational, awaiting, like resting actors, the call of the venture capitalist. They see that the corporation is losing its battle and needs to withdraw; they slowly persuade the startled hierarchy to transfer the Greens from the category of 'alien other' to the more comprehensible one of 'dissatisfied customer'. They do this, not because they have suddenly gone over to vegetarianism and nuclear freezes, but because they know a miserable customer (and eventually) a more profitable product when they see one.

However (and this is the crux of our whole argument), neither the hierarchical nor the individualistic rationality could actually *see* the better product, and switch over to it, until the Greens' rude intrusion forced the non-incremental jump from one development path to another. Without this external pressure, the multinational's obvious capacity to better satisfy each of these aesthetics (for the new high-tech, profitable and environmentally more acceptable product could not otherwise have been developed so quickly) would have remained undeveloped.

The simple but profound message is that the cultural pluralism is *essential*. The three active rationalities – the hierarchical, the individualistic and the egalitarian – structure the world in different and (in the right circumstances) complementary ways.[1] And, lest it appear that, as usual, they have been missed out, we should stress that the fatalists too are essential (in their passive way), because each of the active rationalities seeks to advance its cause by mobilizing them. 'Just get the hierarchists and the egalitarians off their backs', say the individualists, 'and they'll soon lift themselves up by their own bootstraps'. 'Once the inequitable markets and hierarchies have been eliminated', the egalitarians argue, 'there will be no one to poison or otherwise oppress you. Only when we are all meek will we at last inherit our fragile earth'. The hierarchists, pointing to their code of *noblesse oblige*, and to the idea of a ruler being responsive to the (suitably modest) needs of the ruled, argue for the fatalists getting a better deal in the hierarchy than they would in the free-for-all of the marketplace or in the egalitarian millennium (if it ever comes).

By directing our attention to the social influences on cognition, and to the plural rationalities they sustain, this new synthesis tells us that it is our institutions which analyze the inchoate. It is our institutions that are the repositories of our myths: the structures which frame individual awareness (Douglas 1986). And it is in the play of our institutions that wisdom lies, for, as each rationality adapts to the others, so a kind of meta-understanding of the inchoate is generated. Our concern, therefore, should not be with which one is *right* (for that would be to insist that just one rationality had access to 'the truth') but rather with which is *appropriate* to the task at hand. There is no final solution; there is no rationality without its institutional context; there is no complete knowledge. Diversity, contradiction, contention and criticism (the basic ingredients of this 'new synthesis') are the best tools we have for understanding the inchoate. We must learn to husband them and make the most of them. Divided we stand; united we fall.

Notes

[. . .]

1   The ecologist C.S. Holling has captured this complementarity by a meta-myth: nature resilient. Nature resilient focuses on the transformational properties of ball and landscape – the way the movement of the ball actually changes the shape of the landscape through which it moves – and in so doing subsumes the four primary myths as phases within an ever-repeating cycle of transformation.

[. . .]

READING 1.2 RISK SOCIETY: TOWARDS A NEW MODERNITY

U. Beck

Source: Sage, London, 1992: 51–59

Both in the nineteenth century and today, consequences experienced by the bulk of humanity as devastating are connected with the social process of industrialization and modernization. With both epochs we are concerned with drastic and threatening interventions in human living conditions. These appear in connection with definite stages in the development of productive forces, of market integration, and of the relationships of property and power. There may be different material consequences each time – back then, material immiseration, poverty, hunger, crowding; today, the threatening and destruction of the natural foundations of life. There are also comparable aspects, such as the amount of danger and the *systematic nature* of modernization with which it is produced and grows. Therein lies its internal dynamic – not malevolence, but the market, competition, division of labor, all of it just a bit more global today. Just as before, the latency (side effects) can in both cases only be broken through in conflict. Then, as now, people went into the streets to protest, there was, and still is, loud criticism of progress and technology, there was Luddism – and its counter-arguments.

Then came the gradual admission to the problems, as can still be observed today. Systematically produced suffering and oppression become more and more visible and must be recognized by those who have denied them. The law sets its sails to the prevailing wind, by no means voluntarily, but with the powerful support of politics and the streets: universal suffrage, social welfare laws, labor laws and codetermination. The parallels to today are obvious; harmless things, wine, tea, pasta, etc., turn out to be dangerous. Fertilizers become long-term toxins with worldwide consequences. The once highly praised sources of wealth (the atom, chemistry, genetic technology and so on) are transformed into unpredictable sources of danger. The obviousness of the danger places more and more obstacles in the way of the customary routines of minimizing and covering up. The agents of modernization in science, business and politics find themselves placed in the uncomfortable position of a denying defendant breaking into a real sweat because of the chain of circumstantial evidence.

One could almost say, we have seen it all before, there is nothing new. But the systematic differences stick out just as much. The immediacy of personally and socially experienced misery contrasts today with the intangibility of threats from civilization, which only come to consciousness in scientized thought, and cannot be directly related to primary experience. These are the hazards that employ the language of chemical formulas, biological contexts and medical, diagnostic concepts. This constitution of knowledge does not make them any less hazardous, of course. On the contrary, intentionally or not, through accident or catastrophes, in war or peace, a large group of the population faces devastation and destruction today, for which language and the powers of our imagination fail us, for which we lack any moral or medical category. We are concerned with the absolute and unlimited NOT, which threatens us here, the *un- in general*, unimaginable, unthinkable, un-, un-, un-.

But it only *threatens*. Only? Here another essential difference is revealed; we are dealing today with a *threatening possibility*, which sometimes shows a horrified humanity that it is not just a possibility, but a fact *in abeyance* (and not just a chimera of dreamers).

This difference in kind between reality and possibility is further supplemented by the fact that – in the most developed countries with high levels of social security – the immiseration through hazards coincides with the *opposite* of material immiseration (at least if one looks at the images of the nineteenth century and the starving countries in the Third World). The people are not impoverished, but often prosperous; they live in a society of mass consumption and affluence (which can certainly move in tandem with an intensification of social antagonisms); they are mostly well educated and informed but they are afraid, feel threatened and organize themselves in order not to let the only possible test of their realistic-pessimistic visions of the future even happen, or to actually prevent it. A confirmation of the danger would mean irreversible self-annihilation, and this is the argument that actively transforms the projected threat into a *concrete* one. In that sense, the problems emerging here cannot be mastered by increased production, redistribution or expansion of social protection – as in the nineteenth century – but instead require either a focused and massive 'policy of counter-interpretation' or a fundamental rethinking and reprograming of the prevailing paradigm of modernization.

These differences also make it appear understandable how quite different groups are affected then and now. In the past, the affliction was dictated along with one's class fate. One was born into it. It stuck to one. It lasted from youth to old age. It was contained in everything, what one ate, how and with whom one lived, what kind of coworkers and friends one had, and whom one cursed and, if necessary, went into the streets to protest against.

Risk positions, on the contrary, contain a quite different type of victimization. There is nothing taken for granted about them. They are somehow universal and unspecific. One hears of them or reads of them. This transmission through knowledge means that those groups that tend to be afflicted are *better educated* and *actively inform themselves*. The competition with material need refers to another feature: risk consciousness and activism are more likely to occur where the direct pressure to make a living has been relaxed or broken, that is, among the wealthier and more protected groups (and countries). The spell of the invisibility of risks can also be broken by personal experiences, such as fatal signs on a beloved tree, the planned nuclear power plant in the area, a toxic waste accident, media reporting on it, and similar things, which in turn sensitize one

to new symptoms, toxic residues in foodstuffs, and the like. This type of affliction produces no social unity that would be visible on its own and to others, nothing that could
be designated or organized as a social class or stratum.

This difference in how people are affected by class and risk positions is essential.
To put it bluntly, in class positions being determines consciousness, while in risk positions, conversely, *consciousness (knowledge) determines being*. Crucial for this is the type of
knowledge, specifically the lack of personal experience and the depth of dependency
on knowledge, which surrounds all dimensions of defining hazards. The threatening
potential that resides in the determinants of the class situation – the loss of a job, for
instance – is evident to everyone affected. No special cognitive means are required for
this, no measuring procedures, no statistical survey, no reflections on validity, and no
consideration of tolerance thresholds. The affliction is clear and in that sense *independent of knowledge*.

People who find out that their daily tea contains DDT and their newly bought cake
formaldehyde, are in a quite different situation. Their victimization is *not determinable* by
their own cognitive means and potential experiences. Whether DDT is contained in the
tea or formaldehyde in the cake, and in what dose, remains outside the reach of their
own knowledge just as much as does the question of whether and in what concentrations
these substances have a long- or short-term deleterious effect. *How* these questions are
decided, however, decides a person's affliction one way or the other. Whether yes or no,
the degree, the extent and the symptoms of people's endangerment are fundamentally
dependent on external knowledge. In this way, risk positions create dependencies which are
unknown in class situations; the affected parties are becoming *incompetent* in matters
of their own affliction. They lose an essential part of their cognitive sovereignty. The
harmful, threatening, inimical lies in wait everywhere, but whether it is inimical or
friendly is beyond one's own power of judgment, is reserved for the assumptions,
methods and controversies of external knowledge producers. In risk positions, accordingly, features of daily life can change *overnight*, so to speak, into 'Trojan horses', which
disgorge dangers and with them risk experts, arguing with each other even as they
announce what one must fear and what not. Even the decision of whether one will
let them in or ask them for advice at all does not lie in the hands of the afflicted
parties. They no longer pick the experts, but instead the latter choose the victims. They
can barge in and out at will. For hazards can be projected onto all the objects of daily
life. And that is where they are now lodged – invisible and yet all too present – and they
now call for experts as sources of answers to the questions they loudly raise. Risk positions in this sense are *springs, from which questions rise to the surface, to which the victims have
no answer*.

On the other hand, this also means that all decisions on the risks and hazards of
civilization falling within the compass of knowledge production are never just questions of the substance of knowledge (inquiries, hypotheses, methods, procedures,
acceptable values, etc.). They are *at the same time* also decisions on *who is afflicted*, the
extent and type of hazard, the elements of the threat, the population concerned, delayed
effects, measures to be taken, those responsible, and claims for compensation. If it is
determined today in a socially binding way that, for example, DDT or formaldehyde
are dangerous to health in the concentrations in which they appear in ordinary products
and foodstuffs, this would be the equivalent of a catastrophe, since they are present
everywhere.

This makes it clear *that the margins for scientific research become narrower and narrower as
the threatening potential increases*. To admit today that one had been mistaken in setting
the acceptable values for the safety of pesticides – which actually would be a normal
case in science – amounts to the unleashing of a *political* (or economic) catastrophe,

and must be prevented for that reason alone. The destructive forces scientists deal with in all fields today impose on them the inhuman law of *infallibility*. Not only is it one of the most human of all qualities to break this law, but the law itself stands in clear contradiction to science's ideals of progress and critique. [. . .]

Unlike news of losses, in income and the like, news of toxic substances in foods, consumer goods, and so on contain a *double shock*. The threat itself is joined by the *loss of sovereignty* over assessing the dangers, to which one is directly subjected. The whole bureaucracy of knowledge opens up, with its long corridors, waiting benches, responsible, semi-responsible, and incomprehensible shoulder-shruggers and poseurs. There are front entrances, side entrances, secret exits, tips and (counter-) information: how one gets access to knowledge, how it should be done, but actually how it is twisted to fit, turned inside and outside, and finally neatly presented so that it does not say what it really means, and signifies what people should rather keep to themselves. All of that would not be so dramatic and could be easily ignored if only one were not dealing with very real and personal hazards.

On the other hand, the investigations of risk researchers also take place with a parallel displacement in everyone's kitchen, tea room or wine cellar. Each one of their central cognitive decisions causes the toxin level in the blood of the population to shoot up or plunge, so to speak – if one first short-circuits the entire division of labor. In risk positions then, unlike class positions, quality of life and the production of knowledge are locked together.

From this it follows that the political sociology and theory of the risk society is in essence *cognitive sociology*, not only the sociology of science, but in fact the sociology of all the admixtures, amalgams and agents of knowledge in their combination and opposition, their foundations, their claims, their mistakes, their irrationalities, their truth and in the impossibility of their knowing the knowledge they lay claim to. To summarize, the current crisis of the future is not visible, it is a possibility on the way to reality. But as just happens to be the case with possibilities: it is an *imputation* one hopes will *not* occur. The falsity of the claim thus lies in the intention of the prognosis. It is an invisible immiseration in the face of flourishing wealth, ultimately with global extent, but without a political subject. And yet: it is clearly and unambiguously an *immiseration*, if one looks correctly at both the similarities to and the differences from the nineteenth century. Alongside lists of casualties, pollutant balances and accident statistics, other indicators also speak in favor of the immiseration thesis.

The *latency phase of risk threats is coming to an end*. The invisible hazards are becoming visible. Damage to and destruction of nature no longer occur outside our personal experience in the sphere of chemical, physical or biological chains of effects; instead they strike more and more clearly our eyes, ears and noses. To list only the most conspicuous phenomena: the rapid transformation of forests into skeletons, inland waterways and seas crowned with foam, animal bodies smeared with oil, erosion of buildings and artistic monuments by pollution, the chain of toxic accidents, scandals and catastrophes, and the reporting about these things in the media. The lists of toxins and pollutants in foodstuffs and articles of daily use grow longer and longer. The barriers provided by 'acceptable values' seem better suited to the requirements for Swiss cheese than to the protection of the public (the more holes the better). The denials of the responsible parties grow ever *higher* in volume and *weaker* [in] substance. While some of this thesis remains to be demonstrated, it should already be clear from this list that the *end of latency* has two sides, the risk itself *and public perception of it*. It is not clear whether it is the risks that have intensified, or our *view* of them. Both sides converge, condition each other, strengthen each other, and because risks are risks in *knowledge*, perceptions of risks and risks are not different things, but one and the same.

The death list for plants and animals is joined by the more acute *public* consciousness, the increased sensibility to the hazards of civilization, which by the way must not be confused with hostility to technology and demonized as such. It is predominantly young people *interested* in technology who see and speak of these hazards. This increased consciousness of risk can be seen from international comparative surveys of the population in the Western industrial states, as well as from the greater relative importance of corresponding news and reportage in the mass media. This loss of latency, this growing awareness of modernization risks, was a totally unimaginable phenomenon a generation ago, and is now already a political factor of the first rank. It is not the result of a general awakening, however, but is based in turn on a number of key developments.

First, the *scientization* of risks is increasing; secondly – and mutually related – the *commerce* with risks is growing. Far from being just critique, the demonstration of the hazards and risks of modernization is also an *economic development factor of the first rank*. This becomes all too clear in the development of the various branches of the economy, and equally in the increasing public expenditures for environmental protection, for combating the diseases of civilization and so forth. The industrial system *profits* from the abuses it produces, and very nicely, thank you (Jänicke 1979).

Through the production of risks, needs are definitively removed from their residual mooring in natural factors, and hence from their finiteness, their satisfiability. Hunger can be assuaged, needs can be satisfied; risks are a 'bottomless barrel of demands', unsatisfiable, infinite. Unlike demands, risks can be more than just called forth (by advertising and the like), prolonged in conformity to sales needs, and in short: manipulated. Demands, and thus markets, of a completely new type can be *created* by varying the definition of risk, especially demand for the avoidance of risk – open to interpretation, causally designable and infinitely reproducible. Production and consumption are thus elevated to a completely new level with the triumph of the risk society. The position of pre-given and manipulable demands as the reference point of commodity production is taken over by the *self-producible* risk.

If one is not afraid of a rather bold comparison, one can say that in risk production, developed capitalism has absorbed, generalized and normalized the destructive force of war. Similarly to war, the risks of civilization which people become aware of can 'destroy' modes of production (for instance, heavily polluting cars or agricultural surpluses), and therefore overcome sales crises and create new markets, which are expandable to boot. Risk production and its cognitive agents – critique of civilization, critique of technology, critique of the environment, risk dramatization and risk research in the mass media – are a system-immanent normal form of the revolutionizing of needs. With risks, one could say with Luhmann, the economy becomes *self-referential*, independent of its context of satisfying human needs.

An essential factor for this, however, is a 'coping' with the *symptoms and symbols* of risks. As they are dealt with in this way, the risks must grow, they must not actually be eliminated as causes or sources. Everything must take place in the context of a *cosmetics* of risk, packaging, reducing the symptoms of pollutants, installing filters while retaining the source of the filth. Hence, we have not a *preventive* but a symbolic industry and policy of eliminating the increase in risks. The 'as if' must win and become programmatic. 'Radical protesters' are needed just as much for that as technologically oriented scientists and alternative scientists who study hazards. Sometimes self-financed ('self-help'!), sometimes publicly financed, these groups are generally 'advertising agencies in advance' for the creation of new sales markets for risks, one might say.

Fiction? Polemic? A trend in this direction can already be seen today. If it should win out, then this too would be a *Pyhrric victory*, for the risks would actually emerge through all the cosmetics and with them *the global threat to everyone*. A society would come into being here in which the explosive force of risks would spoil and poison *everyone's* taste for profits. Nevertheless, even the *possibility* illustrates the dynamics of reflexive modernization. Industrial society *systematically* produces its own endangerment and a questioning of itself through the multiplication and the economic exploitation of hazards. The socio-historical situation and its dynamic is comparable to the situation during the waning of the age of feudalism at the threshold of the industrial society. The feudal nobility lived off the commercial bourgeoisie (through the fief-dependent granting of rights to trade and economic use, as well as from business taxes), and encouraged it in its own interests. In this way, the nobility involuntarily and necessarily created a successor which grew steadily in power. In the same way, developed industrial society 'nourishes' itself from the hazards it produces, and so creates the social risk positions and political potentials which call into question the foundations of modernization as it has so far been known.

Mistakes, deceptions, errors and truths: on the competition of rationalities

Where the surplus of risks far overshadows the surplus in wealth, the seemingly harmless distinction between risks and the *perception* of risks gains importance – and simultaneously loses its justification. The monopoly on rationality enjoyed by scientific hazard definition stands and falls with this distinction. For it puts forward the possibility of objectively and obligatorily determining hazards in a specialized fashion and through expert authority. Science 'determines risks' and the population 'perceives risks'. Deviations from this pattern indicate the extent of 'irrationality' and 'hostility to technology'.

This division of the world between experts and non-experts also contains an image of the public sphere. The 'irrationality' of 'deviating' public risk 'perception' lies in the fact that, in the eyes of the technological elite, the majority of the public still behaves like engineering students in their first semester. They are ignorant, of course, but well intentioned; hard-working, but without a clue. In this view, the population is composed of nothing but would-be engineers, who do not yet possess sufficient knowledge. They only need be stuffed full of technical details, and then they will share the experts' viewpoint and assessment of the technical manageability of risks, and thus their lack of risk. Protests, fears, criticism, or resistance in the public sphere are a *pure problem of information*. If the public only knew what the technical people know, they would be put at ease – otherwise they are just hopelessly irrational.

This perception is *wrong*. Even in their highly mathematical or technical garb, statements on risks contain statements of the type *that is how we want to live* – statements, that is, to which the natural and engineering sciences alone can provide answers only by overstepping the bounds of their disciplines. But then the tables are turned. The non-acceptance of the scientific definition of risks is not something to be reproached as 'irrationality' in the population; but quite to the contrary, it indicates that the cultural premises of acceptability contained in scientific and technical statements on risks *are wrong*. The technical risk experts *are mistaken* in the empirical accuracy of their implicit value premises, specifically in their assumptions of what appears acceptable to the population. The talk of a 'false, irrational' perception of risk in the population, however, crowns this mistake; the scientists withdraw their *borrowed* notions of cultural acceptance from empirical criticism, elevate their views of other people's notions to a dogma and mount this shaky throne to serve as judges of the 'irrationality' of the population, whose ideas they ought to ascertain and make the foundation of their work.

One can also view it another way: in their concern with risks, the natural sciences have involuntarily and invisibly *disempowered themselves somewhat, forced themselves toward democracy*. In their implicit cultural value notions of a life worth living, statements on risks contain *a bit of codetermination*. Techno-scientific risk perception may resist this through the inversion of the presumption of irrationality, just as the feudal lords resisted the introduction of universal suffrage, but at the same time it has made a decision for them. If not, it would be permanently and systematically arguing in contradiction of its own claims to the empirical correctness of its assumptions.

The distinction between (rational) *determination* of risks and (irrational) *perception* of them also inverts the role of scientific and social rationality in the origin of a civilizational risk consciousness. It contains a falsification of history. Today's recognized knowledge of the risks and threats of techno-scientific civilization has only been able to become established *against the massive denials*, against the often bitter *resistance* of a self-satisfied 'techno-scientific rationality' that was trapped in a narrow-minded belief in progress. The scientific investigation of risks everywhere is limping along behind the social critique of the industrial system from the perspectives of the environment, progress and culture. In this sense, there is always a good bit of the unavowed *cultural critical zeal of a convert* in the techno-scientific concern with risks, and the engineering sciences' claim to a monopoly on rationality in risk perception is equivalent to the claim to infallibility of a Pope who has converted to Lutheranism.

The growing awareness of risks must be reconstructed as a struggle among rationality claims, some competing and some overlapping. One cannot impute a hierarchy of credibility and rationality, but must ask how, in the example of risk perception, 'rationality' *arises socially*, that is how it is believed, becomes dubious, is defined, redefined, acquired and frittered away. In this sense, the *(il)logic* as well as the cooperation and opposition of the scientific and social perception of civilizational risks should be displayed. In the process, one can pursue the questions: what systematic sources of mistakes and errors are built into the *scientific* perception of risks, which only become visible in the reference horizon of a social risk perception? And conversely, to what extent does the social perception of risks remain dependent on scientific rationality, even where it systematically disavows and criticizes science, and hence threatens to turn into a revitalization of pre-civilizational doctrines?

My *thesis* is that the origin of the critique of science and technology lies not in the 'irrationality' of the critics, but in the *failure* of techno-scientific rationality in the face of growing risks and threats from civilization. This failure is not mere past, but acute present and threatening future. In fact it is only gradually becoming visible to its full extent. Nor is it the failure of individual scientists or disciplines; instead it is systematically grounded in the institutional and methodological approach of the sciences to risks. As they are constituted – with their overspecialized division of labor, their concentration on methodology and theory, their externally determined abstinence from practice – the sciences are *entirely incapable* of reacting adequately to civilizational risks, since they are prominently involved in the origin and growth of those very risks. Instead – sometimes with the clear conscience of 'pure scientific method', sometimes with increasing pangs of guilt – the sciences become the *legitimating patrons* of a global industrial pollution and contamination of air, water, foodstuffs, etc., as well as the related generalized sickness and death of plants, animals and people.

How can that be shown? The consciousness of modernization risks has established itself against the *resistance* of scientific rationality. A broad trail of scientific mistakes, misjudgments and minimizations leads to it. The history of the growing consciousness and social recognition of risks coincides with the history of the demystification of the sciences. The other side of recognition is the refutation of the scientific 'see no evil, hear no evil, smell no evil, know no evil'.

VIGNETTE 1.1 COMPLICATING THEORY WITH LIFE . . .

M. Redclift, King's College, London

In a key passage from Schwarz and Thompson (1990) they argue that:

> It is by teasing out these (plural) rationalities that we can begin to make sense of what is going on in all those policy debates that are characterised by contradictory certainties. Though this approach *is* saying that knowledge is socially constructed, it is *not* saying that the world can be any way we want it to be. It is not saying that we can know nothing; only that we cannot know everything and that, within that uncertain and inchoate region, it is our institutions – our social involvements – that lead us to grant credibility to one possible state of affairs rather than another.
>
> (Schwarz and Thompson 1990: 11)

Cultural Theory examines the cultural processes through which decisions about the environment are made. It argues that these cultural processes, rather than the search for substantive evidence, provide a key to unlocking the box of uncertain science. Culture is a device for problem-solving, in the face of the limits of individual action, something not readily accepted by neo-classical economics, for example. This approach focuses on what is shared by people with the same interpretative framework. Such groups are disposed to impose order on reality, in specific ways, to socially construct reality (Douglas *et al.* 1998).

Cultural Theory is about the ways in which *trustworthiness* is established in societies. In many ways the absence of trust represents a much bigger obstacle to policy than the presence of ignorance: it underpins the impossibility of deciding between the competing claims of politicians and scientists. It should not come as a surprise, then, that this approach has enormous appeal to the captains of industry, and the 'opinion formers' who are interested, in different ways, in understanding their markets.

Even sympathetic critics of this position (cultural theory), have commented upon its limitations, as well as its strengths. John Adams, for example, suggests that the four 'ways of life' put forward (individualist, fatalist, hierarchist, egalitarian) by Cultural Theorists cannot be framed as a statistically testable hypothesis. Adherents to each of the four ways of life are defined in terms of 'bundles of social relations, cultural biases and behavioural strategies' (Adams 1995: 200). Although these may be internally consistent, it is clear that individuals often participate in a number of different social contexts, and perform different roles, drawing on each of the four ways of life as appropriate. Individuals may prove to be '. . . egalitarians at home, hierarchists at work and individualists while playing golf . . .' (Adams 1995: 201). They may, of course be exiting one rationality only to enter another, as Thompson contends, in his own defence (Dake and Thompson 1993). One cannot help thinking, however, that an approach which works precisely because it sets out *plural* rationalities, as a set of abstractions, also suffers from mythic status, like the myths of nature it embodies. What works well as *myth* does not necessarily fully satisfy us as theory.

The theory of Risk Society is rather different. Ulrich Beck was interested in providing an account of changes through time in the social context for environmental change. His book, *Risk Society*, first appeared in German in 1986 in the wake of the Chernobyl nuclear disaster in the Ukraine, that had engulfed most of the rest of Europe (Beck 1992). Beck drew attention to a new generation of global risks, which arose from nuclear, chemical, ecological and genetic engineering. These risks were limited in neither time nor space. They could not easily be understood in terms of attaching blame or liability to specific parties. They could not be compensated for, or insured against.

In Beck's view the scientific expertise necessary for exercising control over high-consequence risks, had made the scientists unaccountable to their societies. A new lexicon of 'objective risk assessment' had been developed to try and manage the anxieties, and opposition, that these risks prompted. Efforts were constantly made to convince people that hazards were small or confinable. In recent years a litany of public policy disasters has demonstrated the problems that accompany the need to 'manage' opinion in this way – BSE, HIV and AIDS, the 'foot and mouth' epidemic, all illustrate a breakdown in public confidence in 'science'.

Beck's thesis is that the institutional structures of society have been weakened, leading to increasing personal insecurity and dislocation. The integrative functions – the 'props' – have disappeared from societies. In every respect this view is very different from that of Cultural Theory, which seeks to examine 'the props', and pronounces them 'effective'. In the view of writers like Schwarz and Thompson cultures always provide individuals with 'reasons' for behaving in certain ways. To Beck individualisation has taken the 'reason' (and sometimes the 'reasoning') out of the hands of most human agents. Beck's *reflexive modernisation* does not offer solutions through an awakened consciousness; it merely condemns the individual to the paralysis of relativism. In this sense it is consistent with some of the social theory that preceded it, including some writers from the Frankfurt School (Rosa 2000). Habermas, for example, had argued, in 1981, that the so-called New Social Movements were unable to distinguish between the rationalisation of the life-world and the increasing complexity of the social system (Habermas 1981). What marks out Beck's approach from that of some of his predecessors is that he views the 'counter-experts' – the ecology movement, and citizens' experts – as themselves very much a part of the production of environmental knowledge.

Beck's 'Risk Society', unlike Cultural Theory, suffers from a measure of ethno-centrism. The symptoms he adduces are much easier to identify in Northern Europe, than, for example, in the Yucatan peninsular of Mexico, where I have been conducting research. The processes he observes, such as 'individualisation', privilege specific forms of cultural knowledge and behaviour. In Mexico the role of the Virgin of Guadelupe has appeared to increase as the appeal of modernity seems to recede, for most ordinary people. Religion, both Roman Catholicism and Evangelical, has renewed appeal to a population devoid of secure employment and economic stability. Conventional politics has lost what little appeal it had to most of the population, but this disillusion has not manifested itself in the kind of 'individualisation' noted by Beck. In some respects one might be able to even delineate a new sense of 'community', in the face of adversity. The personal risks these people experience, on an everyday basis – from unemployment, poverty, and life-threatening diseases (such as Dengue Fever) – are understood and feared much more than the prospect of a nuclear accident, or a genetic misadventure.

There is also a rather powerful sting in the tail of cultural theory, despite Schwarz and Thompson's protestations, in the quotation that opened this comment. It is sometimes argued that the admission of difference, the centrality of the subject, and the necessity of interpretation, have all contributed to a pervading epistemological relativism, the curse of post-modernism, perhaps. In writing about the environment, nature and risk, everybody's 'nature' is equally valid. This is the suspicion which Schwarz and Thompson explicitly deny, but it hovers over their approach nevertheless. Since we cannot *know* what sustainability means to others, and we only know what it means to us through our institutional context, (and our lives are compartmentalised in ways that enable us to hold mutually inconsistent beliefs), our ability to interpret is ultimately disempowering. Cultural theory does not fully answer the problems raised by our engagement with the real world: the search for guidance, for our behaviour, in a world full of claims and counter-claims. It offers a paradigm of knowledge in place of the need to know.

VIGNETTE 1.2 ENVIRONMENT CONSTRUCTED: PERSPECTIVES FROM THE SOUTH

L. Le Grange, University of Stellenbosch

In this vignette, I focus on issues around sustainable development in Southern Africa.

Nature constructed

Schwarz and Thompson (1990) assert that institutions adopt strategies based on different interpretations of ecosystem stability. The different interpretations are based on what they refer to as 'four myths of nature', *nature benign, nature ephemeral, nature perverse/tolerant* and *nature capricious*. These in turn are based in different rationalities. Disparate perspectives on nature are generated meanings underpinned by different social, political and economic interests. In other words nature is variously socially constructed, according to different sets of interests/rationalities.

Schwarz and Thompson's (1990) typology of nature is anthropocentric. Nature from all four rationalities is viewed as being separate from human beings, existing for the benefit of, and to be managed by humans, as if 'nature' cannot take care of itself. However, what I wish to write about more specifically in this section is the idea of sustainability. I refer to sustainability with respect to resource use, development and living. I discuss the notion of sustainability because it has been adopted in different sites and discourses of social life in southern Africa. Sustainable development has been placed high on the agenda of many southern African governments as well as intergovernmental organisations in the region. For example, in South Africa sustainable development is central to a new vision for environmental policy:

> We can only achieve this through a new model or paradigm of sustainable development based on integrated and coordinated environment that addresses: . . . the integration of economic development, social justice and environmental sustainability . . . the sustainable use of social, cultural and natural resources.
>
> (RSA 1997)

Sustainable development is an attractive option for environmental management in Africa because it addresses a moral imperative to provide resources for future generations without compromising the need for contemporary development in some of the poorest regions such as southern Africa. In fact sustainable development has also been adopted as central to the vision of an African Renaissance (see Makgoba 1999). Sustainability is most closely associated with the idea of *nature ephemeral* than any of the other myths Schwarz and Thompson identify – the idea of living lightly (sustainably) on the earth. But should Africa follow Western models of development? Will its people be able to do so and still tread lightly on the earth? Should external models of natural resources use inform environmental management in Africa? Can indigenous methods of resource use be effectively revived? How can such methods work together with Western approaches? These remain open questions and challenges for Africa.

Risk constructed

Beck (1992) posits that risk society is concerned with a type of immiseration of civilisation. The immiseration he refers to does not involve material impoverishment, as was the case of the working masses of the nineteenth century, but rather concerns the threatening and destruction of the natural foundations of life. The ubiquity of risk is evident today when apparently harmless things such as wine, tea, beef, pasta etc., can turn out to be dangerous (see Beck 1992: 51). Beck's thesis can reasonably be generalised across the 'developed world', but in my view is only partially applicable to the 'less developed' world. In fairness to Beck, his social analysis was of European society. However, the immiseration experienced by nineteenth-century Europe is now experienced by millions in the 'developing world'. Risks associated with poverty, hunger, crowding, disease etc., continues to characterise their daily plight. A double blow hits people in the 'developing world': the risks associated with material irnmiseration and those brought about by modernisation and industrialisation. The following example is illustrative in this regard. A survey conducted in 1994/1995 showed that respiratory illnesses resulting from air pollution were 7 times higher among African children living in the former Eastern Transvaal (South Africa) than European children (SAIRR 1995). The African children live in informal settlements where domestic fuels such as wood and coal are the main source of energy. They are therefore exposed to air pollutants as a consequence of poor living conditions. These children also live near industrial areas and mine dumps and therefore are exposed to industrial pollutants as well as pollutants emitted by motor vehicles.

Although modern science has alleviated the risk of diseases such as polio and smallpox, those who are already poverty-stricken are particularly vulnerable to the risk of AIDS. Recent estimates from the Joint United Nations Programme on HIV/AIDS (UNAIDS) and the World Health Organisation (WHO) show that 34.7 million adults and 1.4 million children were living with HIV worldwide at the end of 2000. These organisations claim that the HIV/AIDS epidemic has given rise to approximately 13.2 million AIDS orphans. Seventy percent (70%) of the global total of HIV positive people live in Sub-Saharan Africa, one of the world's materially most impoverished regions.

Knowledge, lifelong learning and sustainability

Because our knowledge of the biophysical world is socially constructed, our perceptions of nature are intertwined with social, political and economic interests. It is in the dynamic interaction between biophysical, social, political and economic forces that environmental problems and risk arise and are experienced. Beck (1992) points out that in modem society risks have become pervasive to the extent that many are invisible, present in seemingly harmless things. However, in the developing world there are risks that are conspicuous such as the AIDS pandemic. Risks experienced by millions in the developing world today can be likened to those of the nineteenth-century Western experience – arising from material immiseration. However, today even risks of this kind become distributed across the planet because of globalisation processes.

It would be fair to claim that risk presents challenges to both the developed and developing world. Given the ubiquity of risk in contemporary society, education's response should be to prepare learners to be able to negotiate and live with risk. If sustainable living and/or development are to be desirable goals or foci for education, action towards improving risk positions will be essential. But, the sustainability of education systems might itself be at risk given the exponential growth of AIDS. For example, in South Africa grade 1 enrolments are declining and it is estimated that 40,000 of a total of 350,000 teachers are HIV positive. The changing nature of risk positions necessitates lifelong learning.

CHAPTER 2

███████

THE POLICY CONTEXT

READING 2.1 AGENDA 21: CHAPTER 36

United Nations

Source: United Nations, New York, 1992: 221–227

Promoting education, public awareness and training

Education, raising of public awareness and training are linked to virtually all areas in *Agenda 21*, and even more closely to the ones on meeting basic needs, capacity-building, data and information, science, and the role of major groups. This chapter sets out broad proposals, while specific suggestions related to sectoral issues are contained in other chapters. The Declaration and Recommendations of the Tbilisi Inter-governmental Conference on Environmental Education[1] organized by UNESCO and UNEP and held in 1977, have provided the fundamental principles for the proposals in this document.

A   Reorienting education towards sustainable development

Basis for action

Education, including formal education, public awareness and training should be recognized as a process by which human beings and societies can reach their fullest potential. Education is critical for promoting sustainable development and improving the capacity of the people to address environment and development issues. While basic education provides the underpinning for any environmental and development education, the latter needs to be incorporated as an essential part of learning. Both formal and non-formal education are indispensable to changing people's attitudes so that they have the capacity to assess and address their sustainable development concerns. It is also critical for achieving environmental and ethical awareness, values and attitudes, skills and behaviour consistent with sustainable development and for effective public participation in decision-making. To be effective, environment and development education should deal with the dynamics of both the physical biological and socio-economic environment and human (which may include spiritual) development, should be integrated in all disciplines, and should employ formal and non-formal methods and effective means of communication.

Objectives

Recognizing that countries, regional and international organizations will develop their own priorities and schedules for implementation in accordance with their needs, policies and programmes, the following objectives are proposed:

a) To endorse the recommendations arising from the World Conference on Education for All: Meeting Basic Learning Needs[2] (Jomtien, Thailand, 5–9 March 1990) and to strive to ensure universal access to basic education, and to achieve primary education for at least 80 per cent of girls and 80 per cent of boys of primary school age through formal schooling or non-formal education and to reduce the adult illiteracy rate to at least half of its 1990 level. Efforts should focus on reducing the high illiteracy levels and redressing the lack of basic education among women and should bring their literacy levels into line with those of men;

b) To achieve environmental and development awareness in all sectors of society on a world-wide scale as soon as possible;

c) To strive to achieve the accessibility of environmental and development education, linked to social education, from primary school age through adulthood to all groups of people;

d) To promote integration of environment and development concepts, including demography, in all educational programmes, in particular the analysis of the causes of major environment and development issues in a local context, drawing on the best available scientific evidence and other appropriate sources of knowledge, and giving special emphasis to the further training of decision makers at all levels.

Activities

Recognizing that countries and regional and international organizations will develop their own priorities and schedules for implementation in accordance with their needs, policies and programmes, the following activities are proposed:

a) All countries are encouraged to endorse the recommendations of the Jomtien Conference and strive to ensure its Framework for Action. This would encompass the preparation of national strategies and actions for meeting basic learning needs, universalizing access and promoting equity, broadening the means and scope of education, developing a supporting policy context, mobilizing resources and strengthening international cooperation to redress existing economic, social and gender disparities which interfere with these aims. Non-governmental organizations can make an important contribution in designing and implementing educational programmes and should be recognized;

b) Governments should strive to update or prepare strategies aimed at integrating environment and development as a cross-cutting issue into education at all levels within the next three years. This should be done in cooperation with all sectors of society. The strategies should set out policies and activities, and identify needs, cost, means and schedules for their implementation, evaluation and review. A thorough review of curricula should be undertaken to ensure a multidisciplinary approach, with environment and development issues and their socio-cultural and demographic aspects and linkages. Due respect should be given to community-defined needs and diverse knowledge systems, including science, cultural and social sensitivities;

c) Countries are encouraged to set up national advisory environmental education coordinating bodies or round tables representative of various environmental, developmental, educational, gender and other interests, including non-governmental organizations, to encourage partnerships, help mobilize resources, and provide a source of information and focal point for international ties. These bodies would help mobilize and facilitate different population groups and communities to assess their own needs and to develop the necessary skills to create and implement their own environment and development initiatives;

d)   Educational authorities, with the appropriate assistance from community groups or nongovernmental organizations, are recommended to assist or set up pre-service and in-service training programmes for all teachers, administrators, and educational planners, as well as non-formal educators in all sectors, addressing the nature and methods of environmental and development education and making use of relevant experience of non-governmental organizations;

e)   Relevant authorities should ensure that every school is assisted in designing environmental activity work plans, with the participation of students and staff. Schools should involve schoolchildren in local and regional studies on environmental health, including safe drinking water, sanitation and food and ecosystems and in relevant activities, linking these studies with services and research in national parks, wildlife reserves, ecological heritage sites etc.;

f)   Educational authorities should promote proven educational methods and the development of innovative teaching methods for educational settings. They should also recognize appropriate traditional education systems in local communities;

g)   Within two years the United Nations system should undertake a comprehensive review of its educational programmes, encompassing training and public awareness, to reassess priorities and reallocate resources. The UNESCO/UNEP International Environmental Education Programme should, in cooperation with the appropriate bodies of the United Nations system, Governments, non-governmental organizations and others, establish a programme within two years to integrate the decisions of the Conference into the existing United Nations framework adapted to the needs of educators at different levels and circumstances. Regional organizations and national authorities should be encouraged to elaborate similar parallel programmes and opportunities by conducting an analysis of how to mobilize different sectors of the population in order to assess and address their environmental and development education needs;

h)   There is a need to strengthen, within five years, information exchange by enhancing technologies and capacities necessary to promote environment and development education and public awareness. Countries should cooperate with each other and with the various social sectors and population groups to prepare educational tools that include regional environment and development issues and initiatives, using learning materials and resources suited to their own requirements;

i)   Countries could support university and other tertiary activities and networks for environmental and development education. Cross-disciplinary courses could be made available to all students. Existing regional networks and activities and national university actions which promote research and common teaching approaches on sustainable development should be built upon, and new partnerships and bridges created with the business and other independent sectors, as well as with all countries for technology, know-how and knowledge exchange;

j)   Countries, assisted by international organizations, non-governmental organizations and other sectors, could strengthen or establish national or regional centres of excellence in interdisciplinary research and education in environmental and developmental sciences, law and the management of specific environmental problems. Such centres could be universities or existing networks in each country or region, promoting cooperative research and information sharing and dissemination. At the global level these functions should be performed by appropriate institutions;

k)   Countries should facilitate and promote non-formal education activities at the local, regional and national levels by cooperating with and supporting the efforts of non-formal educators and other community-based organizations. The appropriate bodies of the United Nations system in cooperation with non-governmental organizations should encourage the development of an international network for the achievement of global educational aims. At the national and local levels, public and scholastic forums should discuss environmental and development issues, and suggest sustainable alternatives to policy makers;

l) Educational authorities, with appropriate assistance of non-governmental organizations, including women's and indigenous peoples' organizations, should promote all kinds of adult education programmes for continuing education in environment and development, basing activities around elementary secondary schools and local problems. These authorities and industry should encourage business, industrial and agricultural schools to include such topics in their curricula. The corporate sector could include sustainable development in their education and training programmes. Programmes at a post-graduate level should include specific courses aiming at the further training of decision makers;

m) Governments and educational authorities should foster opportunities for women in non-traditional fields and eliminate gender stereotyping in curricula. This could be done by improving enrolment opportunities, including females in advanced programmes as students and instructors, reforming entrance and teacher staffing policies and providing incentives for establishing child-care facilities, as appropriate. Priority should be given to education of young females and to programmes promoting literacy among women;

n) Governments should affirm the rights of indigenous peoples, by legislation if necessary, to use their experience and understanding of sustainable development to play a part in education and training;

o) The United Nations could maintain a monitoring and evaluative role regarding decisions of the United Nations Conference on Environment and Development on education and awareness, through the relevant United Nations agencies. With Governments and nongovernmental organizations, as appropriate, it should present and disseminate decisions in a variety of forms, and should ensure the continuous implementation and review of the educational implications of Conference decisions, in particular through relevant events and conferences.

Means of implementation

$8–$9 billion, including about $3.5–$4.5 billion from the international community on grant or concessional terms.

[. . .]

In the light of country specific situations, more support for education, training and public awareness activities related to environment and development could be provided, in appropriate cases, through measures such as the following:

a) Giving higher priority to those sectors in budget allocations, protecting them from structural cutting requirements;

b) Shifting allocations within existing education budgets in favour of primary education, with focus on environment and development;

c) Promoting conditions where a larger share of the cost is borne by local communities, with rich communities assisting poorer ones;

d) Obtaining additional funds from private donors concentrating on the poorest countries, and those with rates of literacy below 40 per cent;

e) Encouraging debt for education swaps;

f) Lifting restrictions on private schooling and increasing the flow of funds from and to non-governmental organizations, including small-scale grass-roots organizations;

g) Promoting the effective use of existing facilities, for example, multiple school shifts, fuller development of open universities and other long-distance teaching;

h) Facilitating low-cost or no-cost use of mass media for the purposes of education;

i) Encouraging twinning of universities in developed and developing countries.

B　*Increasing public awareness*

Basis for action

There is still a considerable lack of awareness of the interrelated nature of all human activities and the environment, due to inaccurate or insufficient information. Developing countries in particular lack relevant technologies and expertise. There is a need to increase public sensitivity to environment and development problems and involvement in their solutions and foster a sense of personal environmental responsibility and greater motivation and commitment towards sustainable development.

Objective

The objective is to promote broad public awareness as an essential part of a global education effort to strengthen attitudes, values and actions which are compatible with sustainable development. It is important to stress the principle of devolving authority, accountability and resources to the most appropriate level with preference given to local responsibility and control over awareness-building activities.

Activities

Recognizing that countries, regional and international organizations will develop their own priorities and schedules for implementation in accordance with their needs, policies and programmes, the following activities are proposed:

a) Countries should strengthen existing advisory bodies or establish new ones for public environment and development information, and should coordinate activities with, among others, the United Nations non-governmental organizations and important media. They should encourage public participation in discussions of environmental policies and assessments. Governments should also facilitate and support national to local networking of information through existing networks;

b) The United Nations system should improve its outreach in the course of a review of its education and public awareness activities to promote greater involvement and coordination of all parts of the system, especially its information bodies and regional and country operations. Systematic surveys of the impact of awareness programmes should be conducted, recognizing the needs and contributions of specific community groups;

c) Countries and regional organizations should be encouraged, as appropriate, to provide public environmental and development information services for raising the awareness of all groups, the private sector and particularly decision makers;

d) Countries should stimulate educational establishments in all sectors, especially the tertiary sector, to contribute more to awareness building. Educational materials of all kinds and for all audiences should be based on the best available scientific information, including the natural, behavioural and social sciences, and taking into account aesthetic and ethical dimensions;

e) Countries and the United Nations system should promote a cooperative relationship with the media, popular theatre groups, and entertainment and advertising industries by initiating discussions to mobilize their experience in shaping public behaviour and consumption patterns and making wide use of their methods. Such cooperation would also increase the active public participation in the debate on the environment. UNICEF should make child-oriented material available to [the] media as an educational tool, ensuring close cooperation between the out-of-school public information sector and the school curriculum, for the primary level. UNESCO, UNEP and universities should enrich preservice curricula for journalists on environment and development topics;

f) Countries, in cooperation with the scientific community, should establish ways of employing modern communication technologies for effective public outreach. National and local educational authorities and relevant United Nations agencies should expand, as appropriate, the use of audiovisual methods, especially in rural areas in mobile units, by producing television and radio programmes for developing countries, involving local participation, employing interactive multimedia methods and integrating advanced methods with folk media;

g) Countries should promote, as appropriate, environmentally sound leisure and tourism activities, building on The Hague Declaration of Tourism (1989) and the current programmes of the World Tourism Organization and UNEP, making suitable use of museums, heritage sites, zoos, botanical gardens, national parks and other protected areas;

h) Countries should encourage non-governmental organizations to increase their involvement in environmental and development problems, through joint awareness initiatives and improved interchange with other constituencies in society;

i) Countries and the United Nations system should increase their interaction with and include, as appropriate, indigenous people in the management, planning and development of their local environment, and should promote dissemination of traditional and socially learned knowledge through means based on local customs, especially in rural areas, integrating these efforts with the electronic media, whenever appropriate;

j) UNICEF, UNESCO, UNDP and non-governmental organizations should develop support programmes to involve young people and children in environment and development issues, such as children's and youth hearings, building on decisions of the World Summit for Children;

k) Countries, the United Nations and nongovernmental organizations should encourage mobilization of both men and women in awareness campaigns, stressing the role of the family in environmental activities, women's contribution to transmission of knowledge and social values and the development of human resources;

l) Public awareness should be heightened regarding the impacts of violence in society.

Finance and cost evaluation

$1.2 billion, including about $110 million from the international community on grant or concessional terms.

C   Promoting training

Basis for action

Training is one of the most important tools to develop human resources and facilitate the transition to a more sustainable world. It should have a job-specific focus, aimed at filling gaps in knowledge and skill that would help individuals find employment and be involved in environmental and development work. At the same time, training programmes should promote a greater awareness of environment and development issues as a two-way learning process.

Objectives

    a)   To establish or strengthen vocational training programmes that meet the needs of environment and development with ensured access to training opportunities, regardless of social status, age, gender, race or religion;

    b)   To promote a flexible and adaptable workforce of various ages equipped to meet growing environment and development problems and changes arising from the transition to a sustainable society;

    c)   To strengthen national capacities, particularly in scientific education and training, to enable Governments, employers and workers to meet their environmental and development objectives and to facilitate the transfer and assimilation of new environmentally sound, socially acceptable and appropriate technology and know-how;

    d)   To ensure that environmental and human ecological considerations are integrated at all managerial levels and in all functional management areas, such as marketing, production and finance.

Activities

Countries with the support of the United Nations system should identify workforce training needs and assess measures to be taken to meet those needs. A review of progress in this area could be undertaken by the United Nations system in 1995.

    National professional associations are encouraged to develop and review their codes of ethics and conduct to strengthen environmental connections and commitment. The training and personal development components of programmes sponsored by professional bodies should ensure incorporation of skills and information on the implementation of sustainable development at all points of policy- and decision-making.

    Countries and educational institutions should integrate environmental and developmental issues into existing training curricula and promote the exchange of their methodologies and evaluations.

    Countries should encourage all sectors of society, such as industry, universities, government officials and employees, non-governmental organizations and community organizations, to include an environmental management component in all relevant training activities, with emphasis on meeting immediate skill requirements through short-term formal and in-plant vocational and management training. Environmental management training capacities should be strengthened, and specialized "training of trainers" programmes should be established to support training at the national and enterprise levels. New training approaches for existing environmentally sound practices should be developed that create employment opportunities and make maximum use of local resource-based methods.

    Countries should strengthen or establish practical training programmes for graduates from vocational schools, high schools and universities, in all countries, to enable them to meet labour market requirements and to achieve sustainable livelihoods. Training and retraining programmes should be established to meet structural adjustments which have an impact on employment and skill qualifications.

Governments are encouraged to consult with people in isolated situations, whether geographically, culturally or socially, to ascertain their needs for training to enable them to contribute more fully to developing sustainable work practices and lifestyles.

Governments, industry, trade unions and consumers should promote an understanding of the interrelationship between good environment and good business practices.

Countries should develop a service of locally trained and recruited environmental technicians able to provide local people and communities, particularly in deprived urban and rural areas, with the services they require, starting from primary environmental care.

Countries should enhance the ability to gain access to, analyse and effectively use information and knowledge available on environment and development. Existing or established special training programmes should be strengthened to support information needs of special groups. The impact of these programmes on productivity, health, safety and employment should be evaluated. National and regional environmental labour-market information systems should be developed that would supply, on a continuing basis, data on environmental job and training opportunities. Environment and development training resource-guides should be prepared and updated, with information on training programmes, curricula, methodologies and evaluation results at the local, national, regional and international levels.

Aid agencies should strengthen the training component in all development projects, emphasizing a multidisciplinary approach, promoting awareness and providing the necessary skills for transition to a sustainable society. The environmental management guidelines of UNDP for operational activities of the United Nations system may contribute to this end.

Existing networks of employers' and workers' organizations, industry associations and nongovernmental organizations should facilitate the exchange of experience concerning training and awareness programmes.

Governments, in cooperation with relevant international organizations, should develop and implement strategies to deal with national, regional and local environmental threats and emergencies, emphasizing urgent practical training and awareness programmes for increasing public preparedness.

The United Nations system, as appropriate, should extend its training programmes, particularly its environmental training and support activities for employers' and workers' organizations.

Finance and cost evaluation

$5 billion, including about $2 billion from the international community on grant or concessional terms.

Notes

1 Intergovernmental Conference on Environmental Education: Final Report (Paris, UNESCO, 1978), chap. III.
2 Final Report of the World Conference on Education for All: Meeting Basic Learning Needs, Jomtien, Thailand, 5–9 March 1990, Inter-Agency Commission (UNDP, UNESCO, UNICEF, World Bank) for the World Conference on Education for All, New York, 1990.
[. . .]

READING 2.2 LIFELONG LEARNING FOR ALL

Organisation for Economic Co-operation and Development

Source: OECD, Paris, 1996: 94–97

Towards strategies for lifelong learning

The above review of barriers to the implementation of lifelong learning strategies has indicated a number of weaknesses and problems, which pose major challenges to policy-makers. These problems cannot be appropriately addressed in a piecemeal fashion; meeting the challenges requires system-wide reform. Lifelong learning provides an appropriate framework for pursuing this system-wide reorientation of education and training policies. This section examines the overall feasibility of implementing the all-embracing concept of lifelong learning and proposes the broad outlines of possible strategies. It aims to identify the policy directions that might be considered – guidelines that are analysed in depth in the subsequent chapters.

The policy directions and guidelines are aimed at improving equity, coherence, flexibility and efficiency of the pathways in lifelong learning and work; by improving the relevance and quality of the foundations and extending it to all; by enhancing articulation between the various pathways and system components; by renewing the resources and "assets" of the system; and by improving flexibility and increasing efficiency through better policy co-ordination, new approaches to governance, including new partnerships, and a reassessment of the priorities and means of financing the system.

Building an inclusive learning society will take major and sustained efforts over the long term. Yet, the need for action is urgent, for unless countries are already moving towards lifelong learning now, the likelihood that they will meet these long-term objectives become still more remote. Although the policy guidelines developed below are consistent with this long-term vision for the development of education systems in OECD countries, the focus is also on action that must be initiated in the short and medium term, until the turn of the century. "Long-term" does not mean "dispensable in the immediate term"; it refers instead to the large scale of the undertaking and hence the investment of time and resources in order to see the project fully through into practice. There is a particular value, given the theme of partnerships, of identifying the strategic contribution where each of the main partners has particular responsibilities. It is obvious that the education authorities, by no means the only partner in the lifelong learning enterprise, have a central role; it cannot be realised without the lead and integral involvement of education and training systems.

In considering the scope and content of strategies for lifelong learning, three questions are pertinent. Firstly, what are the goals and objectives a lifelong learning strategy is supposed to serve? Secondly, what are the constituencies for lifelong learning, and what are their respective roles and responsibilities? And thirdly, what are the requirements in terms of monitoring, assessing and evaluating progress towards achieving the goals? These questions imply directions for strategic analyses which are elaborated in the subsequent chapters.

Strategic goals and objectives

A commitment to lifelong learning will necessitate a review of the goals and objectives of education, training and learning more generally. Although the priorities and specific emphases will differ among countries, six interrelated sets of goals deserve attention:

1) *Enlarging access to high-quality early childhood education.* Because the first years of life are crucial for continued learning, and since disadvantage which is not corrected in the early years can persist, enlarging access to high-quality early intervention programmes and early childhood education is a central goal in any strategy for lifelong learning.

2) *Revitalising foundation learning in primary and secondary schools.* Providing a solid and secure basis of learning in primary and secondary schools will require attentiveness to both the capacity and motivation to learn. In order to sustain motivation and develop abilities, "positive" learning environments are needed. Such environments should facilitate the use of individualised teaching and learning strategies, and employ assessment and examination procedures that value and take account of individual progress in learning. A rethinking of the curriculum and the very organisation of schools, continued attentiveness to students with special needs, the underserved and slow learners, and more generally a focus on those who are "at risk" of failure, are further requirements.

3) *Overcoming problems of transition.* In all Member countries, young adults, communities and employers are faced with the individual, social and economic consequences of difficulties in managing the transition from school to work. Building an inclusive learning society requires that the barriers that hinder this transition be removed. Appropriate guidance and counselling services are a major element in any strategy for achieving this.

4) *Encouraging adult learning.* Beyond schooling and initial tertiary education, the most common times for adults to undertake major learning projects have been at points of crisis or substantial change in their lives or careers. There is a need for learning to become a part of the on-going process of everyday life, as a function of continuing self-development and adaptation to new conditions and environments. This highlights the importance of creating a better framework to motivate, facilitate and reward continued learning, and in so doing increase the demand for learning opportunities among adults. Because evidence suggests a strong bias in participation in favour of those who already have a good education, there is a role for governments in securing fairness; this must be reflected in strategic policy decisions. Because over 20 per cent of adults in some of the most advanced OECD countries have literacy skills at only the most basic level [. . .], adult basic education must feature centrally in any strategy for realising lifelong learning for all.

5) *Addressing the lack of coherence in the system.* A comprehensive system of lifelong learning opportunities implies a fluid relationship between learning and work, where an initial period of full-time schooling is followed throughout working life by sequences and combinations of organised learning at school and/or at work, which accompany or alternate with full- or part-time work. Under current arrangements, most of the elements of the system are in place, but the articulation between them is far from perfect. University education exerts a disproportionate influence on the structure of some education systems, and the pathways that should connect general and vocational education are often non-existent or inflexible. Priority must be given to the creation of a framework for linking the formal and non-formal elements of lifelong learning in flexible sets of pathways and progressions in education and working life, taking account of the differing needs and potential of individuals, and including arrangements for the assessment of knowledge and skills which recognise the value of all forms of learning. Important elements of a coherent system are more developed arrangements for the assessment and recognition of acquired skills and competencies, including well-developed mechanisms for assessing prior

learning and validating skills acquired outside the formal sector. Frameworks of standards for assessment, recognition and certification of training are needed to encourage investment in skills and to facilitate mobility.

6)   *Renewing the resources and "assets" of the system.* The goal of creating "positive" learning environments calls for new capital investment in buildings and other physical infrastructures. But the "assets" of education systems lie only partly in their buildings. The greater share is in the knowledge and experience of teachers and non-teaching staff. In many OECD countries these human resources are underdeveloped. Teachers and administrators need access to information and research about the structures they are working in, at local, national and international levels. The continuing professional development of staff, especially but not exclusively teachers, must be taken far more seriously. However, informed decision-making cannot take place in the absence of an adequate information base. Hence there is a need to strengthen the research and information base at the national and international levels.

In order to give substance and focus to the formulation of these goals and objectives, the main purposes of lifelong learning, the "cases" outlined above, come to the fore to ask how each – the "learning economy", "speed of change", "life-cycle redistribution", "active policies" and "social cohesion" arguments – can be implemented on a widespread basis. The focus of each emphasises the need to seek ways in which these broad ambitions are actively developed across OECD countries as: continuous training and retraining on the basis of an advanced foundation of learning; openness to new learning and the ability to manage knowledge "overload"; the promotion of active lives and policies; social inclusion not exclusion; "life-cycle sensitive" perspectives and practices that break away from rigid (and inappropriate) age compartmentalisation patterns.

It is also necessary to recognise that practices and policies that promote one of these may not promote the others in equal measure. Hence the inclusion in the goals and objectives listed above of the need for "visions" that set out the nature and priorities of lifelong learning, bringing in all the relevant partners and players. Obviously, too, objectives by themselves are much easier to identify than to put into practice, for they depend on a range of means and instruments through which they are made possible. Certain of these are elaborated in the following section, focusing on those aspects that are closer to those fields where the education authorities are likely to play a lead or major role.

Means and instruments

The key instruments for implementing a strategy for lifelong learning include: 1) the redefinition of the roles and responsibilities of Education Ministries and their partners; 2) the appropriate human resources, physical infrastructure and knowledge base to provide high-quality lifelong learning; 3) adequate financing arrangements to implement an inclusive programme of lifelong learning and to provide sufficient opportunities and incentives to the partners in the system.

The insight that lifelong learning is not restricted to formal education provides a useful starting point for a strategic discussion about roles and responsibilities. A strategic question is how far the responsibility of governments for education should be extended to the areas of lifelong learning that lie beyond formal education and training, for example continuing vocational education and learning on the job. Instead of extending the role of governments in organising and funding an integral system of lifelong education, extending from pre-school years to old age, policy-makers now tend to opt for a more limited approach, one in which the responsibilities of other interest groups – especially the individual and the social partners – are emphasised. This approach has been accompanied by a tendency to increase the scope for private constituencies to assume more responsibility for provision.

There is wide agreement that governments need to assume a significant role in co-ordinating the provision of lifelong learning: for example, it is clear that governments have a role in disseminating information and guidance on the options that are available. It is the responsibility of governments to establish the appropriate framework conditions for lifelong learning; but governments cannot become monopoly providers. Partnerships are central in any strategy for achieving an inclusive approach to lifelong learning. Notions of partnership differ, however, depending on the levels and sectors of educational provision; partnerships for better schools will be very different from partnerships for adult education and training.

Strategies for lifelong learning must be financed; the success of any strategy stands or falls with its success in mobilising and reallocating resources. Because of the high costs involved, the financing of mass tertiary education is a real issue for governments. If it is widely acknowledged that education and training have the characteristics of investment, little has been done in OECD societies to account properly for human capital. As a result, countries are unable to make appropriate investment decisions. In OECD (1996), it is put this way: "In the context of a growing body of evidence that investment in human capital is playing an even greater role in determining the outcome of competition amongst firms (. . .) the question [arises] of the extent to which the systems for information and decision-making regarding the stocks and flows of human capital impede or facilitate structural adjustment and optimal choices. In the light of today's competitive pressures and pervasive changes in the realm of production (. . .) the need [is] to rethink the rules and traditions that govern human capital formation and decision-making systems."

[. . .]

VIGNETTE 2.1 EDUCATION FOR SUSTAINABILITY

T. O'Riordan, University of East Anglia

Perspective

Education for sustainability means preparing everyone to care for the planet by respecting justice, local identity and fundamental requirements for well being. Tuning into the rhythms of life support is generally the benchmark of many indigenous peoples and sensitive local cultures. By sensing the rhythms of long established ways of living, yet ensuring health, freedom of choice and opportunities to be adaptive for wealth creation in the modern world, it may be possible to link the traditional with the innovative through natural rhythms, social justice and returning waste into new economic options. Education, in this sense, is the emancipation of governing for the insurance of social harmony and shared futures. Education for sustainability is a process of societal transformation in which all learners share and adjust. The classroom becomes the changing roles of experience for co-operation around managing for more well being via less resource use and recyclability. The tools for ensuring this should be tried out in the classroom and transferred to the community, that is, the "community" becomes the child and parent learning from each other. Right now education is not preparing any of us for this perspective, so education for sustainability remains elusive and unful-filled. We need a series of experiments in a host of circumstances, and reliable means of sharing this learning process that will ensue. Only in patterns of governing change will education for sustainability thrive.

This means that education will begin to combine both its purpose (vocation, training) and its process (adaptability, sensitivity, teamwork, farsightedness) into a single trans-formative function. It will also mean that acting and doing would become elements of assessment and educational development as much as studying and communicating. Ideally, the school could become an experimental and experiential laboratory for the transition to sustainability where the pupil creates the kinds of community and styles of governing that sustainability encourages. Maybe, too, the schools inspection service will be able to audit sustainability initiatives and applaud good practice.

Governing for sustainability

Sustainability is a concept which remains ill-defined and ambiguous. In essence, humanity as a whole can only thrive if it does not diminish the capacity of the planet to support its requirements. Since no one knows just what this capacity is, humanity has to act with care, with anticipation and through sharing and caring. We all know that we do not meet these conditions. Indeed all governments operate on the basis of non-sustainability in order to retain a democracy. Their legitimacy emerges through their capacity to secure wealth, by means that do not lead to fairness of treatment, so that the poor always receive less than the wealthy.

In essence, this suggests that education is based on a philosophy of economy and society that is not sustainable. The notion of non-sustainability is based on the requirement to deplete resources, add toxics, breach the replenishment of renewable resources, and spread wealth, opportunity and health unevenly. Report after report states these outcomes from recent studies by the World Resources Institute (2000) to the UN Environment Programme (2000) and the UN Development Programme (1999). Only a lone voice of scepticism (Lomborg 2001) challenges these analyses, and even that author admits he is guided by statistics rather than facts on the ground. For an analysis of how and why governments depend on non-sustainability for their survival, see Held (1996) and Flyvberg (1998). The key issue to grasp here is that schools devise curricula on the basis of a received outlook that relies on being non-sustainable for its maintenance, at least for the short term.

Thus for governments to act to promote sustainability, there needs to be a change in how patterns of power operate. The shape will be towards many centres of decision-taking with governments acting through partnerships of public, private and voluntary sectors. Furthermore, the style of governing will move towards sharing responsibility and accountability from formal governments to a co-ordinative relationship with busi-ness and with civil society via citizens' associations of various kinds. This in turn means a broader based democracy dependent on more direct participation and the inclusion of many kinds of interests via combined patterns of social responsibility and reciprocity.

All this is summarised in Figure 4. The outer spokes represent the notion of multi-centred government, participatory and power-sharing democracy, and the linkage of global to local in thinking and action so that all citizens are both neighbours and plan-etary trustees. All this sounds far fetched. This may be so at present, but education for sustainability should begin the process of helping the picture to emerge.

According to Stephen Sterling (2001: 13) education is

• still informed by a mechanistic and programmatic view of the world, where progress is measured more by wealth than happiness, where quality of life is about cleanliness and security rather than trusteeship and reciprocity, and where learning is geared more to vocation and skills development, than to a sense of inner peace and spirituality;

* largely ignorant of the issues of social care, personal transformation, creative adapt-ability, sensitivity to environmental rhythms and tolerances that may guide humanity in the future;
* blind to the rise of ecological thinking which seeks to foster a more integrative awareness of the needs of people to the planet through a co-evolution of human and natural rights, and a co-responsibility for managing resources and property for both trusteeship as well as personal satisfaction.

> Within this paradigm, most mainstream education *sustains unstainability* – through uncritically reproducing norms, by fragmenting understanding, by sieving winners and losers, by recognising only a narrow part of the spectrum of human ability and need, by an inability to explore alternatives, by rewarding dependency and conformity, and by servicing the consumerist machine.
>
> (Sterling 2001: 14–15)

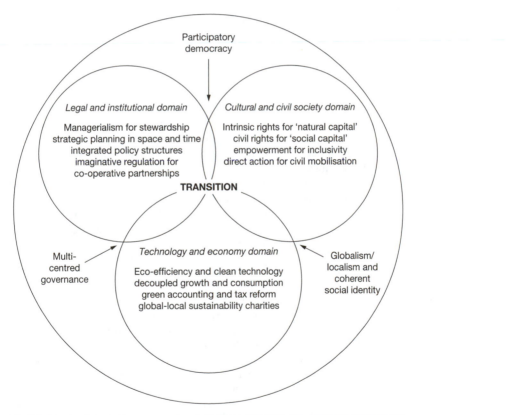

Sustainable development can mean almost anything, including the scope for fundamental contradiction. It is best to regard sustainable development as a constant process of transformation of a society and an economy towards acting as trustees for future generations of a planet that maintain and nurture life and habitability.

Figure 4 The domains of sustainability.

Towards a sustainability science

Science is both a cult and a form of knowing. The cult part is the culture of forming laws and devising theories by testing hypotheses through experimentation, replication, verification, falsification and organised observation. This process has clear rules and roles, and is protected by peer review. Science as a cult both evolves and is self-regulating. On the whole it is conservative in the face of innovation.

But science is also a way of knowing and feeling about the world beyond the conscious. In that sense, science is a process of understanding, revealing, exploring and connecting. The tools are observation, cooperation, intuition and instinct. Most people form views, and strength of opinion, through various personal and social processes of knowing. Many scientists regard much of this as emotional or irrational and certainly non-scientific. We are beginning to recognise that such processes of knowing are deeply important in shaping individual and communal views on matters of enormous importance in building trust in government, belief in community, love and respect for nature, and willingness to live beside and share with those of different incomes, opportunity histories, colour and religion.

Sustainability science is essentially the mix of the more informal, cultural knowing with the formal "science cult" ·acquisition of knowledge and prediction. Just as education should be both instrumental and intrinsic, i.e. gear pupils for vocations and many skills as well as to ensure they are holistic and sensitive to others' needs, so it is important for science to combine its great traditions in the cause of sustainability.

A sustainability science will need to:

*   span the range of spatial scales to encompass cause, effect, cumulative initiating actions and international agreements;
*   account both for short-term inertia where no discernible change is taking place while ecosystem tolerances are being studied, as well as convulsive synergisms whose immediate consequences may be dramatic, but whose longer scale outcomes may not be foreseeable;
*   deal with the complexities of discontinuities and unexpected combinations of processes and social responses in an arena of uncertainty;
*   recognise and appreciate the wide range of ways of knowing and understanding through which societies address nature and cope with dangers and opportunities, including the roles of instinct and intuition.

Sustainability science may not yet be fully defined, or initiated, or even accepted by those now facing the management of global environmental change (see Figure 5). At its heart, whatever its final destination, is the notion of a creative and open-hearted partnership between government, business, civil society and scientists. Such partnerships will be based on combined approaches to acquiring information, on sharing appreciation of differences, in understanding of causes, pathways and consequences, and on joint funding and action.

Sustainability science through partnership also introduces more demanding requirements for research method and policy evaluation. Inclusion of interested parties to the point where they become active co-managers may result in more attention being given to a mix of quantitative data gathering and forecasting, and qualitative means of exhibiting how various possible future states can be displayed. The act of visualisation or representation is likely to be value laden, advocacy driven and subtly coercing. Even if the act of exhibition and portrayal seeks to minimise such biases, there is still the

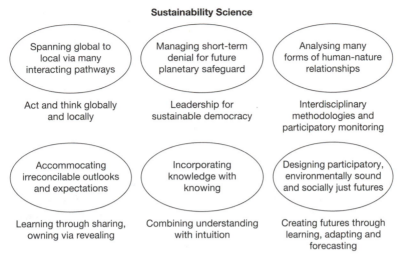

Sustainability Science

Spanning global to local via many interacting pathways	Managing short-term denial for future planetary safeguard	Analysing many forms of human-nature relationships
Act and think globally and locally	Leadership for sustainable democracy	Interdisciplinary methodologies and participatory monitoring
Accommocating irreconcilable outlooks and expectations	Incorporating knowledge with knowing	Designing participatory, environmentally sound and socially just futures
Learning through sharing, owning via revealing	Combining understanding with intuition	Creating futures through learning, adapting and forecasting

The diagram above summarises the six principal components of sustainability science. At its heart lies a fresh role for science in public affairs, as well as more innovative approaches to methodology and enquiry. The most notable extensions to existing transformations in scientific activity are:

- improving the scope for interdisciplinarity among the natural and social sciences as well as between them. There is a growing need to link chemistry to physics to ecosystem processes to discontinuities to sophisticated modelling and prediction. Exciting developments are already occurring, notably around the theme of interactive and integrated assessments of climate change futures;
- widening the basis of knowing and feeling, so that reason and judgement are explicitly connected in scientific enquiry, as much as they are in human experience. This means evolving tools for incorporating quantitative and qualitative approaches to analysis and prediction, as well as to expand the role of intuition and instinct as bases for forming personal outlooks and establishing social bonds;
- including all manner of interests, biases, social networks and political power relationships in the interactive and listening mode of science. These sciences become a partnership network that enhance and strengthen scientific advocacy and legitimacy.

Figure 5 Sustainability science in action.

matter that choices will reveal values, expectations, trust and views on fairness and equity for the well-being of others and ecosystems.

Sustainability science extends interdisciplinarity into the arena of knowledge and feeling, of measurement and judgement, of information and ethics, and of explanation and participation. Interdisciplinarity is built on the premise that there is no distinction between a natural system and human interpretation of that system. The "truth" of nature lies in the unfolding of human understanding, responsiveness and empathy both to the natural world, as revealed, and to the social world, as proclaimed by action through management or protest.

This quality of local empathy to the natural world is an intrinsic component of sustainability science. It places special emphasis on social memory, that is, the collective history of management of an area, the underlying expectations of future benefits for natural resources exploitation, and how various groups share a common identity with the natural world and human cultures.

VIGNETTE 2.2 LIFELONG LEARNING

J. Fien and G. López Ospina, Griffith University/UNESCO

Lifelong learning will hold the key to ensuring that, with the further development of information and communication technology, we avoid the 'have' and the 'have-nots' of the past. At the same time, we must ensure that we use the talent of all, to fulfil the potential of individuals and to ensure our economic survival as a nation. Lifelong learning is also essential to sustaining a civilised and cohesive society, in which people can develop as active citizens, where creativity is fostered and communities can be given practical support to overcome generations of disadvantage.

(UK Department for Education and Skills 1999)

Integrating basic education, adult and community education and appropriate technical and vocational education, lifelong learning is a vital ingredient of capacity building for a sustainable future. Indeed, sustainable development requires that education not only continues throughout life, but also is as broad as life itself; that is, it requires an approach to education that serves all people, draws upon all domains of knowledge, and seeks to integrate learning into all of life's major activities.

The time when education was the activity of childhood and work the pursuit of adults is long over. Education, at all levels, is a continual process in which opportunities for learning are available to people at every stage of life. The foundation of lifelong learning is basic education, which extends beyond preschool, primary and junior secondary schooling, to include basic literacy education for adults who may have missed important educational opportunities earlier in life. Only by taking this view will we successfully include the excluded, and reach those who otherwise could not be reached, in the transition to a sustainable future.

The rapid growth of knowledge has rendered the notion of schooling as a 'once and for all' preparation for life obsolete. Knowledge is advancing exponentially, yet not nearly as fast as the need for understanding and solutions. As the 1999 Cologne G8 Summit charter for lifelong learning argued, the challenge of globalisation is for every country to become a learning society and to ensure that its citizens are equipped with the knowledge, skills and qualifications they need, not just for improved living standards but also for an improved quality of life. As economies and societies become increasingly knowledge based, education and training will become more indispensible to economic success, social cohesion and civic responsibility (see Bourne 2002).

Two key components of lifelong learning for a sustainable future are adult and community education and appropriate technical and vocational education.

Adult and community education

Action towards sustainable development ultimately depends on public awareness, understanding and support. In democratic societies, public policy responds to the will of the people. It is here that public awareness and understanding of the need for sustainable development best expresses itself through support for laws, regulations and policies favourable to the environment, social equity and peace. People express their preferences as they decide how to spend their money, as well as by decisions over whom to vote for. Public action, through consumption, voting or otherwise, however, requires more than 'public awareness'. What is needed is an understanding of the issues.

A key lesson of adult and community education is the realisation that people are not unaware of the social and environmental problems they face. In fact, more often than not, people have learnt quite a lot about them – from the media, social movements, scientists, governments and, most importantly, their daily experience. Consequently, there is a need to move beyond awareness raising, and to engage people critically and creatively in their own communities, planning and participating in action for socially just and ecologically sound development at the local level (Clover *et al.* 2000). This can lead to an appreciation of the root causes of issues and problems, an analysis of whose interests and voices are being served and whose are excluded or marginalised, and a concern for the likely consequences of a given consumer, electoral or other decision. Public understanding of this type is the foundation for people to fulfil their roles as responsible citizens, consumers and public-spirited individuals.

Public awareness and understanding are, at once, consequences of education and influences on the educational process. A public well informed of the need for sustainable development will insist that public educational institutions include in their curricula the interdisciplinary subject matter, values education, and the skills of critical thinking and political literacy needed to participate effectively in activities directed towards achieving sustainable development. The students that emerge from such courses will, for their part, be alert to the need for public authorities to make adequate provision for the protection of the environment and promotion of social justice and peace in all economic, health, education and foreign policy decisions and plans.

The precautionary principle tells us that a major reason for focusing on adult education for sustainable development is that it would be unwise to wait for the present generation of school and college students to grow up and begin applying what they are learning. Indeed, it is today's adults who are the primary voters, consumers, workers, teachers, scientists, and parents. At the Conference on Adult Education (CONFINTEA V), meeting in Hamburg in 1997, members of the International Council for Adult Education's Learning for Environmental Action Program said today's adults: 'must have the opportunity to develop their critical thinking skills, and to use their ideas, knowledge, power and imaginations to begin to make change rather than simply maintaining the ecological status quo' (cited in Clover *et al.* 2000). In this way, education for sustainability is both a key process and outcome of adult and community education.

Appropriate Technical and Vocational Education

Technical and Vocational Education (TVE) is vital to two of the most urgent human resource problems facing global society: the need to develop appropriate skills for sustainable development and the high levels of unemployment and under-employment in many countries.

TVE trains technicians, who are the interface of nature, technology, economy and society and who have a key role to play in helping society resolve environmental and development issues. Challenges such as: reorienting technology and managing risks, meeting essential needs such as food, water, sanitation and, at the same time, conserving natural resources, reducing energy and resource consumption, all have to be tackled by technicians. Technicians, who are aware of and have acquired practical skills for sustainable development, can ultimately apply increasingly sustainable practices, as they are the ones who are involved in production.

Recognising the crucial role of TVE graduates in devising and implementing practical solutions to problems of sustainable development, the UNESCO International

Congress on Technical and Vocational Education stressed that TVE systems should not only focus on economic dimensions but should also incorporate emerging issues such as the use of environmentally sound technology as well as develop the 'whole person' rather than just their knowledge and skills or their potential to earn a living. Thus, it must also provide activities and support structures that encourage self-esteem, basic life skills (saving, credit, etc.), self-protection strategies (from violence, sexual abuse and HIV/AIDS), civic responsibility and electoral enfranchisement.

Formal programmes of TVE are important in countries of both the North and the South. However, non-formal TVE is also important as a strategy for empowering out-of-school youth, the homeless, street children and other marginalised youth. Current education systems are sometimes not serving the best interests of such young people. Programmes are needed to develop practical and entrepreneurial skills in areas such as recycling, alternative energy technologies and handicraft production to stimulate and support young people to apply their creativity, skills and solidarity in income-generating activities, especially in the so-called informal or 'popular' economy.

Indeed, the popular economy is the main sector of productive activity for the majority of the world's poor, especially those living in the world's rapidly expanding cities. The popular economy represents the last resort against extreme poverty, unemployment and social exclusion, and is made up of a multitude of small businesses, often family-run, but also of individual activities run by women and youths. Jobs vary greatly and include: recycling discarded household equipment, repairing machines, sewing, selling and transporting water, making craft goods, and market stalls. To contribute effectively to sustainable development, TVE needs to address training needs for these jobs also.

Conclusion

Lifelong learning for a sustainable future involves much more than adult and community education, and technical and vocational education. These two key components were selected for discussion here because they not only highlight themes particular to these individual areas of concern, but also highlight the fundamentally democratic and egalitarian ethos of both a sustainable future and the approaches to education required to attain it. This democratic and egalitarian ethos also underpins basic literacy education for adults when it is conducted, not just for technical reasons, but so that people can learn not only to read and write words, but also to read and write their world.

CHAPTER 3

LANGUAGE AND MEANING

READING 3.1 WHO DREW THE SKY? CONFLICTING ASSUMPTIONS IN ENVIRONMENTAL EDUCATION

A.W.G. Stables

Source: *Educational Philosophy and Theory* 33(2), 2001a: 250–254

The search for a 'common sense' for EE

The position taken in this paper is inherently post-foundationalist in calling for acceptance of differing positions but retaining a belief in the potential of EE to help bring about some sort of sustainability. Indeed, none of the above positions is necessarily hopeless in this respect. Even a relativist position (after Rorty or Derrida perhaps) calls for deference to an Other. If we cannot know Nature, at least we can defer to its Otherness; perhaps the policy option of leaving well alone is one that has been too little adopted. Neither does the adoption of a post-foundational position infer that there can be no common ground between environmental educators. The *sensus communis* which Gadamer (1975), for example, sees as an important indicator of our historically-effected consciousness (and for which Kant, too, had considerable respect) tells us that there cannot be many with an interest in environment generally who do not share some apparently common concern for a better, cleaner, healthier, or, at least, not-worse biophysical environment. There are not likely to be many people who would not subscribe to such sentiments, though critical realists might see the issues as subsumed within a programme for social, rather than merely environmental, change. At this level of generality (only), there can be some agreement about the aims or, at least, some of the objectives of EE; at this level, EE certainly allows for pluralism.

The recent EE discourse in the UK and several other countries recently has put increased emphasis on 'Sustainable Development Education' (SDE) rather than 'Environmental Education'. It may be the hope of some that this re-orientation will give increased clarity of focus and aims. However, it is already acknowledged in the curriculum development literature that SDE is not an unproblematic term, despite its origins in Brundtland's (arguably narrowly social and anthropocentric) ideal of meeting the needs of the present while not compromising the ability of future generations to meet their own needs. The term is effectively redefined in the latest curriculum guidance provided for teachers in Britain, for example, with seven key concepts held to be central to it (interdependence; citizenship and stewardship; needs and rights of future generations; diversity; quality of life, equity and justice; sustainable change, and uncertainty and precaution: CEE *et al.* 1999). If the term were uni-dimensional and unproblematic across all the language games in which it appears, there would be validity in such a breakdown of its elements. In reality, increased reflection on the term and its uses is unlikely to result in greater consensus, unless there is universal aspiration towards a consensual definition. SDE is particularly problematic in this regard because 'sustainable development' is a good example of a 'paradoxical compound policy slogan' (Stables 1996), the appeal of which is that it can allow those of widely differing views to 'buy into' it to some extent. In the words of Fairclough (1995), it has high 'ambivalence potential'. In this case, on the most obvious level, economic interests are served by 'development' while ecological concerns are addressed by 'sustainable'; at the same time, economic interests are served by 'sustaining' profits, investments etc.; the compound term, however, allows us to feel that the two key terms are unproblematically complementary: that we can 'have our cake and eat it'. Such paradoxical, or oxymoronic, policy slogans have become increasingly popular in British educational discourse in recent years; other examples are 'equality of opportunity', 'multicultural society' and 'parity of esteem'. In each case, widely conflicting interests are combined into what is intended to serve as a single regulative ideal. Practically, of course, much good can be done as a result of such sloganising, and each of the slogans cited above has wide popular appeal (it is perhaps too early to claim this for 'sustainable development'). However, it is important to bear in mind that the implementations and practical outcomes of such policies are highly unpredictable, dependent as they are on what David Corson has referred to as 'secondary elaborations of belief' (Corson 1988: 253). The variety in the existing realisation of EE within school curricula might be seen as compelling evidence of this. Policies work for democratic politicians to some extent merely by allowing those politicians to be re-elected, but the popular appeal of a policy does not predetermine even the nature, let alone the effectiveness, of its outcomes when these are evaluated in any more than crudely populist terms. SDE may, therefore, prove an even more contested field than EE, both because it is a more sophisticated, and thus potentially ambiguous, compound term, and because it currently enjoys even less popular appeal in schools and colleges. Already, some environmental educators have expressed severe doubts about the reorientation of EE as SDE (Jickling 2000).

How should educators, who tend to share the general aspiration towards a better, cleaner, less depleted world but who approach EE/SDE from widely differing perspectives and with differing preconceptions, work with their students within this contested field?

To what extent might the *sensus communis* also allow us to make some general statements in relation to teaching processes? (By 'teaching processes' I mean those generic processes to do with teaching and learning, in whatever field.) In this area we can suppose a degree of loose consensus concerning three areas, though we cannot assume any consensus regarding their appropriate balance: the importance of knowledge (practical and theoretical), the importance of cultural sensitivity (involving some degree of empathy), and the importance of enterprise or empowerment. In EE/SDE, I have suggested in previous papers (particularly Stables 1998) that we might usefully think of such broad educational objectives in relation to the development of functional, cultural and critical environmental literacies, thus enabling us to relate pedagogical processes in EE/SDE to those in other areas.[1]

As a focus of differing disciplinary traditions, the environment can be understood in various ways, so even agreement on what should constitute functional environmental literacy cannot be taken for granted. Nevertheless, given the dominance of instrumental rationality in modern cultural practice and thus in the pursuit of modern science (see Habermas 1971), the teaching and learning of the basics of scientific ecology is an example of one area that is bound to underpin the development of such a 'literacy', especially in advanced technological societies.

However, functionality without cultural sensitivity and critical reflection is potentially as destructive as constructive, even if it is a functionality that takes some account of, say, resource management and social and environmental consequence. Knowing about ecology does not ensure ecologically responsible behaviour, where such knowledge forms part of a tradition that eschews considerations of value, or values only 'progress' as measured in narrowly anthropocentric terms. Certainly, in terms of purely instrumental rationality and arguably, even with respect to social justice, a 'sustainable' ecosystem does not guarantee a world worth living in; a dictatorship could be more ecologically responsible than a democracy, for example. Even 'sustainable development' might be unbearable, if it simply meant the union of economic growth and environmental sustainability – even if it included more equitable distribution of resources – because it might be achieved without any consideration of other important value domains, such as the aesthetic.

For the world to be worth living in, we surely need high levels of both cultural and critical environmental literacies in order that we can acknowledge that we live in an ecosystem, the future of which is dependent on our moral choices, feel empowered to act for the environment in ways that seem apposite and become better able to evaluate the effects of our, and others', actions with respect to the environment. What should the role of the teacher be in such a contested field? In terms of the typology above, it cannot simply be to develop functional environmental literacy, important though this is. Such a simple outcome orientation is untenable when we cannot assume agreement over either ends or means. In effect, the need to develop cultural and critical environmental literacies demands a critical retrospective on the histories that have brought us to an appreciation of ecological crisis: the history of science, for example, and of the increasingly secular humanism that has driven and interpreted it. EE/SDE calls for a critical retrospective on humanist modernity, inspired by a sense that the cultural practices through which we have been nurtured may be, unless modified, inadequate bases for the future, however much we are indebted and attached to them.

In terms of teaching, this implies a reconceptualisation of environment from principally cross-disciplinary to within-disciplinary concern, with inter-disciplinarity acknowledged as driven by specialism rather than *vice-versa*. The search becomes less for an holistic approach to EE and more for the best way to develop, and thus modify, the disciplines in a period of ecological crisis. If we are to take the later Wittgenstein (and others) seriously, environment should be seen as a topic within fields rather than across fields because fields, not topics, define and proscribe meanings. Nevertheless, in each discipline there remains scope for an increased focus on how human and non-human activity are mutually implicated.

Take, for example, the study of literature. A body of eco-critical work has arisen in recent years (e.g. Bate 1991; Buell 1995), some of it looking explicitly at literary approaches to the human–nature relationship, such as Buell's criteria for environmental writing (1995: 7). As I have attempted to show in an essay on Scotland as a 'living nation' in Shakespeare's *Macbeth* (Stables 1993), there is much scope for new and accessible readings of canonical works stemming from our ecological concerns. A recent European Union- (EU-) funded project attempted to develop this and other ideas for creative classroom use (Bishop *et al.* 2000). This project developed five foci based on the various possible relationships between 'environment' and 'text' in literary and media studies, from eco-critical readings of literary texts (Focus 1) to the creation of texts exploring environmental issues (Focus 3) and consideration of the environment itself as text (Focus 4). Thus the aim was to explore the human-nature relationship through good literature and media education rather than distorting the curriculum by studying certain texts merely as the embodiment of environmental and ecological themes and issues (see also Stables 1993). There must be scope for other subjects to give more attention to environmental issues without the crude imposition of 'sustainable development' as a cross-curricular theme or aim assuming validity free of context. For example, the work of Fernand Braudel (1981) and, more recently, of Simon Schama (1995) shows clearly how cultural and social histories can be studied within broader environmental contexts.

Our late-modern, or post-modern, consciousnesses are formed by the ways of thinking that have brought us to the realisation of environmental crisis. Herein lie both the threat of a double-bind and our hope for the future. We are continuously able to reflect on and modify such mental structures, as Kant suggested (whether or not such reflection is driven purely by experience). Given the impossibility of constraining EE within a narrowly defined set of aims and measurable outcomes, we should rather take the ever-present opportunity of examining the cultural, social and academic practices of our recent histories from the viewpoint of our environmentally-concerned present. Alongside developing functional environmental literacy, in part through a basic grounding in scientific ecology, education could be more strongly orientated to developing increased meta-awareness of dominant cultural practices within our own societies and of the cultural practices of others. Above all, as educators, we are aiming to empower those who will live in the world of the future to draw their own conclusions in circumstances that are bound to be different from our own. They should then be better able, individually and co-operatively, to act in ways that seem to them appropriate to purpose.

[. . .]

Note

1   Briefly: functional literacy relates to the ability to 'get by' as circumstances demand; cultural literacy to an understanding of the significance of (for example) places and events within social and cultural practice; critical literacy to the ability to rework cultural and social practices for personal and mutual empowerment. For a more extended overview, see Stables (1998); for a fuller discussion relating to critical environmental literacy, see Stables and Scott (1999).

READING 3.2 ENVIRONMENT AND DEVELOPMENT: THE STORY OF A DANGEROUS LIAISON

W. Sachs

Source: *The Ecologist* 21(6), 1991: 253–257

The marriage between environment and development

However, there was still a long way to go until, in 1987, the Brundtland Report could finally announce the marriage between craving for development and concern for the environment. As the adamant rejection of all "no-growth" positions in particular by Third World governments at the Stockholm Conference demonstrated, the compulsion to drive up the GNP had turned many into cheerful enemies of nature. It was only in the course of the 1970s, under the additional impact of the oil crisis, that it began to dawn on governments that continued growth not only depended upon capital formation and a skilled workforce but also on the long-term availability of natural resources. Concerns about the conservation of inputs to future growth led to development planners gradually adopting a strand of thought which goes back to the introduction of forest management in Germany around 1800: that – in the words of Gifford Pinchot, the steward of Theodore Roosevelt's conservation programme – "conservation means the greatest good for the greatest number for the longest time". Tomorrow's growth was seen to be under the threat of nature's revenge. Consequently, it was time to extend the attention span of planning and to call for the "efficient management of natural resources" as part of the development package: "We have in the past been concerned about the impacts of economic growth upon the environment. We are now forced", concludes the Brundtland Report, "to concern ourselves with the impacts of ecological stress – degradation of soils, water regimes, atmosphere, and forests – upon our economic prospects."

Another roadblock on the way to wedding "environment" to "development" has been an ossified vision of growth. The decades of smoke-stack industrialization had left the impression that growth was invariably linked to squandering ever more resources. Under the influence of the appropriate technology movement, however, this notion of development began to crumble and give way to an awareness of the availability of technological choices. It was, after all, in Stockholm that NGOs had gathered for the first time to stage a counter-conference which called for alternative paths in development. Later, Initiatives like the Declaration of Cocoyoc and the Dag Hammarskjöld Foundation's "What Now?" helped – perhaps unwittingly – to challenge the assumption of an invariable technological process and to pluralize the road to growth. Out of this awareness of technological flexibility grew, towards the end of the 1970s, a new perception of the ecological predicament: the "limits to growth" are no longer seen as an insurmountable barrier blocking the surge of growth, but as discrete obstacles forcing the flow to take a different route. "Soft-path" studies in areas from energy to health care proliferated and charted new beds for the misdirected river.

Finally, environmentalism was regarded as inimical to the alleviation of poverty throughout the 1970s. The claim to be able to abolish poverty has been – and still is – the single most important pretension of the development ideology, in particular after its enthronement as the official priority goal after the speech at Nairobi by the then World Bank President, Robert McNamara, in 1973. Poverty had long been regarded as unrelated to environmental degradation, which was attributed to the impact of industrialization; the poor entered the equation only as future claimants to an industrial lifestyle. But with spreading deforestation and desertification, the poor were quickly identified as agents of destruction and became the targets of campaigns to promote "environmental consciousness". Once blaming the victim had entered the professional consensus, the old recipe could be offered for meeting the new disaster: since growth was supposed to remove poverty, the environment could only be protected through a new era of growth. As it says in the Brundtland Report: "Poverty reduces people's capacity to use resources in a sustainable manner; it intensifies pressure on the environment . . . A necessary but not sufficient condition for the elimination of absolute poverty is a relatively rapid rise in per capita incomes in the Third World." The way was thus cleared for the marriage between "environment" and "development"; the newcomer would be welcomed to the old family.

> Brundtland suggests further growth, no longer in order to achieve the happiness of the greatest number, but to contain the disaster for the generations to come.

The rejuvenation of development

"No development without sustainability; no sustainability without development" is the formula which establishes the newly-formed bond. "Development" emerges rejuvenated from this liaison, the ailing concept gaining another lease of life. This is nothing less than the repeat of a proven ruse: every time in the last 30 years that the destructive effects of development were recognized, the concept was extended in such a way as to include both injury and therapy. For example, when it became obvious, around 1970, that the pursuit of development actually intensified poverty, the notion of "equitable development" was invented so as to reconcile the irreconcilable: the creation of poverty with the abolition of poverty. In the same vein, the Brundtland Report incorporated concern for the environment into the concept of development by effecting "sustainable development" as the conceptual roof for both violating and healing the environment.

Certainly, the new era requires development experts to widen their attention span and to monitor water and soils, air and energy use. But development remains what it has always been, an array of interventions for boosting GNP: "Given expected population growth, a five-to-tenfold increase in world industrial output can be anticipated by the time world population stabilizes sometime in the next century." Brundtland thus ends up suggesting further growth, but no longer, as in the old days of development, in order to achieve the happiness of the greatest number, but to contain the disaster for the generations to come. The threat to the planet's survival looms large. Has there ever been a better excuse for intrusion? New areas of intervention open up, nature becomes a domain of politics and a new breed of technocrats feels the vocation to steer growth along the edge of the abyss.

A successful ambivalence

Ecology is both computer modelling and political action, scientific discipline as well as all-embracing worldview. The concept joins two different worlds. On the one side protest movements all over the globe wage their battles for the conservation of nature, fighting with evidence offered by the scientific discipline which studies the relationships between organisms and their environment. On the other side, academic ecologists have seen with bewilderment how their hypotheses have become a reservoir for political slogans and have been elevated to principles for some post-industrial philosophy. The liaison between protest and science can hardly be called a happy one. While the researchers have resented being called on to testify against the rationality of science and its benefits for humanity, activists have, ironically enough, adopted theorems like the "balance of nature" or the "priority of the whole over its parts" at a moment when they had already been abandoned by the discipline.

> The ecology movement may be the first anti-modernist movement which attempts to justify its claims with the enemy's own means

However, without recourse to science, the ecology movement would probably have remained a bunch of "nature freaks" and never acquired the power of a historical force. One secret of its success lies precisely in its hybrid character. As a movement highly suspicious of science and technical rationality, it plays anew the counter-melody which has accompanied the history of modernity ever since romanticism. But as a science-based movement, it is capable of questioning the foundations of modernity and contesting its logic in the very name of science. In fact, the ecology movement seems to be the first anti-modernist movement attempting to justify its claims with the enemy's own means. It bases its fundamental challenge not on the arts (like the romanticists), on organicism (like the conservatives), on the glory of nature (like preservationists), or on a transcendental creed (like fundamentalists), although all these themes are present, but on ecosystems theory which integrates physics, chemistry and biology. This unique achievement, however cuts both ways: the science of ecology gives rise to a scientific anti-modernism which has largely succeeded in disrupting the dominant discourse, yet the *science* of ecology opens the way for the technocratic recuperation of the protest. This ambivalence of "ecology" is, on the epistemological level, responsible for the success as well as the failure of the movement.

Ecology between organicism and mechanism

While its roots go back to 18th century natural history, ecology became a fully-fledged discipline – with university chairs, journals and professional associations – only during the first two decades of this century. It inherited from its precursors in the 19th century a predilection for looking at the world of plants (and later animals) in terms of geographically-distributed ensembles. The tundra in Canada is evidently different from the rainforest in Amazonia. Consequently, pre-ecology organized its perception of nature, following the core themes of romanticism, around the axiom that place constitutes community. From an emphasis on the impact of climatic and physical circumstances on communities, the attention shifted, around the turn of the century, to the processes within these communities. The competitive/cooperative relations between organisms in a given environment and, under the influence of Darwinism, their adaptive change through time ("succession") emerged as the new discipline's field of study. Impressed by the mutual dependency of species in biotic communities, ecologists began to wonder just how real these units were. Is a given ensemble only the sum of individual organisms or does it express a higher identity? Up to the Second World War, the latter concept was clearly dominant: plant/animal societies were seen as super-organisms that evolve actively, adapting to the environment. In opting for organicism – the postulate that the whole is superior to its parts and an entity in its own right – the ecologists were able firmly to constitute the object of their science.

This anti-reductionist attitude was doomed after the war when, across disciplines, mechanistic conceptions of science again prevailed. Ecology was ripe for a restructuring along the lines of positivist methodology; like any other science, it was supposed to produce causal hypotheses which are empirically testable and prognostically relevant. The search for general laws, however, implies concentrating attention on a minimum of elements which are common to the overwhelming variety of settings. The appreciation of a particular place with a particular community lost importance. Moreover, these elements and their relationships have to be measurable; the quantitative analysis of mass, volume, temperature and the like replaced the qualitative interpretation of an ensemble's unity and order. Following physics, at that time the leading science, ecologists identified energy as the common denominator that links animals and plants with the non-living environment. Generally, the calorie became the unit of measurement for it permitted description of both the organic and the inorganic world as two aspects of the same reality – the flow of energy.

In this way, biology was reduced to energetics. But the holistic tradition of ecology did not wither away. It reappeared in a new language: "system" replaced the concept of "living community", and "homeostasis" the idea of evolution towards a "climax". The concept of "system" integrates an originally anti-modern notion, the "whole" or the "organism", into scientific discourse. It allows one to insist on the priority of the whole without vitalist overtones, while it acknowledges an autonomous role for the parts without, however, relinquishing the idea of a supra-individual reality. This is accomplished by interpreting the meaning of wholeness as "homeostasis" and the relations between the parts and the whole, in the tradition of mechanical engineering, as "self-regulatory feedback mechanisms" steadily maintaining that homeostasis. It was the concept of the ecosystem that thus combined the organicist heritage with scientific reductionism. And it is this concept of ecosystem that simultaneously gave to the ecology movement both a quasi-spiritual dimension and scientific credibility.

Since the 1960s ecology has left the university biology departments and migrated into the common consciousness. The scientific term has turned into a worldview. As such, it carries the promise of reuniting what has been fragmented, of healing what has been torn apart, in short of caring for the whole. The numerous wounds inflicted by modern, goal-specific institutions provoked a renewed desire for wholeness, and that desire found a suitable language in the science of ecology. The conceptual switch that connected the biology circuit with that of society at large was the notion of ecosystem. In retrospect, this comes as no surprise, since the concept is well equipped to serve this function: in scope, as well as in scale, it has an enormous power of inclusion. It unites not only plants and animals – as already the notion of living community did – but also includes within its purview the non-living world on the one hand, and the world of humans on the other. Likewise, ecosystems come in many sizes, small and big, nesting like babouschka dolls, each within the next, from the microscopic to the planetary level. The concept is free-ranging in scale. Omnipresent, as ecosystems appear to be, they are consequently hailed as keys to understanding order in the world. More so, as they appear to be all-essential for the continuance of the webs of life, they call for nothing less than care and reverence. A remarkable career, indeed – a technical term that has strode into the realms of the metaphysical. For many environmentalists, ecology seems to reveal the moral order of being by uncovering simultaneously the verum, bonum and pulchrum of reality: it suggests not only the truth, but also a moral imperative and even aesthetic perfection.

On the other hand, however, ecosystems theory, based on cybernetics as the science of engineering feedback mechanisms, represents anything but a break with the ominous tradition of increasing control over nature. How can a theory of regulation be separated from an interest in manipulation? After all, systems theory aims at control of the second order; it strives to control self-control. As is obvious, the metaphor underlying systems thinking is the self-governing machine, a machine capable of adjusting its performance to changing conditions according to pre-set rules. Whatever the object being observed, be it a factory, a family or a lake, attention focuses on the regulating mechanisms by which the system in question responds to the changes in its environment. Once identified, the way is open to condition these mechanisms so as to alter the responsiveness of the system. Looking at nature in terms of self-regulating systems, therefore, implies either the intention to measure how much more development nature can take or the aim of adjusting her feedback mechanisms through human intervention. Both strategies amount to completing Bacon's vision of dominating nature, albeit with the pretension of manipulating her revenge. In this way, ecosystem technology turns finally against ecology as a worldview. A movement which bid farewell to modernity ends up in welcoming it, in new guise, through the back door.

Survival as a reason of state

In history, many reasons have been put forward to justify state power and its claim on citizens. Objectives like law and order and welfare through redistribution have been invoked time and again. More recently, development has become the goal in the name of which many Third World governments sacrifice the vital interests of huge sections of their populations. "Survival of the planet" is on its way to becoming the justification for a new wave of state interventions into people's lives all over the world.

The World Bank, for instance, sees a gleam of hope for itself again, after its reputation had been badly shaken by criticism from environmentalists: "I anticipate", declared its Senior Vice-President David Hopper in 1988, "that over the course of the next year, the Bank will be addressing the full range of environmental needs of its partner nations, needs that will run from the technical to the institutional, from the micro-details of project design to the macro-requirements of formulating, implementing and enforcing environmental policies". The voices of protest, after finally penetrating the air-conditioned offices in Washington, only led to the Bank seeing a new area for its activities: the demands to stop World Bank activities provoked their expansion!

While environmentalists have put the spotlight on the numerous vulnerabilities of nature, governments discover a new conflict-ridden area in need of political gover-nance and regulation. This time, it is not peace between people which is at stake, but the orderly relations between humanity and nature. To mediate in this conflict, the state assumes the task of gathering evidence on the state of nature and the effects of humanity, of enacting norms and laws to direct behaviour, and enforcing compliance to the new rules. On the one hand, nature's capacity to provide services such as clean air and water and a reliable climate has to be closely watched. On the other, society's innumerable actions have to be kept under sufficient control in order to direct the exploitation of nature into tolerable channels. To carry out these formidable objec-tives, the state has to install the necessary monitoring systems, regulatory mechanisms and executive agencies. A new class of professionals is required, while eco-science provides the epistemology of intervention. In short, the experts who used to look after economic growth now claim to be presiding over survival.

Global knowledge versus local knowledge

Many rural communities in the Third World, however, do not need to wait until specialists from hastily founded research institutes on sustainable agriculture swarm out to deliver their solutions for, say, soil erosion. Provision for the coming generations has been part of their tribal and peasant practices since time immemorial. What is more, the new centrally designed schemes for the "management of environmental resources" threaten to collide with locally based knowledge about conservation.

For example, the Indian Chipko movement has made the courage and wisdom of those women who protected the trees with their bodies against the chainsaws of the loggers a symbol of local resistance acclaimed far beyond the borders of India. Yet their success had its price: forest managers moved in and claimed responsibility for the trees. Thus, the nature of the conflict changed: the hard-nosed woodcutters gave way to soft-spoken experts. These brought along surveys, showed around diagrams, pointed out growth curves and argued over optimal felling rates. Planting schemes and wood-processing industries were proposed, and attempts made to lure the villagers into becoming small timber producers. Those who had defended the trees to protect their means of subsistence and to bear witness to the interconnectedness of life, saw them-selves unexpectedly bombarded with research findings and the abstract categories of resource economics. All along, the "national interest" in "balanced resource develop-ment" was invoked. It mattered little in the face of these priorities what significance the forest had for the villagers, or what species of tree would be most suitable for the people's sustenance. An ecology that aimed at the management of scarce natural resources clashed with an ecology that wished to preserve the local commons. In this way, national resource planning can lead to, albeit with novel means, a continuation of the war against subsistence.

Though the resource experts arrived in the name of protecting nature, their image of nature profoundly contradicts the image of nature held by the villagers. Nature, when she becomes an object of politics and planning, turns into "environment". It is misleading to use the two concepts interchangeably for this impedes the recognition of "environment" as a particular construction of "nature" specific to our time. Contrary to its present aura, there has rarely been a concept that represented nature as more abstract, passive and void of qualities than "environment". Squirrels on the ground are as much a part of the environment as water in aquifers, gases in the atmosphere, marshes at the coast or even high-rise buildings in inner cities. Sticking the label "environment" on the natural world makes any specific and local quality fade away; even more, it makes nature appear passive and lifeless, waiting to be acted upon. This is a far cry from, for instance, the Indian villager's conception of Prakriti, the active and productive power which permeates every stone or tree, fruit or animal, and sustains them along with the human world. Prakriti grants the blessings of nature as a gift; she has consequently to be honoured and wooed.

Cultures that see nature as a living being tend to carefully circumscribe the range of human intervention, because a hostile response is to be expected when a critical threshold has been passed. "Environment" has nothing in common with this view; through its modernist eyes, limits appear as physical constraints to survival. To call traditional economies "ecological" often neglects that basic difference in belief.

[. . .]

VIGNETTE 3.1   ECOLOGY, EDUCATION AND MODERNITY: NATURE AS A SELF-REGULATING MACHINE

M. Peters, University of Glasgow

Writing a decade apart, Sachs (1991) and Stables (2001a) share some interesting assumptions concerning modernity. They both emphasise the need for a scientific ecology (and, for Stables, minimally, a functional literacy based upon it). They both put an accent on the 'successful ambivalence' of 'ecology' and kinship terms like 'environment' and 'sustainable development' that form part of the emerging discourse on the environment. This ambivalence, I shall argue, goes right to the heart of the problem in constructing ecology both as a scientific discipline, on the one hand, and as a metaphysical world-view and popular form of political activism, on the other. Sachs pictures this as an opposition of science and political struggle and Stables, who describes 'sustainable development' as a 'paradoxical compound policy slogan', details the difficulties with overcoming this legacy in education – a problem he attempts to deal with by talk of three environmental literacies: functional (i.e., scientific ecology), critical and cultural. Stables (2001a: 253) also explicitly calls for 'a critical retrospective on humanist modernity' and hints at a post-foundational position that somehow might go beyond modernity. In a similar manner, Sachs (1991: 254) suggests that as a science-based movement, ecology is 'capable of questioning the foundations of modernity and contesting its logic in the very name of science'.

The opposition in question might be better seen in terms of a broader philosophical position that lines up science on one side with a mainstream, 'no-limits-to-growth' economics of development (read 'modernization'), reflecting Enlightenment (and Eurocentric) assumptions about 'change' and 'progress' against a Romanticist anti-modernism that, by contrast, attempts to hold onto organicist metaphors, resists the instrumental rationality that characterises the perceived positivism of the sciences, and courts 'deep ecology' principles, 'local knowledge' and the naturalism of other cultures.

This deep philosophical ambivalence which originates within Enlightenment culture hints at a conceptual and epistemological tug-of-war that has its genealogy, at least in the modern *episteme* (to use a Foucaldian term), from the days well before the disciplinary formation of scientific ecology in the early twentieth century. Understanding this opposition – the whole intersecting matrix of grand narratives of modernism and its oppositional anti-modernist counter-narratives – which, incidentally is still very much part of the ongoing 'culture wars' of the early twenty-first century, is fundamental to understanding how we might break free of this controlling dualism and move beyond modernity. Both Stables and Sachs attempt to formulate the significance of such an epistemological and ethical break and what its importance would be for 'development' and 'survival' (Sachs 1991) and 'environmental education' and education for 'sustainability' and survival (Stables 2001a). Neither, however, uses the term 'postmodernity' to describe this possibility, nor do they frame their arguments in terms of cognate terms – 'modernization' and 'postmodernization' – both of which I think are key descriptive and explanatory concepts to clarifying the stakes of the debate.

Sachs does provide a critical genealogy of ecology: its roots in eighteenth-century natural history (strongly imbued with theological assumptions), its professionalisation and institutionalisation in the academy, its shift in focus from 'geographically-distributed ensembles' where 'place constitutes community' to 'processes within these communities' – a kind of organicism that sat well with romanticism but was replaced by a reductionist science after the war. This epistemological shift to positivist methodology modelled on the physics of the day, Sachs informs us, 'identified energy as the common denominator' and, thus, 'biology was reduced to energetics'. Yet the holistic tradition did not disappear as it was reconstituted in the language of 'system', which Sachs claims 'reintegrates an originally anti-modern notion . . . into scientific discourse'. He shows how the concept of ecosystem, reoriented through mechanical engineering, became 'self-regulatory feedback mechanisms', thus 'combining the organicist heritage with scientific reductionism'. Sachs goes on to suggest that 'ecology' escaped its scientific reductionist straitjacket to become free-ranging and uniting within its purview not only plants and animals, but also the non-living world and the world of humans. Outlining the natural history of the concept of ecology, Sachs remarks, it 'strode into the metaphysical' and became powerful enough to suggest not only the truth but also a moral imperative and aesthetic perfection. Yet, ecosystems theory, based on cybernetic epistemology and the engineering feedback mechanism, simply re-established 'control' (of nature) at the second order and completed Francis Bacon's *modernist* vision of dominating nature.

Ecology, in its very conception and in its current disciplinary understandings, harbours and mirrors the wider contestation and struggle between the cultural forces of modernity and anti-modernity. This broader philosophical contestory dualism is also reflected in a series of oppositions mentioned by both authors: in what Sachs calls 'the marriage of environment and development'; between global knowledge and local knowledge; between First World (modern) state governance of the relations between humanity and nature, on the one hand, and Third World (premodern) subsistence, on the other; between scientific and political models for environmental education and sustainable development education.

This fundamental dualism is also echoed in the opposition between 'environment' and 'development' and Sachs also documents the conceptual shifts that occurred with the challenge to narrow conceptions of growth as an 'invariable technologized process'. Sachs tells the story of the eventual *marriage* of growth and sustainability epitomised in the slogan 'No development without sustainability; no sustainability without development'. As Sachs (1991: 254) argues: 'the Brundtland Report incorporated the concern for the environment by erecting "sustainable development" as the conceptual roof for both violating and healing the environment'. And while 'poverty' also forced its recognition into the discourse of development as part of ecological considerations, 'development remains what it has always been, an array of interventions for boosting GNP' (ibid.). The same story can be told about education, about how education in the era of the knowledge economy has become the main means for modernization, where people treated as 'human resources' or bits of 'human capital' – what Heidegger calls 'standing-reserve' – are seen as sites for state investment. We might paraphrase Sachs in relation to education – 'education has remained what it has always been, an intervention for boosting GNP'. Stables also recognizes how this ambivalence cuts deeply into the edifices of a *modern* education.

The weakness of Sach's and Stables' accounts, in so far as they share the same assumptions, is that they do not explicitly relate the notion of development to the concept of modernization and *modernization* theory (see e.g. Escobar 1995). To do so would have taken the argument a step further and project it into new engagements with the philosophical/historical concept 'postmodernity' and its equivalent development concept, 'postmodernization'. The crucial question is: does postmodernity offer us a way out of the crippling oppositions and deep ambivalences that throw science against ethics and political action, and progress and development against environmental sustainability? And, similarly, does 'postmodernization' offer new 'development' possibilities that differ from the linear, reductionist, and single cause-effect, Eurocentrist cultural model that has so far dominated the world? Perhaps, most importantly, are there forms of education, both at the early and advanced levels that are dedicated to exploring these possibilities? For myself, I would want to answer these questions in the affirmative and have begun my explorations in the writings of what I call 'the prophets of postmodernity' – Nietzsche, Wittgenstein and Heidegger (see e.g., Peters and Marshall 1999; Peters *et al.* 2001; Peters 2001, 2002). Perhaps, we should, like Bateson (1972), recognise that 'There is an ecology of bad ideas, just as there is an ecology of weeds.'

VIGNETTE 3.2 THE CONTACT ZONE. WHOSE NATURE? WHOSE SUSTAINABILITY?

R. Soetaert and A. Mottart, University of Ghent

In his article "Who drew the sky?" Andrew Stables (2001a: 245) warns the reader: "The project of environmental education (EE) is shot through with paradox." Indeed, life is full of paradoxes and it would surprise us if environmental education was free from them. It would even frighten us. Although we really believe society can always change for the better, we also feel the need to problematise all ideologies or meta-narratives even if they promise to bring us a sustainable future.

Apart from teaching all kinds of skills and knowledge(s), all kinds of functional and cultural literacies, all kinds of disciplines, we should also be strongly oriented "to developing increased meta-awareness of dominant cultural practices within our societies and of the cultural practices of others" (Stables 2001a: 254). We are also comfortable with the moderate position taken in his paper: ". . . inherently post-foundationalist in calling for acceptance of differing positions but retaining a belief in the potential of EE to help bring about some sort of sustainability" (Stables 2001a: 245). "Post" is a nice prefix; it suggests we are more tolerant than anti-foundationalists and more flexible than foundationalists. Such meta-awareness is an elegant philosophical solution, but how can it have an impact on the theory and practice of education?

Tradition

In this vignette we want to elaborate on how we can achieve this, focusing on teacher training by suggesting new perspectives on the curriculum. What should the curriculum look like? We should problematise the old curriculum and the knowledge and pedagogy it suggests. As far as pedagogy is concerned traditional education chooses a transmission model: the teacher transmits knowledge to the child – the empty vessel. The perspective on knowledge is fundamentally realist. We teach our pupils what we think they should know about the world (the facts of life). We teach them history as a memory in order for them to think it is *their* memory (identity). We also teach them how we think they should think about the world (morality). Well, we have all been like that (and probably still are). Should we feel remorse? How do we repent? There are perhaps two kinds of repentance: first, we are sorry because we are caught, but that doesn't really count as true repentance; second: there is a change of mind for the better, which produces change of action and conduct: traditionally, this, as it is expressive of true repentance, flows from the understanding being enlightened by the Spirit of God, when the sinner beholds sin in another light. Let us replace God by post-foundationalist theory and let us take seriously the idea of beholding "sin in another light". But the question today is: Whose light? Whose morality? Whose knowledge? Let us first focus on knowledge.

Whose knowledge?

This kind of question is not only theoretical but also practical, since teachers today are indeed confronted with learners who come from different worlds and participate in different social and cultural networks. So teachers also wonder – with Graff (1988: 149) "What should we be teaching – when there is no 'we'?". So the *we*, the *what*, the *how* and certainly the *why* are high on the agenda of education.

All these complex theoretical questions bewilder teachers and very often create a deep nostalgia for the return of "the Arbiter": "he who knows what's good and why, and can place every form of cultural expression in its natural order" (Bérubé 1998: 93 about Bloom 1987). But again, the problem is: whose natural order? As "Human beings can be said to live in a natural environment of meaning" (Hendriks-Jansen 1966: xi), it would probably better to replace *natural* by *cultural*. And then we are confronted with a central question: how are social and cultural forms produced and reproduced? Critical pedagogy today deals with ways of talking about issues surrounding the construction of knowledge and the means through which people come to understand the world (Casella 1998: 187).

Turns

Today, we are confronted with a cultural and anthropologic turn: "There is no such thing as human nature independent of culture" (Geertz 1973: 49). There is also no human culture independent of language. Indeed *language and meaning* are closely intertwined. So, we are also confronted with the linguistic, rhetorical turn. All these turns strip away the foundational status of all knowledge. But that does not imply moral relativism and its "anything goes" philosophy. It makes us realise that our ways of life "depend upon shared meanings and shared concepts and depend as well upon shared modes of discourse for negotiating differences in meaning and interpretation" (Bruner 1990: 25). And it could create "a willingness to construe knowledge and values from multiple perspectives without loss of one's own values" (Bruner 1990: 30).

The (un)learning society

All these turns *unteach* us, they problematise what we have been taught and have learned. So, one of the aims of teaching could be *unlearning*. Some argue that this aim is particularly true in our post-industrial, postmodern society. More than ever we must adapt to ongoing fundamental changes within our lifespan. So, paradoxically, the concept of unlearning has become very important in the learning society. Constructive interaction with change has all of a sudden become essential for survival in the information society. But the same constructive interaction is necessary for the survival of the human species and other life forms on the planet. A life, thriving on diversity and continuous change and an eduction inspired by unteaching and unlearning, suggests we have to look upon our world and ourselves in a fundamentally different way. Things change all the time and so do we.

Tools

We literally create the world in which we live by living in it. Meaning is said to be *constructed* or *negotiated* in interactions between persons constituting their standard practices with artefacts and tools. If culture is described as a product of history rather than of nature, culture becomes the world "to which we had to adapt and the tool kit for doing so" (Bruner 1986: 12). Culture can become a *pedagogical tool* when we examine how culture socialises and disciplines us even as it entertains us. So classes become sites of engagement for critical dialogue regarding how culture works and how we can become critical consumers of culture. What do we study? The construction of meaning, and the role of representation in this construction.

Curriculum

Some suggest that our curriculum is also a moral educator. Education has an oppressive role: maintaining existing power or the status quo. But education can also have enlightening and transformative roles: it enables us to criticize views on the world and so to change that world. But the simple formula – we transfer knowledge and the side effect is goodness or commitment – should be problematised. And also another formula – curriculum teaches the facts – should be deconstructed. Even the progressive correction – teach the facts and students can form their own opinions – should be questioned. Facts and skills are not neutral. The curriculum itself is a representation of facts. So discussing the curriculum is also embedded in a broader debate about the crisis of interpretation, the crisis of representation meaning and language (Hall 1997):

> This expression condenses the broader idea of the existence of a fissure, of instability, of an uncertainty in the very centre of the epistemologies that once governed with such confidence the modern project of domination; of nature, of the world, of society.
>
> (Da Silva 1999: 7)

Whose nature?

We realise we have not mentioned, till now, the central concept in this chapter: environmental education. Our general framework about the complex relation between language, meaning and representation can be combined with environmental education. Both concepts – environment and representation – are said to be in crisis. In the media, in daily conversations, in science, we are confronted with a litany of environmental problems. The crisis of representation is evidenced in the lack of agreement on who is entitled to define what we mean when we refer to an environmental crisis. We are confronted with multiple representations of the problem's context. The idea that nature is a social construction defined by relations of power among discourses and communities (biology, economics, arts etc.) confronts us with the questions: whose nature? whose development? "What development means depends on how the rich nations feel" (Sachs 1991: 161).

Escobar (1998) describes nature as a contested site: "a vast network of sites and actors through which concepts, policies, and ultimately cultures and ecologies are contested and negotiated". The new kind of curriculum can be inspired by the metaphor "a vast network of sites".

Whose education?

The curriculum could become a model site of contest and (re)negotiation. In her essay *Arts of the Contact Zone* Pratt (1991: 34) introduces the concept of the contact zone: "where cultures meet, clash, and grapple with each other, often in contexts of highly asymmetrical relations of power, such as colonialism, slavery, or their aftermaths as they are lived out in many parts of the world today". Bizzell suggests the use of the concept in teaching literature, but it is certainly a handy concept for teaching about the environment. Students can be confronted with a range of presentations and discussions of environmental concerns and learn to understand the arguments in different discourses and disciplines.

Learning environments – with questions and assignments – should be constructed which bring students to "a clearer recognition of the cultural contexts of others' practices and beliefs – and of their own" (Bizzell 1994: 163). Understanding another person's point of view, to see her or his culture from an outsider's perspective, is essential. In the contact zone students can "examine texts which foreground and critique different cultural group's attitudes toward a common issue" (Van Slyck 1997: 155). This common issue could be our environment.

We realise that a lot of work still needs to be done to develop material in the contact zone. In teacher training we developed examples of such a curricular approach. The questions we can ask from the perspective of the social sciences and the arts are: how environmental discourse is produced and circulated through mass media, how nature is represented in art, how landscapes are changed through the tourist's gaze (Bishop *et al.* 2000; Soetaert *et al.* 1996).

Whose sustainability?

We should focus on a dialogue between different discourses as Bakhtin (1981) suggests: dialogism does not allow the authority of one's speech but confronts it with other voices. In the contact zone we can problematise our representations and locate these problems in the curriculum. This anthropological turn (or cultural, linguistic, rhetorical turn) creates the meta-awareness as a basis for change. But change is based on an awareness of different ways of looking at nature. Then we realise that even sustainability is shot through with paradoxes because it confronts us with: whose sustainability?

CHAPTER 4

LIFELONG LEARNING: MAKING THE LINKAGES

READING 4.1 THE CURRICULUM EXPERIMENT: MEETING THE CHALLENGE OF SOCIAL CHANGE

J. Elliott

Source: Open University Press, Buckingham, 1998: 65–73

Social transformation and the liberation of the individual

According to Handy (1995a), the paradoxical consequences of techno-economic development – it has brought enormous benefits to more people in the form of material goods and better health and housing, as well as the negative consequences depicted above – have to be lived with rather than unambiguously resolved. This is no recommendation for a fatalistic attitude and passive inaction. Handy argues that we can do something to 'reduce the starkness of some of the contradictions, minimise the inconsistencies, understand the puzzles in the paradoxes', but we can't resolve them completely, make them go away, or escape from them. What should be done, however, will be far from clear. For Handy, life will 'be best understood backwards' and lived forwards, although such retrospective understandings will offer 'clues' about possible future directions.

The intelligent response to the complexities and paradoxes of living in advanced modern societies is one of imaginative experimentation based on a tolerance of ambiguity and risk. Increasing complexity and paradox in a society enlarges the social space in which its members can participate in the construction of their own and their society's future. Lash and Wynne, in the introduction to *Risk Society* (Beck 1992), commenting on Beck's theory of reflexive modernization, note that it implies more than structural change but a changing relationship between social structures and social agents. When the modernization process reaches the self-reflexive level, 'agents tend to become more individualised, that is, decreasingly constrained by structures' and able to 'release themselves from structural constraint and actively shape the modernisation process' (p. 2).

Beck himself is quite explicit about the changing relationship between social structure and agency which is constitutive of reflexive modernization. He argues that we are eye-witnesses to a social transformation which is freeing people from the social forms of industrial society, such as class-, family- and gender-based roles, and creating 'a social surge of individualisation' where people 'have to refer to themselves in planning their individual labour market biographies' (Beck 1992: 87). The mechanism that 'liberates' individuals from traditional social ties is a labour market which requires 'individual mobility and the mobile individual' (p. 88), and a welfare state which protects people against the harsher consequences of mass unemployment and deskilling.

The individualization of the forms and conditions of existence wrought by dynamic labour markets and cushioned by social welfare implies for Beck (1992: 88) 'the variation and differentiation of life-styles and forms of life, opposing the thinking behind the traditional categories of large-group societies'. Individuals become the units for reproducing society rather than social classes, family groups and gender roles. In the words of Beck, they become 'the agents of their educational and market-mediated subsistence and the related life planning and organisation' (p. 90). However, he is concerned to point out that individualization must not be equated with the emancipation of individuals from all forms of social control. The process of individualization does not necessarily mean that individuals are empowered to create and shape the conditions of their existence, their social life-world. Liberation from traditional ties is accompanied by increasing dependency on the labour market and the institutionalized and standardized ways of life that support its operation; namely, 'education, consumption, regulations and support from social laws, traffic planning, product offers, possibilities and fashions in medical, psychological and pedagogical counselling and care' (p. 90). In this context, the idea of individuals as centres of choice and planning arises from the operation of social power which stands over and against the individual: the social power of a labour market which requires people to become units capable of infinite consumption.

However, Beck (1992: 90) argues that the process of liberation from traditional ties also raises expectations for a 'life of one's own' free from 'industrial and administrative' interference in the personal/private sphere. Inasmuch as the individualization process is self-contradictory, by creating new dependencies while at the same time raising expectations of empowerment, it provides a social space in which individuals can collectively form social movements to resist various forms of dependency on the power of the labour market to shape their lives, and to support their self-chosen experiments in personal and social living. Beck believes that the emergence of such social movements 'are expressions of the new risk situations in the risk society', namely ecology, feminism and peace.

Although the individualization process does little to resolve inequalities in the distribution of wealth – 'the hierarchy of income and the fundamental conditions of wage labour have remained the same' – Beck does not apparently view them as especially significant for the development of personal and social experiments in which people attempt to create and shape their lifeworlds. This is because of the cushioning effects 'of a comparatively high material standard of living and advanced social security systems'.

As we have seen, his analysis of social change in this respect differs from that of Handy, who sees people becoming increasingly disillusioned with traditional legitimations for the unequal distribution of wealth as they become more aware of the self-contradictions inherent in its social production. One reason for this difference of perspective is suggested by Handy himself, although his work makes no reference to Beck (and vice versa). Beck is a German sociologist and Handy an Anglo-Irish economist and organizational theorist living largely in England. Their different origins and locations may give a clue to their rather different views of the significance of wealth distribution issues in advanced modern societies. Handy contrasts attitudes towards the labour market in the USA and Britain with those that prevail in some European countries, including Germany:

> Britain and the US have the most open labour markets and, therefore, the highest number of people in work, but their workers are the least protected and often the worst paid . . . Over the last twenty years the numbers of people in paid work have grown by 30 million in America but only by 10 million in the European Community.

But the Americans and British have to work longer and odder hours, accept more part-time and self-employment and enjoy less protection. Fifteen per cent of British workers put in more than 48 hours a week and 20 per cent regularly work on Sundays. The Continentals think this is mad. Britain and America add on less than 30 per cent to the wage or salary to take care of social security and pensions. Italy, France and Germany add 50 per cent.

(Handy 1995a: 27–8)

The issue at stake, Handy argues, is whether it is best to have fewer workers who are better paid, better educated and better protected, or whether it is best to have more workers who are less well-paid, less well-educated and less well-protected? The continentals believe, says Handy, that only good work is 'tolerable in this modern age' and that no work is better than bad work. On the other hand, the British and Americans, according to Handy (1995a: 28), believe that 'any work is better than no work, even if the result is a progressively down skilled workforce'. He argues that the consequence of American and British policy is a more divided society, illustrating this with the facts that the top 10 per cent of earners in America are paid six times as much as the bottom 10 per cent, while in Germany 'the ratio is just over two'.

I conclude that Beck's view of social transformation in modern societies – the move- ment from a concern with wealth distribution to a concern with risk distribution – assumes a continental perspective on the labour market and the role of the welfare state and social security. On the other hand, Handy's analysis of the self-contradictions in the social production of wealth stems largely, if not exclusively, from his knowledge and experience of the British and American labour markets. Both views have merit in their respective socio-political contexts. However, in the foreseeable future I would argue that, in the UK and USA at least, wealth distribution issues will be coupled with, rather than overshadowed by, issues of risk distribution. In my view, both kinds of issues will be important in supplying the motivation for people to resist the power of the labour market and to take responsibility for their lives by engaging in innovative personal and social experiments. The wealth distribution issues may well, contrary to Beck's thesis, resurface in continental societies, since in many one can discern a trend towards the American and British view of the labour market as they struggle for compet- itive advantage in global markets and find themselves hampered by high levels of investment in social security and protection. The heat surrounding Britain's reluctance in the past to accept a common European currency, 'the minimum wage' and other aspects of the EEC's Social Charter, is perhaps an indication of a crisis of attitude in many continental countries. The British Government certainly claimed that its own attitude to the labour market was more widely shared in Europe than was apparent in Brussels.

It is Handy's contention that transformations in the labour market are paradoxical. On the one hand, business organizations are getting smaller and employing fewer people in proper jobs for shorter periods in their life span, while increasing their use of temporary and part-time labour, whether skilled or unskilled. Hence the problems of mass unemployment, increasing inequities in pay, deskilling of the workforce and the black economy. On the other hand, because businesses are getting smaller by getting rid of slack, they are exercising less control over people's lives and presenting them with emancipatory possibilities; opportunities for people to resist the culture of conspicuous consumption and exercise some control over the conditions of their exist- ence, including the conditions which shape their work.

Handy (1995a) called one of his books *The Empty Raincoat* after visiting the open-air sculpture garden in Minneapolis. One of the sculptures, by Judith Shea, was of 'a bronze raincoat, standing upright, but empty, with no one inside it'. It symbolized for him a 'pressing paradox' of our times:

> We were not destined to be empty raincoats, nameless numbers on a payroll, role occupants, the raw material of economics or sociology, statistics in some government report. If that is to be its price then economic progress is an empty promise. There must be more to life than to be a cog in someone else's great machine hurtling God knows where. The challenge must be to prove that the paradox can be managed and that we each one of us, can fill that empty raincoat.
>
> (Handy 1995a: 1–2)

The 'do-it-yourself' economy

More people in the future, argues Handy, will be 'outside' the employing organizations that drive economic growth and the culture of conspicuous consumption. This need not mean that they have to see themselves as 'out of work', because there are more kinds of work than jobs in employing organizations. The new growth sector for work will reside in the 'do-it-yourself' economy. Some of this work will be paid for and counted when people employ themselves and sell their knowledge and skills directly to the customer. Among the customers of self-employed work will be the new 'slimmed down' business organizations, which prefer to hire in knowledge and skills as and when required rather than stock-pile their slack. Increasingly, their skilled workers will be on the outside of the organization working in, and this gives these workers greater flexibility, independence and control over their working conditions.

In *Beyond Certainty*, Handy relates advice he gave his own children on leaving college:

> 'I hope you won't go looking for a job', I said. I was not advocating the indolent life or a marginal one. What I meant was that rather than scurrying about looking for a corporate ladder to climb or a professional trajectory to follow, they ought to develop a product, skill, or service, assemble a portfolio that illustrates these assets, and then go out and find customers for them.
>
> (Handy 1995b: 26)

The curriculum structures in British schools and even in universities, with their emphasis on traditional academic subjects, have not made it easy for students to develop their particular talents through formal education, although some 'curricular space' has appeared at the level of higher education, particularly within the 'new universities'.

However, for Handy, the 'do-it-yourself' economy covers more than self-employment, and includes unpaid work people do in their own time rather than paying others to do it (e.g. caring for their old and sick, doing their own repairs, growing their own food). Handy (1995a: 30) argues that:

> As more and more people get pushed out or leave organisations, it makes good economic sense for them to do for themselves what they used to pay others to do for them ... Why pay others to do or make what you can do or make yourself, if now, you have more time than money on your hands? Because this new growth sector is invisible, productivity does not seem to be producing the output increases, nor the conventional jobs, which we would have expected.

One might add that unpaid work of this kind also makes good economic sense for the self-employed who have never 'spent time' inside an employing organization, since they are more in control over the use of the time they spend in paid work. Handy coins the phrase 'portfolio living' to depict the life of those who choose to participate in a 'do-it-yourself' economy. A portfolio life will contain a mix of paid and unpaid work, the balance varying at different times depending on personal choice and circumstances. Handy (1995b) suggests that portfolio living involves thinking of life in terms of a circle rather than a line. Abandoning the metaphor of the line 'as the organising design of our autobiographies' means no longer thinking of their line of work up a career ladder or their family line from son/daughter to marriage to parenthood to grandparent. Instead, argues Handy, a portfolio life is like a pie chart:

> with different segments marked off for different occupations, each coloured for kind and degree of remuneration. Some occupations will be paid in money, some in other kinds of reward: love, creative satisfaction, power, joy, and the like. And of course the chart will be constantly changing, the dimensions of the occupation segments expanding or contracting according to the time invested, the remuneration colours fading or brightening according to the returns on the investment, and this not only over the years of one's life but from week to week, even day to day.
>
> (Handy 1995b: 27)

If policy-makers are to take the 'well-being' of their citizens seriously, they may have to give up assuming that progress equals economic 'growth and efficiency' in a formal economy where productivity is controlled by employing organizations. As Handy (1995a: 1) argues:

> Part of the confusion stems from our pursuit of efficiency and economic growth, in the conviction that these are the necessary ingredients of progress . . . It is easy to lose ourselves in efficiency, to treat that efficiency as an end in itself and not a means to other ends.

Basic education in societies with rapidly growing 'do-it-yourself' economies will, in terms of content and outcomes, need in some respects to be more flexible and differentiated, to support the development of the various and diverse interests, talents and capacities individuals possess. It will also, in terms of learning processes, need to foster the more active and dynamic qualities which enable people to take charge of their own lives and see themselves as creators of innovative experiments in living. The scale of the educational problem is indicated by the large numbers of people cast onto the peripheral labour market who passively suffer their fate and appear to be incapable of seizing control over their futures.

Knowledge work

It is not only a growing 'do-it-yourself' economy which begins to put people rather than organizations in control of the economic and social conditions of their lives. Handy (1995a) points out that even proper jobs are of a kind that empowers the employees in relation to the organizations they work in. Technology-driven production is resulting in a reduced need for many kinds of work, except 'knowledge work'. 'Clever workers with clever machines', says Handy (1995a: 23), 'have put to an end the mass organisation'. The 'means of production' are now, he argues, in the hands of the workers in ways Marx couldn't have imagined. 'Focused intelligence', or the ability to acquire and apply knowledge and know-how, is, according to Handy, the new source of wealth and it is not the kind of property which can be owned by the organization. It cannot take intelligence away from someone or own it. It is not a property whose possession can be controlled by those who own the organization. Therefore, says Handy, 'it is hard to prevent the brains walking out of the door if they want to' (p. 24).

The inability of organizations to redistribute intelligence implies that they cannot stop people developing it and using it in ways they determine. If they do not like the way the organization treats their knowledge, individuals can sell it to another, perhaps rival, 'business' or establish their own. It is, according to Handy (1995a: 25), 'a low-cost entry market-place' that makes 'for a more open society'. He argues that it's unfortunate that 'intelligence goes where intelligence is'. The well-educated give their children good educations and thereby secure their access to power and wealth. The most likely outcome of this new kind of property, intellectual property, is, according to Handy, an increasingly divided society unless 'we can transform the whole of society into a permanent learning culture where every one pursues a higher intelligence quotient as avidly as they look for homes of their own' (p. 25). Handy is not very clear what he means by 'focused intelligence' but the concept appears to be similar in some respects to Dreyfus's (1981) idea of 'situational understanding' (see also Elliott 1993), which picks out a cluster of cognitive abilities exercised in making intelligent judgements in particular practical situations.

This kind of practical intelligence is not necessarily best developed through a curriculum organized in terms of the traditional academic subjects which tend to reinforce the passive acquisition of knowledge rather than its use in the practical contexts of living. Such a curriculum may well constitute an obstacle to the equitable distribution of opportunities in society for people to develop their capacities for situational understanding. Traditional standards of academic excellence may provide the criteria for allocating individuals to the best jobs, thereby giving them access to power and wealth, but they may not be the appropriate criteria. As Goodson (1994) argues, a major function of a subject-based 'academic' curriculum could simply be to reproduce a social elite, since only a few may be capable of mastering the bodies of decontextualized and abstract propositions which define school subjects, in comparison with the number of people who could be capable of developing an intelligence which focuses on the problems and issues that arise in concrete human situations. One of the attractions of a subject-based curriculum is that it enables policy-makers to standardize learning outcomes in a way an issues-focused curriculum, aimed at developing capacities for understanding 'human situations', does not.

One implication of Handy's concept of 'focused intelligence', if I have understood his meaning in the terms outlined above, is that it is a form of intelligence that will not only be increasingly exercised in 'proper jobs' inside organizations. A great deal of work in the 'do-it-yourself' economy will also constitute knowledge-work, in which case we will not need to plan a different kind of education for separate categories of workers (i.e. knowledge workers inside organizations and the self-employed portfolio people).

Implications for the curriculum

A curriculum which prepares students for life in the kind of societies described above will look very different to one dominated by nationally standardized learning outcomes that constitute a basis for allocating people to 'proper jobs' in employing organizations that will subsequently control their futures, and are deemed to constitute the essential knowledge and skills required for economic growth. Currently, [. . . many] national curricula specify such knowledge and skills as 'core curriculum' objectives. Priority is therefore given to the *economic ends* of the society as these are conceived in terms of a 'state-steered formal economy'. In the context of an economy increasingly shaped by individual citizens, operating on a 'do-it-yourself' basis or as knowledge-workers or both, priority will need to be given in basic education to enabling all pupils to begin to construct for themselves a positive vision of their own futures in an increasingly complex, less structured and more open and dynamic society. Basic education will need to prioritize the development of those dynamic capacities – cognitive, interpersonal and motivational – associated with the ability to continuously shape and reshape the conditions of one's existence in the light of an unfolding vision of the 'good life' and of how one's natural talents can be developed to realize it.

The curriculum implications of this are two-fold. First, there is a need for a common general education which enables students to use the cultural resources available in society to construct their own vision of the good life and the values they wish to live by. Secondly, there is a need for a more differentiated 'vocational education', in the broad sense of an education which enables individual students to identify and develop their particular talents in ways which reflect their vision of the good life. In this latter respect, students will need access to a curriculum which is more open and responsive to their self-defined learning needs, with respect to both conditions of access and content. This kind of flexible and 'vocationally' orientated curriculum provision will not segregate life and work. It would match the life-concerns of individual students, and while transcending their need to 'earn a living' would not discount it. Such a curriculum would locate their economic well-being in the context of their development as persons capable of constructing their own future in an increasingly dynamic and complex society.

In this book, I am primarily concerned with the implications of social change for the idea of a 'common general education', rather than on its implications for the development of what Rawls (1971: 107) has called 'productive trained abilities', or Stenhouse (1967: 113) calls an education for 'productive enterprise'. The latter requires a separate book to be written. However, the critique of planning by objectives which runs through this book should be seen in this context. I am critical of its use as a basis for planning the curriculum for general education. It may well be appropriate, and this is acknowledged by Stenhouse (1975: 80–81), as a basis for developing productive trained abilities, in a context where students exercise control over which abilities they wish to acquire.

[. . .]

READING 4.2 ORGANIZATIONAL LEARNING II: THEORY, METHOD AND PRACTICE

C. Argyris and D.A. Schön
Source: Addison Wesley, Reading, MA, 1996: 18–25

Productive organizational learning

There are several ways in which instrumental learning may be for ill rather than for good. Some of these are particular to organizational learning; others, applicable to learning by agents of any kind.

First, the *ends* of action may be reprehensible. The value we attribute to an increase in effectiveness or efficiency depends on how we answer the question, Effectiveness or efficiency for what? and how we evaluate the "what." This issue is critically important when the action in question emanates from an organization whose members are eager or unthinkingly compliant participants. During World War II, Eichman's bureaucracy learned over time to become more efficient at sending its victims to the gas chambers.

The value attributed to a particular instance of learning also depends on how we judge its validity. Learning seems to suggest the acquisition of valid, workable knowledge or know-how. But when we treat organizational learning as inquiry that leads to a change in theory-in-use, we open up the possibility that any given change may be based on a lesson that turns out to be false or unworkable. James March (1988) uses the term "superstitious learning" to refer to one such class of lessons: those based on the belief that because events have followed one another in time they are also related to one another as cause to effect. For example, corporate managers may believe that a rise in profits following the institution of a new policy must have been caused by that policy, though it may have been due to nothing more than an improvement in market conditions. March suggests that managers are drawn to superstitious learning because it reinforces the myth of managerial control – a belief congenial to the norms of managerial stewardship but often contrary to fact.

Organizational learning that is valid or workable at the time of its first occurrence may lead to effects that are negative overall. To take a notable example, "competence traps" (also March's term) are situations in which an experience of perceived success leads an organization to persist in a familiar pattern of thought and action beyond the time and conditions within which it yields successful outcomes. The behavior that yields success at time, t, may not yield it at t + 1. Yet an organization lulled by its success and misguided by the lessons drawn from it, may persist in a familiar pattern of behavior long after it has ceased to work. In business strategy, General Motors, IBM, and Digital Equipment Corporation come to mind as recent examples of firms that persevered in following a once-winning strategy that had become a losing strategy, apparently blind to the fact that the competitive environment had shifted out from under it. Such examples should be understood in terms of the webs of interest organizations build up around familiar strategies, technologies, or structures, and the "dynamically conservative" processes (Schön 1967) that reinforce an organization's adherence to the lessons it has drawn from past experience.

Later we will have opportunity to see how people can learn collectively to maintain patterns of thought and action that *inhibit* productive organizational learning. For example, they may learn to respond to error by the use of scapegoating, games of unilateral control and avoidance of control, systematic patterns of deception, camouflage of intentions, and maintenance of taboos that keep critical issues undiscussable. Such patterns of thought and action, learned from experience, often have the effect of inhibiting the kinds of productive learning that yield improved performance or restructured values for performance. Yet members of the organization may develop an attachment to these patterns, even to the point of exclaiming, "It has taken us years to learn to live in this screwed-up world; don't make waves!"

If we were to use learning only in a positive sense, then we would have to qualify the learning involved in all such negative examples with adjectives like dysfunctional, pseudo, or limited. These semantic devices are misleading, since they tend to be applied to learning products after the fact; whereas we are often uncertain in any given situation of action, whether an alleged instance of productive organizational learning is valid and workable. The crucial point is that, as we try to understand or enhance organizational learning, we should keep in mind the variety of ways in which any particular example of it may prove to be invalid, unproductive, or even downright evil.

For these reasons, it is useful to distinguish three types of productive organizational learning:

1   *organizational inquiry*, instrumental learning that leads to improvement in the perform-ance of organizational tasks;
2   inquiry through which an organization explores and restructures the values and criteria through which it defines what it means by improved performance; and
3   inquiry through which an organization enhances its capability for learning of types (1) or (2).

Single- and double-loop learning

By *single-loop learning* we mean instrumental learning that changes strategies of action or assumptions underlying strategies in ways that leave the values of a theory of action unchanged. For example, quality control inspectors who identify a defective product may convey that information to production engineers, who, in turn, may change product specifications and production methods to correct the defect. Marketing managers, who observe that monthly sales have fallen below expectations, may inquire into the short-fall, seeking an interpretation they can use to devise new marketing strategies to bring the sales curve back on target. Line managers may respond to an increase in turnover of personnel by investigating sources of worker dissatisfaction, looking for factors they can influence, such as salary levels, fringe benefits, or job design, to improve the stability of their work force.

In such learning episodes, a single feed-back loop, mediated by organizational inquiry, connects detected error – that is, an outcome of action mismatched to expec-tations and, therefore, surprising – to organizational strategies of action and their underlying assumptions. These strategies or assumptions are modified, in turn, to keep organizational performance within the range set by existing organizational values and norms. The values and norms themselves (related in the previous examples to product quality, sales level, or work force stability) remain unchanged.

By *double-loop learning*, we mean learning that results in a change in the values of theory-in-use, as well as in its strategies and assumptions. The double loop refers to the two feedback loops that connect the observed effects of action with strategies and values served by strategies. Strategies and assumptions may change concurrently with, or as a consequence of, change in values.[1] Double-loop learning may be carried out by individuals, when their inquiry leads to change in the values of their theories-in-use or by organizations, when individuals inquire on behalf of an organization in such a way as to lead to change in the values of organizational theory-in-use.

Organizations continually engaged in transactions with their environments regularly carry out inquiry that takes the form of detection and correction of error. Single-loop learning is sufficient where error correction can proceed by changing organiza-tional strategies and assumptions within a constant framework of values and norms for performance. It is instrumental and, therefore, concerned primarily with effective-ness: how best to achieve existing goals and objectives, keeping organizational performance within the range specified by existing values and norms. In some cases, however, the correction of error requires inquiry through which organizational values and norms themselves are modified, which is what we mean by organizational double-loop learning.

In any particular instance of double-loop learning, the resulting changes in values and norms may not be judged to be desirable: their desirability can be determined only through a situation-specific critique of the changes themselves and of the inquiry through which they are achieved. Nevertheless, it is through double-loop learning alone that individuals or organizations can address the desirability of the values and norms that govern their theories-in-use.

Consider a chemical firm which has set up a research and development division charged with the discovery and development of new technologies [. . .]. The firm has created its new R&D division in response to the perceived imperative for growth in sales and earnings and the belief that these are to be generated through internally managed technological innovation. However, the new division generates technologies that do not fit the corporation's familiar pattern of operations. In order to exploit some of these technologies, the corporation may have to turn from the production of intermediate materials, with which it is familiar, to the manufacture and distribution of consumer products with which it is unfamiliar. This, in turn, requires that members of the corporation adopt new approaches to marketing, managing, and advertising; that they become accustomed to a much shorter product life cycle and to a more rapid cycle of changes in their pattern of activities; that they, in fact, change the very image of their business. And these requirements for change come into conflict with another sort of corporate norm, one that requires predictability in the management of corporate affairs.

Hence, the corporate managers find themselves confronted with conflicting requirements. If they conform to the imperative for growth, they must give up on the imperative for predictability. If they decide to keep their patterns of operation constant, they must give up on the imperative for growth, insofar as that imperative is to be realized through internally generated technology. A process of change initiated with an eye to effectiveness under existing norms turns out to yield a conflict in the norms themselves.

If corporate managers are to engage this conflict, they must undertake a process of inquiry which is significantly different from the inquiry characteristic of single-loop learning. To begin, they must become aware of the conflict. They have set up a new division that has yielded unexpected outcomes; this is an error, a surprise. They must reflect upon this surprise to the point where they become aware that they cannot deal with it adequately by doing better what they already know how to do. They must become aware that they cannot correct the error by getting the new division to perform more efficiently under existing norms; the more efficient the new division is, the more its results will plunge the managers into uncertainty and conflict. The managers must discover that it is the norm for predictable management which they hold, perhaps tacitly, that conflicts with their wish to achieve corporate growth through technological innovation.

Then the managers must undertake an inquiry that resolves the conflicting requirements. The results of their inquiry will take the form of a restructuring of organizational norms and very likely a restructuring of strategies and assumptions associated with those norms; these must then be embedded in the images and maps that encode organizational theory-in-use. There is in this sort of episode a double feedback loop which connects the detection of error not only to strategies and assumptions of effective performance but to the values and norms that define effective performance.

In such an example of organizational double-loop learning, incompatible requirements in organizational theory-in-use are characteristically expressed through a conflict among members and groups of members. One might say that the organization becomes a medium for translating incompatible requirements into interpersonal and intergroup conflict.

For example, some managers of the chemical firm may become partisans of growth through research; while others, committed to familiar and predictable patterns of corporate operation, become opponents of the new, research-based conception of the business. Double-loop learning, if it occurs, will follow from the process of inquiry by which these groups of managers confront and resolve their dispute. They may respond in several ways, not all of which meet the criteria for organizational double-loop learning.

First, the members may treat the conflict as a fight in which choices among competing requirements are to be made, and weightings and priorities are to be set on the basis of dominance. The R&D faction, for example, may include the chief executive who is able to win out over the old guard because of his greater power, or the two factions may fight it out to a draw, settling their differences in the end by a compromise that reflects nothing more than the inability of either faction to prevail over the other. In both of these cases, the conflict is settled for the time being but not by a process that could be appropriately described as learning. If the conflict ends with a power play or a stalemate, neither side is likely to emerge with a new sense of the nature of the conflict, its causes and consequences, or its meaning for organizational theory-in-use.

On the other hand, the adversaries may engage their conflict through inquiry in any of the following ways:

a   They may invent new strategies of performance that circumvent the perceived incompatibility of requirements; they may succeed in defining a kind of research and development addressed solely to the existing patterns of business that offer the likelihood of achieving existing norms for growth. They will then have succeeded in finding a single-loop solution to what at first appeared a double-loop problem.

b   They may carry out a trade-off analysis that enables them to conclude jointly that so many units of achievement of one norm are balanced by so many units of achievement of another norm. On this basis, they may decide that the prospects for R&D payoff are so slim that the R&D option should be abandoned, and with that abandonment there should be a lowering of corporate expectations for growth. Or they may decide to limit R&D targets so that the disruptions of patterns of business operation generated by R&D are confined to particular, segments of the corporation. Here there is a compromise among competing requirements, but it is achieved through inquiry into the probabilities and values associated with options for action.

c   The incompatible requirements may be perceived as incommensurable. In such a case, the conflict may still be resolved through inquiry that gets underneath the members' initial commitments. Participants must then ask why they hold the positions they do and what the positions mean. They may ask what factors have led them to adopt particular standards for growth in sales and earnings, with what rationales, and what are likely to be the consequences of attempting to meet the standards by any means whatever. Similarly they may ask what kinds of predictability in operations are of greatest importance, to whom they are important, and what conditions make them important.

Inquiry of type B or C may lead to a restructuring of corporate values and norms. Or it may lead to the invention of new patterns of incentives, budgeting, and control that take greater account of requirements for both growth and predictability.

In this type of organizational double-loop learning, individual members resolve interpersonal and intergroup conflicts that express incompatible requirements for organizational performance. They do so through organizational inquiry that creates new understandings of the conflicting requirements – their sources, conditions, and consequences – and sets new priorities and weightings of norms, or reframes the norms themselves, together with their associated strategies and assumptions. In such a process the restructured requirements for organizational performance become more nearly compatible and more susceptible to effective realization. And the resulting understandings, priorities, and reframed norms become inscribed in the images, maps, and programs of the organization and are thereby embedded in organizational memory.

[. . .]

Note

1   We borrow the distinction between single- and double-loop learning from W. Ross *Ashby's Design for a Brain* (New York: John Wiley and Sons, Inc., 1960). Ashby formulates his distinction in terms of (a) the adaptive behavior of a stable system, "the region of stability being the region of the phase space in which all the essential variables lie within their normal limits," and (b) a change in the value of an effective parameter, which changes the field within which the system seeks to maintain its stability. One of Ashby's examples is the behavior of a heating or cooling system governed by a thermostat. In an analogy to single-loop learning, the system changes the values of certain variables (for example, the opening or closing of an air valve) in order to keep temperature within the limits of a setting. Double-loop learning is analogous to the process by which a change in the setting induces the system to maintain temperature within the range specified by a new setting. See especially pp. 71–75.

VIGNETTE 4.1 THE LEARNING OF ECOLOGY, OR THE ECOLOGY OF LEARNING?

S. Sterling, author and consultant

The key to creating a more sustainable future is learning. This idea, in various forms, has dominated much environmental education debate since the 1972 UN Stockholm Conference on the Human Environment identified the critical role of education. If people only knew more about the environment, it has been thought, they would be able to make 'informed decisions' and environmental issues would be gradually resolved. I argue here that this simple view, which might be termed 'the learning of ecology', has to give way to a deeper understanding of the relationship between learning, society and sustainability – represented by the term 'the ecology of learning'.

In the thirty years since Stockholm, numerous high-level statements and mandates have pointed to the importance of 'environmental education' (EE) and these have been reflected in policy and practice to a greater or lesser degree at national and local level in many parts of the world. It hasn't made too much difference: either to educational systems or the state of the environment.

So what's wrong? The idea in the opening sentence above is valid – but we need to interpret it in a much more insightful way than it has often been to date. This involves questioning some dominant perceptions and assumptions, such as:

- environmental problems result primarily from ignorance;
- environmental problems are separate from economic, political, social, cultural issues and dynamics;
- learning is a simple, linear process of transmission;

- factual and conceptual learning is key;
- learning, irrespective of purpose or context, is always a 'good thing';
- 'add-on' to existing educational values, policy and practice is sufficient.

However, a degree of social learning has taken place in these last three decades, and such assumptions are not quite as prevalent as they once were. For example, much of the environmental education community has learnt, with varying degrees of resistance, that their endeavours need to be seen within a wider framework of what is often now called 'education for sustainable development' (ESD). Society has broadly learnt, albeit falteringly, that 'environmental problems' are not self-contained, but are a critical and integral part of the 'sustainability' issue which is concerned with the well-being and longevity of interlocking human and natural systems, at a time when both appear increasingly vulnerable. There are some signs then, of significant learning. Indeed, if we are to 'accelerate the transition to a sustainable future' (Brown 2001: 275) it will require further and deeper learning shifts.

To clarify this point, it is important to distinguish between qualities or levels of learning. Using systems terms, learning can serve either to *keep a system stable*, or enable it to *change to a new state* in relation to its environment. These two types of learning are called 'single-loop' and 'double-loop learning' (Argyris and Schön 1996), while other terms include 'first order' and 'second order' change (Ison and Russell 2000), or 'accommodative' and 'reformative' learning (Sterling 2001). These categories are often used to describe organisational change, but they can apply equally to change in worldview or belief systems. The first level of learning is a limited response to a change in the system's environment (which in this case is the whole sustainability imperative). It keeps the system and its 'theory-in-use' (Argyris and Schön 1996) stable, whether we are considering the educational paradigm or our belief system. This *can* be an appropriate response, except where the challenge from the system's environment is so great that second-order learning is required. I would argue that distinction helps us perceive the nature of the learning challenge and crisis we now face. The new postmodern conditions of unsustainability, complexity, and uncertainty require higher-order learning not just by students, but by the whole education community, and indeed, society as a whole.

I suggest that those of us who presume to seek change through learning, are ourselves involved in 'double-loop learning' which is changing our view of what social change through education and learning means and entails: in other words, we are 'learning about learning'. The relative failure of an instrumental approach to environmental education ('people need to learn these concepts, then their behavioural strategies will change'), is leading the education-for-change community to recognise that the sort of assumptions listed above need to be re-examined, and re-cast. It starts with ourselves. But the difficult part is how we engage other educators, policy-makers, and indeed the whole educational system in terms of its implicit assumptions, values, purposes and norms in deeper 'double-loop learning' or 'second-order' change.

For now, most people in the education community – if they recognise the sustainability imperative at all (which is another issue) – think in terms of a need to add something to the existing system, without questioning the bases of this system. This add-on approach is summarised in the title (above) as the 'learning of ecology'. It involves learning concepts *about* environment or sustainability, somewhere in the formal or non-formal curriculum. There is nothing intrinsically wrong with this content-based approach, and one can argue that indeed, people need to become acquainted with the ecological 'facts of life', to learn about concepts like biodiversity, ecological footprinting, sustainable use, *et cetera* or about values such as community, participation, and equity. But single-loop learning does not normally impinge on or change the values of the learner, the educator, the educational institution, or indeed society. It is an adaptive response to the concerns of sustainability based on the values and *modus operandi* of instrumental rationality.

By contrast, double-loop learning, or second order change is so fundamental that the system itself is changed. In order to achieve this it is necessary to step outside the usual frame of reference and take a meta-perspective (Ison and Russell 2000: 229).

From this meta-perspective, we can recognise the insufficiency of the information-based, instrumental approach. Such first order 'education *about* sustainability', does not tend to recognise what learners themselves bring to the learning experience. It tends to dwell on prescribed knowledge, to engage the learner no further than their intellectual response, and to be deterministic. And educational values, policies and practices are left unchallenged. By contrast, at the second level, the emphasis shifts towards 'learning for change' or 'education *for* sustainability'. There is more of a methodological emphasis here, on identifying and exercising the appropriate values and skills as well as conceptual knowledge needed, to meet (what are perceived as) the requirements that sustainability implies. A greater awareness of paradigm leads to an attempt to reorient policy and practice, but change is likely to be piecemeal and there are tensions with dominant norms.

While many individuals and institutions have shifted towards this reformatory, second-order, learning response (evident in the movement to 'green' policies and institutions), it is possible to point to a further learning level: a *transformative response*. This third order level involves epistemic change, that is, a change of worldview and *ethos* from – in my view – the still dominant values and thinking of mechanism and modernism, towards a participatory ecological postmodern worldview which is appropriate to the deeply systemic nature of the world. The education response here is one essentially of continuous inquiry: the *process* of sustainable development is seen as essentially one of systemic learning and change. At the same time, the *context* of learning is seen as sustainability, with emphasis on developing resilience, integrity, and capacity in individuals, groups, communities, organisations and human systems. This links with Elliott's advocacy of a permanent learning culture and self-reliant social actors (Elliott 1998). At this level, we have moved beyond just learning 'about' sustainability, or 'for' sustainability, towards living it in a reflexive and re-creative way. This may be described as 'learning as change' or 'education as sustainability'.

The phrase, 'ecology of learning' represents the nature of this learning level journey, as well as the quality of dynamic learning that sustainable living implies. It is a difficult path of increasing challenge, but also an increasing opportunity as we seek to re-make ourselves and our society. In sum, learning can either reinforce the existing world view, or precipitate the 'movement of mind' (Senge 1990: 13), the *metanoia* or re-perception of meaning that so many now advocate. In the end, transformative learning depends on the nature of the learning experience. We can choose either to achieve it by conscious design, or have it thrust upon us, by mounting crisis.

VIGNETTE 4.2 LIFELONG LEARNING: MAKING THE LINKAGES

M. Strain, University of Ulster

Both people and organizations learn: in what sense, and what for? These are the under-lying questions explored in these two extracts. In Elliott's somewhat idealized account, learning is an aspect of personhood. Through learning, individuals obtain a personal 'version' of the good life, inherent in which is the need to develop their talents. Exercising 'talents' both reflects this vision of the good life and enables each person to realise it in their lives. The key moral condition for and end of learning is freedom. Liberation of each individual through learning ensures that attendant social transformations main-tain necessary conditions of individual freedom.

These propositions support Elliott's argument that society's changing forms and structures require 'a curriculum which prepares students for life'. Such a curriculum needs to be very different from one 'dominated by nationally standardised learning outcomes that constitute a basis for allocating people to "proper jobs" ... that will subsequently control their futures'. If social inclusion and local responsibility for the environment are to be contributory to *individual* well-being, learning must surely have wider aims and benefits than those derived from a subordination of worker pro-ductivity to corporate ends. Robert Putnam (2001), in studies revealing a chronic decline of habits of involvement in community and civic activities in the US, argues that 'the norms and networks of civic engagement also powerfully affect the perform-ance of representative government'. His work has been influential in bringing to prominence the concept of 'social capital', the proposition that investment in the kinds of learning that encourage civic participation will strengthen economic and social life in democracies. Yet it is difficult to see how bonds sustained by adherence to tradi-tional social norms can increase participation in rapidly modernising societies. Schuller and Field (1998) call for a strengthening of 'bridges' between individuals and groups, and a relaxing of 'bonds', which have frequently maintained 'barriers' to learning (Rees *et al.* 2000).

From a more analytical perspective, the need for greater 'inclusivity' arises from two new features of 'late modern' social life: flexibilisation and individualisation. The first stems from what Castells (1996: 277–279) has termed a restructuring of the capital-labour relationship. The explosion of the information age has created a situation where increases in profits follow capital investment only when it also reduces labour costs. 'Lean' becomes a byword for profitable. One effect of the growth of part-time and temporary employment has been to increase the total time available for leisure. Consumption time increases as production/labour time diminishes. Consequently, the sensory and imaginative lives of individuals assume an increasing part of the field of possible economic expansion. The consumption potential of individuals becomes economically and politically more significant than their 'productive' capabilities. Yet these economic, aesthetic and social developments, the exercise of 'choice', respon-siveness to images, and the need to secure positional advantage, induce a sense of becoming 'atomised'. They drive individuals to a position in which life feels not so much like the experience of being a 'free', autonomous individual as an isolated, 'indi-viduated' being, cut off from the linkages of local and inherited forms of sociality, a situation in which 'how one lives becomes the biographical solution to systemic contra-dictions' (Beck 1992: 137). Body shape and habits of care and grooming, for men and women, no longer reveal class origins so much as one's commitment to investing in 'care of the self', as symbolic capital, indicating that one intends to go on personally 'improving' (Field 2000: 46). Part of any consideration of lifelong learning policy and practice must surely examine those aspects of the learning process that derive from and are formative in developing *relations* with others and other groups. In this sense, lifelong learning seems to call for learning to be considered as, in a significant degree, a *rational good*. Following Thrift (1996: 84–93), on the formative relations between space and personality, we may consider whether learning also might be understood as a continuously negotiated and renegotiated enquiry of the social and economic relations that have been constitutive of our personality and social self, and which, except in their most basic aspects, vary inescapably according to locale, region, social class and biographical experience.

Associated with these changes is the emergence of a society that is split according to access to knowledge. Beck (1999: 116–121) has enunciated this as an emerging four-fold population structure in which a highly rewarded elite, and a knowledge class richly paid to serve the technical, knowledge manipulating processes of the new economy, occupy a global space by virtue of their control and deployment of the space-time collapsing capabilities of electronic information and communications technology. Two further groups, one providing flexibilised, knowledge-poor services, the other an under-employed urban 'vagabondage' with time to spare, function chiefly to consume the sensation-packaged products of the globalised economy (Bauman 1998).

Ambiguity regarding *instrumental* benefits from learning is acknowledged, but perhaps not entirely resolved, in the extract from Argyris and Schön. Double-loop learning could support further democratisation of management and working relations and practices. It could also play a part in agreements to redistribute profits/income ratios, stimulate imaginative new efforts to stabilise employment expectations, and be catalytic in implementing international human rights measures to redress the balance of local and global responsibilities. An inescapable interdependence, between the needs of science, industry, the natural environment and politics was exemplified tragically in the notorious accidents at Chernobyl (IAEA 1991) and Bhopal (ICSIR 1985). But demo-cratisation of structures and reflexivisation of learning processes cannot by themselves ensure that the benefits of learning enhance individual and organizational well-being. Critical reflection must be buttressed by shared moral concern for actual and potential victims of technological achievement, and, in contexts of *redistributed* respon-sibilities, be capable of contributing to 'reframed norms' and of becoming 'embedded in organizational memory' (Argyris and Schön 1996: 25).

Elliott's discussion of 'risk', in which he compares Handy's and Beck's approaches to this question, omits one important aspect. Risk, in Beck's sense, is not simply a contingent phenomenon, but an intrinsic aspect of modernity's technological and elec-tronic revolutions. It arises not simply from an increased level of danger, which is avoidable with the help of prudent calculation, assessment, and prediction. In Beck's *Risk Society*, risk has become socialised, so that it permeates, for each individual, their very consciousness and structure of feeling about being in the world. The risks we face are more routinely and characteristically, in this age, the *product* and consequence of human expertise and intervention. This lies at the heart of an argument deployed by Stables and Scott (2001a), that we can no longer rely on principles and practices inherited from pre-modernity; scientific, practical and cultural practices must in future be founded upon *critique* for their 'valorisation'. In a *Risk Society*, we must learn collec-tively to develop our capability, attentive to but unbound by tradition, to assess the moral and social consequences of change, for ourselves and others, even as the work to discover new technological devices, and assess their imaginable technical and productive consequences goes forward.

The context is now one where the globalisation of capital has led to a reconfiguration of the 'capitalist' economy. Capital, in the traditional view, is formed by foregoing present consumption for the sake of later increases in productivity. What linked these two parts of an equation, was a belief system (Elias 2000: 451–483) which *highly valued* the self-denial of current pleasure for the sake of subsequent reward, and privileged a linear conception of time, the irreversible thread of 'clock' time. Economic wealth is now increasingly defined by measures of indicative types of consumption (use of a telephone, PC, free health services) rather than levels of saving, investment and productivity. One neglected dimension of consumption as an economic good is the 'time' consumed in consumption itself. The materially rich are increasingly 'time-poor', while the materially poor, underemployed, 'flexible' workforce has 'time on its hands'. This suggests that we need to consider the notion of a redistribution of time as a key social asset (Gorz 1999). Learning too, may now need to be re-examined as a consumption good, in which all need to participate, for the cultivation of a more rewarding and equitably distributed set of 'public goods' (Quicke 1999; Reisch 2001). Learning of the kind that both requires and contributes to the rewarding use of 'wealth in time' will be an inherently 'reflective' kind of learning, oriented to well-being more than to control and effective performance, to capabilities of participation, pleasure, and connectivity than to acquisition and performativity (Wildemeersch *et al.* 1998). Learning experientially to engage in a variety of 'temporalities', of lifestyles, collectivities and relationships, should perhaps take precedence over individualistic propensities of learning to secure power and protection for the 'self'.

To summarise these suggestions in relation to society's aspirations for learning to contribute to policies and practices which generate *sustainable* social improvement for all, lifelong learning calls for a new conceptualisation of learning both as an individual process and as a relational dimension of individuals in their social lives. To ignore these challenges makes debates about sustainability insufficient. If learning is effectively to promote more inclusive social relations, provide for ecological security, and introduce sustainable new social and economic structures, it should be formative in creating new values and relationships (norms and networks). By so doing, new forms of learning may perpetuate the benefits of new initiatives beyond the foreseeable planning horizons of rationally grounded policy decisions.

▬▬▬▬▬

CHAPTER 5

HUMANS AND NATURE: TENSIONS AND INTERDEPENDENCE

READING 5.1 DEEP ECOLOGY: LIVING AS IF NATURE MATTERED

B. Devall and G. Sessions

Source: Peregrine Smith, Salt Lake City, 1985: 65–70

[. . .]

The term *deep ecology* was coined by Arne Naess in his 1973 article, "The Shallow and the Deep, Long-Range Ecology Movements."[1] Naess was attempting to describe the deeper, more spiritual approach to Nature exemplified in the writings of Aldo Leopold and Rachel Carson. He thought that this deeper approach resulted from a more sensitive openness to ourselves and nonhuman life around us. The essence of deep ecology is to keep asking more searching questions about human life, society, and Nature as in the Western philosophical tradition of Socrates. As examples of this deep questioning, Naess points out "that we ask why and how, where others do not. For instance, ecology as a science does not ask what kind of a society would be the best for maintaining a particular ecosystem – that is considered a question for value theory, for politics, for ethics." Thus deep ecology goes beyond the so-called factual scientific level to the level of self and Earth wisdom.

Deep ecology goes beyond a limited piecemeal shallow approach to environmental problems and attempts to articulate a comprehensive religious and philosophical worldview. The foundations of deep ecology are the basic intuitions and experiencing of ourselves and Nature which comprise ecological consciousness. Certain outlooks on politics and public policy flow naturally from this consciousness. And in the context of this book, we discuss the minority tradition as the type of community most conducive both to cultivating ecological consciousness and to asking the basic questions of values and ethics addressed in these pages.

Many of these questions are perennial philosophical and religious questions faced by humans in all cultures over the ages. What does it mean to be a unique human individual? How can the individual self maintain and increase its uniqueness while also being an inseparable aspect of the whole system wherein there are no sharp breaks between self and the *other*? An ecological perspective, in this deeper sense, results in what Theodore Roszak calls "an awakening of wholes greater than the sum of their parts. In spirit, the discipline is contemplative and therapeutic."[2]

Ecological consciousness and deep ecology are in sharp contrast with the dominant worldview of technocratic-industrial societies which regards humans as isolated and fundamentally separate from the rest of Nature, as superior to, and in charge of, the rest of creation. But the view of humans as separate and superior to the rest of Nature is only part of larger cultural patterns. For thousands of years, Western culture has become increasingly obsessed with the idea of *dominance*: with dominance of humans over nonhuman Nature, masculine over the feminine, wealthy and powerful over the poor, with the dominance of the West over non-Western cultures. Deep ecological consciousness allows us to see through these erroneous and dangerous illusions.

For deep ecology, the study of our place in the Earth household includes the study of ourselves as part of the organic whole. Going beyond a narrowly materialist scientific understanding of reality, the spiritual and the material aspects of reality fuse together. While the leading intellectuals of the dominant worldview have tended to view religion as "just superstition," and have looked upon ancient spiritual practice and enlightenment, such as found in Zen Buddhism, as essentially subjective, the search for deep ecological consciousness is the search for a more objective consciousness and state of being through an active deep questioning and meditative process and way of life.

Many people have asked these deeper questions and cultivated ecological consciousness within the context of different spiritual traditions – Christianity, Taoism, Buddhism, and Native American rituals, for example. While differing greatly in other regards, many in these traditions agree with the basic principles of deep ecology.

Warwick Fox, an Australian philosopher, has succinctly expressed the central intuition of deep ecology: "It is the idea that we can make no firm ontological divide in the field of existence: That there is no bifurcation in reality between the human and the non-human realms ... to the extent that we perceive boundaries, we fall short of deep ecological consciousness."[3] From this most basic insight or characteristic of deep ecological consciousness, Arne Naess has developed two *ultimate norms* or intuitions which are themselves not derivable from other principles or intuitions. They are arrived at by the deep questioning process and reveal the importance of moving to the philosophical and religious level of wisdom. They cannot be validated, of course, by the methodology of modern science based on its usual mechanistic assumptions and its very narrow definition of data. These ultimate norms are *self-realization* and *biocentric equality*.

I Self-realization

In keeping with the spiritual traditions of many of the world's religions, the deep ecology norm of self-realization goes beyond the modern Western *self* which is defined as an isolated ego striving primarily for hedonistic gratification or for a narrow sense of individual salvation in this life or the next. This socially programmed sense of the narrow self or social self dislocates us, and leaves us prey to whatever fad or fashion is prevalent in our society or social reference group. We are thus robbed of beginning the search for our unique spiritual/biological personhood. Spiritual growth, or unfolding, begins when we cease to understand or see ourselves as isolated and narrow competing egos and begin to identify with other humans from our family and friends to, eventually, our species. But the deep ecology sense of self requires a further maturity and growth, an identification which goes beyond humanity to include the nonhuman world. We must see beyond our narrow contemporary cultural assumptions and values, and the conventional wisdom of our time and place, and this is best achieved by the meditative deep questioning process. Only in this way can we hope to attain full mature personhood and uniqueness.

A nurturing nondominating society can help in the "real work" of becoming a whole person. The "real work" can be summarized symbolically as the realization of "self-in-Self" where "Self" stands for organic wholeness. This process of the full unfolding of the self can also be summarized by the phrase, "No one is saved until we are all saved," where the phrase "one" includes not only me, an individual human, but all humans, whales, grizzly bears, whole rain forest ecosystems, mountains and rivers, the tiniest microbes, in the soil, and so on.

II   Biocentric equality

The intuition of biocentric equality is that all things in the biosphere have an equal right to live and blossom and to reach their own individual forms of unfolding and self-realization within the larger Self-realization. This basic intuition is that all organisms and entities in the ecosphere, as parts of the interrelated whole, are equal in intrinsic worth. Naess suggests that biocentric equality as an intuition is true in principle, although in the process of living, all species use each other as food, shelter, etc. Mutual predation is a biological fact of life, and many of the world's religions have struggled with the spiritual implications of this. Some animal liberationists who attempt to side-step this problem by advocating vegetarianism are forced to say that the entire plant kingdom including rain forests have no right to their own existence. This evasion flies in the face of the basic intuition of equality.[4] Aldo Leopold expressed this intuition when he said humans are "plain citizens" of the biotic community, not lord and master over all other species.

Biocentric equality is intimately related to the all-inclusive Self-realization in the sense that if we harm the rest of Nature then we are harming ourselves. There are no boundaries and everything is interrelated. But insofar as we perceive things as individual organisms or entities, the insight draws us to respect all human and nonhuman individuals in their own right as parts of the whole without feeling the need to set up hierarchies of species with humans at the top.

The practical implications of this intuition or norm suggest that we should live with minimum rather than maximum impact on other species and on the Earth in general. Thus we see another aspect of our guiding principle: "simple in means, rich in ends." Further practical implications of these norms are discussed at length in chapters seven and eight [of the reading].

A fuller discussion of the biocentric norm as it unfolds itself in practice begins with the realization that we, as individual humans, and as communities of humans, have vital needs which go beyond such basics as food, water, and shelter to include love, play, creative expression, intimate relationships with a particular landscape (or Nature taken in its entirety) as well as intimate relationships with other humans, and the vital need for spiritual growth, for becoming a mature human being.

Our vital material needs are probably more simple than many realize. In technocratic-industrial societies there is overwhelming propaganda and advertising which encourages false needs and destructive desires designed to foster increased production and consumption of goods. Most of this actually diverts us from facing reality in an objective way and from beginning the "real work" of spiritual growth and maturity.

Many people who do not see themselves as supporters of deep ecology nevertheless recognize an overriding vital human need for a healthy and high-quality natural environment for humans, if not for all life, with minimum intrusion of toxic waste, nuclear radiation from human enterprises, minimum acid rain, and smog, and enough free flowing wilderness so humans can get in touch with their sources, the natural rhythms and the flow of time and place.

Drawing from the minority tradition and from the wisdom of many who have offered the insight of interconnectedness, we recognize that deep ecologists can offer suggestions for gaining maturity and encouraging the processes of harmony with Nature, but that there is no grand solution which is guaranteed to save us from ourselves.

Dominant Worldview	Deep Ecology
Dominance over Nature	Harmony with Nature
Natural environment as resource for humans	All nature has intrinsic worth/ biospecies equality
Material/economic growth for growing human population	Elegantly simple material needs (material goals serving the larger goal of self-realization)
Belief in ample resource reserves	Earth "supplies" limited
High technological progress and solutions	Appropriate technology; nondominating science
Consumerism	Doing with enough/recycling
National/centralized community	Minority tradition/bioregion

Figure 6

The ultimate norms of deep ecology suggest a view of the nature of reality, and our place as an individual (many in the one) in the larger scheme of things. They cannot be fully grasped intellectually but are ultimately experiential. [. . .]

As a brief summary of our position thus far, Figure 6 summarizes the contrast between the dominant worldview and deep ecology.

III   Basic principles of deep ecology

In April 1984, during the advent of spring and John Muir's birthday, George Sessions and Arne Naess summarized fifteen years of thinking on the principles of deep ecology while camping in Death Valley, California. In this great and special place, they articulated these principles in a literal, somewhat neutral way, hoping that they would be understood and accepted by persons coming from different philosophical and religious positions.

Readers are encouraged to elaborate their own versions of deep ecology, clarify key concepts and think through the consequences of acting from these principles.

Basic principles

1   The well-being and flourishing of human and nonhuman Life on Earth have value in themselves (synonyms: intrinsic value, inherent value). These values are inter-dependent of the usefulness of the nonhuman world for human purposes.
2   Richness diversity of life forms contribute to the realization of these values and are also values in themselves.
3   Humans have no right to reduce this richness and diversity except to satisfy *vital* needs.
4   The flourishing of human life and cultures is compatible with a substantial decrease of the human population. The flourishing of nonhuman life requires such a decrease.

5   Present human interference with the nonhuman world is excessive, and the situation is rapidly worsening.
6   Policies must therefore be changed. These policies affect basic economic, technological, and ideological structures. The resulting state of affairs will be deeply different from the present.
7   The ideological change is mainly that of appreciating *life quality* (dwelling in situations of inherent value) rather than adhering to an increasingly higher standard of living. There will be a profound awareness of the difference between big and great.
8   Those who subscribe to the foregoing points have an obligation directly or indirectly to try to implement the necessary changes.

[. . .]

Notes

1   Arne Naess, "The Shallow and the Deep, Long-Range Ecology Movements: A Summary," *Inquiry* 16 (Oslo, 1973), pp. 95–100.
2   Theodore Roszak, *Where the Wasteland Ends* (New York: Anchor, 1972).
3   Warwick Fox, "Deep Ecology: A New Philosophy of Our Time?" *The Ecologist*, v. 14, 5–6, 1984, pp. 194–200. Arnie Naess replies, "Intuition, Intrinsic Value and Deep Ecology," *The Ecologist*, v. 14, 5–6, 1984, pp. 201–204.
4   Tom Regan, *The Case for Animal Rights* (New York: Random House, 1983). For excellent critiques of the animal rights movement, see John Rodman, "The Liberation of Nature?" *Inquiry* 20 (Oslo, 1977). J. Baird Callicott, "Animal Liberation," *Environment Ethics* 2, 4, (1980); see also John Rodman, "Four Forms of Ecological Consciousness Reconsidered" in T. Attig and D. Scherer, eds., *Ethics and the Environment* (Englewood Cliffs, N.J.: Prentice-Hall, 1983).

READING 5.2 THE CHICAGO GANGSTER THEORY OF LIFE: NATURE'S DEBT TO SOCIETY

A. Ross

Source: Verso, New York, 1994: 259–271

[. . .]

To alter the landscape chosen by sociobiologists as the natural habitat for selfish genes, we must consider the significant distinctions in the cultural history of Darwin's legacy. My task here, as elsewhere in this book, is to trace the general influence of these legacies upon the current ecological crisis.

It has often been acknowledged that Darwin's thought about evolution drew primarily upon two conflicting theories of natural life.[1] On the one hand, there was Malthus's dismal picture of a natural economy defined and willed by God as an unequal ratio between population and perpetually scarce resources. What passed from Malthus into popular ideology was the given wisdom that life for most people was fated to be a miserable struggle for existence in a world where there simply isn't enough to go around. Consequently, the backdrop to Darwin's theory of natural selection was a ceaseless war of organic species in competition over limited resources like food and space. Violence, competition, conquest, and scarcity seemed destined, then, to govern the economic struggle over the occupation of nature's finite system of niches. When proponents of social Darwinism like Herbert Spencer and William Graham Sumner took succor from Darwin's naturalist version of the survival of the fittest, they completed the circular logic diagnosed in my earlier discussion of sociobiology. The ideology of classical economics had been absorbed into nature through the Malthus–Darwin connexion, and then projected back onto human society to provide classical economics with an assumed basis in nature.

On the other hand, Darwinism is also indebted to the more Romantic view that nature is imperfect and unfinished, creatively evolving as a realm where species can create new roles and niches for themselves at the expense of no other competing species. According to this view, the key to natural selection lies in the creation of complexity, variation and divergence in a world where codependence and diversity, rather than warfare and limitation, are the rule.

Despite the tension between these two theories of nature, it is clear that competition and scarcity held sway as the dominant Darwinian principles, and that they have left their dismal mark on the subsequent path of the life sciences. While Darwinism was also claimed by the left (Marx himself proposed to dedicate the second volume of *Capital* to Darwin, an honor the naturalist declined; Kropotkin sought to ground the social instincts of cooperation in biology), it most visibly served the immediate needs of Victorian entrepreneurialism. In the USA, Herbert Spencer's own *laissez-faire* version of social Darwinism was particularly well received in the ruthless, individualistic milieu of the Gilded Age, and in ways that appealed directly to captains of industry like Carnegie and Rockefeller who seized for themselves the mantle of the fittest survivors as if it were indeed biologically ordained.[2] Spencer, who saw competition amid scarcity as a healthy, progressive environment for the social evolution of humans, preached optimism to the strongest and most powerful, and sought consent from the less fortunate for their natural subordination. The social Darwinist climate had eroded by the turn of the century and was in intellectual disrepute by the 1920s, thanks to challenges by Socialists, Progressives, and the pragmatist school of James and Dewey, all of whom, to some degree, supported the principle that cooperation, as much as competition, was in accord with evolutionary biology. While popular wisdom has never quite shaken off social Darwinist beliefs, a healthy suspicion set in among social thinkers about the extension of biological analogies to society, especially the application of natural selection to economics. At the same time, however, eugenics was according the same ideas a degree of scientific legitimacy that would provide a basis for future revivals of social Darwinism, even after Nazi race credos had rendered it temporarily *persona non grata*.

As a result, the vestigial influence exercised over biological thought by the doctrines of Victorian *laissez-faire* economics has been quite tenacious. While the law of competition and the condition of scarcity have ceded in part to the functionalist paradigm of nature as a 'system' or set of systems (itself another example of circular logic, since functionalism drew upon physiology for its model of social systems, now projected back onto the natural world), they continue to play a role akin to that of default settings within the life sciences. So, too, the identification of evolution with 'progress' has lent the organic process a highly moral coloring that Darwin himself was eager to avoid: for Darwin, nature had no teleology, apart from the better adaptation of species to their environments.

In certain environmentalist circles, you do not have to look far to see the principle of scarcity being regarded as a rudimentary circumstance of nature. This applies as much to resource-minded environmentalists (heirs of the conservationism of the Progressive era), whose apocalyptic prognoses about 'limits to growth' are pragmatically addressed to the managers of industry, as to biocentric nature activists (heirs of preservationism), morally moved to conserve and redeem sacrosanct areas of wilderness from human contamination. On the one hand, the appeal of the reform environmentalists is to an empiricist model of nature as a limited economy of resources: overuse threatens the survival of all species (and ecosystems) but primarily humans. On the other hand, biocentric fundamentalists view nature as a powerful, if fragile, moral economy which zoologically punishes the human species for its cosmic arrogance. In the first model, there is no account of power, while, in the deep ecologists' model, human domination of nature is simply turned upside down – domination is still dominant. Just as in sociobiology, both of these perspectives project particular social prejudices, whether empirical or moral, into ideas about the natural world. Nature only appears to be 'limited' or 'scarce' if it is conceived as a finite quantity of economic resources that can be renewed or exhausted. So, too, nature only appears to be judgmental if it is endowed with a moral sensibility that defines human activity as competitive and transgressive. Both models are regulated by relatively fixed laws, to which we are asked to subordinate our actions and thoughts.

Whether one believes in the existence of 'laws of nature,' or whether one believes that laws (which are made, and can be changed, by men and women) really only exist in human society, I would argue: (a) that both of these views of nature are full of social theory; and (b) that in so subordinating ourselves, we risk forfeiting any independent or alternative response to perhaps the most consequential debates of our times. To accept (a) and (b) is not to deny that there is an ecological crisis, nor to suggest that our response to that crisis should ignore its empirical and its moral components. It is, rather, to recognize that the way we talk about this crisis and the way we imagine our place within the natural world will determine the (often draconian) social prescriptions advocated in the name of resolving the crisis. This is why, for example, it may be better to think of it as an emergency, from which new ideas 'emerge' as a basis for social change, rather than as a crisis, for which one finds a 'solution' which is more likely to be expediently exploited in the name of the status quo.

To the environmentalist and the biocentrist alike (still accepted in public consciousness as if they were noncontradictory sides of the same coin) we may want to respond in Darwinian ways, not because Darwin holds the truth, but because the contradictions that troubled Darwinism are, in some part, vestigially responsible for these divergent models of nature. To resource-minded environmentalists, we can preach the fundamental historical lesson of evolution – the continuity between humans and nature, and the absence of any special privileges that justify human domination over nature. To the biocentrist or deep ecologist, we can preach Darwin's other lesson – evolution has no directed moral purpose, progressive or otherwise, and the survival of organic species is more a matter of sociable intercourse than it is a result of purposive physical laws. One lesson asks us to acknowledge the similarity between nature and society; the other asks us to acknowledge their differences.

Those who distrust such neat symmetrical analyses, who object in principle to preaching, and who favor a more inclusive and dynamic picture of nature and society, will feel more comfortable with a properly social ecology, by which I mean a social theory of nature that presents itself as such, rather than masquerading as zoological theory (sociobiology), economic theory (environmentalism), or moral theory (deep ecology). First and foremost, a social ecology recognizes the *similarity and the differences* of humans from other species in the natural world. In this respect, we might qualify a few myths that continue to circulate in the lifeblood of popular environmentalist consciousness. It is just not true, for example, that humans are unique in transforming their environment while other species merely adapt to theirs. All organisms enjoy an alloplastic, rather than a simply autoplastic relation to their environments. Whether they are bacteria working on host or neighboring cells, plants changing the composition of the soil where they grow, or birds and beavers building nests and dams, all organisms are a cause as well as an effect of their environments, from which they (and their genes) are indissociable. Humans alone, however, have the intellectual and technological capacity to radically reshape environments in self-consciously purposive ways, and that is what differentiates them from, say, 'social insects.' Nor is it true that pre-humanist, or non-EuroAmerican societies uniquely enjoy a harmonious, nondestructive relation with their environments, many of which they exhausted through deforestation and overuse, or with other species, many of which they hunted to extinction. There is no doubt, however, that the scale of destruction has become nigh catastrophic in modern societies, where special dispensation to devastate the natural world arose out of a combination of the ideologies of humanism and rationalism with the intensive development of industrialism.

Similar myths circulate around the topic of scarcity. Human societies are not governed by natural Malthusian 'laws' of overpopulation and scarcity, *if only because humans alone have the capacity to create societies where such 'laws' are not the primary determinants of survival.* At present, since everywhere in the world scarcity is induced and manipulated in the interest of maintaining power hierarchies, all such 'laws' are used as instruments of social subjugation. They cannot therefore be taken to correspond to actual conditions of physical limitation. It is virtually impossible for us to conceive of conditions of scarcity that would be purely physical in constitution, unaffected, that is, by social decisions about the distribution and consumption of resources. Economically speaking, scarcity figures as a measure of limitation primarily with respect to economic systems of growth and development, and only inasmuch as the calculus of such systems does not incorporate ecological costs except as 'externalities.' (This was as true of the ex-socialist societies which inherited wholesale the religion of growth and development from economic liberalism, and which continued to measure their economic health against the global standards set by Western liberal societies.) The key to resolving the ecological crisis does not lie in the ratios of some zoological/economic calculus that will impose mathematical limits on population and consumption levels any more than it lies in the golden codes of natural morality that will prohibit human intervention while delegating supreme authority to Mother Nature. It lies in the radical reorganization of social life on the planet. An ecological code of ethics that does not incorporate that lesson will not be evolutionary at all.

Most people tend to accept that 'limits,' whether they are socially imposed or socially chosen, are a necessary feature of any ecologically minded reorganization of social life, and indeed that limitation is the cardinal principle of ecological thought. It is assumed that in the West, above all, economists, industrialists and politicians will have to be persuaded to limit growth, while citizens will have to be weaned from the exponentially increasing consumer gratifications that underpin the custom of steady economic growth. It is difficult to argue with the intention of these assumptions, but there are reasons to be cautious about the widespread popular deference to this criterion of limitation, especially when it is advanced as a reason for regulation of social and cultural life. In the first place, we should be wary of any discourse of limits that equates an 'excess' of rights and freedoms with the excesses of material growth and development generally held responsible for the ecological crisis. Material scarcity has long been employed as a justification for imposing punitive and repressive measures upon populations. In the global context today, scarcity is increasingly cited as a basis for imposing drastic policies upon developing countries, where dire population measures are 'introduced' – starvation, disease, forced sterilization – which are seen to be consonant with the sustainability, for some, of a Western way of life.

Many of the classical liberties and rights that are a constitutional part of Western modernity today were won on the back of an expansionist liberal economy. The liberal political institutions of the West were achieved in tandem with the growth of imperialism: classical economics often assumed an abundance in nature that could only have been realized by plundering the resources of the New World and the rest of Europe's colonies. It does not follow, however, that these institutions, liberties, and rights are directly tied to the fortunes of an economic system based on unlimited growth. Indeed, it is precisely *because* of the existence of public freedoms that limits on growth can be democratically chosen and agreed upon. And yet, not only are these principles often considered to be a premature luxury in developing countries, they are also threatened with limitation wherever they exist in the developed world, by the manipulation of material scarcity, by the invocation of national security, or by the strategy of economic recessionism (i.e. a pro-scarcity economic strategy and not an economic consequence of scarcity). The 1993 UN Conference on Human Rights highlighted this situation when representatives of a number of Third World member states argued that, in their societies, human rights ought to be considered secondary to the right to economic development. While this was perceived as a challenge to Western hegemony, it demonstrated how the maintenance of political liberties is directly bound up with perceptions of scarcity and underdevelopment. In times of socially induced crisis, even the most 'universal' rights and liberties are subject to more than the usual limitations.

In recent decades, we have seen the partial achievement of nonuniversalist rights – those pertaining to women, people of color, and sexual minorities – that were tied in part to the economic surplus of the long postwar boom, and consequently to the creation of new consumer identities for the bearers of such rights. In the current recessionary mood, where consent for a step-up in regulation can be more directly elicited, the cry to limit these rights is often heard alongside the call to tighten our belts. The dominant metaphor here is one of paying for the excesses of the past. For conservatives, the excesses are the libertarian permissions of the 1960s and 1970s, while for liberals they are related to the yuppie greed of the 1980s. In either case, the call for frugality, austerity, and rollback sounds across the whole spectrum of civil society, and is consecrated in the 'budget cult' of the postmodern fiscal state. In this milieu of reduced expectations, the mission of 'saving the planet' often serves as a compensatory ideology for a generation of eco-kids perceived to be suffering from the prospect of an ever-shrinking future. The heavily Christianized language of sacrifice and redemption recalls a long history in the West of justifying poverty and social inequality by making promises about the kingdom to come. Every recessionary moment, and the present one is no exception, sees the revival of this language in the form of demands for concessions and forfeits, usually from those with the least wealth and power.

When US-led forces occupied famine-struck Somalia in the name of humanitarianism in the winter of 1993, foreign policy provided its own morality play about the sharing of sacrifice. In contrast to a war in the Gulf fought explicitly over control of natural resources, Somalia was supposed to be the kinder, gentler face of New World Order politics. Humanitarianism (not human rights) was the new interventionist ideology. The international relief NGOs attached to the UN acted as the new political agents. Food aid was the new geopolitical commodity. Never mind that the strife in Somalia was primarily the consequence of over a decade of Cold War client-state manipulation or that the famine was partly the result of the USA's political exploitation, through its own grain surplus, of the international hunger industry. Never mind that. There was something environmentalist about what the troops were doing. Smells like eco-spirit, so give peace a chance.

Operation Restore Hope was as much a public relations exercise in demonstrating the West's capacity for self-sacrifice as a way of securing a new ideological basis for interventionism. These days, the meaning of the spectacle of famine in an African country lies somewhat closer to home than it used to do. Indeed, it is almost a commonplace that the North American economy is increasingly creating conditions of underdevelopment more akin to those of Third World societies. With 35 million North Americans living below the poverty line, and 100,000 children homeless, famine in some distant 'famine-prone' sector of the globe can no longer be talked about in the neo-Darwinian rhetoric of the survival of the fittest – at least not when the fittest are no longer North Americans. With the drastic erosion of a domestic culture of abundance (in the USA, six out of ten incomes fell between 1977 and 1990) it is no longer so easy to obscure the common economic forces that sustain the extreme disparity between affluence and poverty in the First and Third Worlds. The rise of environmentalism has further underscored the structural links between these respective conditions. Everything, we are asked to consider, is globally connected.

But environmental consciousness has not only helped to reinforce the current recessionary messages about self-sacrifice and deprivation in our daily lives. It has also provided some backing for the call to limit freedoms, because it offers an argument about 'natural limits,' based upon empirical projections, which (as in the case of sociobiology) can be used to support discourses of social limits. In the social realm, these discourses have taken the primary form of a conservative backlash against women's and minority rights, but they have been echoed in neoliberals' clarion call to exclude 'special interests,' and also in the hard left's complaint about the 'fragmentation' of old class-based alliances resulting from the growth of the new social movements. In the cultural realm, we have seen the holy war against sex-positive expression in art and popular culture, the moral injunction to 'just say no' to certain forms of cultural experience and experimentation, and the redrawing of social norms around the nebulous quotient of 'family values.' In the latter realm especially, the green ideology of the natural body in a natural environment can very easily translate into drastic prescriptions about social behavior, especially when it appeals to traditional or antimodern values, common to conservatives and greens alike.

While it may be necessary to rebut the call for limits – sounding across a whole spectrum from the economics of corporate environmentalism to the cultural politics of traditional values – it would be historically naive to suggest that cultural freedoms can be uncoupled from the social conditions in which they were won and are maintained today. On the one hand, popular consciousness tenaciously insists that people are less free when they have less to consume even though many consumers recognize that higher levels of consumption involve them in socially constraining networks of dependency and debt that are not always visible or economically quantifiable. But it is rank First World arrogance to suggest that people in nonconsumer societies are somehow more free in their less commodified ways, or more healthy in their freedom from diseases associated with life in high-consumption societies. On the other hand, new forms of cultural expression often find their most fertile soil in the pockets of permissibility created as a marginal offshoot of a free-market economy. Countercultures, alternative cultures, and underground cultures feed off this kind of surplus. Such forms of expression in an 'open' democratic society are as vital to the dynamics of social change as those created out of resistance to more oppressive circumstances in a 'closed' nondemocratic society. Neither enjoys the luxury of conditions of its own making. Not only may it be impossible, it is probably undesirable to abstract cultural freedoms and political rights, even natural rights deemed inalienable, from the social milieu in which they are exercised.

A larger problem, however, lies with our conceptual understanding of 'limits' themselves. Limits, whenever they are invoked, call to mind either a mechanical system with a restricted capacity for production or distribution, or some finite quantity of material resources. Yet neither of these is an adequate representation of the dynamic interplay between human societies and the natural world. More constraining yet is the suggestion of encountering limits or confines on a linear path, along which route we are then obliged to withdraw. This conceptual model, in particular, helps to support atavistic calls for a return to preindustrial infrastructures, or else punitive demands to scale back along the road of consumerist gratification and/or civil rights. The linear model of advance and retreat (there is nowhere else to go) is an equally inadequate way of representing the life of civil rights movements, which diversify their 'gains' almost immediately, each step forward being a step sideways (what Viktor Shldovsky in another context called the 'knight's move') into an alternate world where new and often unforeseen relations of power come into play, and where what had been seen as 'advances' at the previous stage now take on a different and less straightforward appearance. The sexual revolution is a case in point, where the sexuality of bodies has undergone a radical change in social meaning in the age of AIDS. So, too, fighting the battle over reproductive rights in the political landscape of the 1980s and 1990s means something different from the struggles that achieved legal protection of abortion in the 1970s. The clock is never turned back.

Above all, the discourse of limits is best eschewed wherever it implies that our lives and actions are to be reckoned according to some irrefutable calculus or moral cipher of nature. The kind of action needed to address the ecological crisis is not best served by coercive messages about restraint in the face of immutable outcomes. People respond better to a call for social fulfillment than to a summons to physical deprivation, and that is why any social movement that uses self-denial as a vehicle for inducing change is as pathetic as one that uses apocalyptic threats or appeals to Mother Nature's vengeance. A common conception of green politics in general is that the ecology movement aims to make people satisfied with less, and that the green code of voluntary simplicity is a democratic ideal, especially when it can be supported by apocalyptic predictions of material scarcity. The same perception used to apply in crude conceptions about communism, which Marx himself reviled: to wit, that since luxuries and privileges and 'bourgeois' desires were exclusive by definition, they ought to be scaled back and levelled down. Big Bill Haywood, the famous labor organizer, had a better response. When asked by a would-be leveller why he always smoked large cigars, he deadpanned 'Son, nothing's too good for the proletariat.'

Unlike the other new social movements, ecology is commonly perceived as the one that says no, the antipleasure voice that says you're never gonna get it, so get used to going without. Theoretical support for this message can always be found elsewhere. Psychoanalysis is wheeled in as an explanation for psychic craving. Desire is always incomplete, it's founded on an impossible gap between the human drives and whatever reality they are perceived to correspond to – therefore, you're never gonna get it, so get used to going without. Hunting and gathering societies are cited as examples of the original affluent society, proving that the satisfaction of human needs and wants is really quite effortless – why work harder when you're never gonna get it, so get used to going without. The 'false needs' of consumer capitalism are cited as the reason for the inauthentic economy of our desires – no matter what the ads tell us, you're never gonna get it, so get used to going without.

So what are we left with? A dog's breakfast of self-denial, self-restraint, guilt, and disavowal – hardly promising instruments of liberation. Or else, we are barraged with persuasion by threat. Thus, a magazine ad I saw recently for New Cycle Menstrual Lingerie proclaims:

> Mother Earth won't swallow this for much longer! 11 billion disposable, chlorine-bleached menstrual pads buried or burned each year. Use cloth for Menstrual Flow! Confront the Inconvenience! Overcome the Taboo! Beautiful, soft, washable cloth menstrual pads & accessories in organic knit or cotton flannel. Next Time: Tampons as sexual harassment and earth abuse. Stay tuned. Don't stuff it! Reuse it! CALL 1-800-845-FLOW

Don't get me wrong about this ad. I am an advocate of reuse, and share the reservations of many environmentalists about the preference of big business for recycling practices.[3] I submit, however, that people for the most part do not respond favorably to coercive messages of this sort that invoke guilt and self-denial. No more productive is a frontal assault on consumer gratifications. The problem lies deeper. Consumerism has shallow historical roots (only two or three generations in the West), but the concept of perpetual scarcity is deeply entrenched in our minds and cultural memories – there simply isn't enough to go around, sounds the ominous refrain. The history of liberal political economy that runs from Adam Smith and David Hume to Malthus, Ricardo, Marx, Mill and thence onto Keynes, Galbraith, and Marcuse is, from a certain angle, little more than a long debate about the exact ratio between natural scarcity and social scarcity.[4] For those who reject the postulates of classical economics about the permanence of scarcity, it is a debate about whether the postscarcity future of abundance comes about (a) through the market creation of wealth, (b) through some grand post-capitalist transition in social development, (c) through a reversion to premodernist production, or (d) through a simple transcendence of the present structure of inequalities. In recent years, we have seen economic rationalism reinstitutionalize scarcity as a universal condition, rendered tolerable only by the profitable manipulation of markets designed to address the imbalance between supply and demand. The result? The kind of cost-benefit analysis that can accommodate, if it does not serve as an actual blueprint for, corporate environmentalism. Alternately, the ecological crisis has raised the specter of new forms of scarcity not envisaged by any of the thinkers in the classical tradition of liberal politics. The result? Calls to scale back our hard-won liberties, now equated with the excesses of Western privilege and abundance upon which our liberal political institutions were founded.

In this respect, it is easy to see how the practice of wielding the threat of eco-collapse is an activist sword that cuts both ways. It has prompted action in many quarters – communities, institutions, governments – but, like any other political movement partially pursued through coercive, and not liberatory, means, it has also laid the basis for a draconian politics that is not always friendly to civil rights and social freedoms. The eco-apocalypse, however useful as an activist tool, is sometimes only another means of exploiting the category of scarcity – it cannot in itself help us create a politics of liberation. Much better to abolish the concept of scarcity altogether. But doesn't that mean doing away with abundance as well? If scarcity is an invention of modernity, then surely the concept of plenty is equally a myth of modernity's ideas about the future, not to mention the lost golden age? Those of us who still want to retain the idea of a postscarcity future may have to reexamine the content of the 'better world' traditionally promised as a haven of abundance in the tradition of utopian thought. Postscarcity describes a moment when scarcity is no longer an operative concept; it does not necessarily describe an economy where distribution is just and equal, and where scarcity has been temporarily staved off. Getting rid of scarcity is not the same as getting rid of hunger and poverty, although it may coincide with or lead to that happy state of affairs. Getting rid of the concept of scarcity is part of the cultural work that is necessary in order to make a world in which hunger and poverty no longer prevail. In that very different world, scarcity no longer exists conceptually as a default condition, and an ecological society has developed a more democratic way of ordering its priorities. Such a world lies in the future, not in a mythical past to be recreated by simply scaling back current levels of production and consumption.

[. . .]

Notes

1　See Alan Howard's comprehensive history of this obsession, 'Polynesian Origins and Migrations: A Review of Two Centuries of Speculation and Theory,' in Genevieve A. Highland (ed.), *Polynesian Culture History* (Honolulu: Bishop Museum Special Publications, 56), pp. 45–101.
2　Malcolm Crick, 'Tracing the Anthropological Self: Quizzical Reflections on Field Work, Tourism, and the Ludic,' *Social Analysis*, 17 (August 1985), pp. 71–92.
3　In his iconoclastic book, *The Apotheosis of Captain Cook: European Mythmaking in the Pacific* (Princeton University Press, 1992), Gananath Obeyesekere suggests that the thesis of Cook's deification was largely a European myth (drawing upon prior myths about Columbus and Cortes) accepted by or imposed upon Hawaiians in the interregnum between the old and the new religion. Cook was installed, and dismembered, as a Hawaiian chief (and therefore treated 'like' a deity), but no one took him for a Hawaiian, least of all a Hawaiian deity. Obeyesekere argues that the Makahiki festival to honor Lono, with which Cook's arrival coincided, was a minor festival until it was glorified by Kamehameha as 'the main national ritual of integration.'
4　See Valene Smith's introduction to *Hosts and Guests: The Anthropology of Tourism*, 2nd edn (Philadelphia: University of Pennsylvania Press, 1989).

VIGNETTE 5.1　ECOLOGISM: KEY TO SPIRITUAL RICHNESS, OR LEVER OF OPPRESSION?

R.D. North, author and consultant

Our two readings each accept that man's handling of his planet is not ideal and ought to change. "Present human interference with the non-human world is excessive, and the situation is rapidly worsening", say Devall and Sessions; and Ross's text is explicitly about different approaches to the "ecological crisis", which is also assumed. That much is a widely-accepted cliché, a standard modern mantra which it is well worth disputing, but not here. The point now is that our authors' handling of the human implications of this physical circumstance is quite different, and neither is widely-accepted.

For the Deep Ecology text, the hypothesis that there is an ecological crisis is, actually, secondary. These writers' larger concern would exist even if the planet's condition was satisfactory. It suggests that humans have lost touch with "nature" and that this is bad for them on a human level. That's to say: to have lost touch with nature would be bad for us emotionally and spiritually even if it did not lead us to make mistakes in the management of our physical interactions with nature. So Deep Ecology suggests that there is a deep truth, and an illuminating truth, to being human, and it has to do with our being a part of nature. This inner truth enjoins us to treat nature with modesty (and to that extent the view has expedient uses and values), and it suggests that this cautiousness would suit us well even if it did not also safeguard our physical security. This sort of message is popular insofar as its counsels are observed mostly in the breach, as our second text notes.

Ross stands the Deep Ecology tendency on its head. He suggests that whilst there is an ecological crisis, green attitudes – whether pale or deep – as a result of their own grammar and priorities lead us to propose solutions which are useless because they would not work. He doesn't speak directly of Deep Ecology, but his remarks apply even more to deep than pale green thinking. He doesn't say the green prescription would fail by being technically flawed, but because it wouldn't be popular enough to "fly" at a political level. And, anyway, the writer thinks the human trait on display in green attitudes are useless in themselves. "A dog's breakfast of self-denial, self-restraint, guilt and disavowal. . . .", he calls these heartfelt qualities. The essence of his position is that even if "green" policies turned out to be good for the planet, they would be bad for people.

So the arguments of the two texts properly mirror each other: what matters, both say, is the emotional, cultural and historical baggage people bring to thinking about the supposed ecological crisis. They have very different answers to the questions most modern people ponder at some time or other. Is it right to "feel" green or, rather differently, to put "green" thinking at the heart of the premises by which we live and conduct policy?

Ross's case is the more interesting because it is counter-intuitive. Mostly, nowadays, people think the greens are certainly right that the planet is in crisis, probably right about how to put that right, and perhaps right about man's relations with nature. But Ross believes that "alternativism" (which might have been presumed to be the home-territory of the Deep Ecologist) is much more than a reaction to the mainstream. Rather, it reveals and reflects the strengths of the mainstream. It is one of the products of the "pockets of permissibilities created as a marginal offshoot of a free-market economy". He acknowledges that it is the very freedom of democratic, free market societies which allows that "limits on growth can be democratically chosen and agreed upon". But, hold on, he suggests, there are limits to the wisdom of applying this "limits"-based discussion and policy. Abroad, the West can hardly be right when it shoves a "limits" view down the throats of poor countries. He goes on to say that, at home, North Americans have suffered "drastic erosion of a domestic culture of abundance" (that's to say, the old view that Americans were duty bound, and bound, to get richer, has come unstuck). Never mind whether this is really true, Ross uses the argument to suggest that green thinking – a culture of "reduced expectations" – is a dangerous device to clamp down on people's liberties, but also – he implies – their aspirations, including that of getting out of poverty.

Now it happens that this sort of thinking is closely allied to the thinking of the Spiked and Institute of Ideas[1] activists and intellectuals – boldly challenging environmentalism in the UK and the US. Several of these people were close to LM (the reborn *Living Marxism* magazine), and their thinking was substantially reflected in the TV documentary series, "Against Nature" (Channel 4, 1997[2]). They are opaque as to their real agenda but their strands of thinking are important because they function as the only serious opposition to the creeping "green-ness" which has led to the success of very particular readings of ideas such as the Precautionary Principle. This view, and it is found clearly in Ross, is that the greens seek to "shut down" the human urge to better oneself and live freely and to see nature as something to be manipulated for human benefit. That manipulation may need to be savvy and appreciative of nature's rules (as Ross says, "I am an advocate of reuse . . ."). But he believes that thinking about a "postscarcity" future will be the way that an "ecological" society gets past using scarcity as "a default" position which is too often used to crush the "politics of liberation". This leftist view senses that the bourgeois forces in society (and aren't NGOs the very flower of the middleclass?) use greenery (with scarcity as its default position) as a good way of shutting down the mass, progressive, liberation movement which would otherwise flourish, albeit in the unlikely guise of consumerism, but also in a revivified dislike of the controlling, nannying state.

But what of consumerism? Surely there is something to be said for the Deep Ecologist's view that to be enslaved to greed and consumption is at best a very odd way to exercise freedom?

One decent way to attack this view is to suggest that living with a free market in goods, ideas and behaviour is indeed demanding. Enlightenment freedoms are indeed hard to bear – they are tempting, disorientating and so on. But then no-one said that freedom would be easy to live with, only that it is the fully human thing to have to live with. The right's view, and it is shared by the Spiked tendency, is to stress that opportunities, like rights, bring with them obligations.

But Deep Ecology suggests that living with individual freedom is not, really, what we ought to be about. It is not what we are for. Our text discusses the matter as being a description of "the deeper, more spiritual approach to Nature". It is proposing that real "self-realization" (which it accepts as a goal) "goes beyond the modern Western *self* which is defined as an isolated ego striving primarily for hedonistic gratification. . . .".

We might well argue whether Western society's demand that each of its citizens pays between a third and two thirds of his wealth towards the commonwealth is compatible with the idea that we really are devoted to personal hedonism.

But we have deeper problems to face in the Deep Ecologists' argument. They want us to have a "biocentric" view of nature (including human life). Devall and Sessions quote Warwick Fox to the effect that ". . . there is no bifurcation between the human and non-human realms . . . to the extent that we perceive boundaries, we fall short of deep ecological consciousness".

Since we are discussing spiritual life, and how all nature is a borderless zone, it might in passing be worth wondering whether we believe that stones, snowdrops and snakes share with us a spiritual life. Animals, for instance, indeed might have some shard of an emotional, aesthetic, or intellectual life. But do we believe they have a spiritual one? Perhaps it doesn't matter. Maybe humans aren't spiritual either (now *that* would be a blow for the Deep Ecologists). And yet it is interesting that a human might feel "spiritual" about a lion, but the lion would not reciprocate, presumably, in spite of being all one with the human in some way.

Religion is also a problem for the Deep Ecologists. For a start, it is not clear that a non-religious person (even one for whom ecological thinking is a substitute for religious faith) can use the word "spiritual" of himself, since its meaning is bound up with the transcendental. That is to say, it implies the god-given. More importantly, many people have tried to reconcile the deeply ecological with the religious, not least because they have felt that religious spirituality ought to take us nearer to ecological awareness (whilst others hope that ecological awareness will bring us nearer to religious spirituality). This is a perilous path to take. The religious is about seeking some "other" which is worth worship. Deep Ecology says Nature cannot be that "other" thing. All the same, many people who hold strongly green views, also hope that ecologism can triumph within (or over) religion because they believe that religions have tended to be anthropocentric, and thus dangerous.

Actually, of course religious traditions have tended to respect nature at least as much as they tended to trash it. That is to say: you can find most views, and endorsement of most sorts of behaviour, in most religions, according to taste.

Even if one holds up ecologism as a moral, rather than a religious, template, one is in difficulties. Humans can see a moral dimension in the world; non-humans, presumably, do not. Even if the non-human provides us with a moral framework, it can only do so by mistake and coincidentally.

More difficult yet are Deep Ecology's difficulties with intellectual life. The Deep Ecologist view is that "Western culture has become increasingly obsessed with the idea of *dominance*: with dominance of humans over non-human Nature." This is simply not true. The Enlightenment has many traditions and tendencies, but if we read even a few of its core texts (Francis Bacon for instance[3]), we will find that alongside its interest in advancing human freedoms, it is also extremely interested in the "book of nature" as the guide for human discovery and relations with the non-human world.

Our Deep Ecology text is a good account of the attempt to erect a green spirituality, thought and practice; our postscarcity text is a pretty good rebuttal of many of its tendencies. It may be that after the clash of these two opposing mindsets has died down, the reader has – the sadder and the wiser – to find another means to fill what Salman Rushdie called the "God-shaped hole in the heart". But it is the postscarcity thought which presents us with the fresher challenge: to find a post-Puritan approach to the material world, and an approach to environmental policy which does not assume that "environmentalists" know everything or very much.

Notes

1   See www.spiked-online.com and www.instituteofideas.com.
2   See www.ourcivilisation.com/aginatur.htm.
3   "Man is the helper and interpreter of Nature. He can only act and understand in so far as by working upon her or observing her he has come to perceive her order . . . Nature cannot be conquered but by obeying her." Francis Bacon, quoted by Christopher Hill, *The Intellectual Origins of the English Revolution*, Oxford University Press, Oxford, 1965.

VIGNETTE 5.2 HUMANS AND NATURE: TENSIONS AND INTERDEPENDENCE

T.W. Luke, Virginia Polytechnic Institute and State University

Bill Devall's and George Sessions' *Deep Ecology: Living As If Nature Mattered* (1985) and Andrew Ross' *The Chicago Gangster Theory of Life* (1994) take opposing positions on how humans and Nature might coexist. Both books admit to the enduring interdependence of human beings and Nature. Yet, both also see tremendous tensions in the ways in which humanity has used Nature ethically to advance or retard various political projects. This collision of contrary positions can be very instructive.

Both books grapple with how fully humanity's understanding of the natural environment is a construct: Devall and Sessions believe it has been constructed wrongly in shallow ecological terms, while Ross speculates about why politics depends upon how Nature is constructed conceptually and practically. Devall and Sessions would remake Nature in accord with an "alternative paradigm" that bears its own true deep ecological truths. Ross, on the other hand, questions how all rhetorical frames are used to define the environment. For example, his critical questioning of Richard Dawkins' sociobiology of human genes, first, reveals how Dawkins reifies genes as autonomous actors, and then, second, claims they act like selfish Chicago gangsters. This allusion takes up only three pages, but Ross uses it colorfully in the book's title to make a point. Nature never "just is." It needs to be captured in ideas, positioned in a narrative or given an identity to be made comprehensible. How this is done represents entrenched power constructing collective knowledge to suit its own purposes.

Both of these books are loose aggregates of arguments, sometimes written elsewhere for other purposes, only to be assembled into these volumes. Devall's and Sessions' work is a compendium of many different ethical and political statements peppered with borrowings from several world cultures. Ross' book, on the other hand, draws together commentary from *Artforum*, *Boundary 2*, *Social Text* and *South Atlantic Quarterly*, which is then cast as his critical vision of "Nature's debt to society." While this pairing is not quite "the ascetics" versus "the aesthete," Devall and Sessions do not believe industrial society can conquer scarcity. So they do push a program of self-sacrifice, and voluntary simplicity in their appeal to live close to Nature with a spare economy of basic survival. Ross spurns this guidance about scarcity, and he argues why Nature offers no helpful models for human society's well-being. His project instead centers on "the struggle to prevent nature becoming the referee of our fate" (p. 5).

While most of their work concentrates upon wilderness, the outdoors, and Nature itself, Devall and Sessions did not develop the notion of deep ecology. Their work instead has popularized the thinking of Arne Naess (1989), a Norwegian philosopher, who first articulated the principles of deep ecology in the early 1970s (Devall 1988; Sessions 1995; Fox 1990; Manes 1990; Sale 1991). *Deep Ecology* came out in 1985 at the start of the second Reagan administration in the United States. The immobilization of reform environmentalism in the Reagan years, coupled with a reckless disregard for the environment in too many corporate initiatives during the boomtimes of the 1980s, gave Devall and Sessions a very attentive audience around the world. As a result, deep ecology's teachings now inspire many local, national, and global direct environmental action groups on several continents.

For these readers, Devall and Sessions claim the deepening environmental crisis must be understood "as a crisis of character and of culture" (p. ix). The reform movements of the past century have mitigated some of humanity's worst environmental abuses, but those reformers still work within the crisis-ridden categories of character and culture that still cause the problems. Therefore, they see the only way out leading through a fresh "understanding of earth wisdom" (p. ix) which combines an essentially new spiritual consciousness of the Earth with small-group, direct action politics. Their book winds through variations of this idea in an eclectic *tour d'horizon* of all the world's "minority traditions" as they build their case in favor of their alternative visions for a new "ecological consciousness."

In their rambling discussions of deep ecology, Devall and Sessions attribute the contemporary environmental crisis to "the dominant modern worldview" with its deadening commitments to anthropocentrism (or a human-privileged and people-centered set of values), materialism (the earth is a storehouse of natural resources), mechanism (Nature is no more than a vast machine that can be studied, mastered, and then administered), and meliorism (history is the chronicle of human progress made possible by bettering the world). These values, however, all presume an unending exploitation of Nature's bounty. Acknowledging the many critics who have voiced opposition to the dominant worldview throughout history, they then indicate how these minority traditions of resistance mostly drew upon "earth wisdom" to envision more just alternatives to the dominant modern worldview and its intrinsic propensity for ecological destruction.

Andrew Ross in *The Chicago Gangster Theory of Life* expresses his doubts about any environmental credo, like deep ecology, that presumes Nature "always knows best." He rightly observes "the belief that society ought to conform to nature is nothing new" (p. 12). And, then, he worries about how accepting the authority of Nature can quickly lead to a tyrannical curtailment of human rights, individual freedoms, and communal liberties.

Ross makes these points quite tellingly. He first takes on the thorny issues of indigenous authenticity in culture in the face of outside colonial and/or global change in the South Pacific, by focusing, ironically, on popular culture and media imagery. He argues that the European experience with South Pacific cultures, and especially Polynesia, were the ultimate source of Western society's ecological romanticism as well as its Malthusian realism when speaking about the environment. In the end, he plays the rhetorics of preservation against those of development to show how easy binary oppositions, like growth/no growth, native/exotic, and local/global, do not really work well in the Polynesian context where multicultural coexistence, transnational trends, and global conflicts keep bringing the syncretic social complexity of the region up against any simplistic naturalist analysis.

Ross takes up the issue of urban ecology in his "Bombing the Big Apple" section, playing the ideas of civic municipalists, like Murray Bookchin, against urban developmentalists, like the Port of New York Authority, which built the World Trade Center in the 1960s and 1970s. Reading this chapter is particularly poignant after September 11, 2001, but Ross essentially critiques the World Trade Center itself as a sick building, an urban architectural disaster, a sign of the 1970s political economy of stagflation, and finally a target of "the Afghan Mujahideen" (p. 150) in its February 1993 WTC bombing. With this anchor point in Manhattan's urban ecology, Ross also maintains that human ecology must consider other things besides protecting wilderness. Here he considers how the urban workings of Manhattan have been shaped by many environmental forces, ranging from the HIV/AIDs epidemic of the 1980s and its phobias of exclusion in the city's richer, most exclusive neighborhoods to global ethnic diasporas and their settlement in world cities like New York. Ultimately, Ross wonders who assaulted the city worst: the Islamic terrorists of February 1993 or the World Trade Center's planners who "bombed out" Lower Manhattan in their own fashion.

Ross' critique of pop culture continues his ecocriticism as he probes the images of ecology used in the mass media (Haraway 1991; Manes 1990), the men's movement of the 1990s (Bly 1990; Keen 1991; Harding 1992), and genetic sciences in contemporary America (Krimsky 1991; Lewontin 1991). The image war over the destruction of Kuwaiti oil fields in the 1991 Gulf War, the full-blast propaganda machinery of "reality TV" devoted to shows about Nature, and Bravo 20 national park proposal to memorialize humanity's environmental waste at a US Navy bombing range in Nevada permit Ross to discuss how fully "Nature" for most Americans today is composed of images from Discovery Channel specials, *National Geographic* covers, and science fiction dystopias. Ironically, it is people who come of age in such cultures who often end up seeking greater salvation from essentialist teachings in the men's movements or women's movements. Here Ross problematizes the stereotypes used by opposing gender role sets – whether conservative patriarchal or subversive feminism – as he illustrates how Nature is leveraged by ecofeminists and wild men to advance "the most radical reshaping of individualism in the West since Renaissance humanism" (p. 236).

Ross closes his discussion with a look at today's biologistic social philosophies that have returned to genetic engineering, the biotech industry, and genomic mapping for foundational principles. Seeing these neo-Social Darwinian tendencies as a new code of control for corporate interests or the state, he pushes for overthrowing the idea of scarcity permanently. A post scarcity society could lead to a world of common prosperity, but, most importantly, it would disrupt the commerce of liberal political economy in today's public policies with their balancing of natural scarcity and social scarcity in global capitalism. Until environmentalists can think beyond Nature as scarcity, Ross believes, most environmental discourse only will cycle endlessly in debates about whether or not Nature directs humanity toward making new ascetic sacrifices or shifting into greater indulgence in material abundance.

CHAPTER 6

THEORY AND PRACTICE: IDEOLOGY AND PHILOSOPHY

READING 6.1 EDUCATION FOR THE ENVIRONMENT: CRITICAL CURRICULUM THEORISING AND ENVIRONMENTAL EDUCATION

J. Fien

Source: Deakin University Press, Geelong, 1993: 37–44

Ideology critiquing in environmental education

The development of a critical curriculum theory for environmental education is now taken one step further through using the typologies of educational and environmental ideologies outlined above to critique the nature and purposes of education *for* the environment in comparison with education *about* and *through* the environment.

The need for environmental educators to be clear about their intentions and ideologies has been emphasised on a number of occasions. For example, Armstrong asked the following questions when noting the failure of many authors offering definitions of environmental education to be precise about their ultimate goals:

> ... they all avoid something: the end product. What do the authors want to get out of educating people in this way? Do they hope for a prettier world? Do they hope for social change? Do they hope to improve the workings of democracy? Do they want revolution? Or do they merely want every part of the machine to run smoothly?
>
> (Armstrong 1979: 10–11)

Sterling makes this point also:

> What are we trying to achieve in EE [environmental education]? Can it ever change society by 'leading from the front' – or is it more of a 'consolidating operation' reinforcing values that are already changing? ... The global issues facing us are crucial, and if education has a role in addressing them, we need to be clear about what that role is ... it will pay to get our ideas clear if we want to translate them into the most appropriate and effective form of action.
>
> (Sterling 1990b: 1–2)

Huckle (1983) has analysed educational and environmental ideologies to clarify the social assumptions, intentions and effects of education *about* the environment, education *through* the environment, and education *for* the environment. His analysis provides a foundation for identifying the characteristics of education *for* the environment. It also helps explain why education *for* the environment is considered the form

Table 1 The key questions in a conceptual framework *for* education *for* the environment

A Economic production
1 What natural resources are being used or conserved?
2 For what purposes are they being used or conserved? By whom, how and why?
3 What is the impact of economic production on the environment? What environments does it produce?
4 Is the production ecologically sustainable?
5 Is the production socially useful? Does it meet people's basic needs?
6 Who owns and controls the natural resources and technology used in economic production?
7 What power do workers have to decide what is made and how it is produced?
8 In what ways is economic production changing and how is this likely to affect the use of nature in the future?
9 How does the society's history and present position within the world economy shape its production, development and use of nature?

Sample concepts: nature, ecosystem, land, land use, natural resource, renewable resource, non-renewable resource, resource conservation, labour, energy, capital, technology, alternative technology, ecologically sustainable production, economic development, industrialisation, needs, wants, ownership, economic power, economic democracy, division of labour, capitalism, profit, market, socialism, economic planning, state collectivism, world economy, interdependence, commodity chains, multinational company, colonialism, imperialism, terms of trade, global division of labour, dependent development, economic recession, product cycle.

B Distribution and redistribution
1 How are the benefits and costs of economic production distributed and redistributed? What principles determine this and what methods are used to bring it about?
2 What is the level of inequality in society? Are differences in wealth and environmental well-being increasing or decreasing?
3 Is poverty a cause of environmental damage?
4 Does wealth result in wasteful production and environmental damage?
5 What amount of wealth is used for environmental research, management and conservation? How is the charge for this distributed?
6 Would redistribution of wealth, and greater equality within society, assist a transition to ecologically sustainable production and development?
7 How is the society involved in transfers of trade, investment, technology, loans and aid?
8 Do these transfers help or hinder the society in moving towards ecologically sustainable production and development?
9 Would a redistribution of wealth and greater equality between societies assist moves towards ecodevelopment?

Sample concepts: wealth, waste, poverty, environmental poverty, equality/inequality, scarcity/surplus, supply, demand, population, consumption, conservation, trade, investment, aid, social welfare, justice, environmental management, international economic order, competition/cooperation, arms trade.

C Power and decision making
1 How is the society governed?
2 How does government regulate the use of nature?
3 How does government plan and manage the environment? What institutions and procedures exist for this? How are decisions made? How are conflicts over the environment resolved or managed?
4 What power do people have to participate in political decision making? How is political power distributed in society? According to what procedures and rules is it used?
5 In what ways does environmental politics reflect the power and interests of different groups in society? What policies and strategies do environmental groups adopt in seeking to influence the political process?

Table 1 (continued)

6   What forms of economic development does the government support? In what ways are the government's economic and foreign policies related to the society's role in world economy?
7   In what ways do the government's economic, foreign and other policies shape its policies on the environment?
8   In what ways does the international political system seek to resolve global environmental problems? Does competition between nation states prevent international action on environmental problems?
9   In what ways do environmentalists seek to influence the national and international political system?

Sample concepts: politics, power/powerlessness, nation state, local state, international politics, government, forms of government, parties, pressure groups, law, force, authority, manipulation, reason, cooperation/conflict, representation, democracy, consultation, corruption, participation, bureaucracy.

D   Social organisation
1   What distinct groups exist in society and what amounts of economic and political power do they have at their disposal?
2   Are there movements working to extend democracy to give more people some control of economic production and political decision making?
3   What form do these movements take? What are their aims and tactics?
4   Do the movements incorporate environmental goals? What issues do they tackle? How effective are they?
5   What groups work with environmentalists in such movements? What part do women play? What part do ethnic minorities play?
6   Which groups in society oppose such movements for greater democracy and what actions do they take?
7   What have the movements learnt from their campaigns?
8   Do the movements cooperate at all levels, including the international level?

Sample concepts: individual, family, community, class, racism, patriarchy, social order/disorder, consent/dissent, social control, social movements, environmental movement, voluntary groups, pressure groups, trade union, consumer organisations, social responsibility, appropriate technology, cooption, alienation.

E   Culture and ideology
1   What are the accepted ways of interacting with, and thinking about, nature and the environment?
2   In what ways is the society's culture and ideology being changed by economic development? What role do external forces play in this?
3   How does technology reflect and shape people's relations with nature? What alternative or appropriate technologies would alter these relations?
4   How do ideas from the natural and social sciences, and from other areas of knowledge, reflect and shape our relations with nature? What ideas are taught in schools? What ideas are not taught? What ideas act as ideology?
5   What ideas are used by groups and parties engaged in environmental politics? How do these ideas reflect material interests?
6   What messages about nature, the environment and the world does popular culture transmit? What role does popular culture play in consumerism and imperialism?
7   To what extent do news media explain the real causes of problems relating to development and the environment?
8   What elements of traditional, minority and alternative cultures could be useful in creating an ecologically sustainable society?

Sample concepts: cultural needs, communication, language, custom, tradition, religion, myth, values, moral code, world view, knowledge, science, social science, advertising, popular culture, consumer culture, political culture, education, environmental education, culture contact, cultural imperialism.

Table 2 Educational and environmental ideologies in different approaches to
environmental education

Environmental ideology		Educational ideology		
		Vocational/ neo-classical	Liberal/ progressive	Socially critical
Technocentric	Cornucopian	Conservative education *about* the environment		
	Accommodation Managerialism (Light green)		Liberal education *about* the environment	
	Communalism Ecosocialism (Red-green)		Liberal education *through* the environment	Critical education *for* the environment
Ecocentric	Gaianism Utopian (Dark green)		Liberal education *for* the environment	

→ Major ideological direction of less restrictive definitions and analyses of education *about, through,* and *for*
the environment

of environmental education most appropriate to the challenge of the global environmental crisis and, hence, helps to explain the decision to make education *for* the
environment the focus of this book. Table 2 relates educational and environmental
ideologies to these three approaches to environmental education and serves as a summary of the ideological analysis of alternative approaches to environmental education
which follows it.

Ideology and education *about* and *through* the environment

Education *about* the environment emphasises teaching facts, concepts and generalisations about environmental patterns, processes and problems. Its scope and goals are
derived from vocational/neo-classical and liberal/progressive ideologies of education
and from technocentric environmental ideology. These ideologies combine to lead
proponents of education *about* the environment to view both education and environmental management as neutral, but instrumental, processes. Thus, they believe that
increasing the environmental studies content in the curriculum can lead to an improved
understanding of environmental problems and new forms of environmental management (Huckle 1983: 104).

Two forms of education about the environment may be identified. The first, conservative education about the environment, promotes cornucopian environmentalism
and the values of vocational/neo-classical education. Both the overt and the hidden
curriculum of this approach have particular educational implications. For example, the
curriculum content of education *about* the environment emphasises the natural sciences,
especially biology, botany and ecology, rather than the social sciences (Linke 1980;

Robottom 1983). The knowledge chosen for study and the methods by which it is presented to students are based on a technical rationality which promotes a belief in the rights of humans to control nature and the capacity of science and technology to manage the effects of environmental degradation. There is little consideration of the environment as a social construct or of the social contexts or implications of changes in people–environment relationships. Questions of gender in environmental issues are not often considered (Di Chiro 1987). There is a strong framing of the environmental subjects available in the curriculum, with integration or multi-disciplinary perspectives on environmental problems occurring more within individual subjects, or on the initiative of individual teachers, than as a school-wide policy that challenges the positivistic and compartmentalised view of knowledge presented to students in most subjects.

A second type of education *about* the environment program is found in progressive geography, environmental studies, and science, technology and society (STS) courses. Such courses reflect both the liberal/progressive goals of education as the development of the mind and individual growth and light green approaches to environmental management. Liberal education *about* the environment involves concept and enquiry-based investigations that seek to induct students into the modes of thinking of the disciplines (e.g. Bruner 1966) and, sometimes, into multidisciplinary thinking. These programs often have a problem or issue focus which seeks to add relevance to the curriculum. They also advocate enquiry-based learning in order to develop students' higher order thinking and problem-solving skills. These are worthwhile educational developments. However, the environmental ideology behind this approach to education is techno-centric. It promotes a view of environmental problems as issues to which successful accommodations can be made through resource auditing, impact assessment, and improved, scientifically proven management practices. Robottom (1987) argues that this form of education *about* the environment promotes and legitimates a technocratic world view. Central to this view is the belief that environmental problems can be solved through technical and scientific means without a consideration of the social context, the political aspects of environmental decision making, or the 'vested interests' that may exist in a controversial environmental issue or problem. Robottom argues that:

> The technocratic world view promoted by education *about* the environment ignores the important qualitative dimension of the majority of environmental issues which involve 'quality of life' or 'social need' concerns – emotions, beliefs, aspirations, aesthetics and, perhaps most important of all, vested interests. It could be argued that a view of the resolution of environmental problems that stresses the role of technical rationality (i.e. the processes of an objective, applied science method) creates a false impression of the way these issues are resolved . . .
>
> (Robottom 1987: 104)

Sometimes, liberal education *about* the environment may involve elements of dark green and red-green environmentalism. This occurs when decision-making exercises, role plays and values clarification exercises are used to allow students to express their views on appropriate forms of environmental management or to identify aspects of their lifestyles that may contribute to environmental problems. However, these progressive teaching strategies can be used without an analysis of the social context of environmental management or an understanding of the integration of personal and structural change necessary for long-term solutions to environmental problems. When this occurs, this approach has the same ideological effects as conservative education *about* the environment, despite the intentions of its liberal educational and ecocentric environmental orientations.

Robottom (1983) and Huckle (1985) have explored the effects of these conservative and liberal approaches to education *about* the environment within the context of science and geography teaching, respectively. Robottom (1983) argues that the predominance of a positivistic world view in most science education renders it an inappropriate vehicle for environmental education. He argues that the focus on 'technical' solutions to environmental problems in science education disregards the vital human factors involved in their causes and solutions. This can give students a false impression of the way the world works as it masks such value-laden political machinations as negotiation, lobbying, persuasion, bribery and so on, which often play a major role in environmental decision making.

Huckle argues that school geography has tended to be dominated by education *about* the environment and has acted as an agency for social reproduction. This is because it has not helped students to understand how societies and their environments are 'made and remade, and how landscapes and people-environment relationships change in the process . . . [of] the dialectic between social structure and human agency' (Huckle 1985: 302). Evidence of this which he cites includes the teaching of geography as a body of unproblematical facts to be committed to memory; the neglect of issues or interpretations that illustrate the effects of social, economic and political processes, especially the role of historical contexts and capital in environmental issues; an overemphasis on description rather than explanation; interpretation and problem solving; and defining educational success in terms of students' abilities to reproduce ideas, skills and attitudes that support the status quo.

Huckle concludes that students are given a depoliticised and dehumanised view of the world as a result of this uncritical form of pedagogy. He also expresses concern that the hidden curriculum remains conservative even where progressive geography curricula and teaching resources seek to encourage problem-solving and decision-making skills. This occurs because the issues for resolution presented to students are posed within a pluralistic, consensus view of society which emphasises the equality of all values and opinions and ignores the maldistribution of wealth, status and power in society, and the role of conflict and the use of various forms of power in environmental decision making (Huckle 1985: 293). Maher (1988) has also made this point in her critique of the 'equal time for both sides' approach to studying controversial environmental issues.

Education *through* the environment uses the environment as a medium for education, especially in the development of child-centred programs that reflect Gaianist ecocentric values. Such programs are found most often in primary schools in which topic-based work is grounded in the tradition of Rousseau and others who saw the environment as a rationale and a vehicle for children's development. They are found also in much of the perception and townscape approaches of the early Art and the Built Environment movement (Adams and Ward 1982) and behavioural (Slater and Fien 1983) and humanistic geography (Fien 1983; Bartlett 1989; Hall 1989) in secondary schools. Huckle argues that the combination of liberal/progressive educational and Gaianist environmental ideologies in education *through* the environment leads to 'a rather naive respect for both children and nature' (Huckle 1983: 104) in which 'nature and the child are thought to have rights and [it is believed that] education and society should be reshaped to take account of laws of natural development and ecology' (Huckle 1986: 13). He argues that this results in education *through* the environment reflecting 'ideas of natural or ecological determinism that are at best romantic and at worst positively reactionary' for they fail to take account of the material base of society. As a result, education *through* the environment tends to stress personal values, 'cooperation and new ethics but make[s] little mention of politics, conflict and power' (Huckle 1986: 13).

Ideology and education *for* the environment

Education *for* the environment seeks to promote informed and active concern for the quality and preservation of human life and the environment (from which it is inseparable). As Huckle writes about education *for* the environment:

> The curriculum is designed to increase pupils' awareness of the moral and political decisions shaping the environment and to give them the knowledge, attitudes and skills which will help them to form their own judgements and to participate in environmental politics.
>
> (Huckle 1983a: 105)

Education *for* the environment represents an integration of a socially critical orientation in education and ecosocialist environmental ideology. The objectives of critical education *for* the environment include the development of moral and political awareness as well as the knowledge, commitment and skills to analyse issues and participate in an informed and democratic way in environmental decision making and problem solving. Pedagogically, critical education *for* the environment generally begins with the study of environmental issues and problems on a local scale. This is to provide opportunities for students to develop the concepts, procedural values and skills of political literacy so that they may learn how to participate actively in seeking solutions to the problems that concern them. The analysis of local concerns is then extended to consider national and global implications. The global perspective, especially on local issues, that education *for* the environment seeks to develop is often summed up under the rubric of 'think globally – act locally'.

Education *for* the environment is not without its tensions and critics, however. Criticisms focus upon:

1   its anthropocentric nature;
2   the narrow scope of ecosocialist politics compared with the breadth of views in the wide field of green politics;
3   the potential dangers of bias and indoctrination in using environmental education to develop political literacy; and
4   the tension between the values of the New Environmental Paradigm in education *for* the environment and the values of the Dominant Social Paradigm which are so entrenched in contemporary society and schooling.

Relating to the first area of criticism, Gough has challenged the anthropocentric nature of education *for* the environment from an ecocentric, dark green perspective:

> While it has been recognised that environmental education ought not to be merely education *in* or *about* environments, I am not convinced that the popular slogan of 'education *for* the environment' is much of an improvement. Apart from being somewhat patronising and anthropocentric (who are we to say what is 'good for' the environment, and which environment is '*the* environment', anyway?), this slogan maintains the sorts of distinctions that tend to work against a deeply ecological world view – distinctions between subject and object, education and environment, learner and teacher.
>
> (Gough 1987b: 50)

In place of education *for* the environment, Gough (1987b: 50) proposes an ecocentric approach to environmental education based upon the notion that 'we might someday learn to live, and live to learn *with* environments'.

In the second area, Sterling (1990a: 125–6) has made a similar criticism of the ecosocialist orientation of education *for* the environment. He argues that 'valuable insights and principles' of Gaianist ecocentric thinking, such as the integrity and unity-in-diversity of ecosystems and the 'importance and interaction of personal and inner well-being in relation to human and natural systems', are lost in the ecosocialist emphasis on social and economic structures and its dualistic view of people and nature.

[. . .]

READING 6.2   CURRICULUM DEVELOPMENT AND SUSTAINABLE DEVELOPMENT: PRACTICES, INSTITUTIONS AND LITERACIES

S.R. Gough and W.A.H. Scott

Source: *Educational Philosophy and Theory* 33(2), 2001: 137–152

[. . .]

Dead weights and fancy turns

It is well understood by anyone who has ever attempted to carry a heavy pack across country by ski that, once one is travelling downhill at any speed and in a given direction, all attempts to turn, however imaginative, necessary, or skilfully executed will end in failure. The pack will continue in the direction it was going and take you with it. Institutions of both the kinds identified above tend to have a similar inertial effect on those who wish to achieve imaginative, necessary and skilful changes in curriculum. Unlike the pack however, institutions can do this while simultaneously reassuring the would-be innovator of their support for what is intended. Further, even if institutions can be changed, *practices* may display an inertia all of their own. For example, it is very hard to change what teachers do in classrooms even where apparently quite radical reform of education systems has been achieved. As Lundgren (1991: 45) has noted 'the closer we come to the teaching situation, the more stable are the processes of education'. Finally, the different *literacies* that individuals and groups bring to bear in coping with complex and uncertain situations lead them to favour particular interpretations of cause/effect and problem/solution. Further, these incompatible or competing literacies may mean that, rather than being merely *ignorant* of alternative interpretations to their own, individuals and groups may sometimes be aware of and actively *resistant* to such interpretations. An illustration of this is provided by the conservative influence of subject specialisms within the curriculum. Young (1998: 98) sees this influence as one from which education must be rescued in the interests of an integrated curriculum, but insightfully acknowledges that subject specialists themselves can make the reverse case to good effect.

Similar difficulties are recognisable in efforts to bring about change towards sustainable development. For example, analysis of the importance of institutions and their inter-relationships forms an important strand in thinking about environmental management (Schwarz and Thompson 1990; Thompson 1997). This work explicates the influence of individuals' institutional loyalties on their understanding of environmental reality in terms of a 'plurality of knowledges' (Thompson 1997: 142), and was influential in developing the notion of multiple literacies employed in this paper. In education, institutional resistance of various kinds to environmental education has been identified by, for instance, Posch (1991) in his review of the OECD's 'Environment and School Initiatives' programme, and by Scott (1995) from a teacher education perspective, drawing on an EU project. The difficulty of bringing about change in classroom processes in environmental education has been discussed at some length by Fien (1993). The following passage, written about curriculum change, applies with equal force to the project of sustainable development and summarises the essence of the shared problem.

> If the enterprise is to be successful, it is the new logic and not some radically mistaken version of it which must be tried. Yet this is the unlikeliest outcome. . . . For, if the new logic be described in its own terms, its hearers must struggle hard for understanding by whatever means they have. These means, however, are the old modes of understanding, stemming from the old logic.
>
> (Schwab 1978, cited in Reid 1999: 107)

How, in other words, does one implement an innovation for which the need is not universally or even widely acknowledged, the case is not universally accepted, and widespread acceptance of both need and case is likely to be achieved only after a settled period of implementation? In the cases of both curriculum and sustainable development this problem turns out to have (at least) two dimensions.

First, there is the problem of changing everything at once. Unless not only practices but also organisational institutions, cultural institutions and literacies are simultaneously amenable (at least) to change it is likely that, to return to our earlier metaphor, the 'pack' will continue on its own sweet way towing the 'skier' behind it.

Secondly, there is the question of whether and, if so how far, useful change can be built upon local knowledge and aspirations. For example, Westbury (1999) has argued for a curriculum targeted at the expectations of the stakeholders in schooling, and Elliott (1998: 157) for a foundational curriculum focus on 'the problems and issues of everyday living'. A similar emphasis is widely found among advocates of sustainable development. For instance, 'Participatory Rural Appraisal' is an established technique employed by environmental management specialists of various kinds to investigate the knowledge and understanding of local people – and companies such as Shell, which impact heavily on the environment, now routinely make use of 'stakeholder analysis' in their planning. Among environmental educators the work of Robottom and Hart (1993) has been particularly influential through its advocacy of a participatory action research approach. On the other hand Hlebowitsh (1999a: 349–350), for example, argues strongly for a curriculum 'that purposefully goes beyond (or even challenges) local traditions', while efforts to promote Chapter 36 of *Agenda 21*, which deals with the role of education, public awareness and training in sustainable development, identify a need for a more top-down approach to 'disseminate . . . knowledge, know-how and skills' (Hopkins, Damlamian and López Ospina 1996: 3).

We argue that there is no single resolution to these issues, but that they can be understood on a case by case basis by reference to the framework we have proposed (Figure 7). It is perfectly possible for local people, teachers and pupils who share a literacy and a commitment to particular cultural institutions (such as democratic participation, for example) to achieve advances in curriculum and/or environmental practices which simultaneously cause modifications in organisational institutions (Greenall Gough and Robottom 1993). It is also possible for teachers who are attached to the cultural institution of subject-specific teaching to act as a break on inter-disciplinary curriculum innovations (Young 1998) or environmental education initiatives (Posch 1991) planned by, say, imaginative central authorities. Parents may use private tuition as a means to circumvent what

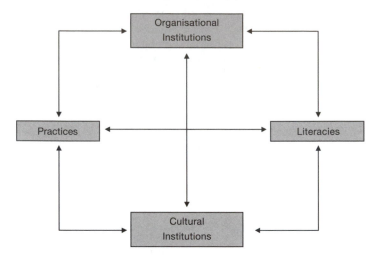

Figure 7 Analytical category framework.

they perceive as social engineering by teachers, educationalists or governments. They may and do also use it to engineer opportunities for their children in the face of state provision that is under-resourced or corrupt (Bray 1999). In every case events will unfold through a complex interplay of the organisational institutions, cultural institutions, practices and literacies that happen to be present in the situation. This unfolding will also occur within, and to a greater or lesser extent, be influenced by, the properties of the physical environment in which it occurs. To return to our tropical island example, the view any interested group takes of both curriculum and sustainable development possibilities is likely to be radically changed by the building and operation of the hotel complex.

Learning societies

We have already noted in passing the significance of uncertainty for the contexts of both curriculum development and sustainable development. If one sets aside the complication arising because terms such as 'uncertainty', 'risk', 'ignorance', 'surprise', 'novelty' and 'catastrophe' are used by different commentators with different degrees of definition and rigour, it is quite clear that inability to enumerate the variables which impact on social change, or to identify ranges of possible outcomes of particular change processes, or to attach probabilities to possible outcomes which *are* identified, is perceived as a crucial strategic parameter by writers across a range of fields. These include business management (Senge 1990; de Geus 1997), environmental management (Schwarz and Thompson 1990; Thompson 1997), curriculum theory (Elliott 1998; Young 1998) and educational management (Strain 2000a, 2000b). Not all these writers are agreed about the origins of this uncertainty (to use this word generically). For Schwarz and Thompson, for example, it is a fundamental characteristic of the human condition. However, educational theorists have tended to build on analyses which see uncertainty as having taken new forms in recent times (e.g. Beck *et al.* 1994; Beck 1999), so developing the case for 'learning societies'. These are characterised, crucially, by 'a self-sustaining beneficial cycle of experience and reflexivity, in which coping with change deepens the capacity to cope with further change' (Wilkins 2000: 346). It will be noted that this formulation seems every bit as appropriate as a key goal of sustainable development as of curriculum development or educational management – a point that is only strengthened by Wilkins' further observation that the 'learning' which characterises a learning society will be 'conscious, largely informal, lifelong, and . . . achieved through dialogue with others rather than in isolation'.

For Strain (2000a: 243–244) the new kind of uncertainty, which is perceived as underpinning the case for learning societies, arises from two fundamental social changes. First, there has been change in our relationship with our environment. Intriguingly, he describes the environment as less 'dangerous' but more 'risky'. The point is that the more we control the environment the less it *actually is* the environment we began by trying to control: or, to return to our earlier terminology, the more we rewrite the environment the less appropriate become our established, taken-for-granted readings of it. This is because our rewriting is mediated through institutions (of both kinds) and practices, *and also* through the imperfectly understood biogeophysical characteristics of the environment itself. Secondly, argues Strain, the notion of an individual's 'self' has changed from being a more-or-less socially and genetically given property into the subject of a more-or-less inescapable process of lifelong negotiation.

The appearance of 'the individual' at this point in the argument is, as we shall argue, interesting: but it is also fairly short lived. In the first place, we have already noted Wilkins' view that the learning in a learning society is necessarily social, a point which has also been powerfully made by Young (1998). In the second place, as Quicke (2000: 301) notes:

> The tendency towards diversity and pluralism may be a cause for celebration, but it also carries with it certain dangers; it may give rise to such pervasive incommensurability and fragmentation that the construction of shared understandings through a common moral discourse might prove to be impossible.

The individual, then, needing to establish a sense of self, may abandon given social reference points (which may be organisational institutions, cultural institutions, practices, or literacies) in order to do so, *but must also* then re-establish other such reference points.

In the previous section we drew attention to the problem of changing everything at once, arguing that resistance to change would be likely to result unless all the four categories of social influences on curriculum development and sustainable development identified in our proposed model (Figure 7) could be changed (or, as a minimum, be made tolerant of change) at the same time. We now argue that although notions of a learning society represent a useful advance in thinking about both curriculum development and sustainable development, they are typically flawed by virtue of a baggage of particular cultural institutions that tend, overwhelmingly, to dominate their prescriptions. It should be noted that our concern is not with the cultural institutions themselves, but with that overwhelming tendency to dominate. Principal among these are the cultural institutions of *collaboration, justice* and *equality*.

We do not want to argue *against* collaboration, justice, or equality. We do want to point out that the valorisation of collaboration in any specific instance involves a (deliberate or unwitting) choice to *exclude* the possibility of progress in that instance through competition and/or conflict. We would ask how, for example, collaborative institutions can extend their influence, or become internally *more* collaborative, without competition and conflict between old and new thinking. Similarly, justice and equality are imperfectly compatible with each other and with liberty. There are trade-offs to be made between all three. Civil society continuously strikes bargains in terms of these trade-offs. It cannot do otherwise, though the 'bargains' can be more-or-less planned and reached through a range of mechanisms that include markets, central planning, local planning and simple default. We would argue that social learning can only progress if the institutions which promote it reserve a valued place for liberty *alongside* justice and equality (and for competition and conflict alongside collaboration) in their practices and literacies. In particular, they should insist on the liberty of individuals to challenge particular practices, institutions and literacies, even where these claim to be grounded in concerns for justice and equality. If that grounding is robust the challenge will fail. If not it will succeed – and social learning will happen.

It will be noted that one effect of the above argument is to create a more meaningful role for the individual who, rather than being merely glimpsed dashing from one piece of institutional cover to the next, now enjoys the possibility of, and some responsibility for, the initiation of change. Such a characterisation is also truer to (original) business thinking on organisational learning and may be a step towards that building of deeper links between learning and production which has been identified by Young (1998: 153) as 'one of the crucial unresolved issues for the learning society of the future'. However much people collaborate at work they are hired, paid, appraised, promoted and fired as individuals by organisations that compete, in one way or another, for resources and customers: and the role of 'employee' or 'employer' is every bit as real a part of a person's life as the role of 'citizen'.

A further consequence is that at least one related dispute becomes less puzzling. For example, the answer to the questions, 'does marketisation of education serve educational purposes?' (Hlebowitsh 1999a; Westbury 1999) and 'does marketisation (of just about anything) promote sustainable development?' is clearly, and firmly, 'Yes' and 'No' in both cases. Abstract arguments about the absolute merit or otherwise of markets are beside the point. What matters in any particular instance concerns the context of practices, institutions and literacies within which such marketisation occurs, and the ways in which it alters the balance of power and influence between them.

Finally, there are further implications for the distinctions between:

* knowledge transmission and creation;
* facts and values.

These turn out to be aspects of a single, larger issue.

The theoretic and the practical

It has not been our intention in this paper to claim that curriculum development and sustainable development are the same thing, though others may have done so (Foster 2001). Rather, our developing argument has been that a professional concern with curriculum development is compatible and probably synergistic with a professional concern with sustainable development. However, it is not by any means obvious what the term 'professional concern' might mean in this context. In fact, its use at this point to some extent anticipates the remainder of our argument and it may be helpful to begin with the observation that any person showing 'professional concern' might be expected, at least on the face of it, to possess *both* a measure of factual knowledge and/or technical expertise *and* a degree of ethical engagement with their task.

The distinction between facts and techniques, on the one hand, and values and ethics on the other is deeply rooted in Western thought, having its origins in Aristotle's distinction between 'technical' and 'practical' thought and action (Kemmis and Fitzclarence 1986). In the simplest terms, technical thought and action are concerned with the instrumental application of established knowledge to achieve known ends. Practical thought and action necessarily involve value judgements, and are concerned with the wisdom and rightness of particular choices in particular circumstances.

This distinction continues to be of great significance with respect to both curriculum development and sustainable development. In relation to environmentalism it divides those who place their 'faith in the application of science, market forces, and managerial ingenuity' from those who have 'faith in the rights of nature and of the essential need for co-evolution of human and natural ethics' (O'Riordan 1989: 85, Table 4.1). In relation to curriculum, it underpinned Schwab's (1969) seminal argument that the field was 'moribund' and required a driving-out of the theoretic (i.e. the 'technical') by the practical. It has been an influence therefore, one way or another, on most subsequent curriculum theorising.

Yet, despite its impressive provenance and extensive influence, the distinction between the technical and the practical is at best incomplete. There is much thought and action that cannot with confidence be assigned to one category or the other.

To say this is, of course, far from original. Thomas Kuhn (1996: 126) in making his case for a view of scientific development as paradigm change rather than as knowledge accumulation, wrote:

> But is sensory experience fixed and neutral? Are theories simply man-made (*sic*) interpretations of given data? The epistemological viewpoint that has most often guided Western philosophy for three centuries dictates an immediate and unequivocal, Yes! In the absence of a developed alternative, I find it impossible to relinquish entirely that viewpoint. Yet it no longer functions effectively, and the attempts to make it do so through the introduction of a neutral language of observations now seem to me hopeless.

The issue, for Kuhn, is not whether facts and values can be separated but the lack of any 'developed alternative' to assuming that they can. In one attempt to develop such an alternative, Tesh (1988) makes the helpful point that just as values may be implicit in facts, so facts may be implicit in values. Hence, ethical relativism should be regarded with as much suspicion as scientific absolutism. Values and facts are not opposites, but rather inseparable properties of our socio-bio-geo-physical world. However, we do not and cannot perceive them from a detached, impartial, or objective vantage point, even if we call ourselves metatheorists in an attempt to appear to do so. We can perceive facts and values only from the perspective of our own, personal, multiple, overlapping contexts at any particular moment in time. These contexts (to be understood, we have argued above, in terms of the interactions of organisational institutions, cultural institutions, practices and literacies, with each other, the individuals who constitute or encounter them and biogeophysical nature) provide us with our perception of where our interests lie. As Schwarz and Thompson (1990: 33) have written:

> If different actors, in the same debate, cognize differently (that is, if they *see* things differently and *know* things differently), then they will inevitably be operating with different definitions of what is there. The debate, therefore, will entail the clash of differently drawn boundaries and the contention of incompatible rules of closure. Means and ends, substantive cases, facts and values, are weapons the protagonists reach for (and define, each to his [*sic*] satisfaction) *not* concepts in terms of which the debate itself can be analyzed. It is the competing *problem definitions*, and their institutional origins, that give us the measure of the debate.

As Schwarz and Thompson themselves point out, this is not to argue that we can never hope to know anything. It is, however, to accept that we can never know everything. Between these extremes, we can learn. Such learning is most likely to be useful if it is not based on an unwavering commitment to *either* knowledge creation starting from the 'subjective' experiences of the learner or knowledge transmission based on the 'objective' certainties of the expert. Rather, it should entertain both learner experience and expert knowledge, *especially* if these seem at odds with each other, and should base its judgements about what is appropriate at any particular time and place on a consideration of context. This is to say that educators should not insist on their own particular preferred combinations of facts and values, but accept that they themselves are just as much in need of learning as anyone else, just as likely to be surprised by what they learn, and not much more likely to turn out to be right in the end.

Once again it should be emphasised that this is to say nothing very new. As an approach to curriculum development the above seems quite consistent with the 'expansive conception of curriculum' advocated by Westbury (1999: 361) and endorsed by Hlebowitsh (1999b), while perhaps suggesting a way forward in thinking about the curricularist's responsibilities in relation to local traditions, customs and beliefs. It is consistent also with the notion of a 'learning society', excepting only our argument that advocates of this concept need more readily to acknowledge their own fact and value preferences, and to subject these to scrutiny along with everyone else's. It is even broadly consistent with much of the spirit of the agreed International Development Target for the environment and sustainable development (DfID 2000a) and in particular its rejection of universal blueprints and advocacy of case-specific action.

However the continuing problem is one of operationalising an approach that not only appears to many to fly in the face of common sense, but appears to do so to different people for different reasons. It is to this task that we hope the framework we have proposed for thinking about the contexts of initiatives in curriculum development and sustainable development can contribute.

Conclusion: a tool for curriculum development and sustainable development

There is an old joke about a driver who asks her passenger for directions to their shared destination and receives the reply 'I wouldn't start from here if I were you'. In effect, this paper suggests that curriculum and sustainable development workers need to accept both that this as a perfectly sensible answer from those they wish to influence and that the destination itself cannot be specified in advance or reached in due course: it has to be *learned*. We believe that our proposed framework is a step towards the facilitation of such learning and conclude with an example of how it might be applied.

Three 'International Development Targets' (IDTs), which have been agreed by the 'international community', are of interest to both curriculum and sustainable development workers. These are:

- the achievement of universal primary education by 2015;
- progress towards gender equality in primary and secondary schooling by 2005;
- implementation of a national strategy for sustainable development (NSSD) in every country by 2005 (DfID 2000a, 2000b).

Thinking about the task of developing curricula that might promote these targets, in the light of the framework illustrated in Figure 7, suggests a preliminary analysis of the form outlined in Figure 8.

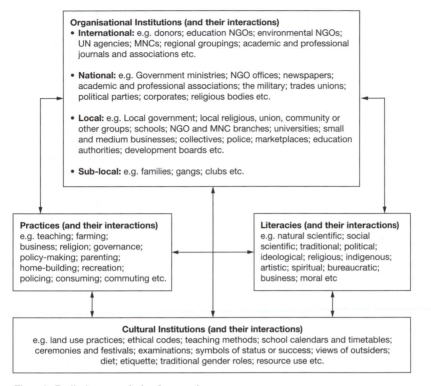

Figure 8 Preliminary analysis of categories.

This analysis would be completed separately, in detail, for each specific context in which an intervention was proposed. It would aim to provide an insight into the likely different problem definitions and expected solutions present in each context (including those of the curriculum developer her/himself), *and* the existing and continuing dynamic interactions between them. It would make possible, in each and every case, a contextually-appropriate choice of curriculum strategy. This might involve subject-specific science instruction, a cross-disciplinary 'connective' (Young 1998: 96) approach, vocational training of one sort or another, basic literacy instruction, participatory action research, and/or something else. An important implication of the approach is that debate about the *absolute* merit of different approaches to curriculum (and sustainable development) is pointless.

Such an analysis will never be easy, complete, or more than partially correct. It will entertain different, often incompatible, problem definitions and solutions. We argue, however, that it will result in curricula which are inherently superior to any which begin non-negotiably from the curriculum developer's or environmental worker's own moral and/or scientific conception of how things are now and how they ought to become. This is because they will be rooted in a *more rigorous* conception of thought and action, purposes and possibilities, and will promote social learning rather than one view or another of what needs to be learned.

[. . .]

VIGNETTE 6.1 FRAMING CHANGE AS A DIALECTIC: DIRECTION ONLY MATTERS IF YOU KNOW WHERE YOU WANT TO GO

P. Hart, University of Regina

Within the broad context of debate and critique of issues concerning how education is environmental, including an assumed need for change in ways we conceive of learning, curriculum, pedagogy and professional development, readings in this chapter proffer heuristics that engage the complexities of this task. Despite reductive tendencies of models and analytical frameworks, each of these heuristics provides openings for critical pedagogical discourse. Each article argues that both theorists (including curriculum workers) and practitioners need to be clearer about their intents and more explicit and critically reflective of their ideologies. Each in its own way attempts to facilitate thinking about the implications of those literacies concerned with human relations with the natural world for curriculum, lifelong learning and sustainability.

Fien's (1993) contribution to this clarification/conceptualization process within environmental education involved critiquing the ideology of "education for the environment" using typologies of educational and environmental ideologies to clarify certain assumptions and purposes of education about, through, and for the environment. What emerges from his analysis is both descriptive of environmental ideologies operationalised using educational terminology (e.g., curriculum implications, learning strategies, pedagogical strengths/weaknesses) and critical of certain structural and functional predispositions (e.g., worldview bias, social context gaps, pedagogical blind spots). Whilst education for the environment appears to provide the greatest potential to address environmental and educational weaknesses, according to Fien (1993), the short-sightedness of restricting oneself to one approach is self-evident.

Despite its contested nature, the three-fold structure of education about, in/through, and for environment has been used by many educators to justify their approach to curriculum theorizing and practice in environmental education (see Palmer 1998). However, simplification of the ideological bases of these approaches to slogans means that the underlying philosophy remains largely unread. The value of Huckle's (1983) analysis of environmental education ideologies and Fien's (1993) critical curriculum theorizing, as a foundation for debate and critique, remains theoretical. Meanwhile, most practitioners are left to choose among the most appealing curriculum materials. Thus, as a practical "tool" for curriculum development in/for environmental education, the heuristic potential of such frameworks often remains tacit as grounding for our understanding of variety in approaches, and in raising our consciousness of the implications of our own environmental preferences and educational decisions.

Gough and Scott (2001), apparently recognizing these complexities of curriculum change, magnified by evolving and contested new education goals such as sustainability, propose a more practical heuristic for rationalizing thinking about theory (i.e., ideologies) which is more directly related to school practices. Acknowledging uncertainties in postmodern times, they question where to begin curriculum development when the destination (i.e., some form(s) of sustainability) is unclear and the curriculum process itself must be learned. Their initial framework for analysis, grounded in the registers of social formation (i.e., cultural and organizational institutions, practices, and literacies), confronts directly the task of developing curricula to meet new educational goals such as sustainability. Juxtaposing technical and practical thought and action within personal, social, and environmental contexts can, within their frame of analysis, work to facilitate thinking about factors that impede change, such as institutional resistance and personal hegemony. They argue that because there is no single resolution to these issues, a framework for analysis of the complex interplay of institutions, practices, and literacies may bring both value judgments and accumulated knowledge together for more informed decisions about education and environment.

The premise for their terminological framework is that analysis, although never easy, complete, or totally correct, can lead to better curricula rooted in a more rigorous conception of both thought and action. Notwithstanding the considerable time commitment, the framework assumes that educators have the backgrounds, capabilities, and inclinations for the kind of analytical and synthetical complexity once envisioned as a dialectical model of critical curriculum theorizing (see Kemmis and Fitzclarence 1986). Whether analysis using this new frame can better bridge the apparent theory-practice gap of practitioner understandings (of facts and values), conceptualization or meta-knowledge (see Stables and Scott 1999) of environmental education than the conceptual frame discussed by Fien (1993) depends on how it can address professional concerns for the application of sustainability goals within educational curricula.

First, while environmental/ecological sustainability (as goal) and curriculum development (as process) have their own internal issues, employing any framework as a means of quieting debate about the absolute merit of one should not preclude the value in considering the relative merit of the other. For example, regarding environmental sustainability as a legitimate (eco)social goal does not reduce the pedagogical necessity of debating its absolute value as a goal of a variety of forms of education. On the other hand, if sustainable development is conceptualised as a process, then the pedagogical debate shifts to one about relative merit of both curriculum and sustainable development approaches within particular contexts. In this latter case, using the Gough and Scott (2001) frame may actually enhance debate, particularly if reconceived as a two-dimensional grid (following Kemmis and Stake's (1988) analysis of Schwab's (1969) curriculum common places). By juxtaposing each of the categories (teachers, students, subject matter, milieu) the complexities of the interactions among various categories could be characterized and debated. Perhaps this is what Gough and Scott (2001) had in mind when including the "and their interactions" component of each of their analytical categories.

My experience with practical application of a similar framework (see Kemmis and McTaggart 1988) in the participatory analysis of an education program (see Hart, Taylor, and Robottom 1994) resulted in practical adjustments of these theoretical categories. As the curriculum process evolved, the intensity of human interactions across multiple dimensions (e.g., faculty, students, curriculum, milieu) became so complex that framework analysis was replaced recursively by phenomenologic and ethnographic analyses. Even then, simple linear text proved inadequate to portray the critical complexities of human interaction (e.g., your account of the situation, my account, my perception of your account, yours of mine, then both of ours about our interactive conversational reaction to the situation, and so on . . .).

So, the challenge of the analytic frame is to find an appropriate image/text balance in its representation of reality (Radnofsky 1996). Frameworks may prove more useful as initial analytical tools, as organizers for thinking about the practical complexity of the process of curriculum development in the face of new sustainability goals. Impediments to educational change in uncertain times make conceptual kinds of tools necessary. Other methods, however, may prove necessary to complete the task, as the recent turn to qualitative methods in educational research testifies (cf. Macbeth 2001; Pamphilon 1999; Schwandt 1999). Change involves searching for qualities beyond those practices, literacies, and institutional considerations that, as Hargreaves (1997) says, go straight to the heart. The answer to the riddle of change is not to be found exclusively in expert-derived knowledge or in practitioner-derived (grassroots) knowledge alone, but, as Gough and Scott (2001) suggest, inside the individual with a social/environmental conscience. Thus, a professionally disciplined reflexive analytic that could attend the uncertainties of representation and competing literacies has much to recommend it, as does sensitivity to the moral-practical experience of understanding others.

Second, within the contemporary move to analytic reflexivity, we need to know more about how to develop and sustain those dialectical cycles by which we become conscious critical thinkers and practitioners. For example, during the past ten years I have met monthly with a group of local "reflective" teachers interested in critical discourse about educational theory and practice. The ideas discussed encompass the dimensions of Gough and Scott's (2001) analytic frame, within the context of critical dialogue among trusted colleagues. We have learned over the years to respect and value competing ideas as much as we do the necessity of moving forward collaboratively to challenge educational dilemmas. We have struggled with institutional hegemony as much as we have with our own ideological biases and predispositions. We have thought about change at many levels but always return to the personal. New curricula, placed before these teachers without accounting for personal beliefs and values (e.g., sustainable environments), will not affect social learning or change. Unless we add personal beliefs and values into the mix of framework dimensions and address change at the personal level, we remain suspended at the analytic/theoretic rather than at a pedagogic level of understanding. Nothing happens if we do not pay more than lip service to the genuine dialectic of theory and practice.

Environmental education, with its associated notions of environmental/ecological sustainability, represents a serious challenge to the field of education whose dominant discourses are complicit in accelerating the degradation of the natural environment. In assessing the value of any curriculum frame we need to ask how it can function to open practical debate about the limits of our dominant ethical/moral discourses (following Fien 1993). Ethical debates about relative merits of different approaches to sustainable development and curriculum development are absolutely required because they are signs of genuine disagreement about the values inherent in conflicting worldviews.

As Gough and Scott (2001) intimate in their example of the tropical coastline, rewriting education as environment seems a function of organizational power, yet every organization operates on an ethic which is a shaping and enframing of the social and natural environment. So, while we need frameworks which can enhance our ability to debate and critique the curriculum and its associated goals within context, we must recognize the ethical/moral underpinnings of those arguments within the context of their modernist origins and provide the scope (within such frameworks) for alternate ethical discourses which might supersede them. Is this not the ultimate aim of Fien's (1993) critical education for the environment, and of Gough and Scott's (2001) framings in more rigorous conceptions of thought and action?

VIGNETTE 6.2 SUSTAINABILITY AND THE IMPLICIT CURRICULUM

J. Foster, University of Lancaster

Fien seeks to distinguish, by reference to his typology of eco-political and educational perspectives, between education *about, through* and *for* the environment. On his view, the first tends to be conservative or technocentric, the second more child-centred and liberal-progressive, while the third, which he evidently prefers, is socially-critical and ecocentric.

There *is*, however, a crucial sense in which all these prepositions are equivalent. They all assume that you can get leverage on the curriculum by appealing to environment or ecology – to how nature works, and thus to the ways in which we do and might interact with it – as in some sense *given*. This is obvious enough for education *about* and *through* the environment, but it should be clear that Fien takes such leverage to be obtainable for his preferred approach too, insofar as that seeks to shape the curriculum around an exploration of what might be desirable in the economic relations, democratic control and social usefulness of production, all considered with reference to its (scientifically measurable) ecological sustainability.

The trouble is that no such leverage is available. The curriculum deeply structures our collective sense-making, and environmental sustainability only exists for us through the sense we ongoingly make. What are to count as environmental problems and their "real causes', and what sustainability parameters are meaningful, are too much artefacts of the implicit curriculum itself to be used as external points of reference for orienting and mobilising curricular development.

Previously (Foster 1999), I have made this point in terms of the prevailing conception of interdisciplinarity in environmental education – which, even while emphasising the need for multidisciplinary understanding, tacitly privileges some disciplines above others. Our current implicit curriculum has a strongly scientistic cast, appearing not only in the ruling assumption that the world for humans is fundamentally describable by natural science, but also in various more or less covert methodological pressures exerted by science even within intellectual disciplines remote from it (in the assumption, for instance, that "modularisation" could be an appropriate study strategy at advanced or university levels in the humanities). I might have generalised this argument, by noting that there are always liable to be social and cultural forces implicitly prioritising among the Hirstian "forms of knowledge" (Hirst 1974), and so structuring the rationality according to which we make sense of environmental, or any other significant, aspects of our situation – including, of course, these very social and cultural forces themselves.

A similar recognition, I think, underlies Gough and Scott's case for "learning societies". Their picture of the relations between the inertial momentum of institutions and the resistances and conductances afforded by literacies and practices effectively models the dynamics by which the implicit curriculum gets configured. Their model applies to both curriculum development and sustainable development just because it applies quite generally to the social processes of sense-making. The curriculum, taken in its widest sense, is at the heart of these processes, but caught up in a constant interplay with their deployment in specific fields of social action, of which sustainability is a prime example. By the same token, the model indicates how any well-grounded changes in the curriculum must come about, we can only develop curricula (including sustainability curricula) through heuristic-reflexive processes of negotiated accommodation among our various literacies, institutions and practices. The "learning society" is then the condition of maximising our openness to this creative interplay: emphasising the dialogical, the reflexive and the cyclic, promoting exploration which doesn't halt itself at particular commitments but remains fluent, confronting all results as new challenges.

This is a powerful picture. But it won't do any more than Fien's, just as it stands. For the *learning* society, promoting curricular and sustainable *development*, must surely be thought of as making cognitive and practical *progress* through such processes – but what could the relevant criteria be? How can we know, for instance, that permanent negotiation and accommodation aren't spreading and deepening ignorance, reinforcing the replacement of commitment by lifestyle and morality by opportunism? How do we know that the environmental values and sustainability parameters which we constitute and refine through all this dialogical interplay are not subtly self-serving, the tacit shaping of possible futures to accommodate and legitimate rather than to constrain present preferences? The heart of man is deceitful above all things, remarked the prophet Jeremiah, and he could well have added that the argument from uncertainty and the absence of fixed points of reference cuts (very sharply) both ways.

Here it seems to me that we need to appeal back to some radically ecological notions. The criterion by which any society claiming *learning* as its distinguishing mark must be judged, is the extent to which it progressively mobilises our best intelligence. This in turn, in conditions of heuristic reflexivity, cannot be thought of as concentrated in any privileged form of knowledge (such as science), but must rather be conceived as the living integration of our full human-natural sense-making endowment. Only a "learning society" empowering and deploying such intelligence could be epistemically justified. Here it is useful to think in terms, not so much of the "forms of knowledge" which Hirst proposed – and which, in any case, are familiarly problematic, so conceived (O'Hear 1981) – as of the fundamental forms of judgement and objectivity which arguably underlie them. The *sui generis* interdependence of private experience and public criteria which informs human sense-making subtends a spectrum of such forms. They range from analytical judgements in logic and mathematics where the appeal to intersubjectivity is purely formal (such judgements inviting wholly impersonal recognition that *this is so*, not any sort of corroboration out of the individual perspective), through empirical and interpretive judgements depending on a generalised common experience, to evaluative and aesthetic judgements where objectivity must rest on the capacity of a shared language to bring the separately embodied organic sensibilities of irreducibly different individuals into a commonality of responsive understanding. If this represents our given natural range as creatures whose *niche* is sense-making, then our best intelligence will consist in fully flexible recourse to this whole repertoire of forms of judgement as we ongoingly constitute the real. Put back into educational terms, it will only be where the implicit curriculum in its widest social realisation is the *whole* curriculum, the full range of disciplines expressing the interactive engagement of all these forms of judgement in heuristic learning, that we shall have a "learning society" in which we could repose epistemic confidence (and the associated authority).

At the same time, since such implicit engagement of our whole repertoire is the only way in which our sense-making could be naturally underwritten, while any explicit account of natural constraint on us must actually be underwritten by our sense-making, we also have in such a learning society the only guarantee available to us of the deeper sustainability of our form of life. (On this, see further Foster 2001.) The juxtaposition of these two extracts thus demonstrates compellingly how sustainable development (living with the grain of nature) and curriculum development (keeping our common sense-making responsively intelligent) must exist in a genuine and necessary symbiosis.

███████

CHAPTER 7

MANAGEMENT OF LEARNING: ISSUES IN CURRICULUM DESIGN

READING 7.1 THE CURRICULUM OF THE FUTURE: FROM THE 'NEW SOCIOLOGY OF EDUCATION' TO A CRITICAL THEORY OF LEARNING

M.D.F. Young

Source: Falmer, London, 1998: 24–33

[. . .]

Curriculum as fact

Most writing and research concerned with the curriculum unavoidably treats it in some way as a topic, thus affirming its external reality rather than explaining it as socially produced. The curriculum becomes something to be preserved or brought up to date for high achievers, modified or made more relevant for low achievers and broadened or integrated for those who specialize too soon, etc. We can also trace features of school organization and administration that sustain the idea of the curriculum as something to be studied, reorganized and analysed. For example, we find deputy head teachers and vice principals for curriculum, professors, journals, degrees and departments of curriculum studies and, of course, the final academic accolade of all otherwise unrecognized activity, attempts to develop curriculum 'theory'. Parallel to this, we find sub-fields, like the sociology and psychology of the curriculum, in which the disciplines apply their respective perspectives and methodologies. Typically, sociology addresses issues around the stratification and integration of different knowledge areas, whereas psychology has been concerned with mental development and stages of learning. I want to suggest that because the starting points of such research have been curricula *as products* rather than the production of curricula in teachers' and pupils' practices but set in their wider social context, problems are created, such as the separation and hierarchies between different knowledge areas, which our theories and methods do not enable us to solve. Educational researchers can be far more naive than teachers. The curriculum is presented as a reality and the language of cause and effect, resistance and change is applied to it; we discover articles with titles like, 'How does the curriculum change?' as if the curriculum was a thing which changed like the weather. There are similarities between such views of the curriculum and references by politicians and journalists to the 'National Interest' or the 'Economy'; in each case, a set of social relations is treated as a set of beliefs about the world. In the case of the curriculum, the social relations are those between teachers and taught and between the classroom context and the wider context in which classroom practices are shaped and the assumptions about knowledge and curriculum embedded in them. It is such assumptions and practices which can become masked by the language of curriculum theory.

This conception of 'curriculum as fact', with its underlying view of knowledge as external to knowers, both teachers and students, and embodied in syllabi and text-books, is widely held and has profound implications for our conceptions of teaching and learning. To say 'I teach history or physics' implies a body of knowledge to be transferred from the teacher who has it to the pupil who has not, whether by rote and test or by enquiries and assignments. It is teachers as well as philosophers who see teaching as initiating children into 'worthwhile' activities. So long as the idea of educa-tion as initiation, with the associated ideas about knowledge and what is worthwhile, is not questioned, educational theory merely confirms what every teacher and pupil knows. The only possible explanations of pupil failure that it provides are either in terms of 'bad teaching' or in terms of the social or psychological deficits that students bring to school or college. Keddie (1971) describes well what is involved in such a conception of curriculum and teaching. She argues that, in order to succeed in school, students must become initiated into the teacher's forms of knowledge and avoid ques-tioning its grounds. I would like to illustrate the link between a view of 'curriculum as fact' and of teaching as 'knowledge to be transmitted' and how they can shape teacher–pupil interactions with an extract from a transcript of a science class for 12-year-olds. The transcript also illustrates how, when such a conception of knowledge prevails, passivity is almost forced on, in this case, a remarkably reluctant pupil.

> (The teachers and pupils have a live worm in a dish in front of them)
> *T:*   Have you ever seen examples of when it [soil] is produced?
> *P:*   No
> *T:*   Earth on the grass
> *P:*   No I just seen holes on the grass
> *T:*   Have you ever seen anything else that might tell you there was a worm on the grass?
> *P:*   Yeah, they're what's called again, the holes they make are called
> *T:*   Have you seen those little piles?
> *P:*   Piles?
> *T:*   Have you seen those little heaps of
> *P:*   Leaves
> *T:*   On the grass, little
> *P:*   Holes
> *T:*   Em?
> *P:*   Dots
> *T:*   Have you seen have you ever come
> *P:*   I've seen holes
> *T:*   Have you heard of something called a cast?

The point of including the transcript here is not just that this could be seen as an example of 'bad teaching' but that it illustrates the consequences of a particular view of teaching, which might be carried out more or less effectively. Assumptions about knowledge as external and 'to be transmitted' can be as much a feature of 'good' teaching than 'bad'; they are integral for both teachers and pupils in creating a sense of pupils as 'not knowing' or at least not knowing until his or her 'knowledge' is confirmed by the teacher.

This conception of 'curriculum as fact' is pervasive, even in sociology. Most sociolo-gists from Durkheim to Parsons treat education as a process of socialization or the acquisition of particular knowledge, skills and values. Thus, the teacher's problem becomes defined as how to devise more effective ways of transmitting these skills and knowledge, whatever they are, to as many pupils as possible. All research from such a perspective can do is to offer a range of explanations, for why schools continue to be unsuccessful with so many pupils. These vary from the cultural inadequacy or the basic lack of ability of pupils to some reference to the 'structure of society'. In each explanation the curriculum remains unquestioned.

The school curriculum is presented as a set of gateways to the adult world, even though the relationships between school and non-school definitions of knowledge and skill are at best tenuous. It is predominantly a subject-ordered world – even when it takes the form of integrated studies. For the learner, there is little to distinguish between integrated science or humanities and physics and chemistry or history. Integration invariably produces an ordering of the world through which the learner has to find his or her way, rather than requiring learners themselves to be involved in the process of integration. Where pupils reject the discontinuity between their knowledge of the world and the way the school orders the world into subjects or themes, they invariably become described as less-able or non-academic. Such descriptions depend for their plausibility on a view of the 'curriculum as fact', which tells us what the terms 'able' and 'academic' refer to. This view of curriculum has not only been an assumption of academic curricula; it is also presupposed in vocational curricula. The difference is that while knowledge is still seen as external to both teacher and pupils, it involves not only ideas about what counts as knowledge but about how knowledge relates to different occupational fields. More generally then, I would suggest that the notions of 'curriculum as fact' expresses particular power relations between teachers and students, and in society, which are designed to reproduce knowledge produced elsewhere by others.

To sum up this section, I have suggested that a view of 'curriculum as fact' expresses many of the prevailing assumptions of educational practitioners, teachers and policy makers. By accepting similar assumptions, curriculum theory does little more than re-describe a world that teachers already know, albeit sometimes in terms they find far from familiar. It also confirms for teachers both the irrelevance of theory for practical change in schools and their own passive role in such changes. Teachers have theories of knowledge, teaching and curriculum that are often remarkably like the ideas of curriculum 'theorists' and which, I shall argue later, play an important, albeit unconscious role in curriculum change or resistance to it. They continue to hold such views because they are congruent with views of the curriculum in the wider society and because, in part, they make some sense of the situation in which teachers find themselves. As a theory, however, 'curriculum as fact', though pervasive amongst academics, administrators and teachers, fails according to the criteria with which I started. It does not enhance the capacity of teachers to become aware of the possibilities of change and of gaining an understanding of the conditions of their own practice. 'Curriculum as fact' presents the curriculum as a thing, hiding the social relations between the teachers, students and curriculum policy makers who have historically and collectively produced it. What then does the 'curriculum as practice', which takes a quite opposite view, have to offer?

Curriculum as practice

The basic premise of the view of 'curriculum as practice' reverses the assumptions of the 'curriculum as fact'. It does not begin with the structure of knowledge but with how knowledge is produced by people acting collectively. In education, the focus of such a view has been on teachers' and pupils' classroom practices and how educational realities such as school subjects or the distribution of student abilities are not external structures or fixed attributes of pupils, but are products of these practices and the assumptions about knowledge, learning and teaching which are embedded in them. From this view, teachers' practices are crucial in both sustaining or challenging prevailing views of knowledge and curriculum. The curriculum thus ceases to be separate from the activities through which teachers devise assignments, produce marks and grades and differentiate between subjects and identify pupil achievements. The implication of such a view is that if teachers subject the assumptions underlying their practices to critical examination, they will understand how to change the curriculum.

Such a theory, while valuable in challenging the view of 'curriculum as fact' and asserting the active role of both teachers and students in the learning process, is misleading both theoretically and practically in locating the possibilities of curriculum change primarily in the interactions of teachers and their students. The concept of 'curriculum as practice' gives teachers a spurious sense of their power, autonomy and independence from the wider contexts of which their work is a part. It thus provides them with no way of understanding their own failure to make changes, except in terms of their personal inadequacies.

The view of 'curriculum as practice' involves a radically different concept of knowledge to that of the mathematician G.H. Hardy. No longer is knowledge viewed as a kind of private property handed down from the academic 'discoverers' for the teacher to distribute or 'transmit'. Knowledge becomes that which is accomplished in the collaborative work of teachers and pupils. In theory, such a view has profound implications for existing school hierarchies and for the organization of education. What might be involved, for example, in seeing the curriculum as a site for the collaborative production of history or science, when we normally think of teaching as the transmission of historical or scientific knowledge, even if it involves a student project? The problem is not just that such possibilities may seem exciting to some and threatening to others but that they remain possibilities only 'in theory', generated as they are from a view of the curriculum as the product of the practice of teachers. Attempts at radical curriculum change based on the idea of 'curriculum as practice' will very quickly face the practical experience that the curriculum is far from being *just* a product of teachers' and pupils' practices. It is also a product of the views about what education should be of parents, employers, administrators and so on. If a group of teachers began to examine critically and reformulate their current practice, there would be two likely outcomes. Either they would immediately come up against external constraints from the Governing Body or Local Authority or, in their attempts to implement alternatives, they would *in practice* be taken outside the context of the classroom and into discussions with local employers and parents. They would be forced, without any theoretical guide, to try and develop a more adequate understanding of their situation than that provided by a view of 'curriculum as practice'.

I would like to illustrate these comments on the view of 'curriculum as practice' by two specific examples, taken from science education. I would argue, however, that the underlying arguments developed from the case of school science are relevant to the question of curriculum change more generally. Innovation in science education in the 1960s and 1970s was virtually synonymous with the Nuffield/Schools Councils Projects. Despite many practical innovations in pedagogy, they tended without exception to sustain rather than challenge existing conceptions of school science and to perpetuate its stratification into 'pure' and 'applied' sciences (Young 1976). The Nuffield perspective was exemplified in a speech at the British Association in September 1974 by Professor Jevons who claimed that, as science teachers 'we are up against something in the cognitive structure of science itself' and that therefore science was not appropriate 'to meet the more radical ideals of education'. This represents a very clear example of the mode of reasoning underlying the view of 'curriculum as fact' discussed earlier. If, however, we go back a century we can see how our contemporary conceptions of school science as a body of knowledge enshrined in textbooks, syllabuses and laboratories gradually gained ascendancy over quite different possibilities. Layton's (1973) well known study brings this out well by describing the fate of a movement during the early days of school science and called by its founder, Richard Dawes, the 'Science of common things'. In the work of this movement, the everyday experiences of pupils of the natural world in their homes and their daily lives formed the basis for developing the school science curriculum. A particular example cited by Layton was the 'radical curriculum' of Arthur Rigg, Principal of Cheshire Training College, in which a major emphasis was placed on the kind of science and workshop skills relevant to an area where most people were employed in the cotton industry. Rigg's experiment was short lived, Layton suggests, because it undermined the separation of teachers from those they taught; it was feared by the Schools Inspectorate of the time that if students investigated their own work context they might come to see it too critically. Furthermore, it was felt that teachers emerging from such a course might become, as one Inspector put it, 'active emissaries of misrule'. Both Dawes and Rigg can be seen as working with notions of curriculum as *practice*, in which school or college science was viewed as the emergent product of the collaborative activities of teachers and students. However, their proposals were perceived by their opponents as raising uncomfortable political questions of significance far outside the classroom or the school laboratory. The ultimate demise of the 'Science of common things' movement can be seen in part as reflecting the limitations of the ideas of its leaders, who thought they could bring outside experiences into the school and leave both the school laboratory and the world outside unchanged. Although it is not possible to draw any direct parallels with science education today, the examples emphasize both the limitations of a view of curriculum as practice and the *social* and *historical* roots and political character of some of the most basic assumptions of what is now taken to be school science.

My second example also illustrates the limitations of the idea of 'curriculum as practice' and suggests how examinations are involved in sustaining particular notions of school knowledge. The example is from an A-Level science syllabus in which part of the assessment involved a project to be devised and written up by candidates and allocated a proportion of the marks in the final examination. In one case, a student chose to investigate problems of streamlining a boat and in doing so she had to learn a considerable amount about viscosity – a topic in most A-Level physics syllabuses of the time. In the context of the student's project, viscosity became a way of understanding and transforming something that was important to her outside school – building a boat. Viscosity was not an external body of knowledge to be learnt because it was on the syllabus. The teacher's advice and the pupil's activities, both theoretical and practical, became in this instance the reality of the student's education in science. However, this *practice*, as a part of teachers' and pupils' activity on a physical science course, was squeezed into one afternoon a week, while the rest of the timetable was used in the 'real' work of reproducing knowledge for the formal examinations which counted for 85 per cent of the marks. It may be, therefore, that such a limited experience of the science 'curriculum as practice' would sustain rather than challenge both for teachers and pupils a view that knowledge of viscosity, like all *real* knowledge, is something to be learnt and reproduced rather than being part of a way of understanding and transforming the world of which we are part. In other words the marginalization of 'science as practice' sustains a view of 'curriculum as fact'.

To summarize this section, I have argued that a view of the 'curriculum as practice' does not offer an adequate alternative to ideas about the curriculum defined in terms of the structures of knowledge. Its weakness is in the limitations of its concept of practice. It replaces a notion of reality located in the structures of knowledge by one located in teachers' classroom practice. Attempts by teachers to develop strategies for changing the curriculum derived from such a theory will confront with the limits of what they can do in their classroom practice. Teachers will also become aware of the limits of a theory that does not enable them to comprehend the origins of such limits or show them how their classroom practice does in part shape the external reality of the curriculum in meaningful ways for their students.

Conclusions

I should like to conclude this chapter by drawing together my critiques of the two curriculum models in relation to my original problem – developing a theory that could assist teachers in transforming the curriculum and so improve the learning experience of their students. 'Curriculum as fact', with its fixed concepts of teaching, knowledge and ability, takes for granted just that which its task as a theory should be to explain. How did curricula based on such assumptions originate and why do they persist? By failing to address this question, such a theory assumes, at least for advanced industrial societies, not only that the organization of knowledge into subjects is in some sense necessary or inevitable but that teachers do not construct the curriculum in the process of interpreting it. The first outcome of such a view of the curriculum is a kind of end-of-history argument in which the past as a dynamic of action and interest which produced the present is forgotten and future possibilities are viewed as the continuation of some kind of universal present. The second outcome is to deny the constructive role of teachers in shaping the curriculum and to underwrite a highly mechanistic view of the curriculum as something to be delivered and tested which flies in the face of much recent research on learning [. . .]. The significance of the view of 'curriculum as fact' is that it is not just a theory produced by academics but that it is the basis on which our education system is organized. In other words, it represents part of the circumstances within which anyone concerned with changing educational practice has to work.

However, such a view cannot be treated as mere illusion, the irrelevant product of ivory tower academics or bureaucratic curriculum developers that is imposed on teachers, To do so is the major weakness of the view of 'curriculum as practice'. Though challenging prevailing conceptions of curriculum, it treats them as arbitrarily imposed on the practices of students and teachers and, as a consequence, it misleads teachers as to the possibilities of change. In doing so it directly contradicts the experience of those about whom it theorizes and contributes, paradoxically, to the very division between theory and practice which its critique would seem to question. In emphasizing the conventionality of prevailing hierarchies of knowledge – academic and non-academic, theoretical and practical, abstract and concrete – it provides no basis for understanding how and why particular educational hierarchies originate in social relations both in and beyond education. Viewing curricular organization as a set of conventions implies that they could be otherwise (which is like equating the ordering of academic knowledge with customs). It assumes that school subjects like mathematics only persist through habit or custom or because that is how those in power define what should be taught. What starts as a critique of the separation of knowledge from the knower, ends up by having to invoke the crudest of mechanistic relations between knowledge and social position. In effect, it explains nothing and not surprisingly offers no strategies for change.

A theory that can provide for the possibilities of curriculum change does not emerge either from the dominant view of 'curriculum as fact' or from its opposite, the idea of 'curriculum as practice' that was proposed by radical educational theorists in the 1970s. The first, by starting from a view of knowledge abstracted from people in history and specifically from the teachers and pupils, denies them any roles except as deliverers of what has been decided elsewhere. The second, in its concern to recognize teachers as conscious agents of change and to emphasize the human possibilities in all situations, becomes abstracted, albeit in a different way, from the constraints of teachers' experience, and therefore, ironically, from their capacity to shape student learning. The idea of 'curriculum as practice' may recognize possibilities in *theory* but their practical implementation is experienced by teachers as little more than utopian. A *theoretical* critique of the *necessity* of hierarchies of knowledge and ability may be exciting in a seminar but is of little use to teachers who experience such necessities as real in *practice*. The problem then is not to deny these hierarchies nor accept them uncritically, but to try and reformulate them as the outcomes of collective and historical actions – and thus render them understandable, potentially changeable and interpretable. This leads me to a number of suggestions for transcending the dichotomy of 'curriculum as fact' and 'curriculum as practice':

1   The prescription to start from teachers' and pupils' practices and the theories that they evolve in their day to day practices can easily itself remain mere theory. This will be so unless there are changes in the relations between 'theorists' based in the universities and those about whom they theorize. This is not an argument against theory, for this could lead to an uncritical acceptance of any tradition and custom currently found in schools or prescribed by government. It is a recognition that the ideas of 'curriculum as fact' and 'curriculum as practice' have their origins in conservative and radical strands of academic debates that were largely removed from educational practice. Whereas the ideas associated with 'curriculum as fact' appealed to specialist subject teachers who wanted to justify what they were doing, it provided no way for them to see what new roles their subjects might have. On the other hand, although the existentialist ideas associated with 'curriculum as practice' struck a chord with teachers resistant to the bureaucratic forms of schooling, they did little to help them locate their practice.

   A genuinely radical concept of the curriculum that would enable teachers to transform their practice and enhance their students' learning cannot be developed in isolation from that practice. Despite the tendency, much evident today in teacher education to dismiss the importance of theory, the new forms of university-school partnership on which teacher education is increasingly based offer the possibility of establishing 'communities of practice' consisting of teachers and academics; they could provide the context for developing more practically informed theories as well as more theoretically informed practice.

2   School learning is often experienced and thought about as if it were either isolated or separate from other types of learning. Furthermore, educational theories rarely challenge this separation and show the interconnections between school and non-school learning. If examining assumptions about the curriculum and its interconnections is to go beyond mere questioning, the broad 'political' problems of the links between different kinds and sites of learning will inevitably be raised for teachers and others involved in education. Prevailing notions about curricula and knowledge, although sustained by the practices and institutional arrangements of formal education, are not sustained by them alone. A more adequate theory of the curriculum would not restrict its concept of practice to that of teachers, nor would it restrict its focus on teachers' practice to their activities in the classroom. If the school curriculum is to become an emancipatory experience for a much

larger section of each cohort of students, this is going to require much greater involvement of many people who currently have no direct links with school, including parents and employers, and many activities by teachers and pupils which are not confined to the school nor, in conventional terms, are usually defined as 'educational' at all.

3   Both views of the curriculum to which I have referred in this chapter tend to obscure the political and economic character of education. This, as I have argued, sets limits on their possibilities as theories of change. They also lack, in common with much educational writing, a sense of history or, more generally, an understanding of the present in terms of the past. One way of reformulating, and so potentially understanding and transcending the limits of specific contexts is to see, as in Layton's example in the history of school science, how such limits are not given or fixed but produced through the conflicting actions and interests of people in history. For example, studies of Trades Councils and Local Schools Boards at the turn of the century suggest a very different strategy for involving working-class parents in the education of their children than the well intentioned paternalism of the Educational Priority Areas of the 1970s (Lynch 1974) or the Education Action Zones and Homework Clubs of the late 1990s.

These suggestions are no more than illustrative as to how aspirations implicit in models of the curriculum might be made real in practice. They argue for more explicit links between learning at work and in the community and learning in classrooms. I see this as recognizing that much school and curriculum improvement will not necessarily begin in schools and that those who work in education need to learn far more about the non-school world that young people experience, how it differs from the world that they experience through the curriculum and how we can help them strengthen the connections.

READING 7.2 COMPLEXITY IN ENVIRONMENTAL EDUCATION

E. Gonzáles-Gaudiano

Source: *Educational Philosophy and Theory* 33(2), 2001: 153–166

[. . .]

Different discourses on the environment

As in any social practice, in the field of environmentalism different discourses co-exist. Within these discourses different conceptions of the world and the roles of nature and the environment are born. Luke (1997: xi) expresses this idea saying that because nothing in Nature is simply given within society, terms such as 'environment', 'population explosion', 'damaged ecosystems' or 'Mother Earth' 'must be given significance by every social group that mobilises them as meaningful constructs'.

Thus, discourses on nature shroud themselves in moral values, religious precepts and scientific fundamentals, which do not usually make themselves clear but materialise in the form of party demands, public policies and citizen manifestos calling for action and 'change'. On the subject, Bookchin (1995: 3) confesses:

I am deeply disturbed by the conservative literature that invokes a 'traditional', usually hierarchical, hidebound past. But paradoxical as it may seem, I am also deeply disturbed by its pseudo-radical complement: the so-called 'new paradigm' or generically 'New Age' literature that 'disenchants' us with our humanity, indeed, that summons us to regard ourselves as an ugly, destructive excrescence of natural evolution – whether as a specie, a gender, an ethnic group, or a nationality.

Academic discourses are not far removed from these standpoints. Moreover, the basis of academic discourses is frequently high *status* in the defence or support of arguments made in the power struggles that characterise the current state of things regarding nature and its resources. Scientific activity is governed by normative paradigms that judge the validity and the potential of research breakthroughs, often with economic and political interests at heart.

> Power relations permeate the most ordinary activities in scientific research. Scientific knowledge arises out of these power relations rather than in opposition to them. Knowledge is power, and power knowledge. Knowledge is embedded in our research practices rather than being fully abstractable in representational theor- ies. Theories are to be understood in their uses, not in their static correspondence with the world. Power as it is produced in science is not the possession of partic- ular agents and does not necessarily serve particular interests. Power relations constitute the world in which we find agents and interests.
> (Rosue 1987: 24, cited in Peters 1996: 139)

As we have seen, the environment, nature, conservation and other associated concepts acquire meanings according to the articulations in the discourse in which they appear. They are, to a certain extent, empty signifiers that have broken free from their specific meanings and have come to have a long chain of equivalent meanings (Laclau 1990: 72). In support of these ideas I turn to the important work of Stavrakakis (1997: 260) on the constitution of Green ideology:

> . . . we have witnessed the emergence of a whole new phenomenon that, although connected to conservationism and environmentalism, is of much greater signifi- cance, at least from the point of view of political analysis. This phenomenon is the development of the field of Green politics and furthermore the articulation of a whole Green ideology. What differentiates this new phenomenon from the preceding forms of conservationism and environmentalism is its universal, 'holistic' and deeply political claims about nature, environmental crisis and its relation to the human world. Ecological radicalism, at least in its 'pure' form, rejects in toto the dominant structures of industrial society and advocates a new order which, as Green claims, will restore the lost harmony between human beings and nature. Moreover, it is suggested that this new order, conceived and planned on the basis of a certain Green conception of nature, will eventually lead to the final solution of problems related to 'strictly' human relations such as class antagonism, etc. The aim of Green ideology is to refound and recreate the political, social and economics foundation of western societies on the basis of a political project that is constructed around a certain conception of nature.[1]

I cannot fail to emphasise the deep essentialist immersion of 'Green' standpoints: the search for universals, valid and transhistoric truths for different contexts, redemption at the end of the journey, the new world order and transcendental man as part of a political project that will free him from his miseries. This green discourse intends to create an all-encompassing system of knowledge and thought, which will underscore the world's constitutive nature, as well as a 'new' scale of values that modify the pernicious relationship we as human beings have established with nature.

Knowledge of the environment

The preceding considerations are important because they help us to understand the role that science, technology and education in general have played in the process of knowledge gathering on the environment where, for example, without putting the ontological nature of existing knowledge in doubt, interdisciplinary sharing of the same type of available knowledge has been encouraged in an effort to deal with the complexity of environmental issues. Thus, it has been sought to use interdisciplinarity as a seam, to close the gaps and to overcome the lacks and deficiencies of current disciplinary knowledge in a renewed attempt to give unity to the available knowledge set: a full identity, another essentialist pretension.

This said, instead of conceiving interdisciplinary approximation as a process of knowledge juxtaposition aimed at stitching up the various problems derived from the generation, articulation, diffusion and use of available knowledge, it is better to take advantage of the interest in interdisciplinary proceedings to create new contexts for environmental research and human resources development not only out of work already done in familiar areas, but more importantly, to strengthen precisely those areas which have been excluded, thereby encouraging the appearance of academic spaces which make the aforementioned articulating practices possible. This most certainly does not imply the surmounting of gnoseological problems to take on environmental issues. Available knowledge would have to be considered a 'residue' of the moment about to be transformed. That is to say, we cannot think of a definitive, complete separation from the disciplinary knowledge set, but rather of the co-existence of different types of knowledge that will interact and antagonise in variable degrees and spaces. It is, however, important to avoid the interdisciplinary *stitch* that some people often inadvertently pursue, because this is the closing mechanism by means of which the world has been built on a foundation of essences, and because it is precisely the 'open character of the context . . . the starting point of a radical anti-essentialist critique' (Laclau 1998: 62).

All of this is happening at a moment of profound and accelerating change; a moment defined by our generation, which has witnessed a reconfiguration of the political and economic geography of the world. It is a moment at which, even though the internet has become a public space where users may share a wealth of diversified information, this information 'superhighway' has also become one of the pillars of globalisation with its resulting impacts on a macro scale and on the daily lifestyles of individuals. It is here that we must exert profound criticism, where knowledge has become information for public consumption.[2]

When Daniel Bell (1973) introduced the concept of post-industrial society in an attempt to identify a change in *social structure*, he described it in terms of three components: a shift from manufacturing to service industries in that sector of the economy, centrality of science-based technological industry development, and the rise of new technological elites and the advent of a new principle of social stratification. Since then, there have been many changes. A rupture on a symbolic and epistemological level between modern and post-modern science is being increasingly recognised; that is to say, a rupture between scientific viewpoints which emphasises ahistoric, foundational knowledge based on a set of dichotomies such as theory/observation, fact/value, schema/content, and the viewpoint that highlights the primacy of history in the understanding of scientific endeavour and recognises that science does not constitute a logical, unified system (Peters 1996: 133).

It is in this context that the environmental problematic has put additional strain on conventional knowledge, causing dislocation of certain branches of knowledge or areas of professional activity whose practice has deteriorated (for example, agronomics). Super-specialisation, rife within the different scientific disciplines, has revealed its own limitations by being unable to provide the expected answers to problems posed by other articulations for which the constituted scientific communities were unprepared. These communities were constituted in terms of specialist topics, single-discipline objects of study and jargon, and were based on a-historic and foundational codes; in short, communities poorly equipped to establish the epistemological and communicative bridges required by problem areas like the environment. This is more serious still in peripheral countries whose precarious scientific communities attempt to fractally emulate the studies and approaches of postindustrial countries, including those lines of research that have already been replaced.

An illustrative example of how the problem of environmental knowledge is being tackled can be found in the World Development Report (Banco Mundial 1999). This report not only conceives knowledge as information, but in the section pertaining to how to approach information problems, particularly in the chapter on 'analysis of our environmental problems', nowhere does it mention the difficulties derived from the complexity of environmental knowledge.[3] Furthermore, in the introduction the importance of knowledge is exemplified and the green revolution is highlighted as a paradigm of knowledge at the service of development, without making any reference whatsoever to the severe environmental problems (salinisation, soil erosion, pollution, aquifer depletion and genetic material loss, among others) brought about by the green movement. This is why 'science has become a reason of state. More closely linked than ever before to the modern notion of development with its connotations of progress, competition and nationalism, science and education as reasons of state have been subjected to a new rationalization designed to optimize its contribution to the system's performance' (Peters 1996: 140).

The pedagogy of environmental complexity

Environmental education has already begun to incorporate elements of this anti-essentialist discourse apparatus (Payne 1999; Gough 1999; González-Gaudiano 1998). In this incipient process, the sedimented discourse promoted by the International Environmental Education Programme (IEEP) since its appearance in 1973 has begun to dislocate. This discourse had placed nature conservation *per se* at the centre of environmental education creating tension in the environmental education field which on the one hand has taken the form of 'a paradigm war', and on the other the appearance of numerous alternative (marginal) proposals on the fringe of the field.

Paradigmatic conflicts

The term 'paradigm war' was coined by Gage (1989) to refer to the existing problem throughout the field of education research. In environmental education the conflict grew between 1990 and 1995, particularly in the North American Association for Environmental Education (NAAEE), where an antagonistic debate took place in the bowels of the Research Commission over different methodological, theoretical approximations which were classified, according to Habermas, as empirical-analytical, interpretative or hermeneutic, and critical.[4]

However, and even though the debate has heightened among researchers, the paradigm war still rages in different educational areas, since field practices respond to articulated environmental and educational discourse. Thus, Gough (1999: 47), faced with the fact that existing approximations have tended to prefer particular forms of knowledge frequently related to natural sciences and ecology, called for a self-critical revision of the way environmental and environmental education discourses were constituted and encouraged resistance to the particular forms of subjectivity and 'objectivism' which many environmental education researchers have brought over from educational research. Similarly, Jickling (1997: 87) called for a rethinking of environmental education, 'it is time for renewal – time for environmental education to be revitalized. These are not just my words, but the sentiments of others who hold different perspectives and represent different research traditions.'

Although I do recognise that this dispute has contributed to shaking up the field and dislocating some of the most structured precepts, in my opinion, the problem cannot be reduced to a paradigm war. As in the case of interdisciplinarity, attributing the problem to the adoption of a paradigmatic stance could operate as a seam which immobilises or diverts the tendencies to put the field off centre to generate other nodal points more in keeping with our open, shifting reality.[5] Thus, and as I mentioned in a recent paper (González-Gaudiano 1998: xiii), to consider nature conservation *per se* as the quintessence of environmental education could lead to serious conceptual and strategic errors in the field, especially in the case of peripheral countries like Mexico.[6]

Faced with the paradigm war, there have been attempts to find a way out without causing ruptures in the field, since during the last ten years alternative, qualitative viewpoints have started to gain momentum. Among the most frequently recurring are the eclectic stances that, despite their tendency to counteract the dominant applied sciences viewpoints that have subjugated the field, do not exclude the descriptive, experimental and quantitative approximations on which most environmental education researchers spend their time, at least in post-industrial countries. In this respect, Tilbury and Walford (1996: 53) point out that:

> No single paradigm can incorporate the complexity and interdisciplinary nature of a field which covers such areas as ecology, environmental ethics, and global and outdoor education. Environmental education is not only diverse but also dynamic, interdisciplinary and interactive. . . . However, environmental education is still to discover the unique and valuable perspective which the 'grounded theory' method . . . can offer on its crucial curriculum question in the 1990s.

Other critiques (Scott and Oulton 1999: 118) emphasise aspects, albeit operational, which are contributing to the dislocation of the fundamental principles of a field that had considered itself to be unified:

> schools, teachers, students and communities attempt to find their own path through a bewildering mixture of often contradictory instruction, guidance and advice, amid doubts about what approaches are effective and what purposes are appropriate, mostly operating within an education system where school success continues to be measured in terms of traditional academic, rather than more environmental criteria.

In all this discussion, it is important to clarify that the paradigmatic issue in educational research is a problem of the first order when defining educational content on the environment (as it is in relation to curriculum design). What perspectives does the complexity of environmental knowledge promote with respect to research strategies, the design of educational processes and their implementation, and are these in line with positivist assumptions? Is the schooling system properly equipped for the implementation of processes such as those proposed even in less radical plans? If not, what should be done?

Rushkoff (1997: 3, 8, 263) points out that children, whom he calls *screenagers*, who have lived in front of the television and computer screens, are undergoing experiences in which they could be described metaphorically as 'immigrants exploring new territories'. We therefore need to change our obsolete institutions to be able to respond to the children's new rituals, media and fantasies at this chaotic moment. Obviously, traditional schools do not respond to the interests of our children as they move through virtual, intercultural spaces; nor do they respond to indigenous children, who find themselves in such dissimilar circumstances as might resemble another era.

The Organisation for Economic Co-operation and Development (OECD 1997: 194) mentions that, in a study carried out in six member countries, environmental education was still found to be a marginal and isolated topic within schooling systems despite international agreements and the place it was supposed to have been given in institutional discourse, and says that if what is required is a 'new environmental education paradigm' 'with full political legitimacy, solid epistemological bases and research and teacher training funding – as is the case in certain branches of mathematics and science – then standard procedures are not yet up to the challenge ... [and therefore] it is necessary to create an innovative conceptual support mechanism which will master the inherent, multidisciplinary complexity of the environmental issue.' I do not wish to give the impression that the idea is to construct an environmental education field without conflicts; nothing is further away from my mind since I consider that the conflict is what inherently constitutes the field. It is the conflict with its varying plans and dimensions that has allowed for the desedimentation of the dominant conception of environmental education promoted by the IEEP. It is the conflict that has brought about the appearance of other forms of environmental education. It will be the conflict that generates the movement needed by the pedagogical complexity of environmental issues.

Marginal pedagogy

As previously mentioned, another way of consolidating hegemonic environmental education discourse is by means of alternative proposals made on the edge of the field and articulated in critical, popular, pedagogical, Latin-American tradition (Simon Rodriguez, Mariátegui, Freire, etc.). In a recent paper (González-Gaudiano 1999), the field organisation is developed from a different perspective, beyond summit meetings and the scope of the references mentioned below, in which it is precisely these alternative proposals, which give the environmental education field in our region a particular profile unlike any other, which are highlighted.

Articulations with popular education have given rise to a Latin-American current, which has been called popular environmental education and is labelled among the so-called *pedagogías de la liberación* (liberation pedagogies), and even if they have not been exempt from criticism from their own promoters (Esteva 1997; Gudynas 1992), they do represent a different space for construction from that allowed by institutional or conventional environmental education.

Esteva and Reyes (1996: 108, 109, 118), questioning environmentalist standpoints that place ecological deterioration at the centre of the debate and with which the political potential of the struggle is neutralised, recognise the popular environmental education stream:

as one of the political expressions within the widest field in environmental education, which is to say that it is made up of very different tendencies, most of which take a completely or practically uncritical stance regarding industrialist rationality. In environmental education, educational proposals for different environmentalisms are articulated; it is [a] field in which different perspectives confront and complement each other and in which the popular current expresses its conviction that the popular sectors are those which can construct an ecologically sustainable, politically democratic, and socially just society.

In this line, numerous Environmental Education proposals have been tied in with different types of premises which go from dependence theories (Teotonio dos Santos, Samir Amin, Vania Bambirra), development styles (Gligo, Sunkel), political ecology (Mires) to liberation theology (Boff), constructing different, open, proposals that are appropriate and specific to the different Latin-American realities.[7] They all agree however on at least three very important aspects:

1   They conceive the environment field in general and the environmental education field in particular as part of a wider arena of political strife, where hoisting the flag of environmental quality and the use of natural resources in benefit of the local townships is a symbol of the highest order, but not the only one, much less the one which raises most public interest.
2   They recover traditional, popular wisdom and community values as a starting point in the formulation of pedagogical proposals (key words, ethnic know-how, etc.) for the gathering of other knowledge which provide them with better intellectual instruments to move in the world.[8]
3   They consider that the conditions for the possibility of an education for our times, including environmental education, lie in the construction of open proposals, fractured proposals that do not claim to be constituted in universals. Puiggrós (1996: 12) puts it this way: 'These imperfections admit the possibility that new future alternatives suggested by new people may be produced. Transmission must be imperfect so that the future is possible.'

This last idea is a very unconventional one. Accustomed as we are to receiving 'finished' models with the assurance that all of them possess the required answers, the desired efficiency, the correct direction, just to think of the convenience of working on a proposal that does not promote the illusion of 'complete closure, of the elimination of all error, of completeness, of universal will and the all-inclusiveness of societies' (Puiggrós *idem*) dislocates our referents, but transports us to a new realm of possibility.

We cannot arrogantly state that we are in the position to formulate a suitable environmental education programme in the face of so much uncertainty and insufficient available knowledge, although, as Angel Maya states (Angel Maya 1995: 11), 'uncertainty is the root of cultural creativity'.

From a different but equally marginal perspective, new premises appeared as long ago as the 1930s regarding what would later be known as Chaos Theory, through which different approximations in different fields, like meteorology, economics and ecology, have been worked. Findings have shown that the non-linear dynamic, that is, one not founded on proportionality, allows for a better explanation of the behaviour of phenomena.[9] But this is not on the school curriculum yet, at least not on that of average schools. Teaching is still done through classic physics and a scientific methodology through which the student is led to believe that by following a mechanical sequence of steps he can create science, and that knowledge is replete with certainty and in a progressive process of accumulation and accuracy. Social issues are tackled from a Natural Sciences perspective, and the world is still seen in the form of discrete phenomena and deterministic equations about which we believe we have the capacity to make predictions. The so-called 'butterfly effect', whose technical name is sensitive dependence on initial conditions (Lorenz), was derived from the figure of a three-dimensional spiral (which looks like a butterfly with its wings spread) which represented total disorder, so long as its trajectory did not repeat itself. The system was unpredictable on a local level though stable globally, creating an unusual and unknown kind of order. From there came the famous phrase that the flap of a butterfly's wing in Hong Kong could cause a hurricane in New York. This scientific development has upset our familiar world, which has been in constant construction since the Enlightenment itself, and desediments our knowledge of numerous topics about which we thought we had definitive answers.

Both the knowledge accumulated since Chaos Theory and that gathered from popular education and community protest, despite the great differences between them, have come to the fore on the edge of institutionalised systems, in the folds of social setting, giving fresh hope to believe optimistically that it is possible to dislocate the entrenched discourse of essences and certainties (apodictic) and to find new articulations to construct cognitive alternatives, which afford us the possibility of getting to know the complexity of environmental issues.

Notes

1 Also see Stavrakakis (1999).
2 See Peters and Roberts (1998: 18–25) for an essay on Lyotard's 'The postmodern condition' on the same subject.
3 'The difficulties caused by insufficient knowledge of these issues receive the name of *information problems*. The mechanisms which could contribute to its resolution – product quality specs, training certificates and credit classification reports – are less numerous and effective in developing countries. Information problems and market dysfunctions they give rise to have particularly harmful effects on poor countries' (p. 1).
4 The debate was taken up in a monograph edited by NAAEE (Mrazek 1993).
5 The problem could be reduced even more if it were seen only as something methodological; a risk we take from the premises of some of the participants in the aforementioned controversy which restricted them to methodological discrepancies: quantitative *vs* qualitative.
6 From a coincidental standpoint, Esteva and Reyes (1996) say that to put environmental degradation at the centre of the debate suppresses the possibility of linking ecology with politics. See also Mires (1990), Mires *et al.* (1996) and Guattari (1997).
7 See, for example, the work of Fernando Mires (1990) and Leonardo Boff (1996).
8 See: Prakash and Esteva (1998) and Esteva and Prakash (1998).
9 For more information see: Prigogine (1996).

VIGNETTE 7.1 SUSTAINING DEMOCRACY AND UNCERTAINTY IN THE LEARNING SOCIETY

J. Quicke, University of Sheffield

The idea of a 'learning society' certainly appeals as a vision of a 'better' world. As Hyland (1994) points out, it comes with all the 'positive connotations associated with learning and development' (p. 138). It conjures up images of a society which is open, democratic, progressive and modernized, where citizens are provided with opportunities for lifelong learning, and where organizations and institutions are in a state of 'permanent reflexivity' about their strategies for sustainability and development in an unpredictable environment.

What sort of curricula would reflect and help to realize such a society? The question requires us to examine models of the curriculum and suggest what might constitute an appropriate way forward. In the reading, Young looks at two widely held views of the curriculum in schools – one the traditional 'curriculum as fact' with its view of knowledge as external to the knower and the other (allegedly more radical) 'curriculum as practice' with its assumption that knowledge is produced by teachers and students in their classroom practices. The shortcomings of both models are explored by Young.

Young's suggestions for 'transcending the dichotomy' between the two forms reflect his own position on the need for changes in the school curriculum so that it becomes 'an emancipatory experience for a much larger section of each cohort of students' (p. 32). He refers to the need to link theory and practice and the development of a radical concept of the curriculum which enabled teachers to transform their practice; the development of a conception of learning which encompassed out of school learning; and the need for an understanding of the essential political and economic character of education.

These proposals have a critical and democratic thrust to them but there are some problems. On training courses, theories of knowledge, teaching and learning are themselves treated as 'curriculum as fact' and precisely because of that are not critically 'conversed' with by teachers. Political and economic theories are beyond the pale of most training courses which in the UK at any rate have become too grounded in practice. Another issue here is what one might describe as the 'poverty of theory' or at least of the theoretical perspectives of those very academics who would be involved in Young's school-university partnerships. For example, the international school improvement and school effectiveness movement, which originated in universities, has a number of deficiencies in this respect. As I have pointed out elsewhere (Quicke 1999), whilst claiming to recognize the need for schools to become learning organizations and for teachers to become reflective practitioners, the movement fails to theorize the political and cultural complexities of schools, the way power operates through the curriculum or the way teachers are constructed as learning professionals.

Young's second proposal requires elaboration for, as it stands, it seems to suggest that exploration of the links between different sites of learning e.g. school/work, school/home would *inevitably* raise political issues. On the contrary, in the context of a hegemonic free market liberalism, there is nothing inevitable about it. The only dialogue between sites is likely to be technical rather than political, and to be confirmatory of the existing instrumental role of education in the reproduction of existing political and economic elites. As Green (1994) has acknowledged, the extent to which new technologies and new work organization have generated a highly skilled, reflexive workforce, even in rich Western countries, is highly exaggerated. What has emerged in recent years is a social differentiation which looks like a new class structure, with the majority having little control over the production process, being less secure in their occupations and having less opportunity for being 'critical'. Teachers, parents, employers and policy-makers have all contributed to this state of affairs.

The third proposal also requires further analysis because, from a democratic perspective, we need an understanding of history, economics and politics which will identify areas of concern for progressive development that would need therefore to be addressed in the curriculum. Young carries out this analysis in the rest of the book from which the reading is taken. He states that the theory of society which underpins his argument is 'reflexive modernization' and he is well aware of some of the possible contradictions – resulting, for example, from the constraints of a capitalist economy, and the 'conservative' and bureaucratic assumptions which underpin many educational reforms. However, I feel that his version of curriculum debate is largely about 'form' rather than 'content'; we learn a great deal about frameworks and processes, particularly in relation to assessment and qualifications, but little about the content of the curriculum for lifelong learning.

In thinking about curriculum content as well as process, the reading from Gonzáles-Gaudiano is clearly instructive. The progressive curriculum would need to be critical in the sense that it should address areas of concern which involve 'hot spots' of contestation particularly relevant for the realization of the democratic learning society. One such area is the 'environment' and in particular the notion of 'sustainability, and, as we would expect in a plural and differentiated culture, our understanding of the latter will be a function of different and competing discourses of the environment. Like Young, Gonzáles-Gaudiano probes discourses which claim to be radical as well as those regarded as traditional. A version of the former, Green Ideology, is seen as just as problematical as the latter. It shares with more traditional notions 'deep essentialist immersion' and an 'entrenched discourse . . . of certainty' which, he alleges, impedes an understanding of the complexity of environmental issues. As an alternative to these essentialist discourses Gonzáles-Gaudiano advocates what he calls 'the critical, popular, pedagogical Latin-American tradition' where there are different perspectives but general agreement that environmental education is part of a wider arena of political conflict, that popular wisdom and community values are significant and should be taken into account, that 'uncertainty' is at the root of cultural creativity and that theoretical models are always unfinished.

These suggestions share with broader analyses of globalization like Gray's (1998) a critique of the 'one size fits all' model of development, which in effect has meant that (a) the American model of the free market is universalized, and that (b) environmental considerations are always secondary to market driven economic policies. Whilst engaging in international trade on a competitive basis, different societies should be encouraged to develop their own sustainable relationships between the environment and the social, political and economic spheres.

There are no certainties here. For Gonzáles-Gaudiano even the *science* which is most appropriate in conditions of uncertainty needs to be of a different form, with marginal forms like Chaos Theory becoming more influential as a guide to methodology and pedagogy. I think, however, one has to be careful not to throw the baby out with the bath water! If there are no universals and no absolute truths in science or any other discipline, there is a socially constructed consensus on what constitutes 'good' science, which is a prerequisite for rational policy making. In fact I would go as far to say that what Gonzáles-Gaudiano would regard as mainstream science, has always involved the principle of uncertainty and, moreover, has an in-built ethical concern about the nature of its impact on the environment and the wider community. This is not to say that western scientific knowledge always supersedes local knowledge but rather neither should be ignored and there should always be a dialogue between them.

VIGNETTE 7.2 MANAGING LEARNING IN THE REAL WORLD

J. Smyth, University of Paisley

Perhaps you know the apocryphal tale of a temperance-minded teacher who wanted his class to learn about the dangers of alcohol. He put an earthworm in a beaker of water and another in water with some alcohol added to it, and his pupils watched them both wriggling. The next day the one in water was still alive but the one in alcohol was dead, so he asked the class what that taught them. The reply came like a shot – "If you've got worms drink gin." Evidently a badly managed learning experience, especially deficient in its understanding of the real world of the learners.

How far can learning be managed? So much of it happens by chance. No learner comes to the task with a mind like a completely flat, blank sheet. Even in the mind of the youngest learner there are always personal, individual genetic factors, developmental features and prenatal experiences of which we can predict little, but which may tilt the plane of the sheet or part of it, even just slightly, in one direction or another, so that learning will tend to move in that direction if nothing else deflects it. As development proceeds the learning surface becomes an ever more uneven landscape, and of a peculiarly individual kind. To impose a topography on it from the outside can never be more than partly successful, and often it fails. And no two topographies are likely to be the same, so one external event can leave different impressions on different learners side by side.

This topographic metaphor of a learning surface is a limited visual way of representing a complex learning system in which learning outcomes are the products of an interplay between qualities of the input and qualities of the physical and mental state of the learned, both of which quality-sets may vary in short or long term. The nature of an experience may be set by the curriculum but the quality of its presentation and its reception by the learner are things which only the manager of the interaction can hope to judge or influence, and that to a quite limited extent. The influence of the learning environment beyond the curriculum is also likely to be in play, offering experiences and setting examples often with the authority of the real world, not segregated for something on the edge labelled education. The guidance of a learning experience whether by a parent, teacher, friend, employer or whoever, is thus a potentially delicate operation calling for a level of perception and preparation which would usually be quite impracticable. It will also be coloured by individual attributes of both the educator and the learner. Is such diversity manageable?

Diversity, especially biodiversity of which this is one small facet, is looked upon nowadays as a quality to be valued, not as a problem. In the natural world it is the diversity of ecosystems, organisms, genes, processes and relationships which enables a complex life support system to go on running in spite of both short- and long-term changes in its operating conditions. In the same kind of way diversity of outlooks and skills helps a community to cope with the varying circumstances in which it functions. This is the foundation for sustainability and, when recognised and properly deployed, it is also the raw material of democracy. The whole community plays a part in the guidance of learning, often unwittingly, but we should do well to recognise this role.

Whatever preparation is offered to young people for life in a diverse and rapidly changing world it should therefore take account of this condition of life. We should be grateful that different people are nursing different interests, talents and skills, and not try to squeeze them into a common pattern. We should not pretend that there is only one route to a learning objective and should welcome different kinds of approach. Both the papers featured in this chapter encourage this point of view. We might wish to provide learners with opportunities for as wide an enrichment as possible of their individual experience, but then be content when they focus in on what suits them. Within a community, however defined, strength and resilience should be gained from a broad repertoire of qualities. Where people most often fail is in discriminating unfairly between qualities, and valuing others for what they have not rather than for what they have. A hierarchy of importance cannot be safely equated with a hierarchy of lifestyles.

Alas, in practical terms this all sounds like very untidy idealism, or worse – learners selfishly pursuing personal inclinations without a care for what their society needs, and missing in the process some of the best gifts it has to offer. A curriculum is a means of protecting education against well-meant disruption, setting up a structure around which to organise experience, better than no structure at all and more secure than something which constantly changes to fit the fashion of the times. People belonging to a wide diversity of world views still need lines set out by others in recognised authority even if they do not agree with them. Then at least they can communicate meaningfully with each other, within the same outlines, even if meanings are sometimes compromises between a range of interpretations. One can argue about order but disorder can be an unmanageable mess.

All this soul-searching comes at a time when growing numbers of people packed closer together are finding they have less personal space than they feel they need. Constraints of this sort easily exert stress on a community whether natural or urban, and on its members. Opportunism is favoured over structure, short-term over long-term considerations, quantity over quality. Intolerance grows of deviance from norms, information content declines, and a self-preservative outlook settles in where a commitment to reconstruct would lay out human capacities to better advantage. But the materials for building, and the tools to use, are no longer as predictable as they were. We have learnt a lot about satisfying the basic needs of humanity in progressively more complex ways and for more people at less cost, but we have not become so much better at predicting and providing for the consequences, either social or environmental. Our culture has been focused on understanding the measurable and hoping the immeasurable will take care of itself. Many of our concerns are now near the cutting edges of hard science, where scientists cannot offer more than guarded opinions, and also at the cutting edge of politics which has more immediacy. Society may settle for the voices which are loudest. In these turbulent times educators can no longer deal in certainties. They must help people to learn how to manage uncertainties.

Balancing out influences and obstacles, probabilities and risks, in a system which includes a whole range of biophysical and socio-economic elements interacting together, calls for the development of special skills. The reductionist approach which has hitherto protected us from confusion in this jungle of contending issues, and allowed our society to make such spectacular advances in its control over nature, is not so much help in understanding systems where the whole is greater than the sum of its parts. Learning to approach our world systemically as well as reductively may be where curriculum designers should now be helping us to go. It might also help other less formal channels of learning to be plotted in more productively.

Through all the complexities runs the arrow of time. We may never understand the present if we do not also have some idea of how it came to be. Nor can we practise sustainability if we do not follow the arrow's track into the future. There is another quality here for educators to nurture, a faculty for creativity. It is a compound of perception, understanding, values and commitment, intuitive so far as we can judge, a product of body, mind and spirit working together which may be as old as human-kind itself and is too vital a quality to be submerged in the anxious detail of modern life.

Can we manage learning to do all this for us? Can we create the right conditions for social learning which will manage itself? Can we take the further step of inter-locking it with the environment in which it operates and which has its own lessons to present – and contrive that people can hear them? If so the alcoholic worm may not have died in vain.

CHAPTER 8

CURRICULUM AND PEDAGOGY

READING 8.1 WHY I DON'T WANT MY CHILDREN EDUCATED FOR SUSTAINABLE DEVELOPMENT

B. Jickling

Source: *Journal of Environmental Education* 23(4), 1992: 5–8

[. . .]

There is considerable debate about *the merits of sustainable development* and the actions it requires; it is a contested concept (e.g., Huckle 1991; Disinger 1990). As we enter the 1990s, this term has become, for many, a vague slogan susceptible to manipulation. For some, it is logically inconsistent. For others, there are concerns that efforts to implement sustainable development will obscure understanding of the economic, political, philosophical, and epistemological roots of environmental issues and adequate examinations of social alternatives. This raises questions about the idea that anyone should educate for such a thing in the first place. With this in mind, I wish to examine two concerns.

The first concern arises from my observations of the "research seminar" held during the North American Association or Environmental Education's (NAAEE's) 1990 conference in San Antonio. Amid discussions about quantitative, qualitative, and action research, talk about philosophical analysis was conspicuous by its absence. The lack of attention to educational philosophy, and the research methods employed by philosophers, has been an impediment to the development of environmental education. This is a matter of considerable importance. The second concern relates to the proposed relationship between education and sustainable development, particularly as it is described in the term *education for sustainable development*. I will argue that this locution epitomizes a conceptual muddle amidst which environmental educators find themselves.

These two concerns are, of course, related. It is precisely the lack of attention to philosophical analysis of the concepts central to environmental education that allowed the expression and proliferation of such questionable ideas. I will begin by briefly talking about environmental education and the importance of philosophical analysis in this field of study. I will then critique education for sustainable development and in so doing will try to illustrate the importance of philosophical research that employs techniques of conceptual analysis.

One of the problems in environmental education has been the failure of its practitioners to reconcile definitions of environmental education with an a priori conception of education. It would seem peculiar, if not logically incoherent, to speak of environmental education in a way that was not consistent with a broader concept of education. It is important to understand that concepts such as *education* and *environmental education* are abstractions, or ideas that describe various perceptions. Further, one comes to understand concepts when one identifies those qualities that appear to be central to their meaning. For example, a person would understand the concept *table* or what constitutes *tableness* when he or she understands what qualities tables have in common. Similarly, one can come to some understanding of education when one identities those qualities that appear central to the idea of being educated. Analysis can therefore, be described as attempts to identify the most useful criteria to delineate the concept in question.

Although studying how a word functions will provide some understanding about the enterprise or phenomena that it represents, the analysis remains an interpretation of an abstraction in people's minds. It is a mistake to think of concepts as objects or concrete entities; they are nothing more than conventional signs or symbols. This is not a precise business. For this reason, the idea of a true, correct, or perfect statement about a concept is implausible. Analysis of concepts is essentially a dialectical business and such analyses are in constant need of reexamination and clarification (Wilson 1969).

These points can be illustrated by attempting to identify some of the criteria useful in describing the educated person. For example, we might ask ourselves if acquisition of knowledge is a necessary condition. Many would affirm this, claiming we would not normally say that someone is educated but does not know anything. However, although the dissemination of information is an important function of schools, we might continue our analysis by asking if the accumulation of mere facts and disconnected information is enough. For example, my son at 9 years of age could go to a map of the world and identify an astonishing number of countries, but this was hardly sufficient to convince me that he was educated. We expect the educated person to have some understanding of the relationships between those bits of information that enable a person to make some sense of the world: the educated person should have some understanding about why a relationship exists. We might also wonder if the ability to think critically is a necessary criterion for the educated person. Again, we would expect to find considerable agreement; we would be reluctant to say that a person was educated if we judged that he or she could not think for him or herself.

Although this constitutes an abbreviated analysis, it does provide a glimpse at the general approach taken in this kind of research. The philosopher, thus, attempts to find out which of the possible criteria are necessary. It is important to note that this analysis cannot provide a definitive or complete answer but only a collection of logical arguments of greater or less merit. This point is frequently misunderstood. For example, one of the pitfalls for researchers working in fields such as education and environmental education is to think as if abstract nouns were

> the names of abstract or ideal objects: as if there were somewhere, in heaven if not on earth, *things* called "justice," "love" and "truth" [and environmental education]. Hence we come to believe that analysing concepts, instead of being what we have described it to be, is really a sort of treasure hunt in which we seek for a glimpse of these abstract objects. We find ourselves talking as if "What is justice?" [or environmental education?] was a question like "What is the capital of Japan?"
>
> (Wilson 1969: 40)

What this means for environmental education is, of course, that the claim environmental education "does have definition and structure" (Hungerford, Peyton, and Wilke 1983) is unlikely. Or, to attempt to *solve* the so-called definitional problem in environmental education in any fashion, let alone by the American Society for Testing and Materials (Marcinkowski 1990–1991), is misplaced. In the field of environmental education, we appear to be witnessing a treasure hunt for an infinitely illusive abstract object. Environmental education will surely continue to wallow along rocky shores until this field allows an important place for conceptual analysis within its research community.

My preview of conceptual analysis also identifies some criteria useful for understanding the term education. Having identified such essential criteria, in this case the acquisition of knowledge, understanding, and the ability to think for oneself, I can now introduce the next task of the philosopher. This job is to examine the implications that logically follow from use of the concept to see if application of the term is consistent with those essential criteria teased out during analysis. Although this analysis of education is by no means complete, the criteria proposed are sufficient to illustrate this task. At the same time, the adequacy of educating for sustainable development can be examined.

While environment education is in the midst of a conceptual muddle, the same can be said for *sustainable development*. For example, at the 1990 NAAEE conference, Slocombe and Van Bers (1991) reminded us that this term is only a concept and that it is characterized by a paucity of precision. Their observations are not unique. Like D. Scott Slocombe and Caroline Van Bers, some researchers acknowledge that there is no agreement about an overall goal for sustainable development (e.g., Huckle 1991; Disinger 1990; Rees 1989). Analysis of the term has not yet been able to identify sufficient criteria to elucidate common meaning and coherence.

It is also possible that that conceptual coherence cannot be achieved. For Huckle (1991), the term sustainable development has entered the dialectic that characterizes modern environmentalism. For him, it has taken different, and possibly irreconcilable, meanings for technocentrists and ecocentrists. According to this view, the term is contested and its shared understanding is rendered impossible by inherent contradictions arising from these divergent world views. Disinger (1990) reports views that reinforce those doubts. He states, "To some, the term sustainable development is an oxymoron – a self-contained non sequitur between noun and modifier" (p. 3). It appears that there are those who are troubled by questions of logical consistency when *sustainable* is juxtaposed against *development*. If such inconsistency is borne out, the conceptual muddle that surrounds sustainable development will be perpetuated.

The observations reported in the previous two paragraphs accentuate the need for philosophical research, particularly conceptual analysis. Clarifying common understandings of sustainable and development and examining the logical coherence of their association will help to assess the usefulness of sustainable development. In the meantime, disagreement exists. The implication of this reality upon education is foreshadowed by planner William Rees (1989), who argued that a prerequisite to developing acceptable policies and plans for sustainable development is a satisfactory working definition of the concept. It seems equally improbable that we can accept any educational prescription in the absence of an adequate conceptualization of sustainable development. To borrow an analogy, "the situation seems to be parallel to someone wanting to be a shoplifter while not knowing what 'shoplifting' means" (Barrow and Woods 1988: 8). It therefore seems unlikely that I should want anyone to educate my children for sustainable development when it is not clear what on Earth it is that they are aiming for.

Even if an adequate conceptualization of sustainable development were argued, we would still be concerned with the educational appropriateness of aiming for it. In spite of such misgivings, there does appear to be considerable momentum amongst environmental educators who wish to promote education for sustainable development. For example, John Disinger in his article "Environmental Education for Sustainable Development?" (1990) discusses the development of this momentum in North America.

Noel Gough (1991) suggests that much environmental education in Australia is concerned with land protection and is often associated with *conservation for sustainable development*. And, the United Nations Educational, Scientific, and Cultural Organization (UNESCO) has looked to environmental education as a vehicle to promote "training, at various levels, of the personnel needed for the rational management of the environment in the view of achieving sustainable development" (UNESCO 1988: 6). In Canada, the National Round Table on the Environment and the Economy has stimulated the establishment of a Sustainable Development Education Program (SDEP). This program has been identified as part of the "new partnerships for education for sustainable development" (SDEP 1992: 2). And its guiding principles include the development of "attitudes supportive of sustainable development through a process of animating meaningful change within the formal education system in Canada" (SDEP 1992: 5). However, this momentum is not without anomalies, which should raise our suspicions.

Disinger (1990) also reports that many environmental educators have difficulty identifying their own positions, particularly with reference to the ecoanthropocentric continuum. However, he claims that educators generally place greater emphasis on "wise use" rather than on non use perspectives. Though the implications of these observations are not perfectly clear, they suggest that teachers have sought to identify their preferences in order to determine what perspectives to espouse. Gough (1991) was more explicit. According to his view, environmental education has been overcome by promoters of instrumental land values that are frequently associated with sustainable development. Does this mean that environmental education has frequently become a promotional tool? It seems thus far that many educators implicitly or explicity assume that their task, education for sustainable development, involves the advancement of a particular agenda.

Inspection of comments in *Our Common Future* illustrates this problem:

> Sustainable development has been described here in general terms. How are individuals in the real world to be persuaded or made to act in the common interest? The answer lies partly in education, institutional development, and law enforcement.
>
> (World Commission on Environment and Development 1987: 46)

This statement suggests that sustainable development is in the common interest, and the public must be persuaded, or made, to pursue this end. Further, education can contribute to the process of persuasion or coercion required. This raises the following questions: Should education aim to advance a particular end such as sustainable development? Is it the job of education to make people behave in a particular way?

To seek answers to these questions, we must consider first the idea that environmental education should promote "training for the rational management of the environment in the view of achieving sustainable development" (UNESCO 1988: 6). As I have argued elsewhere (Jickling 1991), training is concerned with the acquisition of skills and abilities and frequently has instrumental connotations. We generally speak of training for something; we might be training for football or training for work in a trade. Further, training tends to be closely associated with the acquisition of skills that are perfected through repetition and practice and are minimally involved with understanding. Thus, the capacity for rational management is inconsistent with the means suggested for its achievement.

In contrast, we speak of a person being more or less well educated indicating a broader and less determinate understanding that transcends immediate instrumental values. We would not normally speak of educating "for" anything. To talk of educating *for* sustainable development is more suggestive of an activity like training or the preparation for the achievement of some instrumental aim. It is important to note that this position rests on several assumptions. First, sustainable development is an uncontested concept, and second, education is a tool to be used for its advancement. The first point is clearly untrue and should be rejected; there is considerable skepticism about the coherence and efficacy of the term. The second assumption can also be rejected. The prescription of a particular outlook is repugnant to the development of autonomous thinking.

As we have seen in the earlier analysis, education is concerned with enabling people to think for themselves. Education for sustainable development, education for Deep Ecology (Drengson 1991), or education for anything else is inconsistent with that criterion. In all cases, these phrases suggest a predetermined mode of thinking to which the pupil is expected to prescribe. Clearly, I would not want my children to be "educated for sustainable development." The very idea is contrary to the spirit of education. I would rather have my children educated than conditioned to believe that sustainable development constitutes a constellation of correct environmental views or that hidden beneath its current obscurity lies an environmental panacea.

However, having argued that we should not educate *for* sustainable development, it is quite a different matter to teach students about this concept. I would like my children to know about the arguments that support it and attempt to clarify it. But, I would also like them to know that sustainable development is being criticized, and I want them to be able to evaluate that criticism and participate in it if they perceive a need. I want them to realize that there is a debate going on between a variety of stances, between adherents of an ecocentric worldview and those who adhere to an anthropocentric worldview. I want my children to be able to participate intelligently in that debate. To do so, they will need to be taught that those various positions also constitute logical arguments of greater or less merit, and they will need to be taught to use philosophical techniques to aid their understanding and evaluation of them. They will need to be well educated to do this.

For us, the task is not to educate for sustainable development. In a rapidly changing world, we must enable students to debate, evaluate, and judge for themselves the relative merits of contesting positions. There is a world of difference between these two possibilities. The latter approach is about education; the former is not.

[. . .]

READING 8.2   EVOLVING TOWARDS EDUCATION FOR SUSTAINABLE DEVELOPMENT: AN INTERNATIONAL PERSPECTIVE

C. Hopkins, J. Damlamian and G. López Ospina

Source: *Nature and Resources* 32(3), 1996: 2–11

Refining the concept of education for sustainable development

One of the items in the CSD work programme is to 'refine the concept and key messages of education for sustainable development', and in so doing to integrate environmental, demographic, economic, social and a range of other concerns inherent in the complex notion of sustainability. This part of the work programme has been given special emphasis since April 1996, in response to the urgency given by the Commission

Table 3 Work Programme of the Commission on Sustainable Development: Education, Public Awareness and Training*

Priorities agreed upon by the CSD	*Key actors cited by the CSD*
A Develop a broad international alliance, taking into account past experience and promoting networks	UNESCO as task manager, in partnership with UNEP, IUCN and other key institutions
B Integrate implementation of recommendations concerning education, public awareness and training in the action plans of the major UN conferences and conventions	UN system. Governments, major groups
C Advise on how education and training can be integrated into national educational policies	UNESCO, in co-operation with other governmental and non-governmental organizations
D Refine the concept and key messages of education for sustainable development	UNESCO
E Advance education and training at national level	Governments, with assistance from the UN system and others
F Provide financial and technical support	Developed countries, international organizations, private sector
G Develop new partnership arrangements among different sectors of society. Exploit the new communications technologies. Take into account cultural diversity	Educators, scientists, Governments, NGOs, business and industry, youth, the media, other major groups
H Work in partnership with youth	Governments and all relevant stakeholders
I Analyse current investments in education	Bretton Woods institutions
J Take the preliminary results of the work programme on Chapter 36 into account in the 1997 review	Secretary-General of the United Nations
K Make relevant linkages with the CSD programme of work on changing production and consumption patterns	UN system. Governments, NGOs

* Summary of the decision of the fourth session of the UN Commission on Sustainable Development (New York, May 1996) concerning Chapter 36 of *Agenda 21*, prepared by UNESCO as Task Manager.

to moving rapidly from the general definitions and phrases of uniting environment, economy and human development to the specific content of such education. At the same time, the CSD identified the need for concrete, realistic suggestions for teachers and trainers in order to deliver ESD in school and community organizations. The first step in this process is to identify the scope of ESD and then to devise a method for both building upon the existing expertise of teachers and trainers as well as illuminating a way forward as individuals become more competent.

A still evolving concept

While some concepts of 'sustainable development' have been practised in indigenous cultures for centuries and more recently debated on the world scene since the early 1980s, it is still an evolving notion.

Likewise, reorienting 'education for sustainable development' is still an emerging concept that needs to be clarified at the national and international levels, a lengthy process that must involve all stakeholders. 'Environmental education', which emerged after the United Nations Conference on the Human Environment (Stockholm, 5–16 June 1972), and which focused primarily on the environment and its protection, is seen as an important part of education for sustainable development but not its equivalent. The concepts of human development, social development and economic development need to be integrated with environmental concerns in a holistic, interdisciplinary conceptual framework, which is now increasingly referred to as 'Education for sustainable development'. Once this conceptual framework is developed and understood, the existing disciplines of formal education must then be reoriented to shed their particular knowledge and skills to the overall attainment of sustainability. The challenge, therefore, is far broader and deeper than the mere conversion of environmental education to education for sustainable development.

The evolving nature of the concept is quite predictably of concern to educators and communicators, and sometimes a source of confusion or disagreement. Some question whether there is really a need for this new broad focus. Others question the use of the preposition 'for' in the term 'Education *for* Sustainable Development' (ESD). Is educating 'for' something an education or merely indoctrination? Still others go so far as to question whether our formal education system can teach education for sustainable development, when the schools themselves seldom provide good examples of the sustainability they espouse. There is concern for usurption of the concept of sustainable development by business as synonymous with eco-efficiency. The talk of wilderness as a key component of cultural diversity as expressed by indigenous populations clashes with this narrow concept of eco-efficiency, which hints at everything being usable as long as it is used in an efficient manner. Much is yet to be resolved but waiting for the resolutions before addressing the problems is not a luxury society can afford.

The content of ESD

There is also uncertainty, and sometimes confusion concerning the content of education for sustainable development. Numerous questions are being raised, including: Is it possible to identify key messages of universal validity? How should the scope of ESD be defined in order to reflect the multiple facets of the notion of sustainability? How can such a concept be dealt with in formal education systems, taking into account the lack of training in teaching holistic concepts for nearly all of the world's more than 50 million teachers? What is the most realistic approach in order to achieve progress quickly despite the difficulty and scale of the task?

In order to avoid tremendous time delay, it is proposed that the initial content of ESD be simply what has already been identified and ratified by world leaders. Hence, at this moment (late 1996), the essence of ESD can be seen as an understanding of the major issues outlined in the forty chapters of *Agenda 21* (Box 1 [see pp. 142–144]), together with the action plans of the subsequent UN conferences concerning sustainable development, notably the Cairo conference on population, the Copenhagen conference on social development, and the Beijing conference on women. The conventions on biological diversity, climate change and desertification as well as the statement on forest principles provide added substance. In addition, ESD should not overlook issues such as war and militarism, governance, discrimination and nationalism, renewable energy sources, multinationals, refugees, nuclear disarmament, human rights, consumption, media and world views. While defining the content of ESD in this way is intended to bring focus, it simultaneously shows the scope and hence the scale of the way forward. It also shows the need for a multi-sectoral approach.

Infusing existing disciplines

Perhaps the greatest potential to move forward rapidly lies in the concept endorsed at Rio of reorienting the major disciplines of formal education to address sustainability. In this process, existing strengths of teachers in such subjects as mathematics, language, science, geography and history can be built upon. By encouraging the existing disciplines to incorporate elements into their curricula, a major infusion of sustainability can be injected in a relatively short time frame on a global basis.

In other words, individual teachers and trainers in both formal and non-formal settings will identify areas within the broad scope of ESD that they will feel comfortable discussing and including in their programme or discipline. This model builds on the fact that most educators will know or feel comfortable discussing at least one aspect of ESD from the many chapters addressed in *Agenda 21* and the other emerging issues. The viability of this approach is even more convincing if one considers that ESD can begin with education about the issues, without necessarily dealing with how to solve them. To begin, one needs only to identify the issues and show people where they can learn more. The stage of becoming involved and taking action will follow once leaders and students become more comfortable and certain with the material.

The pedagogy of ESD

As well as having identified the factual content of ESD, an integral part of communicating sustainability will be the approach or pedagogy. Step one is to relate global concepts to local realities (Box 1). There will be need therefore to identify for each of the global issues dealt with in the various chapters of *Agenda 21*, a relevant local example that is appropriate for the person being taught or trained. An example would be to move from the chapter on combating deforestation to developing a project on paper recycling in the primary classroom. Another would be to move from demographic dynamics and sustainability to the knowledge of issues and skills involved in reproductive health for a more mature training class.

Also from a pedagogical viewpoint it will be necessary to draw the connections between these seemingly isolated topics in various disciplines so they combine to form holistic concepts. This is the creative synergy that will come from a transdisciplinary approach that is the key to achieving sustainability.

Much work remains to help institutions cope with developing the strengths of both disciplinary research with its accurate information, and transdisciplinary assimilation of this knowledge for informed application in a real setting. Formal institutions are themselves having difficulty working within both the traditional structure of the disciplines and also ensuring students graduate with a holistic interdisciplinary understanding of these highly interrelated issues. Most success has come from work in thematic teaching where a relevant local issue is selected for study by the staff and students. Then teachers contribute their particular expertise – usually from their disciplinary perspective but identifying the connections to the other disciplines. This team teaching and integrated learning approach most parallels real life situations to be found in later years in the worlds of work and family.

Teacher training facilities, professional associations and non-governmental organizations must be mobilized to develop these new strategies and additional units of instruction in the established, globally delivered disciplines. While the task of developing a holistic overview showing the interrelationship of these various aspects will still remain, the infusion of a critical mass of information at various grade levels will already be a major step forward.

The need for content backed by sound science

Another major concern in developing education for sustainable development is the gap between the content of education and the available scientific knowledge. Much of what is communicated today, through both formal and non-formal channels, is inaccurate, out of date or biased. This bias may reflect a single disciplinary approach, culture or geographic area. Education for sustainable development needs to be based on sound science, on the new knowledge which is being acquired by experts to understand the functioning of the Earth system, the complexity of environment, population and development interrelationships, and other still emerging aspects of sustainability.

There is, therefore, a strong need to involve the scientific community (both the natural and the social sciences) in ensuring the accuracy of the emerging messages of education for sustainable development. There are many barriers that will be difficult to overcome, not the least being the challenge of articulating complex theoretical ideas in simple language that people can understand and relate to their daily lives. Education for sustainable development must also grapple with new unproven theories and hopes. Yet the difference between fact and 'perhaps' must be clearly maintained in people's minds. This is not easy for a formal education system that 'marks' and 'grades' in terms of right or wrong. The notion of evolving truths is difficult to cope with.

The key role of environmental education

In facing the difficult challenge of reorienting education towards sustainable development, which needs to be accomplished with little time and limited resources, it is imperative to consider how to maximize the experience acquired and the investment already made thus far in existing movements such as conservation education, population education, development education, energy education, etc. One of these examples is environmental education for which UNESCO and other international institutions have acquired considerable experience which should be built upon.

It is clear that the roots of education for sustainable development are firmly planted in environmental education. While environmental education is not the only discipline with a strong role to play in the reorienting process, it is an important ally. In its brief twenty-five year history, environmental education has steadily striven towards goals and outcomes similar and comparable to those inherent in the concept of sustainability.

Box 1   Education for sustainable development

MOVING FROM GLOBAL CONCEPTS AND ISSUES OF *AGENDA 21* INTO CONCRETE ACTIONS AT DIFFERENT SCALES AND LEVELS

This matrix conveys two important ideas concerning the emerging notion of education for sustainable development: first, the scope of *Agenda 21* and related conventions and issues which could constitute the essential content of ESD; second, the need to relate global concepts to local realities, in order to mobilize people to bring about the needed change. Hypothetical examples are provided for each of the issues highlighted.

SOCIAL AND ECONOMIC DIMENSIONS
- International co-operation
- Combating poverty
- Changing consumption patterns
- Population and sustainability
- Protecting and promoting human health
- *Sustainable human settlements*
- Making decisions for sustainable development

CONSERVATION AND MANAGEMENT OF RESOURCES
- *Protecting the atmosphere*
- Managing land sustainably
- Combating deforestation
- Combating desertification and drought
- Sustainable mountain development
- Sustainable agriculture and rural development
- Conservation of biological diversity
- Management of biotechnology
- Protecting and managing the oceans
- Protecting and managing fresh water
- Safer use of toxic chemicals
- Managing hazardous wastes
- Managing solid wastes and sewage
- Managing radioactive wastes

INTERNATIONAL REGIONAL
e.g. Nations identify the major issues concerning sustainable human settlements and agree on actions required which are reflected in an international action plan approved by governments (Habitat II).

NATIONAL STATE PROVINCIAL
e.g. National/State governments in co-operation with other stakeholders identify the relevant recommendations of the international action plan that they feel need to be understood by the public at large. Appropriate media strategies are designed and implemented.

LOCAL MUNICIPAL PERSONAL
e.g. Students carry out a neighbourhood study as a part of their geography course. They identify a need in their community that is within their competence of rectifying or addressing.

INTERNATIONAL REGIONAL
e.g. Nations agree upon targets for CO_2 reduction and develop a national or regional strategy to achieve these targets.

NATIONAL STATE PROVINCIAL
e.g. National and State or provincial governments in conjunction with relevant stakeholders develop a media strategy that will make the general population and target groups in the work force aware of the need for CO_2 reduction.

LOCAL MUNICIPAL PERSONAL
e.g. A coalition of NGOs and other stakeholders begin a media campaign to reduce car usage and mobilize support for public transportation.

Box 1 *(continued)*

STRENGTHENING THE ROLE OF
MAJOR GROUPS
- Preamble to strengthening the
  role of major groups
- Women in sustainable
  development
- *Children and youth in sustainable
  development*
- Strengthening the role of
  indigenous people
- Partnerships with NGOs
- Local authorities
- Workers and Trade Unions
- Business and industry
- Scientists and technologists
- Strengthening the role of
  farmers

MEANS OF IMPLEMENTATION
- Financing sustainable
  development
- Technology transfer
- Science for sustainable
  development
- *Education, training and public
  awareness*
- Creating capacity for sustainable
  development
- Organizing for sustainable
  development
- International law
- Information for decision-
  making

INTERNATIONAL REGIONAL
e.g. National governments agree on
the Rights of the Child in terms of the
right of future generations to a quality
life and livelihood.

NATIONAL STATE PROVINCIAL
e.g. A multisectoral consortium
distributes a handbook on developing
youth environmental clubs to schools
and community organizations on a
state or national basis.

LOCAL MUNICIPAL PERSONAL
e.g. Local school starts an energy
conservation club that monitors
energy consumption within the school
and makes recommendations to the
staff and concerned officials regarding
possible reductions. Some of the
savings from increased energy
efficiency are passed on to the
club.

INTERNATIONAL REGIONAL
e.g. Nations at the CSD agree upon the
need for and the components of a work
programme to develop ESD at the
international level and within countries.

NATIONAL STATE PROVINCIAL
e.g. A coalition of sectors contribute
funds and other resources to start a state
or national effort to promote ESD by
developing policies, curricula and staff
training.

LOCAL MUNICIPAL PERSONAL
e.g. A university faculty of education
launches an initiative to reorient teacher
training to address ESD.

Box 1　*(continued)*

CONVENTIONS AND STATEMENTS
RELATED TO *AGENDA 21*

OTHER PERTINENT ISSUES

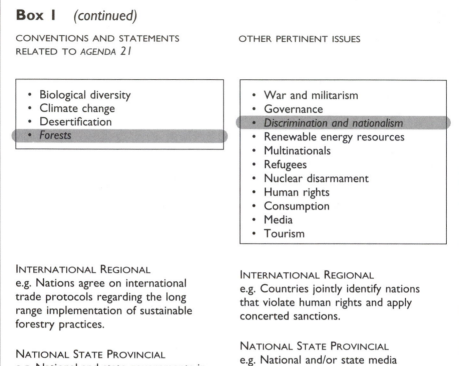

- Biological diversity
- Climate change
- Desertification
- *Forests*

- War and militarism
- Governance
- *Discrimination and nationalism*
- Renewable energy resources
- Multinationals
- Refugees
- Nuclear disarmament
- Human rights
- Consumption
- Media
- Tourism

INTERNATIONAL REGIONAL
e.g. Nations agree on international trade protocols regarding the long range implementation of sustainable forestry practices.

NATIONAL STATE PROVINCIAL
e.g. National and state governments in conjunction with industry and NGOs develop tax incentives and laws which favour employee training that leads to the adoption of sustainable forestry practices.

LOCAL MUNICIPAL PERSONAL
e.g. A forest industry company in co-operation with NGOs and other stakeholders launches a community based information programme that targets employees, spouses and local schools so that all members of the community understand the issue and can be a part of the solution.

INTERNATIONAL REGIONAL
e.g. Countries jointly identify nations that violate human rights and apply concerted sanctions.

NATIONAL STATE PROVINCIAL
e.g. National and/or state media campaigns are developed showing the impact of racism and extreme nationalism in the past while fighting the disparities in society that fuel these movements.

LOCAL MUNICIPAL PERSONAL
e.g. A school board not only enforces strict legislation against bias but launches proactive programmes at all levels to promote understanding of cultural diversity and respect for various world views.

Environmental education has therefore been a sound investment and a solid beginning with respect to the challenge which must now be met. Thousands of workshops and training programmes have been held in the past twenty years, covering most of the countries of the world. Print and audiovisual materials in a host of languages have been disseminated, organizations have been established in the majority of nations and a great deal has been accomplished regarding institutional capacity-building. Networks among specialists, institutions, non-governmental organizations and national governments have been developed.

There is much to build upon and much to learn from these past critical years that can help formulate future action in education for sustainable development.

[. . .]

VIGNETTE 8.1 SUSTAINABLE DEVELOPMENT IN EDUCATION: CONSENSUS AS AN ETHICAL ISSUE

L. Sauvé,
Université du Québec à Montréal

The core argument put forward by Charles Hopkins, Jeanne Damlamian and Gustavo López Ospina (1996) to justify "sustainable development" as the central goal of education, is the "new international consensus" among "experts" on the importance of education to promote sustainable development. To demonstrate the strength of this consensus, they refer to international conferences held in the 90s (funded and thus legitimated by UN agencies) that did promote "sustainable development". This argument, based on the authority of experts and organisations, sets the railway of thought and practices towards global educational reform. What remains to be done is to "refine" the concept. Minimally, this idea of a consensus as the core argument for this world wide reform needs to be critically appraised. Why is the idea of a consensus so seductive? Is there really such a consensus amongst educators? Is a consensus an appropriate basis for educational reform and environmental action? What are the core elements of this consensus?

The proposal of "sustainable development" was framed by the World Commission on Environment and Development as a compromise negotiated between a number of privileged actors across economical, political and environmental spheres (WCED 1987). Vaillancourt (1992) remembers that in this negotiation round, any explicit reference to "environment" or any expression including eco- (like eco-development) was discarded because it was an irritant for many participants: the focus had to be on (economic) development. This compromise was then presented as a universal consensus.

In this way, following Delruelle (1993), consensus has become a new frame of reference for decisions, a "new ethical and political paradigm". It is then much more than a "democratic" strategy to facilitate cooperation between social actors; consensus also brings an impression of certainty against the anguish and stress caused by the dissolution of previous ideologies, the collapse of "truths" and the decline of religions.

The problem arises when consensus becomes a universal prescription, as "the touchstone of truth and the guarantor of correctness in matters of decision and action" (Rescher 1993: 7). Nicholas Rescher develops a rigorous argument to demonstrate that consensus is not a criterion of truth, is not a standard of value, is not an index of moral or ethical appropriateness, is not a requisite for co-operation, is not a communal imperative for just social order, is not, in itself, an appropriate ideal.

(ibid.: 199)

Moreover consensus as a dogma does not consider the diversity of other visions, desires, signification, possibilities. The search for consensus should not overshadow pluralism and dissension which can become important creative forces in a society. Considering diversity is not only an ecological strategy to promote richness and equilibrium in a social system, but it is also an ethical imperative. Such an ethical process specifically requires us to take into account what is outside of "common sense" (decreed by consensus), of "normality", and to listen to difference (Delruelle 1993). In this perspective, to reframe indigenous cultures as an expression of sustainable development reveals a lack of cultural sensitivity and an ethical myopia.

Amongst educators, there exists a rich diversity of world visions, of conceptions of environment, society, development, education, for example the alternative treaty on environmental education resulting from the Global Forum (Council of the Earth 1992) and the different views and criticisms expressed during the regional meetings organised by UNESCO in preparation for the Thessaloniki Conference (Orellana and Fauteux 2000). It has to be considered also that more than half of the participants in the recent International Debate on Education for Sustainable Development agreed that "Education for Sustainable Development has to be abolished as a concept" (Hesselink *et al.* 2000). Still the promoters of ESD maintain that there is a consensus for this proposal; and this consensus should be the world-wide basis of education. "Whose interests are being served?" asks Jickling (2000).

Bob Jickling is one of the dissident researchers and educators who call for a critical analysis of "sustainable development" and the derived "sustainability" proposal, as values and goals for education. To understand such dissent, it is necessary to examine the discourse of Chapter 36 of the Action 21 (WCED 1993) and the proposal of the Thessaloniki Declaration (UNESCO 1997). In these documents (whose guidelines are promoted by Hopkins *et al.* 1996 and Hopkins 1998), environment is essentially seen as a reservoir of resources for development; conservation practices are unavoidable constraints to sustain development; the human relationship to the environment is one of management; development is associated with sustained growth in a new world economic order; education (as a communication and training process) is an instrument to promote sustainable development; following this "new vision of education", the "populace" will be "informed" and "prepared to support changes" determined by experts and world leaders (Sauvé *et al.* 2000).

These views, "wrapped in a generous rhetoric of equity for sustainability" (Sauvé and Berryman 2001) confirm the economisation of all human activities and legitimate "development" as the new cultural and ethical paradigm, based on the historically constructed occidental belief that "development" is the universal key to save humanity (Rist 1996). The core content of the conceptual framework of sustainable development is illustrated by the three interrelated poles of economy, society and environment; it promotes a vision of the world where the economy is outside the social sphere and imposes its goals on society's relationships with the environment. ESD brings people to adopt this "new cosmology" (Berryman 2000). The language is normative: all the teachers over the world "must" "deliver" sustainable development.

It is not surprising if many environmental educators feel uncomfortable with this global and hegemonic educational project characterised by "determinism" and "exclusivity" (Jickling 1999). Environment, our shared house (*Oikos*) of human and non-human life, woven with the interlaced treads of nature and culture, cannot be reduced to "raw material" for economic growth. Development cannot be the only reference framework to interpret our desires, initiatives, activities, etc. Education is not an instrument to promote an exogenous project: it is "concerned with enabling people to think for themselves" (Jickling 1992), which implies critical thinking. Finally, environmental education is not a "discipline" and does not "focus primarily on the environment": it is an essential dimension of fundamental education whose object is the reconstruction of the complex web of relationships between persons, social groups and the environment (Sauvé 1999).

The idea is not to set environmental education and education for sustainable development one against the other, nor to try to integrate them one into the other. Before positioning both, there is still work to be done to examine the evolving ESD proposal, as in the *Environmental Education Research* journal's special issue (7: 2). As noted by Jickling (1999), sustainability appears to be a seductive idea: "it has the capacity to capture important issues and inspire imagination". Considering its universal claim, ESD is an important socio-historical phenomenon that deserves critical appraisal; there is a need "to examine its gestation, incubation and evolution" (Berryman 2000).

Consensus, however, will never suffice as its legitimation. Consensus arises from diversity, which implies divergence and dissension, and reflects a moving and evolving social reality. As an argument for hegemony, "consensus" can bring tensions, dysfunction and ruptures. In a real democratic context, it can help co-operation, but still it is not an essential precondition of collaborative work in a society: mutual understanding, respect and empathy are much more important (Rescher 1993: 179). The search for consensus, if considered to be possible and needed, should be an evolving, reflexive and critical process, with ... "some humility please!" (Jickling 1991).

VIGNETTE 8.2 LIFESPAN LEARNING FOR SUSTAINABLE EDUCATION

J.E. Heimlich, Ohio State University

In comparing these two readings, it becomes clear that the concept of "lifespan education for sustainability" (US Global Change Research Information Office 1997) is rife with definitional problems. Based on economic constructs, the Brundtland Commission (1987) presented sustainable development as that which "meets the needs of the present without compromising the ability of future generations to meet their own needs." Yet, as Jickling (1992) notes, the term "sustainability" remains vague and susceptible to competing definitions, and Hopkins *et al.* (1996) reflect that sustainable development continues to be an evolving notion. Jacobs (1993) attempted to unify definitions of education for sustainability by commenting that all definitions have a consistent core meaning. This comprises a consideration of environmental issues and objectives interdependently with economic issues and objectives; commitment to social equity and fair distribution of environmental benefits and costs – including intergenerationally; and an enlarged view of development to include qualitative improvements in daily life. Even so, "nothing can be taken for granted as regards either our conceptions of sustainability ... or the best curricular and pedagogic responses to them" (Stables 2001b: 126). The definitional challenge is not eased with the apparently simple change of "sustainable development" to "sustainability," but begs that the argument continue on what is or is not sustainability, and the scale at which sustainability operates. Just such a challenge is reflected in the entire issue of *Environmental Education Research* (7:2) devoted to the language of sustainability.

Even if there were a consistency within the language of what it means to be sustainable, we still need to consider the purposes of education. If we are to educate, what are the objectives of the learning, and who is it for? It is entirely possible that education for sustainability will become mired in the debate that has plagued environmental education for decades, i.e. is it education *for, about, in,* or *with* the environment (sustainability)? Further, is altering the focus to sustainable development a solution or a complication? A fundamental issue in how we conceptualize the relationship between education and sustainability is that of needing to get beyond thinking of education as social reproduction, and to view it more as a means of engendering critical thinking and facilitating democratic social change. Both readings represent different views on how this might be achieved and, of course, other perspectives exist. A crucial issue is the need to avoid indoctrination. This argument is central in Jickling's paper, but the concept of indoctrination must to some degree be implicit in Hopkins *et al.*'s (1996) use of the term "training".

The question remains as to what education for sustainability would look like. Hopkins *et al.* (1996) support the "infusion" model, which has been used in the environmental education literature since the late 1970s (see, for example, Disinger 1987a, b; Engleson and Yocker 1994). However, the suggested linearity between curriculum activities and social involvement and action is clearly not always supported in the educational research literature (e.g., Hungerford 1996; Jensen and Schnack 1997), and psychology has long presented arguments against assuming linear relationships between cognitive learning and actual behavioral changes in the learners (Lefebre-Pinard 1983; National Science Board Commission on Precollege Education in Mathematics, Science and Technology 1983). Another question is what is truly new or different about education for sustainable development. Is it different from what is good environmental education, as implied in both readings? What, exactly, does it mean to "build on environmental education" (Hopkins *et al.* 1996), and what would be the role of various emerging and historic approaches such as Earth Systems Education, Science/Technology/Society, Peace Education, Global Studies and the like?

Both texts strongly emphasize the formal school system, and lack reference to, or inclusion of, nonformal and informal education where a great amount of what is actually learned about the environment occurs, and where adult learners tend to obtain information they need or desire. Thus, neither presents an argument for andragogy, in any sense beyond that of training for adults. The constructs of adult learning (Merriam and Caffarella 1991; Merriam and Clark 1993; Laurillard 2002) are not the same as the constructs of training. Adults choose to learn based on their immediate life needs, seek information that supports their perception of life and social roles, bring increasingly larger reservoirs of knowledge with them; are increasingly self-directed, and are increasingly intrinsically motivated (Knowles 1980). For adults, learning is considered to be correlated more with what the learner does/wants than what the teacher does, which imposes upon the educator the responsibility for helping adults make meaning from the education experience (Merriam and Caffarella 1991; Carlsen 1988). One major outcome of adult learning is critical awareness of how and why presuppositions constrain the way the individual thinks, perceives, and feels about the world (Mezirow 1991), and the success of an adult learning transaction is in part dependent upon the educator helping the learner at whatever point the learner is in the learning process (Vygotsky 1962; Tharp and Gallimore 1988, 1991). This lack of reference in both readings to education outside formal schooling and training (ie, by not addressing the larger society through non-school learning) has the effect (whether intended or not) of imposing the responsibility for sustainability on future generations.

The ideal of "life-span education for sustainability" has appeal because it reminds us that sustainability is something to be worked on through the living of our lives – rather than something to be learned once, and then applied intelligently. Yet the literature focuses us away from operationalizing this construct, and steers us into a debate on language, purpose, means, and structures for education. Changing society implies a changing focus within the educational system, but it is not possible to change society solely through education. For sustainability to become a societal norm, and therefore an outcome of lifespan educational systems, both the social structure and educational systems must work toward the same end, and it is this which is at the heart of the challenge which we all face.

VIGNETTE 8.3 EDUCATION FOR SUSTAINABILITY: A REGULATIVE IDEA AND TRIGGER FOR INNOVATION

F. Rauch, IFF, Austria

Sustainable development, and based thereon, Education for Sustainability are dynamic and multi-faceted notions as well as still evolving concepts. The two key readings in this chapter are examples of the ongoing debate. The major difference that I see in the two readings is the different perspective from which Education for Sustainability is reflected upon. Bob Jickling (1992) argues from an educational theory that is oriented towards the individual, and rightly rejects any indoctrination and unthinking action orientation, which the notion of Education *for* Sustainability implies. He writes: "Education is concerned with enabling people to think for themselves. Education for sustainable development . . . is inconsistent with that criterion" (Jickling 1992). Education for sustainable development suggests a predetermined mode of thinking to which the learner is expected to subscribe as "for" suggests training or the preparation for achieving instrumental aims.

Hopkins *et al.* (1996) begin by taking up several points of criticism raised vis-à-vis education for sustainability, including that of Jickling (1992). Then, however, they adopt a rather pragmatic line of reasoning: "Much is yet to be resolved, but waiting for the resolutions before addressing the problems is not a luxury society can afford" (Hopkins *et al.* 1996). Against this backdrop, this paper briefly outlines *Agenda 21* and addresses implementation strategies for more sustainable living conditions. From this perspective, pedagogy is dealt with from the angle of a relatively pragmatic-technical rationality, in terms of solving problems by using local examples and by involving all stakeholders. Learning processes and specific improvements towards sustainable development are to be interlinked. Existing subject-matter competencies (e.g. of teachers and academics) and structures of the organisations involved (e.g. schools) are to form the basis for transdisciplinary communication processes that are to be newly developed. However, this approach places exacting demands on the development capacity of individuals and organisations without according a prominent position to the role of reflection, as was done by Jickling.

The authors of the two readings draw markedly different conclusions from the open and unfinished nature of the sustainability concept without, however, transgressing the idea of sustainable development. Let me develop my line of reasoning on a number of common features. A sustainable society will only be achieved through a social process of searching, learning and shaping. It is critical to organise this process in a way that allows different conceptions and interests to be contributed in a constructive manner. Jurg Minsch (2000) points out that this is not a novel phenomenon: "Not even ... the idea of human rights can be finally and concludingly operationalised, but must be reinvented again and again, in its historic context." Like human rights, sustainable development may be regarded as a "regulative idea" which inspires social learning and shaping processes. The notion of regulative idea is derived from the German philosopher Immanuel Kant and may be understood as an epistemological construct. Kant (1787/1956) writes: "In this way, the idea is nothing but an heuristic and non-ostensive notion and indicates not how an object is made up, but how we, guided by the same, are to explore how the objects of our experience are made up and linked to one another"[1]. Regulative ideas thus help us to organise our knowledge and to link it systematically with normative elements. Regulative ideas serve as heuristic structures for reflection. They give direction to research and learning processes and in this way prevent the individual from groping about in the dark without orientation or appropriate context. Regulative ideas can also be understood as pre-concepts without which no reasonable question can be asked and no problem identified. Therefore, uncertainty is a constituent element of this regulative idea without which consensus would be impossible. In terms of sustainability, this implies that the contradictions, moral dilemmas and conflicting targets inherent in this vision need to be constantly re-negotiated in a process of discourse between participants in each and every concrete situation. The consensus which is expressed in the idea of sustainable development is not static, but one that needs to be re-established time and again in given situations and between different groups. The tentative and emerging nature of the idea can delineate an extremely creative, manifold and dynamic field, which is nevertheless oriented towards a particular direction.

Education for sustainability as a trigger for innovation in education

The idea that education for sustainability can be a pre-concept or regulative idea goes hand in hand with a responsiveness in many social areas. Responsiveness, however, does not suggest a complete alignment of the idea of sustainability to those to whom it is addressed; rather, it looks for overlaps with visions and objectives which already exist there. For school education this means, for example, that sustainable development must tie in with existing conceptions of teaching, school life and the relation of the school and its environment. Thus, dealing with the topic becomes appealing and worthwhile from the inner perspective of a school, as it not only implies new, additional tasks, but also results in solutions for current problems (De Haan and Harenberg 1999).

Furthermore, the interdisciplinary nature as well as the present and future relevance of the sustainability debate, with all its inherent dilemmas, uncertainties and confusions, may constitute fertile ground for educational innovation. It is of utmost importance to address the twofold challenge of the vast complexity which results from sustainability and related uncertainties in order to retain a capacity for action without lapsing into simplistic dogmas. While on the one hand sustainability issues are used as a vehicle for innovation by these initiatives, they are also meant to trigger concrete sustainable social development processes (Rauch 2002).

It follows that it makes sense to link the regulative idea of sustainable development with ideas of school reform and development, not least because one may then draw parallels between their characteristic features. The following basic theorems apply to current educational reform concepts (De Haan and Harenberg 1999):

- a reflective understanding of education, which focuses on independence, self-determination, communication, cooperation and reflection;
- autonomy for schools to design matters independently as a concept of democratisation and differentiation;
- school development plans as dynamic instruments to develop teaching and schools;
- openness of schools towards shaping the relation of schools and their environment.

It is also important to critically examine the sustainability concept. Jörissen *et al.* (1999; quoted in Minsch 2000) have formulated criteria to concretise the dimensions of ecology, society, economy and institutions. For the institutional-political dimension, their criteria include:

- responsiveness: institutions contribute to strengthening the responsiveness of society vis-à-vis ecological, economic and social problems;
- reflexivity: institutions contribute to enabling a reflection of social action beyond the limits of particular social contexts;
- self-organisation: the manageability of society depends on the self-organising potential of social systems;
- balance of power: institutions contribute to balancing the different scopes for articulation and interference of the different players or groups of players.

The parallels and overlaps between the two sets of characteristic features demonstrate that schools which deal with sustainable development in the context of school development might be able to develop in that area and make a contribution to a more sustainable design of society.

One example in the school development arena is the "Ecologisation of Schools" project, which is being carried out within the OECD–ENSI Project in Austria and several other countries. In the "school development" context, environmental education culminates in the concept of a sustainability-oriented further development of the school as a place of teaching and learning. The school development process which is prompted by environmental initiatives is called the ecologisation of schools. Ecologisation is targeted at awareness and behaviour, at social structures and impacts on environmental quality. The ecologisation of schools is the environment-oriented design of work, teaching and learning at school and in the school environment on a human scale which involves all players (pupils, teachers, school head, non-teaching staff, parents, citizens). It implies the development of new forms of teaching and learning, school development as a culture of communication, co-operation, conflict and decision-making, as well as the opening to the outside world (the local community as a place of teaching and learning for school, school being a cultural centre in the community). For this, it is imperative that knowledge and the enormous wealth of information are used critically and reflectively, and that dynamic (key) skills are developed (Posch 1999; Rauch 2000a,b).

Note

1   The German quote was translated by the author of this article.

CHAPTER 9

MEASURING LEARNING: ASPECTS OF ASSESSMENT

READING 9.1 CHANGING LEARNER BEHAVIOR THROUGH ENVIRONMENTAL EDUCATION

H. Hungerford and T. Volk

Source: *Journal of Environmental Education* 21(3), 1990: 8–17

[. . .]

Goals and objectives for instruction in environmental education

Behavior in the environmental dimension can be perceived as so very complicated as to make instructional planning difficult. This difficulty (as well as a lack of research into the precursors of behavior and instructional strategies designed to change behavior) probably resulted in the model that knowledge leads to awareness which leads to behavior.

There has been a great deal of criticism about the lack of direction in EE over the past 15 years. The lack of emphasis upon objectives that focused on helping students actually solve environmental problems and develop problem-solving skills is contrary to the recommendations for environmental education objectives contained in both the 1977 Belgrade Charter and the 1977 Tbilisi Intergovernmental Conference Report.

The answer to some of these concerns might be found in instructional goals for environmental education that incorporate the variables related to "ownership" and "empowerment." Such a set of goals was developed in the early '80s and has subsequently been used throughout the world as a guide for curriculum development and research. This set of goals identifies a "superordinate goal" which follows:

> *The superordinate goal*: . . . to aid citizens in becoming environmentally knowledgeable and, above all, skilled and dedicated citizens who are willing to work, individually and collectively, toward achieving and/or maintaining a dynamic equilibrium between quality of life and quality of the environment.

Four major goal levels as well as subgoals were developed to help accomplish the superordinate goal. The goal levels are presented below [. . .].

Goal Level I: The Ecological Foundations Level. This level seeks to provide learners with sufficient ecological knowledge to permit him/her to eventually make ecologically sound decisions with respect to environmental issues.

Goal Level II: The Conceptual Awareness Level – Issues and Values. This level seeks to guide the development of a conceptual awareness of how individual and collective actions may influence the relationship between quality of life and the quality of the environment and, also, how these actions result in environmental issues that must be resolved through investigation, evaluation, values clarification, decisionmaking, and finally, citizenship action.

Goal Level III: The Investigation and Evaluation Level. This level provides for the development of the knowledge and skills necessary to permit learners to investigate environmental issues and evaluate alternative solutions for solving these issues. Similarly, values are clarified with respect to these issues and alternative solutions.

Goal Level IV: Action Skills Level – Training and Application. This level seeks to guide the development of those skills necessary for learners to take positive environmental action for the purpose of achieving and/or maintaining a dynamic equilibrium between quality of life and quality of the environment.

Educating for a change in behavior

What are the critical educational components?

Given all that has preceded this section, one should be able to identify a number of critical components of a total educational program for environmental education if changes in learner behavior are desired. Among these critical components are ones which can be facilitated by formal and nonformal educational agencies (see Table 4).

Comments on implementing the critical components

Certainly, there is no one best way to implement these components in an instructional setting even though the research provides the reader with some meaningful clues concerning important and successful strategies. And it may be that it will take a concerted, cooperative effort among educational institutions to meet the challenge of changing learner behavior. Certainly, an articulated implementation across grade levels and the cooperation of nonformal educational agencies as well as local and regional educational resources would maximize the opportunity for success.

What are some successful strategies for meeting the implementation challenge? What are some cautions that should be kept in mind while implementing the important components? Most of the components listed in Table 4 will be discussed here in some detail. However, first let us focus on at least one overall strategy that seems to be especially critical.

The need for a reinforcement strategy. Educators must not assume that one course or one unit or one year of training will accomplish the task needed even though a number of studies have shown that certain strategies for changing behavior are successful (Holt 1988; Klingler 1980; Ramsey 1989; Ramsey *et al.* 1981; Simpson 1989). Associated with one of these studies (Ramsey *et al.* 1981) was an important but unpublished follow-up investigation conducted three years after Ramsey measured the effects of three different treatments on the environmental behavior of eighth-grade students.

Three years after Ramsey completed his initial investigation, he trained several graduate students to act as interviewers and took them to the secondary school where the original subjects were students. The interviewers were trained to assess the extent of student involvement in environmental issues and environmentally appropriate behavior. The interviewers were not told which students had been in the experimental group and which had been in either of the control groups. Interestingly, the interviewers

Table 4 Critical education components.

It appears that we can maximize opportunities to change learner behavior in the environmental dimension if educational agencies will:

1   teach environmentally significant ecological concepts and the environmental interrelationships that exist within and between these concepts;

2   provide carefully designed and in-depth opportunities for learners to achieve some level of environmental sensitivity that will promote a desire to behave in appropriate ways;

3   provide a curriculum that will result in an in-depth knowledge of issues;

4   provide a curriculum that will teach learners the skills of issue analysis and investigation as well as provide the time needed for the application of these skills;

5   provide a curriculum that will teach learners the citizenship skills needed for issue remediation as well as the time needed for the application of these skills; and

6   provide an instructional setting that increases learners' expectancy of reinforcement for acting in responsible ways, i.e., attempt to develop an internal locus of control in learners.

could identify each of the students who had been in the experimental group. The subjects were *involved in more environmentally appropriate behaviors* than their counterparts. However, it was clear that the original behavior observed in the eighth grade had eroded over time. There had been no intervening educational reinforcement for the students over a three-year period. Thus, it seemed obvious that, even though the experimental subjects were more environmentally involved, some sort of intervening treatment would have been needed to maintain the original level of involvement.

In light of Ramsey's follow-up study, it seems obvious that learners need to be reinforced for positive environmental behavior over time. No definitive recommendations about the extent of instructional reinforcement will be made here. There is simply no research to validate how much is needed. However, it is evidently imperative that learners get in-depth educational experiences over a substantial amount of time.

Thoughts on the sensitivity component. Environmental sensitivity is a particularly troublesome variable for many educators who understand its importance. The variables associated with sensitivity are often not associated with formal education.

Several research studies have focused on "sensitivity" (Peters-Grant 1987; Peterson 1982; Scholl 1983; Tanner 1980). These studies yielded similar results concerning the precursors to environmental sensitivity. It appears that "environmental sensitivity" is a function of an individual's contact with the outdoors in relatively pristine environments either alone or with close personal friends or relatives. The environmentally sensitive individuals reported hunting, fishing, and other outdoor activities as important variables. Of great importance is the fact that they reported that these activities took place over long periods of time.

Numerous sensitive individuals reported that some experience with severe environmental degradation substantially increased their environmental sensitivity. Some sensitive individuals reported the importance of teachers who acted as sensitive role models for them. Others reported being raised in an environmentally sensitive social environment. Only a few reported the importance of educational courses or books.

If these research studies are to help us make educational decisions about developing environmental sensitivity, it seems important that learners have environmentally positive experiences in nonformal outdoor settings over long periods of time. And, in the formal classroom, we must look to teachers who are, themselves, sensitive and willing to act as positive role models for learners. Both of these conditions, for millions of learners, are hard to meet.

Accomplishing the issue of investigation, action, and knowledge components: two recommended approaches. These variables are collapsed together in this heading because there is research evidence that these can be met simultaneously in a formal instructional setting (Holt 1988; Klingler 1980; Ramsey 1989; Ramsey *et al.* 1981; Simpson 1989). In each of these studies, behavior changed positively as a consequence of instruction that focused on ownership and empowerment. Of great importance is the fact that, in all cases, students were shown to participate in more environmentally appropriate behaviors out of school after instruction.

The instruction used in each of these studies focused on the goal levels cited earlier with the exception of the ecological foundations goal. That particular goal (ecological foundations) was met earlier in the learner's schooling. Thus, Goals II, III, and IV were part of the instructional design. In all cases, the instruction involved the use of one of two curricular strategies (Hungerford *et al.* 1988; Marcinkowski *et al.* 1990; Hungerford *et al.* 1990).

Two curricular strategies: the issue investigation and action model and the extended case study model

In the issue investigation and action model, the student learns to discriminate between environmental events, problems, and issues. The impact of beliefs and values on issues is emphasized, and an issue analysis strategy is introduced and practiced. Students then learn how to identify environmental issues, write research questions focused on these issues, and learn how to obtain information about issues using secondary sources. They also learn how to compare and evaluate secondary information sources. They then learn how to develop surveys, opinionnaires, and questionnaires and how to sample populations in order to obtain scientifically valid information. In addition, they are taught how to record data, interpret the data, make inferences about the data and draw recommendations from these inferences. At this time, each student chooses an issue of particular interest to him/her and investigates that issue in depth. Subsequently, the student prepares a report on that investigation and tenders a written report to the instructor and an oral one to his/her peers.

After the students have completed their issue investigations, they learn the major methods of citizenship action, analyze the effectiveness of individual action versus group action, and develop issue-resolution action plans. This action plan is evaluated against a set of criteria designed to assess the social, cultural, and ecological implications of the action. Finally, the students decide whether they want to actually implement the plan of action. If they choose to implement their action, the instructor helps to facilitate this citizenship behavior.

In the extended case study model, the students learn some of the same skills that were learned in the other model except that they do so focused on a predetermined issue, sometimes chosen by the class but most often chosen by the instructor. The research indicates that the extended case study model, although successful, is not as powerful an instructional model as the issue investigation and action model.

[. . .]

READING 9.2 ALTERNATIVE PERSPECTIVES IN ENVIRONMENTAL EDUCATION RESEARCH: PARADIGM OF CRITICAL REFLECTIVE INQUIRY

P. Hart

Source: North American Association for Environmental Education, Troy, OH, 1993: 8–13

The guiding principles and key characteristics of environmental education establish particular kinds of pedagogical practices as being necessary to achieve the stated goals. For example, learners should work toward the resolution of environmental problems; teaching and learning are intended to be cooperative processes involving inquiry into and action on environmental issues; the development of knowledge, skills, and values is not only directed towards action, but emerges in the context of preparing for (i.e., the inquiry) and taking action; curriculum and pedagogical planning need to be highly flexible. However, common knowledge indicates that in most classrooms there is a markedly different, yet consistent, pattern to current pedagogical practices than the guiding principles of environmental education advocate. Typically teachers act as dispensers of factual information, students respond to teachers' questions, and knowledge is acquired individually for future use (i.e., in later life). The teacher is frequently the only participant who actively engages in high order thinking processes.

Observable surface-level discrepancies between theory and practice betray deeper, more fundamental pedagogical contradictions between environmental education and schooling as follows:

- While an environmental education curriculum should be interdisciplinary and focus on real practical problems, school curricula, especially in science, are discipline-based and emphasize abstract theoretical problems.
- Whereas a curriculum in environmental education is emergent and problematic in that the content arises as students are involved in specific environmental problems, most school curricula are predefined since they are designed to serve predetermined behaviorally specific ends (that is, ends whose attainment can be readily assessed).
- Whereas pedagogy in environmental education ought to be problematic in the sense that the way for students (and teachers) to solve environmental problems is uncertain, most school programs embrace an unproblematic pedagogy of information dissemination. This results from instructional means being clearly defined by the criterion of the efficient achievement of the desired ends.
- Whereas a function of knowledge in environmental education is immediate use for the social value of a sustainable and emancipated quality of life, the major function of school knowledge is storage for future use and the enhancement of individual status and economic well-being.
- Whereas environmental education advocates learning that is holistic and cooperative, school learning tends to be atomistic and individual.
- Whereas in environmental education rhetoric, students are active thinkers and generators of knowledge, in schools students are usually in the passive position of spectators and recipients of other people's knowledge and thinking.
- Whereas learning and action should proceed hand in hand according to environmental education theory, the acquisition of knowledge precedes its application in most school practices.

- Whereas the mastery of relevant knowledge and skills is demonstrated in environmental education by students' actions in real situations (that is, their performance in exerting influence on environmental decision making), in schools students write about theory in artificial situations (that is, their performance in "influencing" the teacher).

(Stevenson 1987: 75–76)

Given these issues that reflect the "gap" between schooling and the goals and advocated processes of environmental education, how can environmental education be organized for reconstruction of [the] school curriculum?

Recently, McClaren (1987) has argued for the importance of participation of the teacher in improving environmental education.

The implementation of curriculum ultimately depends on teacher support and commitment. The classroom teacher is at the center of the transaction of public schooling. No matter how much curriculum theorists and developers may believe in the value of the importance of their programs, and no matter how elegant their designs may be on paper, in the final analysis no curriculum can be (or should be, in my opinion) teacher-proof. The proponents of mandated curriculum, whether in environmental education or arithmetic, all too often forget this. To them, the curriculum is simply a technology to serve their purposes, and teachers are merely cogs in the machinery (McClaren 1987: 53).

It is apparent that environmental educators have focused their attention on the development of environment-related goals and have neglected to probe deeply enough into pedagogy, particularly at the level of the teacher. The process problem remains in environmental education because environmental educators have not focused on the real-life working conditions of teachers, their perceptions about change, and the support system needed to facilitate change in teaching method demanded by these new curriculum materials.

In my view, the key issue in efforts to organize for more and better environmental education is not simply one of producing more or better curriculum project materials, but one of creating the conditions for participatory action research as a prerequisite to curriculum planning and professional development. The central problem in environmental education change is lack of teacher involvement. It is a problem because educational change has pedagogical and political dimensions. Our failure to recognize the importance of the political nature of the process of educational decision making has resulted in a dismal record in past attempts to stimulate change. The process issue of whether to integrate or segregate will absolve itself in the larger process of resolution of conflicts surrounding the process of teacher change. And a key aspect of teacher change is teacher participation. Rather than being mere "cogs in the machinery" teachers have influential theories and values about environment and education which guide their actions in environmental education. The real life working conditions of teachers need to be taken into account both in research (theorizing) and in curriculum development (practice). Authentic teacher participation in curriculum research and development must be supported.

Posch (1988) has argued for a "participatory research" role for teachers in environmental education curriculum development.

Teachers who take on this (curriculum development in environmental education) duty need to communicate with each other and need external support . . . This, however, is not enough . . . When a teacher no longer contents himself [herself] with imparting systematic knowledge, but exceeds the limits set by the school and accepts to cope with unstructured situations, he [she] increasingly needs to be aware of what he [she] does, a kind of systematic reflection on his [her] own actions, in order to keep a check on the risks connected with environmental projects, and in order to facilitate communication on his [her] actions and further development. Therefore, we want to encourage teachers to evaluate their work with the pupils themselves and to write about it . . .

I think that this aspect of "research" as a sort of systematic reflection on one's own actions will become increasingly important and is not only apt to contribute to the building up of a stock of practical professional knowledge, but will also improve the social status and the autonomy of the teaching profession.

As regards the further development of environmental project instruction, I personally attach particular importance to three perspectives:

- The improvement of teacher-teacher communication and the integration of a greater number of teachers/schools into this exchange of experiences,
- The production of knowledge on environmental project instruction by the teachers themselves, and
- A more dynamic and innovative design of infrastructural conditions for this sphere of work.

(Posch 1988)

An example of participatory action research within a paradigm of critical inquiry

The question naturally arises: What specific forms would participatory action research take in "real-life" situations? The example of a project currently in progress in southeastern Australia illustrates some apparent correspondences between an action research project in environmental education and socially critical education (Greenall Gough and Robottom 1993).

Seven schools along the southeast coast of Australia engaged in developing environmental education curricula focusing on water quality in nearby streams, lakes and ponds, and in the sea off local swimming beaches. The schools were linked with each other and with Deakin University by electronic mail.

There were three dimensions to teacher activities in the overall project: engagement in scientific study with students, participation in an international computer conference, and involvement in a form of participant research focusing on educational issues.

Some features of the project illustrate its alignment with the participant research approach to curriculum development in environmental education:

1   The project engaged critical environmental education. The environmental education engaged in by the school was interested in environmental accountability – it was environmental education for environmental responsibility.
2   The project attracted significant support from the local community. As the school developed environmental education programs in response to perceived local environmental concerns, community interest, and support were forthcoming. In one instance, the local Water Board provided assistance with water sampling and the local press provided public visibility to the role of the schools in addressing this environmental issue of concern to the community.
3   The project was consistent with principles of participation and responsiveness. Teachers were involved in the study of the project itself through data collection (diaries, computer logs, field notes, and photography) and in processes of identification of technical, teaching, and curriculum issues of interest and concern to themselves.

4   The project embodied a range of structures for enhancing communication between participants. Individual visits by university personnel, project newsletters, computer conferences, and project workshops were all part of the project and supported the views of Posch (1988) that in environmental education it is important to work towards the improvement of teacher-teacher communication.

Greenall Gough and Robottom (1993) describe characteristics of this participatory action research project that suggest a common ground between environmental education and the critical inquiry paradigm. For example, in relation to epistemology of practice, the project embodied a constructivist view of knowledge simply by exhibiting fidelity to the key principles of the rhetoric of environmental education, albeit with a distinctive critical orientation. That is, the substantive knowledge of the programs engaged in by the schools was "working knowledge" generated by the participants themselves. The environmental critique in this case was an action-based, community-embedded form of inquiry yielding "working knowledge" that was transactional rather than transmissive, generative/emergent rather than preordinate, opportunistic rather than systematic, and idiosyncratic rather than generalizable . . . School activities were exemplified as interactive involvement in socially significant politically-relevant participant-negotiated tasks focused on student participation in community change, and employing consultants as required for communication and methodological problem solving (Greenall Gough and Robottom 1993).

Greenall Gough and Robottom (1993) acknowledge that, although classes were conducted in the spirit of collaborative research communities, some conditions for critical self reflection aimed at improving the relationships of teacher/student practices, understandings and situation were lacking. Nevertheless, the project illustrates the practicality of participatory action research as a natural method for environmental education.

The restructuring and reconstructing of environmental education, as illustrated by the Australian action research project, can help to bring about the changes needed to make society more actively and effectively environmentally responsible. The forms that this reconstruction takes will need to involve concentration on teachers' reflection on their own practice and active participation in new curriculum development. Not only must curriculum development in environmental education be considered in terms of the materials and methods that are really the "product" but also in terms of the process whereby the teacher becomes the "researcher".

Environmentalism has evolved to the point where conflicting messages could lead to a confusion of environmental education goals and directions (Gough 1987a). If environmental educators are able to get beyond the dictates of environmentalist contradictions and focus on the pedagogical process by involving teachers in reflective practice and curriculum reconstruction as a means of professional development, environmental education may yet provide a crucial core in the education of an environmentally responsible citizenry. The key element in all this is the process – get that right and the product will take care of itself. This paper contends that teacher involvement is a key element in the process of environmental education renewal in the field of education.

Conclusion: environmental education as critical inquiry – aligning theory and practice

Gough (1987b) describes how education must change in order to align with an ecological worldview. As a foundation for educational inquiry, it is the critical action research paradigm that most closely aligns with the ecological worldview that underlies mainstream environmental education rhetoric but does not align with environmental education activity. For example, the influential and widely accepted environmental education policy statements that emerged from international conferences at Belgrade in 1975 and Tbilisi in 1977 established goals for environmental education that include the intellectual tasks of critical appraisal of environmental issues and the formulation of a moral code concerning such issues, as well as the development of a commitment to act on one's values by providing opportunities to participate actively in environmental improvement (Stevenson 1987). In addition to prescribing the development of critical thinking, problem-solving, and decision-making skills within the context of quality-of-life issues, the Tbilisi Declaration emphasized that students should be actively involved in all levels of working toward resolution of environmental problems (UNESCO 1978: 18). However, there appear to be few examples of environmental education practice that authentically enact this educational philosophy policy.

Admittedly, environmental education is a product of both the older and the emerging worldviews and to some extent reflects the contradictions and conflicts that accompany a major paradigm shift. This mixture of environmental ideologies is particularly evident in the variety of courses variously labeled environmental science or environmental studies, which often embody uncritical assumptions about scientific and applied science research methods in resolving problems of environmental "management". Even when intentionally labeled environmental education, many of these courses have preserved teaching practices and learning experiences that embody an earth-centered ontology based on a scientific worldview (Zais 1976). For example, environmental education in schools tends to reproduce the industrial model of schooling dominated by the authority of teachers, textbooks and timetables, by trivial pursuits of memorizing information and routinely performing technical tasks. In the 1960s educational philosophers and curriculum theorists such as Schwab and Bruner attempted to broaden this rather narrow epistemology base to include an epistemology of discovery. What appears to be happening in the 1980s and 1990s in environmental education is a shift in the epistemological base to an epistemology of constructed knowledge based on a man-centered ontology. Current arguments in the field of science education (especially within the science-technology-society environment movement) reflect this tension of competing worldviews as seen in arguments for the extension of the science curriculum base to include values, morals, ethics, and aesthetics as legitimate components of the real (authentic) world of science.

Whereas historically schools were not intended to develop critical thinkers, social inquirers, and problem solvers, or active participants in environmental/social decision making, contemporary environmental education imposes a revolutionary purpose on schools – one which intends to transform the values that underlie our decision making through educational practices that can only be described as action research. For example, there is a distinct alignment between the principles of action research described earlier and the following pedagogical and curriculum practices which Stevenson (1987) embeds within guiding principles (UNESCO 1978) and key characteristics (Fensham 1978; Hart 1979, 1987) of environmental education.

Teaching and learning are intended to be co-operative processes of inquiry into and action on real environmental issues. Such an inquiry process demands that students actively engage in critical or complex thinking about real problems. The development of knowledge, skills and values is not only directed towards action, but emerges in the context of preparing for (i.e., the inquiry) and taking action. Consequently, curriculum and pedagogical planning need to be highly flexible. For example, as well as adapting to students' own social constructs, the teacher should be amenable to students' decisions in relation to both their learning and their actions (Stevenson 1987: 75).

Clearly, action research methods recommended for practitioner-researchers align with a pragmatic epistemology of constructed knowledge, based on a man-centered ontology (Zais 1976) and an ecological (as opposed to applied science) worldview (Gough 1987a). Although this worldview also aligns with environmental education rhetoric, it unfortunately does not yet characterize environmental education activity in schools. Perhaps it is only when practitioners themselves decide to practice education within an action research (critically social) paradigm that environmental education activity in schools can finally align with its now aging rhetoric.

VIGNETTE 9.1 LIFE'S RICH TAPESTRY

A. Reid, University of Bath

A tapestry-making analogy for sustainability invites us to consider our role in the 'fabric' and 'fabrication' of sustainable development. In line with the Brundtland Commission (1987), *Agenda 21* (United Nations 1992) and the 2002 World Summit on Sustainable Development, the analogy suggests we have all been commissioned to engage in producing the world's most significant tapestry, and that it will be our life's work. But in this instance, there is one crucial difference from standard tapestry-making: *we cannot have full access to the front of the fabric.* We can only weave sustainability from behind – from the present – and we can have only limited understanding of the future and the consequences of today's actions on the 'other side'. Given this constraint, the processes and products of our present work towards sustainability are rendered problematic: we have little appreciation of the outcome of our labours, working with, or without, a 'template' – or perhaps more appropriately, a 'greenprint'. We may receive occasional encouragement and correction from the messengers of Rio de Janeiro or Johannesburg, but at heart this work remains inspired more by conviction than absolute fact. In other words, restricted contact with the textures and tensions that create patterns of sustainable and unsustainable development means that the value of working on our designs for sustainability must be taken on trust in the short term at least.

The challenges presented by this metaphor derive from explorations of the existential dimensions to educating for sustainable development. As with the medieval tapestry, history becomes the arena, hindsight the tool, and the viewers and values of later generations rather than those of the commissioners' or workers', the ultimate – if sometimes unforeseen – assessors of the merits of current work against a paradigm of 'unsustainability'. Whether we regard the 'weft' added to the 'warp' or particular 'yarns, loops or knots' as representing the various economic, political, socio-cultural or environmental processes involved in sustainable development, assessing the tapestry from one side alone, and only in the context of one's own lifetime, means that at best, what might be seen and felt by others from the 'front' can only be inferred. In this analogy, as in reality, there is neither foundation or Archimedean point that acts as the final source of reference for evaluating approaches to and progress towards sustainable development, whether they be top-down, bottom-up or some points in-between. In the final analysis, assessing progress towards sustainable development remains as much socially constructed as it is culturally situated.

What of assessing sustainability-related learning, as proposed by Hungerford and Volk, and Hart? Continuing with the tapestry-making analogy is not entirely out of place. Recasting the 'worker' as 'lifelong learner', the comparison suggests that recommendations by these authors fit with an ideology of assessment in environmental education:

- that privileges the criteria of educators and their authority in deciding and applying them over those of the learner(s); for example, in relation to specific learning contexts and the nature of the learning goals, tasks or demands, Hungerford and Volk, and Hart tend to circumscribe 'education' as something 'happening to' learners in the context of schools, and not taking place in self-directed and negotiated ways, or in other settings, e.g. the workplace, home, trade union or community, as befits lifelong learning (Rainbird 2000);
- where stipulated learning outcomes, whatever their apparent worth or consensus, can neither be universal, fully achieved in practice, or necessarily meaningful to those living and working with(in) the present – let alone, future – dynamics of sustainability, as lifelong learners living around a diverse, unequal world; or, as Bown (2000) highlights, '*Learning beyond school is not an option for those who have never been to school*';
- where some criteria for the learner and educator – the 'tapestry maker' and 'commissioner' – remain unworkable and unknowable without dialogue and acknowledgement of the limits of both the sustainability exercise and that of lifelong learning. That is, with conceptions of lifelong learning focusing on the need for the individual to take responsibility for his or her own learning, including its order, focus and analysis, such elements remain contextualised within a range of competing interests, such as those related to the learner's relationships with others (like family, employers etc.), the relative abundance of (and access to) time and resource, and the learners' dispositions towards the merits of lifelong learning (Carr and Claxton 2002).

Read allegorically then, texts on the assessment of sustainability-related learning might do well to avoid presuming clear and regular access to the front of the tapestry – the products of a 'sustainable development education' in progress or in finished form – neither of which the analogy or reality appear to allow. Unsettling though it is for those working with education and sustainable development, the connectedness of educational activities with sustainability outcomes cannot be confirmed or predicted absolutely, a situation that highlights the futility of assuming that either the immediate or lasting worth of sustainability-related learning can be easily assessed (Scott and Reid 2001).

So, what might frame discussion of assessment and lifelong learning in the context of sustainability, or the portmanteau concept, 'Assessment for Lifelong Sustainability Learning', as it will be termed here? For writings like Hungerford and Volk's, and Hart's, immediate questions to consider are:

- In the context of measuring progress towards sustainability, how necessary and adequate are current understandings of assessment, where their focus and 'technologies' centre on measuring knowledge, capacities, qualities and dispositions (Carr and Claxton 2002)?
- What is effective lifelong sustainability learning, whether we consider this in terms of purpose, conduct or engagement with the learning process? And, how situated, stable and transferable is it (Scott 2002)?
- (How) will our thinking and techniques regarding assessment change to address the challenges of developing the formative and summative dimensions to assessment for lifelong sustainability learning?

- Will contemporary testing regimes simply be replicated for sustainable development (e.g. transferred from environmental education or science education), such that they do little more than generate new methods of labelling in classifying learners (Broadfoot 2002)?

But, expressed in the form of terse statements, issues in lifelong sustainable learning might also emerge around the 'truth value' of the following propositions:

1   It is a truism that what is assessed is what educators and learners themselves come to 'value'. It is not true that all learning is desirable, or all assessment leads to learning (see Carr and Claxton 2002).
2   Assessments of learning and sustainability are perspectival: people are situated within a range of contexts, they make assessments at unique periods of history, their vision and frames of reference are bounded and partial (see Broadfoot 2002).
3   What is assumed to be sustainable and worth learning to sustain are contestable within a generation, and by other generations, now and in the future (see Scott and Reid 2001).
4   As with learning, so with sustainability: there is no transcendent position from which to evaluate, what is achieved or successful in absolute terms or assess what has been learned (see Bown 2000).
5   Education is fundamentally anthropocentric; people constitute what is to be learned and are constituted by their learning. The same may be said for sustainability, though this may seem counter-intuitive: that sustainability, like learning, is anthropocentric. 'Wanting to sustain being sustained' is a human project and not one that can be attributed to Nature, 'Gaia', the cosmos or some 'Other' without qualification (see Scott and Reid 2001).

It is unhelpful to confuse lifelong sustainability learning with environmental education in school settings, even if they overlap or contribute to each other. Lifelong learning often implies individuals who are willing, committed and able to go on learning throughout their lives, who are capable of coping with uncertainty, diversity and the need for collaboration with others (see Broadfoot 2002). Each characteristic is fundamental to effective learning in the context of sustainable development, and in sustainable development supporting, rather than hindering, learning (Scott 2002).

In conclusion, we do well to remind ourselves that faith in the meaningfulness of assessing education for sustainability may prove to be misplaced, mistaken or misguided. Furthermore, despite our best efforts or intentions, current conceptions of educating for sustainability will not necessarily endure as the discourse on sustainable development and education evolves or changes profoundly. The challenges raised by the tapestry analogy support notions of lifelong learning that shift the focus from product to process, from 'assessment *of* learning' to 'assessment *for* learning'. Indeed, in the context of lifelong sustainability learning, the process may be more worthwhile than the product.

VIGNETTE 9.2 ASSESSING ACTION COMPETENCE?

B. Bruun Jensen and K. Schnack, Danish University of Education

For a number of years now, we at the Research Programme for Environmental and Health Education at the Danish University of Education have expressed our criticism of the many campaigns, information projects and teaching projects that aim to change people's behaviour. In fact, the modification of behaviour has been the overall aim of perhaps the majority of measures taken in areas of environmental and health education.

When people are worried about the ecological crisis and/or the living conditions and quality of life of people it is easy to make the classical failure of letting good ends legitimate questionable means. From a democratic educational perspective the ideal must be to encourage students' action competence, even if doing this is difficult, and produces few easily measurable outcomes.

Action competence as an educational ideal

Action competence is an educational ideal. It is therefore neither a teaching method nor a prescribed and well-defined objective to be reached, and for this reason its development can be difficult to measure. Individual elements of it can perhaps be monitored, but as a whole, action competence is difficult to pin down. Nor is it possible to operationalise the concept by converting it into a set of observable phenomena. This is connected with the fact that it is an ideal within the framework of critical liberal education (Schnack 2000).

Environmental and health problems are primarily social problems that have to be solved at the political level. It is not the task of the school and teaching to solve society's political problems, nor to improve the world through the behaviour of pupils. While it is a good idea for schools to save energy, to collect batteries and to sort waste for recycling, in the educational context, the decisive factor must be what the pupils learn by taking part in such activities – or, perhaps, by being involved in the making of decisions to do something else.

Action and action competence

The action competence approach is related to schools' work with open social questions, such as the health and environmental problems in our societies. As the term indicates, the goal of the approach is to improve, support and qualify pupils' commitment, will and abilities to take action. Pupils are thus involved in developing visions for the future and in clarifying the kind of personal and societal changes and actions necessary to move towards their visions. Pupils should among other things acquire:

Insight and knowledge: coherent and action-minded understanding of environment and sustainability.
Commitment: motivation to become involved in change regarding one's own life and in the processes of a dynamic society.
Visions: ability to go "behind" the environment issues and think creatively regarding ideas for a healthy and sustainable development. This also includes their critical thinking – not taking everything – or anything – for granted.
Action experiences: real experiences from participating individually or collectively in facilitating changes within a democratic framework and considering how barriers can be overcome.

The fourth component, action experience, stresses the benefit from taking concrete action during the learning process. Teachers' and pupils' experiences within many development projects in Denmark seem to support the view that participating in a wide range of different types of actions is a vital step in the development of action competence, and perhaps such competence might only be acquired through action.

Pupils' actions are therefore crucial in environmental and health education. Before an action, there must always be a conscious making up of one's mind. This is the inner component of the action concept. Secondly, in order to be characterised as an action, pupils' activities must be directed towards a solution of the problem in question. This is the outer component of the action concept. In other words an action is targeted at change: a change in one's own life style, in the school, in the local society or in the global society. And an action is intentional (Jensen and Schnack 1997).

Two cases

In connection with an evaluation project for the Development Council for the Danish Folkeskole, we visited a number of schools and observed teaching and interviewed teachers and pupils (Christensen and Schnack 1992). The focus was on environmental issues and at several schools the pupils had collected batteries, but at none of them had the pupils any idea what happened to these batteries after they had been collected. One particular school was proud of the fact that they had won a competition concerning who could collect most batteries, but interviews with some of the boys revealed that their class had achieved this "imposing" result by fetching already collected batteries from chemists and suchlike places in the neighbouring towns.

Our immediate reaction was one of indignation, but after this we began to examine more closely in what sense these children had actually "cheated". The boys had agreed to take part in a competition, and they actually did exhibit action competence in terms of initiative, creativity and co-operation with those grandparents who had driven them to the neighbouring towns. The point is, however, that the boys' actions have no meaning outside the logic of the competition itself. Those who had organized the competition were certainly convinced that it would lead to good habits, but the boys referred to here had at no point accepted such a pursuit. So in a way, one could maintain that the boys did not "cheat" at all, but that by their conscious actions, which brought home the promised reward of 5000 Danish Krona (US$700) to their class, they indirectly revealed the deceit that is built into so many campaigns and competitions.

At a school in Northern Jutland, a group of teachers developed a Health Promoting School project on pupil participation and pupil action (Jensen 1998). The pupils were to work with a number of different phases: (1) choice of a real-life health situation that meant something to them; (2) a critical investigation to find out how they could have an influence on this situation; (3) the development of their own ideas and visions for a healthier future; and (4) the initiation of actions with the aim of changing reality in the direction of the visions set up at the outset.

Some pupils started talking about alcoholism and loneliness, and outlined a vision of a local community with a wide variety of existing leisure activities. They set up a club for schoolchildren outside school hours. Other pupils discussed exercise, and ended up by building a cycle-cross track close to the school. Another group wanted to lobby for the building of a swimming pool in the area, and so on. In total there were more than 10 different projects going on as part of the project.

The pupils (aged 13) who started to work with the swimming pool tried out a lot of different activities and actions. Firstly they wrote directly to the mayor and got a negative response. Then they discussed the power relations in the community and got ideas for working out a more comprehensive strategy. They approached the other pupils at the schools and got their approval for the idea. They held a meeting with their parents – where they introduced their ideas and plans – and got their support as well. Finally, they approached the municipality and got professional support in designing the swimming pool, making a proper budget etc. In the end they sent in the application, now with all the materials and back up included. After a few weeks they got the answer from the municipality where they were congratulated for the nice work and for their contribution to the local democracy. But they were also told that the municipality simply didn't have the finance for taking such a big project on board. So, once again the response was negative.

Issues for discussion

From the examples it is clear that what has been achieved cannot simply be measured and assessed by documenting and describing pupils' actions. In order to understand the value of such actions in the educational context it is necessary to explore how they influence pupils' future competence to take action. And that involves among other things being aware of the context (seen from the eyes of the pupils) in which the actions are placed.

It is also clear that the degree to which the pupils succeed in changing the "real world" should not be confused with the improvement of their action competence; very often there will be no linear relation between these two "outcomes" and sometimes the reverse might even be the case. Interviews with pupils from the different projects in the health promoting school revealed that the pupils from the swimming pool group had the highest degree of motivation, they acquired the most sophisticated insight about how a local democracy works and they also developed a strong sense of ownership as well as insight into the area of "strategy building". When we compared with other groups who succeeded in reaching their goals (the youth club, the cycle cross track etc.), they didn't show the same kind of development. One of the important distinctions might be that the swimming pool group met a lot of barriers which they had to discuss how to overcome. Many of the other groups simply didn't have the opportunity to meet barriers during their projects and to learn from these kinds of challenges.

The different approaches and educational ideals make a difference even if they are in themselves rather abstractly articulated. You cannot assess action competence itself, but by accepting it as the overall aim you will prioritise other factors and you will ask other questions. Too often educational aims are chosen because they are easy to measure. However, this often involves a reduced and uni-dimensional assessment procedure where you only assess the degree to which students have learnt what you want them to learn. From an educational perspective it is, however, most often more important what else they have learnt – and, especially, what they have learnt by learning what they have learnt.

CHAPTER 10

MEASURING EFFECTIVENESS: MONITORING AND EVALUATION

READING 10.1 EVALUATING ENVIRONMENTAL EDUCATION

H. Stokking, L. van Aert, W. Meijberg and A. Kaskens

Source: IUCN, Gland/Cambridge, 1999: 19–23

As an organisation, what do you have to evaluate and why should you do it?

Evaluation means making a critical examination of what something is worth. What the 'something' may be has already been examined [. . .]. The main objects of evaluation are likely to be:

- the functioning of all or parts of the organisation;
- the 'market position' of the organisation compared with other providers;
- the quality of and/or interest in the current range of provision as a whole;
- one or more products for particular client target groups;
- one or more activities for particular participant target groups.

The question of why such things should be evaluated has already been discussed [. . .]. In brief, the possible purposes of evaluation include:

a) reporting to a funding body (accountability);
b) to be able to provide participants and target groups with information (PR function);
c) to monitor quality (keeping a finger on the pulse);
d) to improve quality (learning from experience).

Reasons for carrying out more, or more systematic, evaluation as an organisation relate to combinations of the above. For example, it might be to determine whether an activity corresponds sufficiently to the interests of the target group, to determine what participants learn from it, to discover what aspects of a product can be improved, to make the value of your work clear to administrators, clients and others and so on. In short, as an organisation you only carry out evaluation if it is in your interests to do so.

A survey of educational establishments a few years ago showed that many appreciate the value of evaluation and are implementing it but that there are three recurrent problems:

- lack of time;
- lack of funds;
- lack of expertise.

In addition there are establishments which question the purpose of evaluation. This may simply be due to a lack of knowledge and experience.

However, it can also be due to unsuccessful attempts or a negative experience, or the difficulty of striking a proper balance between what evaluation can deliver and what it costs.

These problems can only be solved by targeted investment. However, the situation will vary according to the size of the establishment. A large organisation may decide to free up time, funds and personnel for, say, a year, in order to gain insight into what evaluation can mean for the establishment and what it would cost to introduce it. A small organisation would often be hard put to make such an investment. However, in that case there is probably scope for obtaining a special temporary budget allocation. Educational organisations which, for example, are part of a local authority, can attempt to make use of budgets for professional development, quality control, improving market orientation, efficiency or effectiveness or whatever 'label' may suit the purpose.

Organisations which receive support from, say, a government department, can try to put forward a case for a one-off investment.

A proposal stands more chance if it is described in a short but clear plan, setting out the objectives, activities, costs, benefits and planning. One possible benefit is an operational plan for evaluation within one's own organisation. Another is a description of the steps followed to reach this point because it will probably be of interest to other parts of the authority or to other institutions associated with the department.

Both small and large organisations need to get to grips with, and make decisions about what can and should be evaluated. This then needs to be translated into a small project for a limited period. The project should enable you to answer the following questions:

- What are the main reasons for the organisation to consider introducing more systematic evaluation? What aspects of the organisation, the work or the services offered, does it seem particularly appropriate to evaluate?
- What conditions must you be able to meet in an organisation in order to carry out such an evaluation and obtain results? To what extent does the organisation meet these conditions already and on which points can the organisation meet the conditions in future and what needs to be done to effect this?
- Assuming that you have decided to implement on-going evaluation, how can this be approached? (It is most effective if a pilot study is used to create a plan of action, since that is the best aid to concrete decision-making.)

The first question is addressed elsewhere. Here we will restrict ourselves to answering the second and third questions.

What conditions must be met in order for an organisation to introduce regular evaluation?

If you wish to tackle evaluation seriously, you must meet certain conditions. If certain conditions are not being satisfactorily met, it is advisable to address this problem first of all. Furthermore, in considering all the conditions, it is not a matter of whether they are met in full, but whether they are fulfilled to the necessary extent. There is always room for improvement. It is up to the organisation to decide what is 'sufficient' at any given point, given the time and means available, and given the purpose the evaluation is to serve. If the aim is to produce an official report or if an activity which is strategically important to the organisation is due for a radical overhaul, you will be inclined to set more stringent requirements and to make a greater investment.

In short, it is not necessary to meet all the conditions in order to make a useful start on evaluation.

The list can be used preferably with the team, to determine the extent to which you would like to fulfil certain conditions better. At first sight it may seem that it will require considerable time and effort. In practice, however, many of the conditions relate to 'having given a good deal of thought to your work'. And that is very important in itself, irrespective of evaluation.

The conditions relate to the following four categories:

- products and activities which are suitable for evaluation;
- clear division of responsibilities and cooperation and openness in the team;
- time, material, space;
- expertise.

Products and activities which are suitable for evaluation

The product in general

1 Activities and products of sufficient importance

Organisations which carry out many fragmented activities and/or have only fleeting contact with the participants or which restrict themselves, say, to the distribution of short pamphlets, must question whether it is worthwhile to carry out systematic evaluation. That is, whether it is worthwhile to do any more than run through a simple checklist from time to time or ask members of target groups, clients or participants very briefly about their satisfaction and requirements.

Products such as teaching materials or a course can be evaluated with relative ease by experts and users. If you wish to determine the extent to which target groups learn from a product, the evaluation begins to resemble that of an activity, since one is then evaluating the use of a product within the framework of an activity. For this reason we will refer only to 'activities' below.

The activity in general

2 Clear definition of the activity

It must be possible to describe an activity clearly. It must be clear where and when the activity takes place.

The activity should be reasonably stable overtime, in other words not always being set up and implemented differently. Evaluation of a one-off activity is possible, but you would not invest so much in it.

It is also important to be able to assume that the activity will be implemented as planned or that you can determine the extent to which it was or was not done. Also, when evaluating the effects of the use of a product, it is important to determine the extent to which the product was actually used.

The objectives of the activity

3 Clear objectives

An activity is always evaluated against certain criteria. Often the most important criterion is whether the activity has any effect. The intended effects are referred to as objectives and the evaluation determines if the objectives were achieved. That can only happen if these objectives have been clearly formulated.

4   Measurable results

Objectives must not only be clear, they must be measurable. For example: 'to contribute to the development of a sustainable society' is not an easily measured objective.

The implementation of the evaluation

5   Availability of suitable times

The scheduling of the activity must make it possible to collect data prior to, during and/or after the activity.

6   Accessibility of participants

Where data must be collected before or after an activity, you have to know how to contact the participants.

7   Willingness of participants to cooperate

Participants must be willing to help with providing information or to assist in collecting data from others, for example asking teachers to collect data from their pupils.

8   Language skills of participants

All methods of data collection, apart from observation and assessment by third parties, require some language skills on the part of the participants.

Interpreting and using the results

9   Expectation of learning results

You must have some expectation that the participants will achieve certain learning results. Without such an expectation there is no point in evaluation and you probably would not even embark on the activity. However, this is not entirely self-evident. Sometimes participants already have the skills and knowledge at which the activity is aimed. Sometimes the majority of people who sign up for an activity are already very active and come more for the social contact than to learn anything new. Sometimes participants are not very open to the planned learning processes due to lack of interest or motivation, for example, when participation is compulsory.

10   Assessment of the learning results

The significance of the results is not always obvious. You must be able to make a comparison with something else. For example, are they roughly what you could have expected? If an activity has not previously been systematically evaluated, it can be diffi-cult to determine whether you should regard the results as good or poor. Only by carrying out several such evaluations or by using experience gained elsewhere can you obtain comparative material.

11 Clear relationships between cause and effect

As long as you are only evaluating to determine to what extent objectives are achieved and to present a justification based on that, the measurement of the results is sufficient. The only complication is that you must be able to establish that the results really are the effect of the activity and not of something else.

There are various ways of making a reasonable case to say that the results could not have been caused by something else. For example, it is plausible that the results were not obtained elsewhere:

- if the activity takes place in a relatively short, continuous period then the participants will have little chance to learn similar things in the meantime;
- if the activity is aimed at fairly specific goals then the knowledge and skills [. . .] cannot easily be picked up elsewhere;
- if clear links can be established between the means used (content, working methods, materials, activities) and the objectives.

It is even more useful if you have some idea of how the involvement of the participants in the activities can lead to the desired learning results. In other words, how the participants can acquire the envisaged knowledge, skills and attitudes. We are now in the realms of educational psychology.

[. . .]

READING 10.2 EDUCATION AND CONSERVATION: AN EVALUATION OF THE CONTRIBUTIONS OF EDUCATION PROGRAMMES TO CONSERVATION WITHIN THE WWF NETWORK

World Wildlife Fund

Source: WWF International and WWF-US, Gland/Washington, 1999: 15, 17–20

[. . .]

It is appropriate here to briefly outline what we see as the scope and purpose of education within conservation for this view shaped our deliberations.

Environmental education is a process for facilitating the development of the knowledge, skills, attitudes and values that people can use to contribute positively to conservation. As such, it addresses a wide range of audiences in formal, nonformal and informal education settings. It is as relevant for political and business leaders as it is for members of the general public whether they be attending schools or learning from TV and newspapers, attending various sorts of community meetings and discussions, or participating in a conservation action group.

Environmental education combines strategies from pedagogy (the processes of teaching and learning), behavioural research, social marketing, gender analysis and participatory methodologies, as well as information and communications. These strategies are integrated in education projects – in particular combinations – in order to encourage people to explore and evaluate their actions around specific environmental issues as well as develop the knowledge and skills required to undertake a broad range of longer-term changes in the social and economic settings that challenge sustainability.

Environmental education can be a pivotal process within conservation. Conserving biodiversity depends on creating practical policies and programs that are based on a sound understanding of human motivations and behaviour. Environmental education programmes can help to uncover the intrinsic logic of human behaviour which, in turn, can reduce uncertainties in programmes, thereby helping conservation managers anticipate the problems and fears of local people, and weigh the costs and benefits of alternative conservation processes.

(Adapted from Foster-Turley 1996)

[. . .]

Evaluation terminology

The following clarification of evaluation terminology explains the definitions used in the analysis of the achievements of educational work throughout this report.

> Evaluation is the key to improved programming. It suggests how the programme may be modified and help direct long term planning. The power and efficacy of education can be realised as programmes are evaluated, the results reported to all concerned, and the information used to make future education programmes even better.
>
> (Blanchard 1995)

Outputs

Outputs are the material products of a programme or project. They normally do not have value in and of themselves but rather as tools for, or contributions to, the achievement of outcomes and impacts.

Outcomes

Outcomes are the achievements or changes brought about by a programme, project or activity that, although potentially short-term, provide a supportive context or infrastructure for longer-term cumulative effects, or impacts.

Impacts

Impacts are the longer-term cumulative effects of a programme, project or activity and embody lasting changes. These could be in conservation practices, the conservation status of an area, in education provision, and in the ways in which people think and live.

Using this terminology, the achievements of educational work in WWF may be analysed in the following [. . .] categories.

1   Conservation outcomes

Conservation outcomes relate to the conditions necessary for the achievement of conservation impacts/goals. That is, they constitute improvements in the capacity to plan and manage strategies for conservation and normally provide conditions that enable the achievement of an intended or potential conservation impact. Examples include: raised levels of public understanding and support for biodiversity, improved management of an environmental reserve, a new Local *Agenda 21* plan, ISO 14001 accreditation for a company, or new legislation or policies for environmental protection and conservation.

2   Conservation impacts

Conservation impacts are the result of the sustained achievement of conservation goals. Examples of conservation impacts include: long-term improvements in the biodiversity status of an ecoregion, the effective and long-term management of natural resources, increased numbers of an endangered species, sustained improvements in stream quality, a well-managed fishery, etc. Education can be integrated with other strategies for conservation to achieve these impacts. Indeed, it is very important to recognise that conservation impacts are only feasible where understanding, commitment and other aspects of social capacity have been developed to ensure their sustainability.

3   Educational outputs

Educational outputs are generally seen by education and conservation staff in WWF as comprising publications such as textbooks, posters, stickers, teaching units, guides and kits, videos, CD-ROMs and a great variety of similar materials. They also include: baseline studies, training courses, and the variety of materials produced for the informal education of the general community such as books, brochures, Internet sites, public displays and exhibitions, radio and television programmes, and public service announcements.

However, unless teaching and learning processes – directed at enhancing environmental understanding and sensitivity, and motivating people to participate actively in conservation – are embedded in these outputs, they are not really *educational* outputs. Instead, they are closer to being information or communication outputs and, as such, require further development and enhancement if their educational value is to be maximised.

Conservation outputs include:

* wildlife surveys
* environmental legislation
* a set of Global 200 maps
* scientific reports and conference papers

Education does not play a major role in the achievement of such conservation outputs. However, the credibility of WWF's education programmes depends upon the credibility of WWF's science. Education programmes can also make effective use of conservation outputs.

For example: *Exploring Europe's Environment* is a multimedia resource (an educational output) that has been developed to encourage students in Europe to explore local and regional environmental issues. The product draws extensively on *Europe's Environment: The Dobris Assessment* – the most detailed and comprehensive review available on the state of the environment in Europe. Four themes are covered: water and rivers, coasts and seas, forests, and urban areas. The educational materials include: a teacher's handbook and two diskettes containing text, photos, maps and statistical data. The project builds on the experience of WWF-UK (as leading partner), WWF-Belgium, WWF-Italy, WWF-Spain and WWF-Sweden who are participating in the project. The resource is available in English. A CD-ROM in Spanish and English is under production and other language versions are planned.

(Minutes of the 1998 WWF European Education Network Meeting)

4   Educational outcomes

Educational outcomes include: increased levels of knowledge and understanding of conservation issues and principles, strengthened commitment to biodiversity values, and an enhanced capacity to work for the achievement of conservation goals. Educational outcomes are both people- and system-focussed, and support the ability of individuals and communities to analyse conservation issues in their ecological, political and socio-economic contexts, to envision and evaluate alternative solutions and scenarios, to make action plans, and to work cooperatively with others to implement them effectively.

Educational outcomes can be viewed as capacity building within educational and related systems. Educational outcomes help to establish the policy as well as the institutional and human capacity to support the realisation of educational impacts and, in turn, conservation outcomes and impacts.

Educational activities tend to have their greatest impact on conservation goals in the long term. Indeed, like conservation impacts, educational impacts tend to be realised only over the longer term.

This means that educational outcomes are rooted in present issues and contexts, but are also future oriented – towards the time when they will have developed the capacity to resolve the environmental problems that concern them and, in so doing, reduce the impacts of human activities on ecosystems.

Educational outcomes that support this capacity-building goal include the development of appropriate social and educational infrastructures. Such system-focussed outcomes include:

- the integration of conservation and sustainability goals into wider social and educational policies, core curricula, syllabuses, and schemes of work;
- the development of related strategic plans and learning resources;
- the creation of a network of supporters and donors for environmental education work;
- the preparation of professional development guides and their integration into a regular programme of training for conservation and education officers, teachers and teacher educators;
- the development and servicing of networks of environmental educators;
- the promotion of evaluation studies and processes for learning from them; and
- research into effective planning strategies and resources for improving education work.

5   Educational impacts

As long-term educational goals, educational impacts are mostly expressed in general terms, such as the 'cultured individual', the 'active citizen', the 'good parent', or the 'technologically literate worker'. Conservation equivalents would be the 'environmentally literate individual', the 'environmentally concerned citizen', someone who lives a 'sustainable lifestyle', and so on.

Such goals have to be expressed in general terms for a number of reasons. Firstly, it is not possible to specify in advance what such future-orientated goals will mean in any detail because circumstances and contexts change so much over time. Secondly, because many are value-laden it would be improper to specify what these should be in the many different cultural contexts in which WWF operates. The participatory and democratic foundations of the sustainable society upon which conservation depends demands that we not be too explicit about what these long-term goals mean as they must remain relevant not just to different geographic and cultural contexts but also to future contexts in which people will live.

What should we evaluate?

Threatened Species Network – WWF-Australia

The Threatened Species Network (TSN) is a community education and action programme funded by the Endangered Species Program of the Natural Heritage Trust of the Australian government and WWF-Australia. TSN aims to facilitate the recovery of threatened species and ecological communities by assisting concerned citizens to "participate in and enjoy activities that promote the recovery of our threatened flora and fauna".

The ideal *conservation impact* of the Network would be the recovery of a number of threatened species and ecological communities to the point where they met criteria established in their recovery plans to be down-listed or removed from the Endangered Species Act schedules. We are yet to achieve this and, nationally, only one species so far has been de-listed from the Act due to conservation work.

Our *conservation outcomes* include the development of recovery plans for a substantial number of endangered species and ecosystems. We also have developed a strong network of local action groups across the country who are skilled in implementing these plans. The level of media coverage of the Network is recorded and is growing substantially in terms of both quantity and quality. Political support for the Network is growing also, as indicated by the 200% increase in annual Natural Heritage Trust (government) funding from 1996 to 1998.

> Educational evaluation within WWF must focus upon both:
> - educational and conservation outcomes,
> and
> - measures of achieved and potential impacts in conservation and education.

The Network also measures a number of *conservation outputs*. For example, the Network undertook conservation activities directed at 86 species, groups of species, ecological communities and mitigating threatening processes in 1997/98. In South Australia, 115 community conservation projects were promoted during the year and, in the six months prior to January 1999, the South Australian Threatened Plant Action Group spent more than 40 volunteer days undertaking substantial recovery action for 24 threatened plant species and 5 ecosystems, mostly involving intensive weeding, covering 370 hectares.

In terms of *educational outputs*, project statistics show that, in the month of June 1998 alone, the Network answered 444 enquiries; contacted around 303,000 people through its activities and publications; had 73 inquiries about volunteer and work experience; referred 32 people to government agency programs; and gave 10 presentations to a total of 335 people.

Our main *educational outcome* is an increase in the popular awareness of, and participation in, conservation of threatened biota. Regrettably, we have not yet commissioned any sort of baseline survey to ascertain future change attributable to the Network, although one is planned.

(Source: Jamie Pittock, WWF-Australia)

Two dilemmas for evaluators

The process of evaluation is often fraught with conceptual and practical difficulties. Two that were significant in seeking to identify, and find evidence of, the outputs, outcomes and impacts of education across the network in this evaluation were: (i) the close relationship between these measures of achievement, and (ii) the timing of evaluation in relation to these different achievements.

While it is generally easier to achieve (and measure) an output or outcome than to ensure that education work has an impact, all three are closely related. For example, in relation to WWF-UK, it could be argued that the quality and range of its extensive publications programmes (outputs) and its role in the development of national-level policy support for environmental education (an outcome) have led to some schools moving away from 'green tokenism' to teaching about deeper issues of local and global sustainability (an impact). While such an impact is a long-term aim of WWF-UK, it would take a brave evaluator to claim that there is a causal link between the outputs and outcomes and this impact, and that these are also having an impact on the conservation status of school grounds and their neighbouring environments.

Nevertheless, when appropriately focused and developed, educational activities can lead to enhanced social capacity for achieving conservation outcomes and impacts. However, this brings a second dilemma for evaluators, especially those with a fixed time limit. Evaluations can only be made of past and present activities and existing outcomes. Good intentions and potential outcomes and impacts cannot be evaluated.

Conservation is a long-term process and its impacts usually take many years to achieve. It is the same with education. Thus, two key questions that must be faced are: 'How can long-term conservation and education impacts be measured?' and 'How long do you have to – or can you and stakeholders afford to – wait for actual evidence?'

This dilemma means that evaluators have to identify and use 'proxy measures' or impact in the form of educational and conservation outcomes in the meanwhile. As a result, the evaluation of educational activities must focus upon both (i) educational and conservation outcomes and (ii) measures of achieved and potential conservation and education impacts. This is what has been done in this evaluation.

[. . .]

VIGNETTE 10.1 LEARNING ABOUT LEARNING

J. Braus, World Wildlife Fund

I don't pretend we have the answers. But the questions are certainly worth thinking about.

(Arthur C. Clarke)

Both readings highlight many of the dilemmas of evaluation. *Evaluating Environmental Education* points out that clear and measurable evaluation targets are needed, and goes on to suggest that trying to measure "how a program contributes to the development of a sustainable society" is not an objective that you can easily measure. The problem is that's exactly what many environmental educators want to measure. We know that we can show that people learned something about the creatures that live in a forest or how a bill becomes a law, and we can show how much people like our programs or materials. It is much harder, however, to show how educational experiences influence attitudes and behaviors and whether they will ever lead to environmentally positive behavior or a more sustainable future. For example, will our education efforts result in more people who reduce their use of toxic chemicals, volunteer for a restoration project, recycle, or buy a low emissions car? And if we can't show the connection between education and conservation, how can we justify spending limited resources on an activity that might be a good thing to do, but not necessarily a critical one in slowing biodiversity loss in the immediate future?

This raises the issue of long-term change. Some people say we can't wait for education to work: biodiversity is disappearing before our eyes – we don't have time to educate. We might have time for a communication campaign – but what we really need are more policies, parks, business deals, and treaties. But supporters of education say that we need both. We can't afford *not* to educate because we need people to care enough to protect the environment, uphold the laws, and demand environmentally-sound business practices. Because educators can't prove that the money they spend on their education programs will eventually (2–50 years on) lead to a more concerned and caring constituency, there's a constant debate about the value of education. Thus, it often comes down to a conviction about education and the importance of engaging citizens, communities, and stakeholders.

The WWF report, *Education and Conservation: an evaluation of the contributions of education programmes to conservation within the WWF Network*, tried to evaluate the effectiveness of environmental education throughout the WWF network over the past decade. Trying to evaluate this across 40 countries was no easy task, especially when interviews revealed a wide range of ideas about what education was for. Similarly, there were very different perceptions about *education, communication*, and *capacity building*, with terms often used interchangeably. The evaluation examined educational achievements throughout the WWF network by looking at outputs (material products such as posters, workshops, books, stickers), outcomes (achievements or changes that occur as part of a program), and impacts (the longer-term, cumulative effects of a project or activity that contribute to lasting changes), and did this for both education and conservation. The easiest to measure are outputs. The hardest are impacts. While most of us will evaluate the things we produce, few evaluate short-term achievements, and hardly any of us successfully measure the long-term conservation impacts in ways that are realistic and/or convincing.

Even if you're not trying to show conservation impacts, evaluation is still tricky. For example, the tips outlined in *Evaluating Environmental Education* are helpful and make perfect sense. However, evaluating things like curriculum is never easy to do. If you choose to measure student knowledge gain, a formal assessment can cost a lot of money. Does it really make sense to spend $25,000 or more to prepare a pretest and post-test just to confirm that students learned something? Many programs around the world don't have that kind of money for their implementation, let alone evaluation. And what of the harder questions such as how long will students retain the information? Was it the right information that would contribute to greater understanding and insight? Did it change or influence attitudes and worldviews? Would something else have been more effective?

The two evaluation readings also highlight a number of questions that environmental educators, evaluation experts, funders, and others still need to sort out if we want to have the greatest impact with our efforts. These questions include:

- *What's most important to evaluate?* If program managers have limited funding, their first priority will probably be to show the funder that their money was well spent, or to show that what they're doing contributes to the mission of the organization. However, that often means focusing on numbers of people reached, workshops held, and so on, which can leave unanswered questions that might ultimately be far more important in helping to create a more sustainable society. For example, interviews with participants, action research techniques (where learners continually reflect on what they did), and smaller, in-depth, qualitative studies are often more insightful than generalized surveys and tests. Although we need different evaluation strategies, many who make decisions about a program haven't been trained in evaluation and don't know what their options are, or how to interpret qualitative results.
- *Do individuals count?* The two readings touched on an environmental education problem that doesn't directly relate to evaluation. Some people have difficulty with judging the worth of education programs that create individual learning because

they don't believe individuals matter in long-term conservation efforts. People who believe this are more concerned with changing policies, governments, and other societal and institutional structures, rather than reaching individuals who vote for policies, use natural resources, and make up those institutions. Without individuals how can we ever achieve our conservation mission? It seems that our society needs to be clearer about why education is important – for conservation and for achieving a more just and sustainable world. But for those people who don't think that individuals count, no evidence of individual change will likely convince them that education is important.

- *Is communication faster and better?* Many people point to social marketing and other communication efforts as more effective strategies than education because they can reach more people in less time, and they use market research more strategically, with specific actions in mind. They point to communication success with health issues (e.g., campaigns with messages such as use condoms, don't smoke, wear a seat belt). Educators have not been able to convincingly show that education and more in-depth experiences are also critical if we want to create lasting change, and it's still not clear to decision makers about when to use social marketing, when education, when information, and when something else, and why all these strategies have a role.

- *If we can't measure impact, is it worthwhile?* People aren't lab experiments and they don't all react in the same predictable way after having an educational experience. Education takes people on a journey, without a specified outcome. But you can take the pulse along the way (and revise and adapt as needed) and help provide experiences that might influence worldviews, attitudes, and beliefs. We also know that research shows that if people have more hands-on experiences with nature, good mentors, and success in taking part in environmental action projects, they are more likely to care about the environment and be engaged citizens.

- *How much knowledge?* We do a better job of measuring knowledge gains because that's easier than measuring changes in attitudes and behaviors. But what types of knowledge are most critical (and who decides)? And if we don't know how knowledge gains will contribute to attitudes and behavior changes, how do we decide what knowledge is most critical? We also know that behavior change doesn't follow a linear model, so bombarding people with information won't necessarily lead to behavior change. However, many learners are swayed by knowledge – and it can form a foundation for our beliefs and attitudes. So we need more discussion about when to measure knowledge gains and when to focus on attitudes and behaviors and how we can best decide when to do what.

One day we'll realize that education is actually our fulcrum for conservation success. Information, communication, and other tools may give us short-term conservation successes enforced by policies, but as the editors note elsewhere, "no policy objective can be (or has ever) been sustained over 50–100 years in the face of popular indifference or opposition. Education engages learners in terms of their own knowledge, beliefs, and interests." If done well, it pushes individuals to think, reflect, debate, challenge the status quo, and become empowered players in creating their own future. And evaluation, if done well, can help ensure that we're on the right path with education. We need more of both.

VIGNETTE 10.2 EVALUATING ENVIRONMENTAL EDUCATION: THE MEANING OF STANDARDISATION AND THE LANGUAGE OF INSTRUMENTALISM

A.E.J. Wals, Wageningen University

Evaluation has always been a prime topic of educational research and has preoccupied many experts and professional organisations. One could argue that the field of environmental education has been somewhat slow in developing this area of expertise or in benefiting from the work done in related educational fields. Nonetheless, whether driven by the demand for "proof" by sponsors of environmental education or by criticism by conservative lobbying groups (Sanera 1998) or by a more intrinsically felt need among environmental educators to improve practice, there now seems to be increased attention in the field to evaluation. The recent works published by the IUCN (Stokking *et al.* 1999) and by WWF (1999) are just two examples of sponsors of environmental education seeking to promote evaluation by presenting sets of evaluation guidelines. These two works are interesting since they take on quite a different perspective on evaluation. Regrettably these perspectives are not always made explicit, but they tend to reveal themselves when critically examining the language that is used to describe the evaluation activity.

In order to examine this language, it is helpful to recognise one of the dichotomies running through many environmental education programmes, namely, the one running between instrumental and emancipatory approaches. It can be argued that this dichotomy leads to varying degrees of openness of the evaluation process, goals and intended outcomes, as well as varying degrees of participation and ownership (Wals and Jickling 2000). In the past these tensions have been reduced to a somewhat overly simplified distinction between behaviourist and non-behaviourist environmental education. Educating within the behaviourist paradigm implies a specific view on the role of education in society, as does operating within a non-behaviourist paradigm. One could argue that the current environmental or ecological crisis is deeply rooted in a deterministic world view and its positivist and behaviourist science traditions (Plant 2001). It is then questionable that the same world view and science tradition is able to solve the very crisis to which it contributed. When the design (i.e. establishing causality, standardising responses) and purpose (i.e. accountability, comparison and transferability) of evaluation mimics such a world then evaluation could easily become an extension of unsustainable practice.

In the world of positivism or, as Gough puts it "in an arena in which legitimation and management are routine prerequisites of successful change" (Gough, S.R. 2001: 119), setting standards may seem logical, desirable and feasible. Basically the setting of standards is an issue of reaching some kind of expert-driven consensus on universal goals, objectives, methods, learning outcomes and the ways of measuring them. One could even design some kind of benchmarking or accreditation system for environmental education. Such standardisation would also lead to standardised evaluation procedures which would allow for comparisons. One could argue that for emancipatory environmental education the setting of standards and the homogenisation of evaluation procedures is somewhat contradictory since human needs and interests – fortunately, perhaps – vary with context. This implies that the act of evaluation is not, in the words of Stables, "a culturally neutral or value-free package that can be 'delivered'" (Stables 2001b: 121). Evaluation then should recognise, as the WWF publication does, that all actors have unique perspectives on what constitutes an improvement.

> As knowledge and understanding are socially constructed, they are functions of each individual's unique context and past. There is, therefore, no single "correct" understanding. What we take to be true depends on the framework of knowledge and the assumptions we bring with us.
>
> (WWF 1999: 15)

When scrutinising the work published by the IUCN (Stokking *et al.* 1999) the language of instrumentalism reveals itself quite clearly in the chapter titled *Introducing evaluation as a regular activity in an organisation: What do you need and how do you approach it?* The chapter begins by telling the reader what kinds of objectives one – to borrow from the chapter title – needs: These include: the ability to compare *the market position* of the organisation with other *providers*, the evaluation of one or more *products* for particular *client target groups*, *accountability* and *public relations*. The chapter continues by outlining the conditions that need to be met in order for an organisation to introduce regular evaluation, one of them being that there should be *clear relationships between cause and effect* (p. 23). The authors write here that *you must be able to establish that the results really are the effect of the activity and not of something else* (p. 23). Apparently the authors are firmly grounded in the belief that human ideas, experiences, and intentions are objective things like molecules and atoms that are related through some kind of billiard ball causality that can be manipulated, measured and controlled.

The WWF publication is far less prescriptive in terms of telling people what they need or should do, more explicit in terms of the author's own perspective of environmental education and the role of evaluation, and less deterministic in terms of stating, in advance, the intended outcomes of an activity. The authors recognise the open-ended nature of the educational process: "the participatory and democratic foundations of *the* [italics mine] sustainable society upon which conservation depends demands that we not be too explicit about what these long-term goals mean . . ." (WWF 1999: 19). A distinction is made between outcomes, impacts and outputs. The educational impact – with long-term aspects – of an environmental education programme is considered by the authors as being the most important, but also the hardest to evaluate. The authors seem to recognise that "What you cannot measure, still exists" (Wals 1993) and that one should not put all one's evaluation eggs in the measurement basket. The latter is supported by Rickinson who, in his extensive report on the "evidence base" on learning and learners in environmental education, notes that the evidence base, ". . . while considerable in size, is less diverse in terms of methodological and theoretical approaches . . ." (Rickinson 2001: 207). The WWF work hints at a more contextual approach that allows for diversity of evaluation methods and ownership of the evaluation process by those engaged in the educational process, and not by those external to the process, i.e. outside "professional" evaluators.

Many researchers and evaluation-experts have tried to structure environmental education by using hierarchical levels of universal goals and objectives (Wals and van der Leij 1997). Outside experts determine what the learners need in terms of knowledge, attitudes, values and skills; design a curriculum or programme of activities that consists of measurable/quantifiable goals and objectives; implement the programme; test to what extent the goals and objectives are realised; modify the programme and re-instruct the teacher. In the worst case scenario, the students become a database or an "input" while the teacher becomes an implementation instrument. The IUCN publication seems to underscore this. This widely used positivistic approach to educational research and development often results in ignoring the learners' own ideas and experiences, as well as those of the facilitator of learning. The primary participants in the educational process apparently are not viewed as capable of determining the content of their own education, of setting their own goals and objectives and, finally, are not allowed to evaluate their own teaching and learning. Alienation, for instance, between outside evaluators and the school community and disempowerment of teachers and students who have been denied a role in shaping and evaluating their own education, often is the result.

At the same time we must recognise the tension between the need for contextual appropriateness and relevance on the one hand, and the call for universal evaluation guidelines and standards on the other. The WWF publication at least appears to be struggling with this tension, whereas the IUCN publication fails to recognise it. One way to resolve this tension might be to raise some critical questions with regards to the content, outcomes and process of evaluation and with regards to the use of standards (see Wals and Jickling 2000):

- *Question with regards to content*: Who selects the content of the learning process? Does the content of the learning process meaningfully relate to the world of the learner? Does the content motivate and challenge the learner? Does the content of the learning process stimulate active participation?
- *Questions with regards to outcomes*: Who determines the learning outcomes? What is the nature of the outcomes sought? Are they of a behavioural change nature or of a human development nature (i.e. a focus on critical understanding, heightened awareness, personal values, social norms, etc.)? What process is used to determine the learning outcomes? How are the learning outcomes evaluated? Are the outcomes fixed or can they be adapted as the learning process moves on and the context transforms?
- *Questions with regards to process*: Does the learning process depart from the participants' own ideas, interests, values, etc? Does the learning process allow for active participation, democratic process, ownership and empowerment to emerge? Does the learning process allow for multiple perspectives to enter? Is there room for outcomes that cannot be predicted in advance?
- *Questions with regards to standards*: Questions can be raised about the use of "standards": Are they used in a universal or more contextual way? Are they used to serve a specific political agenda, a basis for comparison or rather as a means to work towards excellence? Are they dynamic and flexible or static and carved in stone? Are they prescriptive (providing rules, rights and wrongs, do's and don'ts) or more descriptive (encouraging reflection, raising questions, providing a range of possibilities and choices). Have they been determined by outside experts or by a community of learners through an open process (which does not exclude the input by experts!)?

From an emancipatory point of view, emphasis in evaluation is placed on documenting and describing human experience and intentions, using a variety of methods. The main objective is not to find out or prove the kinds of changes that occur in the learner as a result of an educational activity, but to find out whether the activity and the context in which it was carried out provided for such change. When taking on such a perspective it can also be argued that the evaluation of any activity should have a pedagogical end in itself, in the sense that the participants themselves should somehow benefit from the evaluation. Thus, evaluation should not just be an attempt to learn about people, but to come to know with them the reality that challenges them.

CHAPTER 11

BUILDING CAPACITY: DEVELOPING AGENCY

READING 11.1 OUR COMMON FUTURE

World Commision on Environment and Development
Source: Oxford University Press, Oxford, 1987: 358–367, 370–374

[. . .]

Getting at the sources

National policies and institutions

The way countries achieve sustainable development will vary among the many different political and economic systems around the world. Governments differ greatly in their capacity to monitor and evaluate sustainable development, and many will need assistance. Several features should be common to most countries.

Sustainable development objectives should be incorporated in the terms of reference of those cabinet and legislative committees dealing with national economic policy and planning as well as those dealing with key sectoral and international policies. As an extension of this, the major central economic and sectoral agencies of governments should now be made directly responsible and fully accountable for ensuring that their policies, programmes, and budgets support development that is ecologically as well as economically sustainable.

Where resources and data permit, an annual report and an audit on changes in environmental quality and in the stock of the nation's environmental resource assets are needed to complement the traditional annual fiscal budget and economic development plans.[1] These are essential to obtain an accurate picture of the true health and wealth of the national economy, and to assess progress towards sustainable development.[2]

Governments that have not done so should consider developing a 'foreign policy for the environment'.[3] A nation's foreign policy needs to reflect the fact that its policies have a growing impact on the environmental resource base of other nations and the commons, just as the policies of other nations have an impact on its own. This is true of certain energy, agricultural, and other sectoral policies discussed in this report, as well as certain foreign investment, trade, and development assistance policies and those concerning the import or export of hazardous chemicals, wastes, and technology.

Regional and interregional action

The existing regional and subregional organizations within and outside the UN system need to be strengthened and made responsible and accountable for ensuring that their programmes and budgets encourage and support sustainable development policies and practices. In some areas, however, especially among developing countries, new regional and subregional arrangements will be needed to deal with transboundary environmental resource issues.

Some countries already enjoy comparatively well developed bilateral and regional structures, although many of them lack the mandate and support required to carry out the greatly expanded role they must assume in the future. These include many specialized bilateral organizations such as the Canada/USA International Joint Commission; subregional agencies in Europe such as the different Commissions for the Rhine River, the Danube River, and the Baltic Sea, and organizations such as the Council of Mutual Economic Assistance (CMEA), the Organisation for Economic Co-operation and Development (OECD), and the European Economic Community. These bodies provide member countries with a strong foundation on which to build. Although most of them have effective programmes for international co-operation on environmental protection and natural resources management, these programmes will need to be strengthened and adapted to new priorities. The regional organizations in particular need to do more to integrate environment fully in their macroeconomic, trade, energy, and other sectoral programmes.

> All governments should develop a 'foreign policy for the environment' as one major way of improving the international co-ordination of national environmental policies.
>
> But in the long-term perspective, and here I think the World Commission could have an important message, I think that it will be politically sound and wise to get support from the NGOs to prepare for changes that have to take place anyway sooner or later. So I think it would be politically wise to look into that in a much broader way than what has been done so far.
>
> (Segnestam 1985)

Similar organizations among developing countries should be strengthened, particularly at bilateral and subregional levels. Organizations such as the Organization of African Unity, the Southern Africa Development Coordination Conference, the Gulf Cooperation Council, the Arab League, the Organization of American States, the Association of South East Asian Nations, and the South Asian Association for Regional Cooperation could work together to develop contingency plans and the capacity to respond quickly to critical situations and issues. They need in such bodies to develop comparable economic and environmental statistics, base-line quantity and quality surveys of shared resources, and early-warning capabilities to reduce environment and development hazards. They could develop and apply in concert basic common principles and guidelines concerning environmental protection and resource use, particularly with respect to foreign trade and investment. In this respect, developing countries have much to gain through sharing their common experiences and taking common action.

A new focus on the sustainable use and management of transboundary ecological zones, systems, and resources is also needed. There are, for example, over 200 distinct biogeographic zones in the world. Moreover, most non-island countries in the world share at least one international river basin. The entire national territories of nearly one-quarter of those countries is part of an international river basin. Yet over one-third of the 200 major international river basins in the world are not covered by any international agreement, and fewer than 30 have any co-operative institutional arrangements. These gaps are particularly acute in Africa, Asia, and Latin America, which together have 144 international river basins.[4]

Governments, directly and through the UN Environment Programme (UNEP) and the International Union for the Conservation of Nature and Natural Resources (IUCN), should support the development of regional and subregional co-operative arrangements for the protection and sustained use of transboundary ecological systems

In retrospect, even if the institutional and policy goals of the decade had been achieved, one is left with the feeling that most developing countries would be only marginally better off than they are today. The reason for this is a striking and humbling one. Although governments, environmentalists, and the aid agencies kept their eye on the environmental ball during the 1970s and the early 1980s, recent events have starkly demonstrated that they were watching the wrong ball. While the world was worrying about the environmental impacts of investments, controlling pollution, and conserving resources, we collectively failed to notice the dramatic decline in what had complacently been called 'renewable resources'.

(Runnals 1986)

with joint action programmes to combat common problems such as desertification and acidification.

Global institutions and programmes

At the global level, an extensive institutional capacity exists that could be redirected towards sustainable development. The United Nations, as the only inter-governmental organization with universal membership, should clearly be the locus for new institutional initiatives of a global character.

Although the funds flowing to developing countries through UN programmes represents a relatively small portion of total official development assistance (ODA) flows, the UN can and should be a source of significant leadership in the transition to sustainable development and in support of developing countries in effecting this transition. Under existing conditions the UN system's influence is often fragmented and less effective than it might be because of the independent character of the specialized agencies and endemic weaknesses of co-ordination. However, recent moves towards organizational reform and greater economy and efficiency could improve the capacity of the UN to provide this leadership, and should include sustainable development as an important criterion.

All major international bodies and agencies of the UN system should be made responsible and accountable for ensuring that their programmes and budgets encourage and support development policies and practices that are sustainable. Governments, through parallel resolutions in the respective governing bodies, should now begin to reorient and refocus the mandates, programmes, and budgets of key agencies to support sustainable development. They should also insist on much greater co-ordination and co-operation among them.

Each agency will need to redeploy some staff and financial resources to establish a small but high-level centre of leadership and expertise. That centre should be linked to the programme planning and budget processes.

Each agency should be directly responsible for ensuring that the environmental and resource aspects of programmes and projects are properly taken into account when they are being planned, and that the financial resources needed are provided directly from its own budget. In line with these new responsibilities, the following bodies should also assume full financial responsibility within their own budgets for certain programmes presently supported by the Environment Fund of UNEP: the World Health Organization on 'Environmental Health', the Food and Agriculture Organization (FAO) on 'Agricultural Chemicals and Residues', the UN Disaster Relief Office on 'Natural Disasters', the UN Industrial Development Organization on 'Industry and Transport', the International Labour Organization on 'Working Environment', the UN Department for Disarmament Affairs on 'Arms Race and the Environment', the Department for International Economic and Social Affairs on 'Environmental Aspects of Development

Planning and Cooperation', the UN Educational, Scientific, and Cultural Organization (UNESCO) on 'Education', and the UN Development Programme (UNDP) on 'Technical Cooperation'. UNEP (discussed extensively in the next section) should continue to co-operate closely with these agencies and help identify new programme needs and monitor performance.

As in each agency, there is also a need for a high-level centre of leadership for the UN system as a whole with the capacity to assess, advise, assist, and report on progress made and needed for sustainable development. That leadership should be provided by the Secretary-General of the United Nations Organization.

Governments at the UN General Assembly should therefore take the necessary measures to reinforce the system-wide responsibility and authority of the UN Secretary-General concerning interagency co-ordination and co-operation generally, and for achieving sustainable development specifically. This will require that the representatives of those same governments in the governing bodies of all major UN organizations and specialized agencies take complementary measures. This could be done as an integral part of the parallel resolutions just proposed on building sustainable development objectives and criteria into the mandates, programmes, and budget of each agency.

To help launch and guide the interagency co-ordination and co-operation that will be needed, the UN Secretary-General should constitute under his chairmanship a special UN Board for Sustainable Development. The principal function of the Board would be to agree on combined tasks to be undertaken by the agencies to deal effectively with the many critical issues of sustainable development that cut across agency and national boundaries.

Dealing with the effects

Governments should also strengthen the role and capacity of existing environmental protection and resource management agencies.[5]

National environmental protection and natural resources management agencies

Strengthening of environmental agencies is needed most urgently in developing countries. Those that have not established such agencies should do so as a matter of priority. In both cases, bilateral and multilateral organizations must be prepared to provide increased assistance for institutional development. Some of this increased financial support should go to community groups and non-governmental organizations (NGOs), which are rapidly emerging as important and cost-effective partners in work to protect and improve the environment locally and nationally, and in developing and implementing national conservation strategies.

Industrialized countries also need greatly strengthened environmental protection and resource management agencies. Most face a continuing backlog of pollution problems and a growing range of environment and resource management problems too. In addition, these agencies will be called upon to advise and assist central economic and sectoral agencies as they take up their new responsibilities for sustainable development. Many now provide institutional support, technical advice, and assistance to their counterpart agencies in developing countries, and this need will grow. And, almost inevitably, they will play a larger and more direct role in international co-operation, working with other countries and international agencies trying to cope with regional and global environmental problems.

Strengthen the United Nations Environment Programme

When UNEP was established in 1972, the UN General Assembly gave it a broad and challenging mandate to stimulate, co-ordinate, and provide policy guidance for environmental action throughout the UN system.[6] That mandate was to be carried out by a Governing Council of 58 member states, a high-level UN interagency Environment Coordination Board (ECB),[7] a relatively small secretariat located in Nairobi, and a voluntary fund set initially at a level of $100 million for the first five years. UNEP's principal task was to exercise leadership and a catalytic influence on the programmes and projects of other international organizations, primarily in but also outside the UN system. Over the past 10 years, the Environment Fund has levelled off at around $30 million annually, while its range of tasks and activities have increased substantially.

This Commission has recommended a major reorientation and refocusing of programmes and budgets on sustainable development in and among all UN organizations. Within such a new system-wide commitment to and priority effort on sustainable development, UNEP should be the principal source on environmental data, assessment, reporting, and related support for environmental management as well as be the principal advocate and agent for change and co-operation on critical environment and natural resource protection issues. The major priorities and functions of UNEP should be:

- to provide leadership, advice, and guidance in the UN system on restoring, protecting, and improving the ecological basis for sustainable development;
- to monitor, assess, and report regularly on changes in the state of the environment and natural resources (through its Earthwatch programme);
- to support priority scientific and technological research on critical environmental and natural resource protection issues;
- to develop criteria and indicators for environmental quality standards and guidelines for the sustainable use and management of natural resources;
- to support and facilitate the development of action plans for key ecosystems and issues to be implemented and financed by the governments directly concerned;
- to encourage and promote international agreements on critical issues identified by Earthwatch and to support and facilitate the development of international law, conventions, and co-operative arrangements for environmental and natural resource conservation and protection;
- to support the development of the institutional and professional capacity of developing countries in all of these areas and help them develop specific programmes to deal with their problems and advise and assist development assistance agencies in this respect; and
- to provide advice and assistance to the United Nations Development Programme, the World Bank, and other UN organizations and agencies regarding the environmental dimensions of their programmes and technical assistance projects, including training activities.

Focus on environmental protection issues

UNEP has been a key agent in focusing the attention of governments on critical environmental problems (such as deforestation and marine pollution), in helping develop many global and regional action plans and strategies (as on desertification), in contributing to the negotiation and implementation of international conventions (on Protection of the Ozone Layer, for example), and in preparing global guidelines and principles for action by governments (such as on marine pollution from land-based sources). UNEP's Regional Seas Programme has been particularly successful, and could serve as a model for some other areas of special concern, especially international river basins.

UNEP's catalytic and co-ordinating role in the UN system can and should be reinforced and extended. In its future work on critical environmental protection issues, UNEP should focus particularly on:

- developing, testing, and helping to apply practical and simple methodologies for environmental assessment at project and national levels;
- extending international agreements (such as on chemicals and hazardous wastes) more widely;
- extending the Regional Seas Programme;
- developing a similar programme for international river basins; and
- identifying the need for and advising other UN organizations and agencies in establishing and carrying out technical assistance and training courses for environmental protection and management.

Priority to global environmental assessment and reporting

Although more is known about the state of the global environment now than a decade ago, there are still major gaps and a limited international capability for monitoring, collecting, and combining basic and comparable data needed for authoritative overviews of key environmental issues and trends. Without such, the information needed to help set priorities and develop effective policies will remain limited.

UNEP, as the main UN source for environmental data, assessment, and reporting, should guide the global agenda for scientific research and technological development for environmental protection. To this end, the data collection, assessment, and state of the environment reporting functions (Earthwatch) of UNEP need to be significantly strengthened as a major priority. The Global Environment Monitoring System should be expanded as rapidly as possible, and the development of the Global Resource Information Database should be accelerated to bridge the gap between environmental assessment and management. Special priority should be accorded to providing support to developing countries to enable them to participate fully in and derive maximum benefits from these programmes.

> The environment has quickly deteriorated in certain areas and we don't know where to put the thresholds for nature's tolerance. We must move very fast towards a consensus on the necessity for taking urgent action. There is a strong popular support for this in our country. The findings of several opinion polls tell us that ecological issues have heightened priority. People feel anxious about the legacy our generation will be passing on to the next one. A new environmental awareness has germinated among large sections of the community and mainly among young people.
>
> (Nagy 1981)

Strengthen international environmental co-operation

The UNEP Governing Council cannot fulfil its primary role of providing leadership and policy guidance in the UN system nor have a significant influence on national policies unless governments increase their participation and the level of representation. National delegations to future meetings should preferably be led by Ministers, with their senior policy and scientific advisers. Special provisions should be made for expanded and more meaningful participation by major non-governmental organizations at future sessions.

Increase the revenue and focus of the environment fund

The UNEP voluntary funding base of $30 million annually is too limited and vulnerable for an international fund dedicated to serving and protecting the common interests, security, and future of humanity: six countries alone provided over 75 per cent of the 1985 contributions to the Environment Fund (the United States, Japan, USSR, Sweden, the Federal Republic of Germany, and the United Kingdom).[8] Considering the critical importance of renewed efforts on environmental protection and improvement, the Commission appeals to all governments to substantially enlarge the Environment Fund both through direct contributions by all members of the UN and through some of the sources cited later in this chapter in the section 'Investing in Our Future'.

A substantial enlargement of the Environment Fund seems unlikely in the current climate of financial austerity. Any additional funds made available by states for UN development programmes and activities will likely be channelled largely through UNDP and the development programmes of other UN agencies. Moreover, as recommended earlier, the budgets of all of those agencies should be deployed so that environmental considerations are built into the planning and implementation of all programmes and projects.

The Environment Fund can be made more effective by refocusing the programme on fewer activities. As other UN agencies assume full responsibility for certain activities now provided through the Environment Fund and finance them entirely from their own budgets, some resources will be released for other purposes. These should be concentrated on the principal functions and priority areas identified earlier.

Expanding support and co-operation with NGOs capable of carrying out elements of UNEP's programme will also increase the effectiveness of the Environment Fund. Over the last decade, non-governmental organizations and networks have become increasingly important in work to improve environmental protection locally, nationally, and internationally. However, financial support from the Environment Fund for co-operative projects with NGOs declined in both absolute and relative terms in the last 10 years, from $4.5 million (23 per cent of the Fund) in 1976 to $3.6 million (13 per cent) in 1985.[9] The amount, and proportion of Environment Fund resources for co-operation and projects with NGOs should be significantly increased by using the capacities of those NGOs that can contribute to UNEP's programmes on a cost-effective basis.

[. . .]

Making informed choices

As is evident from this report, the transition to sustainable development will require a range of public policy choices that are inherently complex and politically difficult. Reversing unsustainable development policies at the national and international level will require immense efforts to inform the public and secure its support. The scientific community, private and community groups, and NGOs can play a central role in this.

Increase the role of the scientific community and non-governmental organizations

Scientific groups and NGOs have played – with the help of young people[10] – a major part in the environmental movement from its earliest beginnings. Scientists were the first to point out evidence of significant environmental risks and changes resulting from the growing intensity of human activities. Other non-governmental organizations and citizens' groups pioneered in the creation of public awareness and political pressures that stimulated governments to act. Scientific and non-governmental communities played a vital role in the United Nations Conference on the Human Environment in Stockholm.[11]

These groups have also played an indispensable role since the Stockholm Conference in identifying risks, in assessing environmental impacts and designing and implementing measures to deal with them, and in maintaining the high degree of public and political interest required as a basis for action. Today, major national 'State of the Environment' reports are being published by some NGOs (in Malaysia, India, and the United States, for instance).[12] Several international NGOs have produced significant reports on the status of and prospects for the global environment and natural resource base.[13]

The vast majority of these bodies are national or local in nature, and a successful transition to sustainable development will require substantial strengthening of their capacities. To an increasing extent, national NGOs draw strength from association with their counterparts in other countries and from participation in international programmes and consultations. NGOs in developing countries are particularly in need of international support – professional and moral as well as financial – to carry out their roles effectively.

Many international bodies and coalitions of NGOs are now in place and active. They play an important part in ensuring that national NGOs and scientific bodies have access to the support they require. These include regional groups providing networks linking together environment and development NGOs in Asia, Africa, Eastern and Western Europe, and North and South America. They also include a number of regional and global coalitions on critical issues such as pesticides, chemicals, rain, seeds, genetic resources, and development assistance. A global network for information exchange and joint action is provided through the Environment Liaison Centre (ELC) in Nairobi. ELC has over 230 NGO member groups, with the majority from developing countries, and is in contact with 7,000 others.

Only a few international NGOs deal on a broad basis with both environment and development issues, but this is changing rapidly. One of them, the International Institute for Environment and Development, has long specialized in these issues and pioneered the conceptual basis for the environment/ development relationship. Most of them work with and support related organizations in the developing world. They facilitate their participation in international activities and their links with counterparts in the international

If the NGO community is to translate its commitment to sustainable development into effective action, we will need to see a matching level of commitment from the governmental and intergovernmental communities, in genuine partnership with NGOs. The success and cost-effectiveness of NGO action is to an important degree a function of their spontaneity and freedom of action.

Both among NGOs and amongst governments, we must find ways to engender a new period of international co-operation. The urgency of our tasks no longer permits us to spill our energies in fruitless and destructive conflict. Whilst we fight our wars of ideology on the face of this planet, we are losing our productive relationship with the planet itself.

(Bull 1986)

community. They provide instruments for leadership and co-operation among a wide variety of organizations in their respective constituencies. These capabilities will be ever more important in the future. An increasing number of environment and development issues could not be tackled without them.

NGOs should give a high priority to the continuation of their present networking on development co-operation projects and programmes, directed at the improvement of the performance of NGO bilateral and multilateral development programmes. They could increase their efforts to share resources, exchange skills, and strengthen each other's capacities through greater international co-operation in this area. In setting their own house in order, 'environment' NGOs should assist 'development' NGOs in reorienting projects that degrade the environment and in formulating projects that contribute to sustainable development. The experience gained would provide a useful basis for continuing discussions with bilateral and multilateral agencies as to steps that these agencies might take to improve their performance.

In many countries, governments need to recognize and extend NGOs' right to know and have access to information on the environment and natural resources; their right to be consulted and to participate in decision making on activities likely to have a significant effect on their environment; and their right to legal remedies and redress when their health or environment has been or may be seriously affected.

NGOs and private and community groups can often provide an efficient and effective alternative to public agencies in the delivery of programmes and projects. Moreover, they can sometimes reach target groups that public agencies cannot. Bilateral and multilateral development assistance agencies, especially UNDP and the World Bank, should draw upon NGOs in executing programmes and projects. At the national level, governments, foundations, and industry should also greatly extend their co-operation with NGOs in planning, monitoring, and evaluating as well as in carrying out projects when they can provide the necessary capabilities on a cost-effective basis. To this end, governments should establish or strengthen procedures for official consultation and more meaningful participation by NGOs in all relevant intergovernmental organizations.

International NGOs need substantially increased financial support to expand their special roles and functions on behalf of the world community and in support of national NGOs. In the Commission's view, the increased support that will allow these organizations to expand their services represents an indispensable and cost-effective investment. The Commission recommends that these organizations be accorded high priority by governments, foundations, and other private and public sources of funding.

Increase co-operation with industry

Industry is on the leading edge of the interface between people and the environment. It is perhaps the main instrument of change that affects the environmental resource bases of development, both positively and negatively. (See Chapter 8.) Both industry and government, therefore, stand to benefit from working together more closely.

World industry has taken some significant steps through voluntary guidelines concerning industry practices on environment, natural resources, science, and technology. Although few of these guidelines have been extended to or applied regionally in Africa, Asia, or Latin America, industry continues to address these issues through various international associations.

These efforts were advanced significantly by the 1984 World Industry Conference on Environmental Management (WICEM).[14] Recently, as a follow-up to WICEM, several major corporations from a number of developed countries formed the

International Environment Bureau to assist developing countries with their environment/development needs. Such initiatives are promising and should be encouraged. Co-operation between governments and industry would be further facilitated if they established joint advisory councils for sustainable development – for mutual advice, assistance, and co-operation in helping to shape and implement policy, laws, and regulations for more sustainable forms of development. Internationally, governments in co-operation with industry and NGOs should work through appropriate regional organizations to develop basic codes of conduct for sustainable development, drawing on and extending relevant existing voluntary codes, especially in Africa, Asia, and Latin America.

The private sector also has a major impact on development through commercial bank loans from within and outside countries. In 1983, for example, the proportion of the total net receipts of developing countries from private sources, mostly in the form of commercial bank loans, was greater than all ODA that year. Since 1983, as indebtedness worsened, commercial bank lending to developing countries has declined.[15]

Efforts are being made to stimulate private investment. These efforts should be geared to supporting sustainable development. The industrial and financial corporations making such investments, and the export credit, investment insurance, and other programmes that facilitate them, should incorporate sustainable development criteria into their policies.

Providing the legal means

National and international law has traditionally lagged behind events. Today, legal regimes are being rapidly outdistanced by the accelerating pace and expanding scale of impacts on the environmental base of development. Human laws must be reformulated to keep human activities in harmony with the unchanging and universal laws of nature. There is an urgent need:

- to recognize and respect the reciprocal rights and responsibilities of individuals and states regarding sustainable development,
- to establish and apply new norms for state and interstate behaviour to achieve sustainable development,
- to strengthen and extend the application of existing laws and international agreements in support of sustainable development, and
- to reinforce existing methods and develop new procedures for avoiding and resolving environmental disputes.

[. . .]

Notes

1 L. Gagnon, Union Quebecoise pour la Conservation de la Nature, Quebec, 'Pour Une Revision des Sciences Economiques', submitted to WCED Public Hearings, Ottawa, 1986. See also the review of the state-of-the-art concerning natural resource accounts, including detailed case studies from Norway and France, in OECD, *Information and Natural Resources* (Paris: 1986).
2 T. Friend, 'Natural Resource Accounting and its Relationship with Economic and Environmental Accounting', Statistics Canada, Ottawa, September 1986.
3 The need for an explicit 'foreign policy for environment' was raised in different ways in the discussion at many WCED public hearings, but originally in a joint submission by Nordic NGOs to the Public Hearings in Oslo, 1985.

4 See 'Report of the Secretary-General: Technical and Economic Aspects of International River Basin Development', UN E/C.7/35, New York, 1972. An updated list of relevant international agreements was provided by the IUCN Environmental Law Centre. See also Department of Technical Cooperation for Development, *Experiences in the Development and Management of International River and Lake Basins*, Proceedings of the UN Interregional Meeting of International River Organizations held at Dakar, Senegal, in May 1981 (New York: UN, 1983).

5 In 1982, there were environment and natural resource management agencies operating in 144 countries. At the time of the 1972 Stockholm Conference, only 15 industrial countries and 11 developing countries had such agencies. World Environment Center, *World Environment Handbook* (New York: 1985).

6 See General Assembly resolution 2997 (XXVII) of 15 December 1972 on 'Institutional and financial arrangements for international environmental co-operation'.

7 The Environment Coordination Board was abolished in 1977 and its functions assumed by the Administrative Committee on Coordination (ACC). See General Assembly Resolution 32/197, Annex, para 54. The ACC subsequently established a Committee of Designated Officials for Environmental Matters (DOEM).

8 In addition to the Environment Fund there were 18 special Trust Funds with contributions totalling $5–6 million in 1985. See UNEP, *1985 Annual Report* (Nairobi: 1986).

9 Ibid., Annex V, Table 8.

10 The importance of involving youth in nature conservation and environmental protection and improvement activities was emphasized in many presentations at WCED Public Hearings. See, for example, the report 'Youth Nature Conservation Movement in the Socialist Countries' to the Public Hearing at Moscow, December 1986.

11 For an overview of the role and contribution of NGOs to environment and development action at the national and international levels, see 'NGOs and Environment-Development Issues', report to WCED by the Environment Liaison Centre, Nairobi, 1986. It includes a selection of 20 case studies of successful NGO environmental action around the world.

12 NGOs in Chile, Colombia, the Federal Republic of Germany, and Turkey have also published 'State of the Environment' reports. Official reports have appeared in Australia, Austria, Canada, Denmark, Finland, France, Ireland, Israel, Japan, the Netherlands, Poland, Spain, Sweden, the United States, and Yugoslavia.

13 See, for example, the annual *State of the World* report by Worldwatch Institute, the *World Resources Report* by World Resources Institute and the International Institute for Environment and Development, and the *World Conservation Strategy* by IUCN.

14 *Report of the World Industry Conference on Environmental Management*, sponsored by the International Chamber of Commerce and UNEP, 1984; see particularly the principles adopted by OECD in 1985 as a clarification of the OECD Guiding Principles for Multinational Enterprises in *International Legal Materials*, Vol. 25, No. 1 (1986); see also the presentation to WCED Public Hearings, Oslo, June 1985, on 'World Industry Conference Follow-Up' by the Chairman of the Environment Committee of the International Chamber of Commerce.

15 See P.S. Thacher, 'International Institutional Support: The International System, Funding and Technical Assistance', presented to the World Conservation Strategy Conference, Ottawa, Canada, June 1986.

READING 11.2 INQUIRY AND CHANGE: THE TROUBLED ATTEMPT TO UNDERSTAND AND SHAPE SOCIETY

C.E. Lindblom

Source: Yale University Press, New Haven, CT, 1992: 216–219, 224–230

Dimensions of the self-directing society

What are the specific distinctions between the two models of social problem solving?[1] Outlining them will to a degree recapitulate and to a degree extend the analysis of all preceding chapters.

Probing

The self-guiding model centers of course on lay investigation or probing, a wider variety of inquiries than those of social scientists. The self-guiding model also pictures its wide inquiries as much less conclusive than those of the scientific model. Probing, again, suggests accepts a never-ending inconclusiveness while science pursues closure. As for ends – usually standing volitions – the self-guiding model neither takes any as given, as in some versions of the scientific model, nor regards them as discoverable. For no one can dis- or uncover a volition; and instead people form, choose, decide upon, or will. This they do through a mixture of empirical, prudential, aesthetic, and moral probes. Among more numerous lesser questions, probing pursues great existential and moral questions, working answers to which join with the unexpected to shape people and society.

Social science in aid of probing

Consequently, the self-guiding model rejects social science as an alternative to ordinary inquiry and sees it instead as an aid, refiner, extender, and sometime tester of it, always a supplement, never broadly embarked on a program to displace or replace it. No less present in the self-guiding model than in the science model, social science pursues an adaptive strategy in the former instead of trying to set out on its own course as in the latter. Even on most empirical questions, problem solving in the self-guiding model remains more often dependent on lay inquiry than on scientific investigation.

Lay learning

In the science-guided model of social problem solving, for every social problem sufficient analysis can almost certainly find at least one solution. The other model makes no such assumption. Given certain institutions, social processes, established patterns of behavior, a problem may be beyond hope of solution or amelioration. Acknowledged problems – say, prison reform, some forms of juvenile delinquency, or environmental decay – for which knowledge of appropriate techniques for solution lies at hand, persist because neither political functionaries nor ordinary citizens will bear the costs of remedy. For such problems, all solutions remain closed off unless and until people experience sufficient distress to induce them to reconsider the institutions, social processes, or behavioral patterns up to that moment regarded as parameters. Expert opinion and social research on policies for such problems come to nothing in the absence of a reconsideration of volitions, nor can social scientists or experts of any other kind themselves accomplish the reconsideration. If achieved, it comes as an outcome of a diffuse social process in which at least politically active citizens examine their relevant volitions. Consequently, lay probing as a social process can cope with problems intractable to social science.

Sensitivities

[. . .] Statistics on unemployment do not make it a problem, and it does not become a problem except to those who for some reason care, are disturbed, or feel badly about it. That the origin of problems lies in sensitivities, feeling, or affect continues to be an embarrassment to the model of a scientifically guided society, for such a model aspires to more objective indicators of the existence of problems and to analyses of problems that can be stripped of sentiments, feelings, or emotions. The self-guiding society model takes for granted that no escape from feeling can be found. If people do not feel an aversion to a situation or state of affairs, they cannot formulate it as a problem, nor will they seek to escape from that state of affairs, nor is there any reason why they should or would. Even a person who sees inefficiency as a problem and claims to be coldly analytical in analyzing it cannot make it into a problem without some feeling of aversion to it or to its results.

No correct solutions

In some forms of the scientific model, by a good solution one means, in principle, an approximation to the correct solution, even if in practice one cannot determine correctness. One regards "best," "ideal," and "correct" as synonymous. The assumption that complex social problems have correct solutions has a long history.[2] When Rousseau says that under appropriate circumstances, the "common good will then be everywhere evident," he may intend an assumption that there exists a common good and a correct order of society.[3] The Webbs often made such a claim explicit, and some social scientists still dare to make it: for example, Maslow in seeking a scientific ethic. In Marxist thought it appears frequently. Thus the Chinese Communist party achieves "correct policies, and the Constitution of the Communist Party of China declares the Party to be great, glorious, and correct."[4] Or a Soviet writer offers Soviet science as "the only correct approach."[5]

Among advocates of the self-guiding model, the claim seems naive. Except for solutions to extremely simple problems, any such claim to correctness would have to assume that volitions are in principle empirically discoverable rather than created, an assumption which the self-guiding model rejects. In the self-guiding model, the usual test of a good solution is instead that it has been well probed. Competent opinions will differ on whether it has. Judgments about the quality of probing will be supplemented retrospectively by examination of the solution's consequences as they in fact unfold. And any one observer's appraisal of the solution will reflect his substantive volitions. One may, for example, regard a solution as unethical or in some other way unacceptable even if those who reached it probed it well. In particular, one may evaluate a solution as unacceptable because it blocks the continued investigation of the problem area, for one may think the preservation of inquiry itself more important than the solution to any given problem subjected to probing.[6]

Learning from error

In the science model, the problem solver aims for a solution; in the self-guiding model he tries a step toward amelioration, a step very likely containing a significant element of failure but leaving the situation open for another, now better informed step. The one model tries to avoid error; the other feeds on it, engaging in indefinitely prolonged change of course in which both means and ends change in the light of newly informed probes. While the science model always at least hints at aspiration to closure, equilibrium, or stasis, the self-guiding model envisages a constant reconsideration, including endless problem redefinition in which a "solution" forever recedes, like "Neurath's sailors who must rebuild their ship on the open sea without discerning its ideal design."[7]

A learning from action

In the model of scientific guidance, problem solving is entirely cerebral. In the alternative model, the acknowledged impossibility of anyone's ever achieving a full grasp of the relevant complexities of society compels action in ignorance. Hence the model counts on strategies like trial and error, in which the trial serves not simply as an action to attempt a solution but provides feedback information to illuminate subsequent attempts. In this model, citizens, functionaries, social scientists, and other experts do what they have learned and then learn what they have done.[8]

[. . .]

Time-bound, place-bound

The two models offer another choice: between the timeless problem solutions of the scientific model and the time-bound solutions of the self-guiding model. Spinoza "supposes that the rational answer to the question of what is the best government for men is in principle discoverable by anyone, anywhere, in any circumstances. If men have not discovered these timeless solutions before, this must be due to weakness, or the clouding of reason by emotion, or perhaps bad luck: . . . Hobbes . . . equally dominated by a scientific model, presupposes this also. The notion of time, change, historical development, does not impinge upon these views."[9] And a contemporary sees social science as "the chance to escape the obsessions of time and place and to see things in the aspect of eternity."[10] By contrast, advocates of the self-guiding model hold that problem solving "is not the science of setting up a permanently impregnable society, it is the art of knowing where to go next in the exploration of an already existing traditional kind of society."[11] What a people can do about a problem follows as the product of a specific historical experience.

Not a Burkean argument that through historical experience good problem solutions emerge, compete with less good solutions, and survive only because of their merits, the argument maintains only that appropriate or best problem solutions, if found at all, are appropriate or best to a time and a place. In this respect – not in some others – social problem solving looks like biological evolution: "the interplay of local opportunities – physical, ecological, and constitutional – produces a net historical opportunity,"[12] which for human beings consists often of an opportunity for choice. The timeless universal solutions sought in some versions of scientific problem solving do not exist.

Nor is this a Marxist argument that historical changes move in predictable sequences that a science of social change, such as Marx attempted, can capture. Granting that societies share some universal characteristics, and granting too that some aspects of change social science can grasp and predict, the model of the self-directing society postulates a great deal more indeterminacy than does the science model.

Institutions

In the model of the scientifically guided society political institutions authorize and implement solutions but do not decide on them, for ideally scientific inquiry instead discovers them. Determining a solution requires only the assignment of social scientists to the task. Advocates of the self-directing model see, though often only obscurely, the need for institutions that not only implement but reach solutions. The market mechanism provides the great example. It solves mammoth allocational and distributional problems without their appearing on anyone's desk or agenda, thus discharging the same problem-solving tasks as would be assigned to social scientists in a science-guided society. Similarly, the self-guiding model locates problem-solving tasks in parties, legislatures, cabinets, and courts. Idealized models aside, the two visions differ in the consequentiality they find in institutional, political, and social procedures for reaching problem solutions.

No holism

At least back to ancient Greece one can trace an aspiration, powerfully revived by Descartes, that "a single system of knowledge, embracing all provinces and answering all questions, could be established by unbreakable chains of logical argument from universally valid axioms."[13] Persisting through the Enlightenment, it eventually ran head-on into the articulation of the fact-value distinction and shrank to become an aspiration, as in Alexander von Humboldt, Lord Kelvin, and T.H. Huxley, among many others, for a comprehensive or unified scientific theory of the empirical world alone,[14] such as gave rise to the later "unity of science" ambitions of the logical positivists.

Not even theoretical physicists have, however, attempted a comprehensive theory; Einstein is among those whose pursuit of a key segment of it ended in failure. On the state of physical theory he says: "The greater part of physical research is devoted to the development of the various branches in physics, in each of which the object is the theoretical understanding of more or less restricted fields of experience, and in each of which the laws and concepts remain as closely as possible related to experience."[15]

In the social sciences, such explicit proposals as Horkheimer's for "theoretical consideration of society as a whole"[16] are uncommon, though they perhaps persist unspoken in the minds of many social scientists. More commonly one hears pleas from both lay people and social scientists for broad and complete analyses of vast phenomena and clusters of problems. Either way, holistic ambitions for social scientists and citizens alike often mark the scientific model of society, ambitions beyond those of the self-directing model both for social scientists and ordinary investigators.

Limited faith in reason

Not entirely but in large part, the foregoing differences between the two models turn on a difference in faith in reason to solve social problems. Advocates of the science model have great faith in reason or human cognitive capacity: as already noted in Plato's concept of the philosopher-king, Bacon, Descartes, the Enlightenment, Bentham, the Webbs, Marx, and many of the "new Utopian" enthusiasts of contemporary formal systems of analysis like systems analysis. In Descartes' words, "There is nothing so far removed from us as to be beyond our reach, or so hidden that we cannot discover it." In advocates of the self-guiding model, a contrary sense of human cognitive incapacity dominates: in Hume and Burke, liberal concerns about human fallibility, and liberal advocacy of the market system as a device for reducing the otherwise unbearable burdens of economic planning. To these we can add recent and contemporary explicit argument on human cognitive incapacities from Hayek, de Jouvenel, Michael Polanyi, and Herbert Simon, among many others, as well as mountainous testimony, on human cognitive incompetence for complex problem solving displayed in the retreat from over-ambitious economic planning for development in the third world, in the dismal record of city planning in many countries, and in the disrepute of Soviet and Chinese economic planning, even in Soviet and Chinese circles. Between the supply of competence and demands for solutions lies a tragic discrepancy. Rationality, as social scientists now say, is bounded;[17] the best human minds can cope well only with greatly simplified problems.

A faith in reason can take the form of faith in the capacity of excellent minds to discover inexorable social laws that paradoxically reveal limits on man's capacity to change the social world. Such a faith in reason tells some people that poverty is ineradicable or ordinary citizens forever incompetent in public affairs. But the faith in reason may also take the form of faith in the capacity of scientists, other intellectuals, and experts to discover leverage points in society and thus design and effect solutions to social problems. Hence, the faith in human cognitive capacity opens either the road to powerlessness or the road to social control. It is not possible for both positions to be correct, unless one modifies each to approach the other in an appreciation of what can and cannot be changed in social organization. In the model of the scientifically guided society, the inconsistency between the two forms of faith in reason often embarrasses advocates of the model who want to have it both ways.

Insofar as an advocate of the science-guided society believes that reason can solve problems, just where does he find reason? It might appear in the capacity of millions of reasoning people to live cooperatively with each other with only a hint of the coercions of the state, thus, in a kind of reasoned harmonious anarchy or near-anarchy, as anticipated by many of the figures of the Enlightenment. Or, as other figures of the Enlightenment believed, it might appear in the form of intellectual capacity of no more than an elite, which must then find the authority to effect its reasoned solutions to social problems. Advocates of the self-guiding model need make no such choice. Their vision of society calls neither for harmonious anarchy nor benevolent authority, but for political institutions and leadership, and for a citizenry of investigators who turn again and again to politics to reach problem solutions because of the many conditions in which inquiry, discussion, and persuasion cannot reach a solution without the additional element of imposition.

The connection between reason and democracy

A complex connection joins a greatly limited faith in reason to a belief in democracy in the self-guiding model. Arising in the Enlightenment, one great tradition in liberal democratic theory identified liberal democracy with government reason instead of authority or coercion, as in the concept of "government by discussion."[18] A now parallel younger tradition identifies, to complete the picture, communism with force, authority, and the suppression of inquiry. Yet from another perspective, not inconsistent with this first perspective, the identification of democracy with reason and communism with force and authority reverses.

However much actual communist societies constrain discussion and inquiry, communist doctrine has continually displayed a faith in elite intellectual capacity in sharp contrast to the troubled concern about fallibility that is characteristic of liberal democratic society as represented in Mill. The liberal democrat's faith in reason looks strong only in contrast with earlier traditionalism and authoritarianism in science, religion, and politics. Compared to the Marxian and communist faith in reason, it looks puny. Marx's scientific socialism was meant to be scientific; the term was not just a slogan.

The version of democracy as "government by discussion" identified democracy less closely with the self-guiding model than with the scientific model. As, roughly coincident with the later Enlightenment, the egalitarian democratic idea emerged in France, democrats were typically admirers of science, rationalist, turning against traditionalism, authority, and superstition. They might believe, as a result of their new faith in rationality and science, in the possibility that they – or even better minds – could find harmony in the universe, each person potentially no longer in conflict with others, the intellect consequently capable of discovering "correct" solutions.[19]

This earlier faith, both in human intellectual capacities and in harmony, has declined for numerous reasons, including, among other intellectual influences, Freud's investigations of human irrationalities. Many thoughtful people also lost faith in reason when they recoiled from the Terror of the French Revolution and the later demands and counter-revolutionary bloodshed of the Paris Commune, a "pivotal event in European political thought."[20]

Thus, a once confident movement of thought that somehow amalgamated enlightenment, science, democracy, and equality, divided. Down one road, liberal democratic thought allied itself with classical economic thought and became increasingly skeptical of man's capacity to reshape his world. It therefore turned toward institutions that would hold fallible leaders responsible but would not grant them authority to create "correctly" an egalitarian world. Down the other road, the communist movement, armed with Marxian "science," marched behind leaders not held responsible to an inhibiting electorate but granted authority to create by "correct" design an egalitarian world.[21] The earlier tie between science and democracy came loose, and a model of a self-guiding society began to emerge.[22]

The two models present fundamental alternatives in strategies for social problem solving, and with particular respect to the place of social science in the social process as a whole. Almost everyone mixes elements of the two in developing his own picture or way of participating in social problem solving. The choice requires an inquiry – a probe into one's political and social philosophy. That should not, however, call up only the traditional problems in political and social philosophy – of achieving order, authority and obligation, or even distributive justice. It should call up problems in how to use intelligence in social problem solving.

Is it foolish to regard the model of the self-guiding society as a working ideal? Less so, it would seem, than so to regard the science model with its trust in a disinterested intellectual elite and its peripheral hostility to democracy, to say nothing of its other disabilities outlined above. On many counts, contemporary democracies approach the self-guided model in their bouts of hostility to elites, their broad scope for both politics and "politics," their occasional demands for aspirations to greater popular participation, and their intermittent veneration of the popular will. Not on these points can the self-directing model be dismissed as foolishly utopian. It is its postulate that masses of people probe and can greatly improve their probing that stirs disbelief in some quarters.

To that disbelief, John Dewey replied in commenting on judgments of citizens in political life: "Until secrecy, prejudice, bias, misrepresentation, and propaganda as well as sheer ignorance are replaced by inquiry and publicity, we have no way of telling how apt for judgment of social policies the existing intelligence of the masses may be. It would certainly go much further than at present. In the second place, *effective* intelligence is not an original, innate endowment. No matter what are the differences in native intelligence (allowing for the moment that intelligence can be native), the actuality of mind is dependent upon the education which social conditions effect."[23] Improving the quality of inquiry by citizens and functionaries does not rest on improbable or improbably successful positive efforts to promote better probing – strained proposals, for example, for neighborhood or workplace forums, new adult education programs, or new pressures on citizens to read serious books. It rests on what might be called negative reforms – reducing impairment, getting the monkey of impairment off the citizen's back. Societies do not need to urge citizens to probe; they need only to permit them to do so. They need only to reduce the disincentives to probe the diversions and obfuscations that muddle or dampen probing, the misinformation and indoctrinations that misdirect it, and the intimidations and coercions that block it. If none of that looks easy, none is impossible nor, in the long future, even unlikely.

Notes

[...]
1 The distinctions revise an earlier list in C.E. Lindblom, *Politics and Markets* (New York: Basic Books, 1977), pp. 249–260.
2 See the discussion in Alvin W. Gouldner, *Enter Plato* (New York: Basic Books, 1965), p. 281.
3 Jean-Jacques Rousseau, *The Social Contract*, trans. Charles Frankel (New York: Hafner, 1947), p. xviii.
[...]
4 Gong Yuzhi, "Deng Xiaoping and Party's Intellectual Policies," *Beijing Review* 27 (March 19, 1984), p. 16.
5 L.V. Golovanov, "Socialism and the Scientific and Technical Revolution," as quoted by James N. Danziger, "Power Is Knowledge," in Kenneth E. Boulding and Lawrence Senesh, *The Optimum Utilization of Knowledge* (Boulder, Col.: Westview Press, 1983), p. 266.
6 In advocating in this book a society's commitment to probing, I must weigh heavily a continuation of probing as a condition to be met by any solution to a problem.
7 Laurence H. Tribe, "Ways Not to Think about Plastic Trees," *Yale Law Journal* 83 (June 1974), pp. 1340f.
8 At an extreme is the deliberate social experiment, on the justification of which social scientists as well as lay people differ. See Alice M. Rivlin, *Systematic Thinking for Social Action* (Washington, D.C.: Brookings Institution, 1971) chap. 5; and Donald T. Campbell, "Reforms as Experiments," *American Psychologist* 24 (April 1969).
[...]
9 Isaiah Berlin, *Against the Current* (New York: Viking, 1980), p. 87.
10 Charles Frankel, "The Autonomy of the Social Sciences," in Frankel, ed., *Controversies and Decisions* (New York: Russell Sage Foundation, 1976), p. 30.
11 This is what Oakeshott says of politics: Michael J. Oakeshott, *Rationalism in Politics* (London: Methuen, 1962), p. 58.
12 François Jacob, "Evolution and Tinkering," *Science* 196 (June 10, 1977), p. 1166.
13 Isaiah Berlin, *Against the Current* (New York: Viking, 1980), p. 3.
14 Shirley R. Letwin, *The Pursuit of Certainty* (Cambridge: Cambridge University Press, 1965), pp. 325f.
15 Albert Einstein, "The Fundamentals of Theoretical Physics," in L. Hamalian and E. L. Volpe, eds., *Great Essays by Nobel Prize Winners* (New York: Farrar, Straus and Giroux, 1970), p. 220.
16 Max Horkheimer, *Critical Theory* (New York: Herder and Herder, 1972), p. 4.
17 Herbert A. Simon, *Models of Man* (New York: Wiley, 1957), pp. 196–197.
[...]
18 Frank Knight, *Freedom and Reform* (New York: Harper and Brothers, 1947), p. 190. Ernest Barker, *Reflections on Government* (Oxford: Oxford University Press, 1942), p. 40.
19 Carl L. Becker, *New Liberties for Old* (New Haven: Yale University Press, 1941), p. 106.
20 Edmund Wilson, *To the Finland Station* (Garden City, N.Y.: Doubleday, 1947), p. 283.
21 J.L. Talmon, *The Rise of Totalitarian Democracy* (Boston: Beacon Press, 1952).
22 Five paragraphs have been taken almost verbatim from Lindblom, *Politics and Markets* (New York: Basic Books. 1977), pp. 252f.
23 *The Public and Its Problems* (Chicago: Gateway Books, 1946), p. 209.
[...]

VIGNETTE 11.1 CHALLENGING FORMULAIC APPROACHES
TO ENVIRONMENTAL THINKING

C.A. Bowers, University of Oregon

The world has changed in fundamental ways since the appearance of the *Brundtland Report* in 1987, and the publication in 1992 of Charles Lindblom's *Inquiry and Change*. Most of the scientific community has reached consensus that global warming is occurring, and that many life-supporting ecosystems are being seriously degraded. The World Trade Organization, which was founded in 1995 as a result of the GATT Uruguay Round, has been given the power to overturn any nation's laws and other barriers that limit the free-market practices of corporations. In effect, the decisions of the WTO now supersede national sovereignty in such areas as domestic agricultural practices, tariffs and trade, intellectual property rights, and foreign investment. At the same time critics of globalization and the WTO have become well organized and articulate proponents of cultural and biological diversity. Additionally, religiously based conflicts, combined with the economic stresses connected with globalization, have re-emerged in a way that threatens to marginalize efforts to undertake cultural reforms that contribute to greater ecological sustainability.

Each of these changes brings into question the relevance of the recommendations presented in the *Brundtland Report* as well as the more convoluted analysis in Lindblom's *Inquiry and Change*. While the scientifically based, hierarchical and highly bureaucratic system of UN agencies proposed in the Report now appears hopelessly out of touch with today's realities, it nevertheless represents a way of thinking about global solutions still prevalent today – in spite of decades of failure.

The emphasis on basing sustainable development on scientific data, and a "high-level centre of leadership" within the UN still has adherents. Unfortunately, they continue to ignore that sustainable development is always situated in a particular cultural and bioregional setting. And they ignore the limitations of scientific knowledge. Scientists are, for the most part, only educated to study the dynamics of natural systems, and thus lack a deep knowledge of culture, their own as well as non-western cultures that would enable them to understand the different expressions of intergenerational knowledge and practices that contribute to local self-sufficiency – and to maintain a smaller ecological footprint. This limitation is further exacerbated by their general prejudice against non-western ways of thinking. Their insensitivity to local traditions of knowledge (the exception being knowledge of medicinal plants that can be patented) can be seen in their introduction of the Green Revolution in Bali – which the Balinese subsequently abandoned in favor of their traditional temple system of controlling the cycle for allocating water to their rice paddies (Lansing 1991). It can also be seen in the way western doctors used the physical development of children in the West as the standard for evaluating the development of children in Ladakh (Norberg-Hodge 1992). The prejudice against local knowledge can also be seen in the universities of Peru where the hegemony of western science leads to agriculture classes that omit any references to the agricultural practices of the Quechua, even though the Quechua have created the second most diverse center of seed plants in the world (Apffel-Marglin 1998).

The reliance on western science to provide the data for eco-management by "high-level" centres of leadership, as the Report recommends, is problematic for other reasons as well. Scientists have only recently become aware of the ecological crisis – and few of them understand the connections between maintaining cultural diversity and biodiversity. Scientists have a long history of providing the knowledge that led to technologies needed for the expansion of the Industrial Revolution. The latest expression of their complicity in furthering the current phase of the Industrial Revolution can be seen in the direct role they now play in the industrialization both of food production and human reproduction. In addition, influential scientists are turning the theory of evolution into an ideology that supposedly provides scientific justification for the creation of a world monoculture. Hans Moravec and Ray Kurzweil claim that we are now entering the phase of evolution where a global network of computer-based intelligence will replace humans – and thus differences in cultural ways of knowing. E.O. Wilson, Francis Crick, and Richard Dawkins envision a world monoculture that will be dictated by the better adapted genes. Not wanting to leave the determination of cultural patterns ("memes") entirely to the process of natural selection, Wilson argues that scientists will have to make the final determination for all cultures of what constitutes a valid belief and social practice (1998: 265). Lee Silver, a molecular biologist at Princeton University, even predicts the emergence of two types of humans: the genetically engineered human he refers to as "GeneRich," and the non-engineered type he calls "Naturals". These scientists have made important contributions to their field of inquiry, but they also stand out as examples of why scientific data should not be given the central importance accorded by the *Brundtland Report*. Cultural influences enter into the process of framing the questions that eventually lead to scientific findings. In addition, scientists are increasingly willing to accompany the data with recommendations that are cultural in nature – and too often ill informed about the intergenerational knowledge of the local culture.

UN agencies continue to be highly useful in many areas: peacekeeping, distribution of food and medical services, providing education, and so forth. But the UN, like other international organizations, is subject to political forces – forces that often represent the interests of the more powerful western countries that also promoted the establishment of the WTO. One result is that the effectiveness of UN agencies is now being overshadowed by the hyper-capitalist orientation of the WTO. The global spread of western technologies (particularly the western style media, computers, and medical technologies that enable the gender of fetuses to be determined and thus aborted – leading to significant gender imbalance in parts of the world) has also diminished the ability of UN agencies to create a more peaceful and sustainable world. It might even be argued that its global perspective complements the WTO as well as the continued domination of western scientists in framing the discourse on ecological sustainability. Unless the cultural roots of the ecological crisis are addressed in a way that takes account of cultural differences, the eco-management approach of scientists will continue to represent only stop-gap measures in the downward cycle of degraded ecosystems.

The analysis in Lindblom's *Inquiry and Change* (1992) is also outdated. The two models of problem solving he offers the reader – the scientific and the self-directing model – are theoretical constructs that contain all the limitations of abstract thinking. When we see examples of his two models being practiced in the real world it is easy to recognize how Lindblom misrepresents their complexity. To refer to the "model of scientific guidance" as entirely cerebral is a wild over-generalization, and to suggest that science always leads to "setting up a permanently impregnable society" is also unsupportable. Similarly, there is much to criticise in Lindblom's description of the self-directing model – especially when he claims that the "market mechanism" is the best example of solving problems. The limitation that Lindblom shares with the authors of the *Brundtland Report* is that both ignore differences in decision making that result from profound differences in cultural ways of knowing. Local decision making (Lindblom's self-guiding model) among the Hopi of the American Southwest is profoundly different from decision making in Islamic cultures (which have their own variations); and both are different from local decision making in English speaking countries – which also have their differences. Lindblom, like so many writers of his era, ignores that there are over 6,000 languages still spoken in the world, and that there are important differences among the language communities in how knowledge is encoded, who is looked to as a source of special knowledge, and how this knowledge affects the self-directing process of the community.

Lindblom's reference to Dewey as a guide to understanding the nature of the self-directing community is also problematic in ways overlooked by Dewey's followers. While Dewey is identified with promoting democratic decision making at the local level, he recognized only one method of intelligence, assumed that change is progressive in nature, and continually denigrated cultures based on moral values that had not met the test of his system of experimental inquiry. As I explain in *Educating for Eco-justice and Community* (Bowers 2001), Dewey's democracy required conformity to the western assumptions he took for granted. Even though well intended, Lindblom's analysis and prescriptions also reflects the western ethnocentrism that Third World cultures are now challenging so vigorously.

VIGNETTE 11.2 BUILDING CAPACITY, DEVELOPING AGENCY: WOMEN DON'T PLAY XYLOPHONES

B. Golder, WWF International

Women don't play xylophones (and) there is a distinction between who dances and who sings. If there is a party and there are no men to play the drums a woman will play the drums. But never a xylophone.

(MacDonald *et al.* 2002)

It might seem strange that consideration of who can or can't play the xylophone is a topic for consideration by conservation practitioners. After all conservation organizations are not interested in the musical decisions or traditions of local communities. Or are they?

In a world where the state of the environment and the state of people are inextricably linked, it is increasingly the business of conservation practitioners to understand and respond to the multiple dimensions of human behaviour and the patterns of tradition, superstition and status that guide it. No longer are we able – as the Brundtland Report suggests – to make institutional or prescriptive recommendations that will shape or determine the fate of the environment because it has been deemed by data or policy instruments as the right thing to do. Conservation organizations today live in a world where beyond the façade of the policies, mandate and institutional capacity promoted in the 1980s, it is recognized that less well-defined constituencies exist that need to be acknowledged, respected and engaged.

These are the constituencies of women who won't play the xylophone. The same women who are responsible for harvesting crops, gathering fuel-wood for cooking, and raising five or six children who will all too soon assume responsibility for extending the boundaries of land on which the family sustains itself. And they are the women who, when given the room and support to make informed choices, may choose to have fewer children, use solar stoves instead of fuel wood, and commit themselves to getting their children through school so that they can pursue a future beyond the further exploitation of natural resources. To help them achieve that future reality the conservation worker of today must deal with their current reality as embodied in the story of the xylophone: a story that sits outside the biological surveys, reports and assessments of governments and official agencies charged with achieving sustainable development across the biodiversity rich regions of the world.

There are also the constituencies of men and women who honour their ancestors by having as many children as possible. They are the traditional communities who see land as a symbol of power and therefore seek to inhabit as much of it as possible – and as quickly as possible – irrespective of its identified biodiversity values. For these constituencies the rational pursuit of gender equity, family planning and land zoning systems matter little. Indeed, even if the messages of science and of politicians were to reach these constituencies the logic that they promote and follow is often so alien to the values that these communities subscribe to, they would be rejected out of hand.

Governments and non-governmental organizations of today are having to grapple with the uncertainty, complexity and variability that comes with recognizing that the social and cultural values of those whose lifestyles and livelihoods are firmly entwined with the state of biodiversity are ultimately the determining element of conservation success and sustainability. In a world where communications and transportation have made everywhere accessible and nowhere isolated from information or the temptation of profit, organizations are coming to recognize that science and politics alone cannot determine the continued wellbeing of the global environment. Rather, today's reality is that while foundations of institutional will and capacity of the type proposed by Brundtland can help communicate messages and lessons to those in positions of power (political or financial), it is the will of the individual or their community that will ultimately shape the state of the environment. And in coming to that recognition, the decision-making processes and traditions of the women who don't play the xylophone – and the self-guiding model of social problem solving – come to centre stage in the race to sustain the world's biodiversity.

As conservation and development practitioners listen to the stories of men and women for whom the state of biodiversity has an overwhelming resonance, it is critical that they have the perspective and capacity to probe the values, interests and needs of the people with whom they wish to reach a negotiated settlement. Ultimately that settlement – irrespective of the goals of science and politicians who drive it – will be based in the reality that drives human action; the immediate, personal and community need and desire to secure food, shelter, and if possible, economic gain. In regions identified by the best science as distinct, unique and irreplaceable, the conversation today is less about the application of global principles or implementation of policies articulated by Brundtland, and more and more about the social and cultural values that are driving exploitation. The recent introduction of mechanisms like the citizen jury (Coote and Lenaghan 1997) or socio-economic scoping to conservation planning is recognition of this reality. As the unsustainability of political visions is acknowledged in a world of legally protected areas that in reality are neither protected nor managed, and consumer demand for rare and endangered species grows, despite international regulations, it is the voice of those whose lifestyles and livelihoods are sustained by local biodiversity that conservation practitioners are motivated to listen to and understand. It is those people, driven by need or aspiration, whose opinion and incentives – to learn and act – will ultimately shape whether our seas, forests and rivers continue to flourish for generations to come.

Conservation practitioners working in isolated and poor communities around the world have learnt first hand that the road to change is one that of necessity must respect social, cultural and economic traditions. It is a journey that more often than not requires educated, skilled and well-resourced individuals to "lose their education" (WWF 2002) as they engage with, and gain the trust of, the men, women and children who inhabit the world's biologically rich and unique regions. It is about understanding the incentives for living of people whose reality is a distant reach from the educated and powerful. Listening to the women and men of the conservation community who spend their days pursuing the most ambitious of conservation visions by embracing those who have few resources or options is a lesson in the true – and effective – nature of lay investigation or probing. The solutions these practitioners identify and pursue can seem odd in a world where so many argue that changing foreign policy, building globally responsible institutions and building a legal capacity for enforcing sustainable development is critical to the future of the world. But for the farmer and his wife who want more children to populate the land around them, or the women of socially and religiously conservation communities who have no access to education or health services, it is the understanding of the "probing" field worker who will probably make the difference to their future – and ours.

One need only look to the conservation initiatives in a country like Namibia to see the impact that listening to people can have on the prospect for sustainable development. Building on socio-ecological surveys and efforts to meet community needs (and address their fears) Namibia's Community-based Natural Resource Management Programme is testament to an approach to conservation and learning that "empowers local people to make their own decisions about their own resources while enabling them to benefit from these resources" (NACSO 2002). While institutional frameworks exist to support this innovative approach to conservation, it is the will of the people who depend on the region's resources for survival that gives shape to the country's conservation programme and the pursuit of sustainability.

So what in the end do any of these examples say about conservation and the call to build "capacity" and "agency" for sustainability? Clearly the world of conservation needs a strong foundation – of institutions, policies and laws – that can support and sustain actions to protect the natural environment. But it also needs institutions and practitioners who are prepared to support and undertake the meandering journey that explores patterns of action and learning and embraces "constant reconsideration (and) endless problem definition . . ." (Lindblom 1992).

The goal of organizations working with communities around the world should not be to give women the capacity to play the xylophone – even though we believe in equity and have the funds and skills available to ensure that all women can play the instrument. Rather, the goal must be to understand why women won't play the xylophone in some societies, and what that reality means to how they and those around them make decisions about the rest of their lives. With that understanding it should be possible for practitioners, politicians and educators to forge forward in a way that meets the needs and aspirations of the many rather than the few. It will not be a straightforward path, but it should be one that builds the capacity all of society – practitioner and community member – to make an informed and sustainable difference.

VIGNETTE 11.3 DEVELOPING AGENCY – BUILDING CAPACITY

M. Singh, University of Western Sydney

We live in a dangerous and endangered world of unsustainable and ecologically hazardous overdevelopment: agricultural chemical residues, desertification, the arms race, marine and air pollution, deforestation, genetic engineering, ozone depletion, acidification, indebtedness. Developing the investigative capacity of citizens and building the civic agency of scientists are important goals for those engaged in the provision of lifelong learning directed at the problems of the unsustainability of overdevelopment. Using Lindblom's (1992) problem-solving models this vignette critically analyses the Brundtland Commission (1987) report's orientation to effecting environmental solutions. To begin, Brundtland's construction of scientists and their state institutions is reviewed. This gives rise to the argument that their science-guided model of problem-solving now needs supplementation through the development of the civic agency that is associated with the self-guided model of problem-solving. After briefly summarising Brundtland's construction of citizens and the organisations of global civil society, it is argued that their self-guided model of environmental problem-solving also needs extending to build their investigative capacities.

Developing scientists' civic agency

Brundtland constructs the science-guided model of problem-solving used by scientists, their professional organisations (e.g. The Royal Society, or the American Academy of Sciences) and formal State structures as the source of common, world-wide solutions to the problems of unsustainable overdevelopment. Within this model *the* solution lies in the refinement and standardisation of the scientific techniques of governing problems – locally, nationally, regionally and internationally. The suggested accountability regime includes integrating ecologically and economically sustainable objectives into economic policies; action planning; (reoriented) program budgeting; constructing principles, guidelines and indicators; performance monitoring; conducting audits and surveys; generating statistics and early-warning capabilities; and producing annual reports.

Many advocates of such science-guided models tend to mistakenly believe that "reason" can be detached from political or economic interests in order to solve environmental problems. However, Brundtland encourages scepticism about this model of problem-solving in pointing to the consequences of the variability of political and economic systems. Brundtland notes the absence of, and difficulties in, securing transboundary environmental agreements and contingency plans for redressing unsustainable and ecologically hazardous overdevelopment, especially of international river basins. Official development assistance is ineffective because it is fragmented by endemic weaknesses of inter-agency rivalry, because of gaps between assessment and management, and/or due to a lack of government participation. The very construction of these problems and their resolution is biased towards the centralisation of control and the science-guided model of problem-solving. International funding of environmental problem-solving is too limited, vulnerable and has levelled off as the tasks have increased markedly. Any substantial funding increase is unlikely given government rhetoric of "financial austerity." And despite the effort and resources invested in techniques of governing for environmental and economically sustainable consumption, Brundtland

(1987, p. 365) argues for more. There is, however, no analysis of the political economy underpinning the fragmentation, gaps and limited capability for monitoring and collecting comparable data for authoritative overviews of environmental issues.

Lifelong learning may augment and re-focus the scientific problem-solving model of governance through the development of scientists' civic agency using Lindblom's self-guided model of problem solving. This model of environmental problem solving assumes that for some problems there may be no hope of a solution, in part, because neither functionaries and/or citizens will bear the political or financial costs involved. Moreover, it recognises that a "problem" only exists as such when some functionaries and/or citizens have reason to care, be disturbed or feel concern about an issue. If no one feels any aversion to a given situation then they cannot construct it as a problem, nor will they seek to change that state of affairs, nor have any reason for so doing.

Within the self-guided model "solutions" are pursued by learning from the errors made in attempts to ameliorate the problem; this learning creates a basis for a more informed next step in a lifelong process. Consequently, this implies that both means and ends change in the light of the new learnings produced in the process of probing possible improvements. The "problem" itself is continuously redefined and the "solution" is always open to question. Since it is impossible for anyone ever to achieve a full and complete grasp of the complexities involved in any environmental problem, the action of solving a problem proceeds by learning that is immanent in, and derived from, engagement with the problem itself. Lindblom's self-guided model of social problem solving uses trials as strategic actions aimed as finding a solution and in full anticipation that feedback from these will provide learnings to better inform future actions.

The self-guided problem-solving model offers "solutions" that are indeterminate because they are bound by time and space. It recognises that any "appropriate solution" is a product of specific geographical, social, economic and historical opportunities, and so encourages the continuing exploration of solutions that may be chosen for their appropriateness to new times and new places. The self-guided model locates problem-solving tasks in institutions – political leadership, parties, legislatures, cabinets, courts, investigative citizens – being concerned less with technical implementation than with reaching solutions through making productive use of the resources of politics.

Building citizens' investigative capacities

Brundtland (1987, p. 363) constructs citizens and the organisations of global civil society as important "cost-effective partners" in environmental protection and the implementation of conservation strategies. This effectiveness is to be achieved by co-opting these organisations to carry out elements of the international environmental programme, despite the decline in funds directed to such supportive cooperation. Increasing the use of these non-government organisations, locally, nationally and internationally, is seen as a strategy for improving the cost-effectiveness of the not-so-United Nation's efforts. Despite the problems of governance identified above, Brundtland's discussion of the complexities and political difficulties inherent in public policy choices is linked solely to informing the public and securing its support. This is despite the acknowledgement that "non-governmental organizations and citizens' groups pioneered . . . the creation of public awareness [of ecological risks] and political pressures that stimulated governments to act" (Brundtland 1987, p. 370). The capacities required for building and maintaining public interest, regional citizen networks and global coalitions for the long life of the planet in order to secure political action are not detailed; consequently there is no attention given to how these might be strengthened.

The self-guided model of environmental problem solving used by informed and active global citizens may now be widened to build their investigative capacities. As Brundtland (1987, p. 372) implies this could include using the scientific model to investigate problems such as government refusal to recognise and extend citizens' right to know and access information; their right to be consulted and to participate in decision making; and their right to remedies and redress for serious environmental problems. For Brundtland, these are necessary investments if there is to be a solution to the problem of gaining the support of organisations of global civil society in the provision of cost-effective and efficient projects. The science model of problem solving sets out to create timeless solutions that make the world permanently impregnable to a given environmental problem. However, as Brundtland goes on to observe, voluntarism is not without problems. For instance, while world industry has developed voluntary environmental guidelines, few of these have been extended to, or applied in, Africa, Asia or Latin America.

There is a role for lifelong learning in addressing the complex problems of unsustainable overdevelopment. Analysis of the Brundtland report suggests that lifelong learning can be used to improve the capacity of citizens to engage in social inquiry, to enhance the capacity of scientists to engage in democracy through education, and to educate both citizens and scientists about the role of national and transnational institutions in permitting, authorising and legitimating their work of solving environmental problems. However, as Lindblom warns, this is not a once-and-for-ever solution, but a lifelong journey in a quest to learn what the problems are and what problems are created by our solutions.

CHAPTER 12

ECONOMIC BEHAVIOUR: VALUE AND VALUES

READING 12.1 COEVOLUTIONARY AGRICULTURAL DEVELOPMENT

R.B. Norgaard

Source: *Economic Development and Cultural Change* 32(2), 1984: 528–535

[. . .]

A coevolutionary model of agricultural development

The ecological concept of coevolution provides a new entrée for linking ecological and economic models. Coevolution in biology refers to an evolutionary process based on reciprocal responses of two closely interacting species.[1] The evolution of the beaks of hummingbirds and the shape of the flowers they feed on, the behavior of bees and the distribution of flowering plants, and the biochemical defenses of plants and the immunity of their insect prey have all been given coevolutionary explanations. The concept can be broadened to encompass any feedback processes between two evolving systems. For agricultural social and ecological systems, man's activities modify the ecosystem while the ecosystem's responses provide cause for individual action and social organization. Thus, agricultural development can be viewed as a coevolutionary process between a sociosystem and an ecosystem that, fortuitously or by design, benefits man. Indeed, if the gains from agricultural development are real, not simply this generation living at the expense of the next or one region or group living at the expense of others, it is difficult to imagine how the gains from development could arise other than by a process of positive feedbacks between the sociosystem and ecosystem, whereby these systems coevolve in a manner favorable to man. In this view, sociosystem options compatible with coevolutionary development are constrained by characteristics of the ecosystem; but development is not simply ecologically determined.

Coevolutionary feedback need not benefit man. In the Amazon, for example, repeated attempts to establish well-developed, market-oriented agricultural systems through directed settlement have degenerated in a reciprocal process with the responses of the tropical rain forest ecosystem to a subsistence interaction based on limited farming, fruit and nut gathering, and hunting and fishing.[2] The terms, to coevolve, coevolution, and coevolutionary are value free in this paper and merely refer to the reciprocal process of change. The term coevolutionary development is used to refer to coevolution that benefits man.[3]

Sociosystems and ecosystems are maintained through numerous feedback mechanisms. Change occurs when these feedbacks are changed. With coevolutionary development, maintenance feedback systems frequently shift from the ecosystem to the sociosystem. The history of paddy rice culture in Asia provides an interesting example. Increased productivity under paddy technology has been achieved through investments in dikes, terraces, and irrigation facilities and through the management of water for weed control and nutrient retention. At the same time, paddy technology necessitated more socially demanding property, water-management, and labor-exchange institutions to maintain the paddy rice ecosystem in its more productive state.[4] Thus, contrary to the view of growth as a process of overcoming environmental constraints, the coevolutionary perspective emphasizes an increasingly important, and frequently more complex, interaction between man and his environment.

The idea that the sociosystem frequently assumes the complementary activities and regulatory functions that were either previously endogenous to the ecosystem or maintained by the individual farmer cannot be overstressed. From an ecological perspective, Odum characterizes agricultural development as an ecosystem transformation involving reduced numbers of species and usually lower combined efficiency of nutrient recycling, higher but less stable rates of production, and low biomass stocks relative to natural conditions.[5] As man pushes an ecosystem in directions that meet his own needs, he intervenes in some of the nutrient cycles and disturbs some of the equilibrating mechanisms evolved previously. Coevolutionary development occurs faster, or is perhaps only possible, if the sociosystem compensates for these natural system changes. For example, new sociosystem functions may entail both fertilizing and managing legumes to replace lost nutrient cycles, weed control to offset natural succession, and insect control to compensate for displaced equilibrating mechanisms. These new sociosystem functions are costs because they involve manual labor, managerial effort, knowledge acquisition, the use of natural resources, and institutions (including markets) to provide and allocate these inputs. Ecosystem modification need not necessarily entail more sociosystem involvement, but when it does, the costs of these new activities must be deducted from the gross surplus of the new interaction.[6]

Agriculture in western Europe and North America was once a small-scale, labor-intensive, polycultural, near-subsistence interaction with the ecosystem. From this, it coevolved to a large-scale, mechanized, energy-intensive, monocultural commercial farming interaction buoyed by implement and agrochemical industries; a highly developed marketing system; and government institutions to generate and disseminate knowledge, develop new inputs, regulate markets, absorb risk, limit distributional impacts of adjustments, and control environmental and health-related externalities. The various sociosystem elements evolved, in part, in reaction to the nature of ecosystem responses to man's activities. While monocultural systems brought increasing returns to scale with mechanization, their ecological instability encouraged the development and use of agrochemicals and of risk-spreading institutions. Similarly, ecosystem responses to agrochemicals have led to new pesticide and water pollution regulatory institutions as well as new research programs in agricultural experiment stations.[7] Equally important, the institutional responses typically encouraged further changes in similar directions. Crop insurance and regulated markets, for example, reduce the risks of monocultural production and make it even more attractive. Today's agroecosystems have soil features, weed dynamics, and insect-crop interactions that reflect coevolution with the social system much the same as today's agricultural institutions reflect the vulnerability of disturbed soil to wind and water erosion, the dynamic adaptations of insect populations to chemical control, and the susceptibility of monocultural systems to variations in weather.

In western agriculture, there has been a dramatic increase in the productivity of the few individuals we still label "farmers working the land." This increase is frequently attributed to a relaxation through technology of the environmental constraints that once reduced the farmer's productivity. The coevolutionary perspective emphasizes the increase in individual task specialization and the increase in the organizational complexity of maintaining feedback mechanisms between specialized actors within the sociosystem and with the ecosystem. These perspectives are not incompatible. The coevolutionary perspective, however, stresses social and environmental feedbacks and the evolution of both agroecosystems and agricultural social systems.[8] Neoclassical economics' neglect of feedback processes may account for many of the difficulties in western agricultural, resource, and environmental policies today.

Coevolutionary agricultural development can be envisioned as a sequential process in which a surplus of energy and human capital, beyond what is necessary to maintain the ecosystem and sociosystem in their present states, is directed to establish a new interaction between the systems. If this new interaction is more favorable to man and a surplus can be directed to further beneficial changes, then coevolutionary development is underway.

A surplus can result from transforming the ecosystem so that it captures a greater portion of the sun's energy or transforming it so that it uses less energy for maintenance. Similarly, a surplus can occur by changing technologies, institutions, or values so that the social system uses less energy for maintenance.[9] Stock resources, or the low entropy of the existing order of the world (in Georgescu-Roegen's view), can be used for consumption or as an input to affect coevolutionary development. This latter opportunity significantly alters how we should view the optimal exploitation of stock resources or, more precisely, their optimal exploitation in conjunction with flow resources.

The coevolutionary view challenges the pessimistic entropic determinism of Nicholas Georgescu-Roegen.[10] Although we cannot deny the universal applicability of the Second Law of Thermodynamics, the possibilities for local entropy decreases must be admitted. Georgescu-Roegen acknowledges the incredible energy and long life of our sun and its importance to economic well-being over the long run. His references to biological processes and evolution, however, tend to be limited to the directionality or irreversibility of biological processes, phenomena he associates with the directionality of the Second Law.[11] What Georgescu-Roegen does not fully acknowledge is that man could not have existed on earth 4.5 billion years ago, before life began to evolve an order – through the use of solar energy – that had low entropy for man. The oxygen we breathe, the plant and animal life we eat, and the hydrocarbons we tap to fuel our industry all arise from biological processes. Even the ordering of minerals has improved for man over eons by various physical processes stemming from solar energy and the gradual cooling of the earth. From a perspective limited to man and the earth, the evolution of life has been a negentropic process.[12]

This seemingly optimistic view, however, must be tempered by three severe caveats. First, evolution and man's position therein have largely been a process of chance. Unless man learns how to influence the process, his favored position will go the way of the dinosaur sooner rather than later.[13] Second, though no available data are adequate, many scientists are persuaded that man is currently exploiting the accumulated low entropy of his environment, through both extraction and pollution, to the detriment of future generations far faster than he is coevolving with nature to the benefit of future generations. In this sense, Georgescu-Roegen may be quite correct; most of the technologies we associate with development may simply allow us to utilize low-entropy stocks faster.[14] Third, too little of our current knowledge and research efforts are directly applicable to the immense task of influencing coevolution to our benefit. Indeed, not only the research but the social organization of the developed and developing world are being structured around the exploitation of low-entropy stocks and the correction of related social and environmental problems.[15] A coevolutionary path of progress will not be easily found or followed.

The coevolution of western agriculture may not even coincidentally fit the coevolutionary development mold. One can argue that what we think of as development could simply be a system dislocation associated with the temporary exploitation of hydrocarbons. Even if appropriate energy substitutes are found, the chemical approach to agriculture seems to be collapsing as pests develop resistance and the environment reaches pollution thresholds. Furthermore, the high-yielding cultivars that are nearly dependent on the energy-intensive approach may be extinguishing significant future options through the extermination of diverse traditional strains. Focusing on the social system, one can argue that agricultural coevolutionary change has involved such complex interactions between specialized technical experts, private interests, and bureaucratic empires – in short, a form of advanced coevolution with unusual niche specificity and interdependence – that there are few remaining options for further coevolutionary responses to the problems that will occur inevitably as low-entropy stocks are depleted or if by chance climate should change.[16] These doubts are a realistic complement of the coevolutionary perspective.

The difference between coevolving to a new interaction and adopting a new low-entropy exploiting technology will forever be fuzzy. The introduction of miracle rice varieties, for example, induced phenomenal associated technical and institutional changes.[17] The distinguishing characteristic of the new varieties, however, is their responsiveness to fertilizer, especially nitrogen. To the extent that fertilizers largely come from low-entropy stock resources, the introduction of miracle varieties represents an acceleration of low-entropy resource exploitation largely within the existing sociosystem-ecosystem interactive framework. On the other hand, in conjunction with the recent recognition and adoption of rice-paddy algae that host nitrogen-fixing bacteria, the miracle varieties and associated technical and institutional changes take on the appearance of coevolutionary agricultural development.[18] The pest susceptibility and dependence on water control of the miracle varieties also have implications that put the new rice somewhere between coevolutionary and low-entropy-exploiting technologies. Clearly, the general idea of coevolutionary change cannot be transformed to a simple distinguishing taxonomic characteristic of a new technology.

Though a coevolutionary perspective gives relatively more emphasis to ecological processes, it can also enhance our understanding of the importance of economic organization, political power, and values. Man affects coevolutionary development initially through changes in his social system. These changes can range from subtle shifts in values to minor adjustments in market mechanisms to major power transformations such as a significant land reform. Whether or not there is a net surplus, a new interaction is initiated, and this is seen as coevolutionary development ultimately depends on the distribution between groups in society of the positive and negative effects of a new interaction with the environment, on the historical distribution of power between these groups, and on the values of these groups. Power, the ability to affect or impede change, is also not an absolute; it depends critically on the types of changes under consideration. Otherwise analogous opportunities to interact with an ecosystem might be chosen by one society and shunned by another because of differences in their economic organization, power structures, or values.

The coevolutionary explanation of agricultural development is no more value free than any other view but is somewhat more positive. It emphasizes the opportunities for and the processes of change given the organization, power, and values of the actors involved, while other views start with value-laden objectives of development and proceed to explain why these objectives are not being met or how they might be.

Whether or not coevolutionary development ever gets started depends on some initial compatibility between the social and ecological systems. The failure of planned development of the Brazilian Amazon, for example, can be characterized as a classic sociosystem and ecosystem mismatch.[19] The key characteristics of the ecosystem are incredible species diversity, a highly specialized system of nutrient recycling, uncertain succession responses, and rapid rates of growth. These characteristics suggest that an initially compatible social system would emphasize (1) a multiple-product, regional, near-subsistence economy, (2) participation of native people with knowledge of the natural system, (3) technologies that evolved in the tropics, (4) formal and informal risk sharing, and (5) decision-making power in the hands of people close to the dynamic ecosystem. Instead, Brazil has attempted to implant social systems that (1) produce a few crops for distant markets, (2) transplanted peasants and capitalists from the south of Brazil, (3) use temperate zone technologies, and (4) share decision-making power with government bureaucracies and large corporations extending to Brasilia and São Paulo. In spite of extensive transfers from the south of Brazil, the implanted social structure has broken down as corporations leave after their development subsidies terminate and as peasants find multiple cropping of subsistence crops combined with hunting and gathering – in essence, the pattern of the indigenous population – to be a more suitable approach.

Using temperate-zone approaches to agriculture in a tropical rain forest entails high transactions costs. The social system must maintain better roads, storage facilities, and exchange systems for cash crops using produced inputs. More sophisticated credit, risk-sharing, and extension programs are required to counteract the unpredictable yields of monocultures of crops unsuited to the ecosystem. The necessary layer of businessmen, bureaucrats, and technicians on top of an otherwise agrarian society also increases the diversity in education and values and, hence, the difficulties of defining and attaining social goals. The resulting high transaction costs are symptoms of the social and ecological mismatch. They more than absorb any surplus that has been transferred to the rural sector or that perhaps could be internally generated to promote coevolutionary development. The consequent process of social degeneration is shared with the environment. The consequent transformation, species extinction, and soil destruction have been the environmental costs.

The coevolutionary framework is compatible with the induced innovation framework of Hayami and Ruttan that was extended to institutions by Binswanger, but the two approaches have some distinctly different emphases. Ruttan starts with relative scarcities of productive factors, treating natural resources such as land and water as separable inputs. The coevolutionary view includes such more or less separable inputs, but stresses ecosystem characteristics. How ecological components connect, interact, and respond to perturbations – how nutrients recycle, weeds succeed, and insects populate when man changes his role – are important in coevolution. In both views, technologies and institutions develop in response to some initial conditions – relative scarcities in the induced innovation and institutions framework and ecological characteristics in the coevolutionary perspective. Most descriptive studies that start with the induced innovation framework acknowledge the feedbacks from the social system to the ecosystem, but the framework itself is basically linear, moving from relative factor scarcities, to technologies, to institutions. The coevolutionary perspective, however, looks more closely at the feedback of technological and institutional changes on the ecosystem as part of an on-going reciprocal process. The various responses of the ecosystem to this feedback determine the ways in which the innovation is successful and not successful and provide new signals for the social system to respond to.

Model specifics and policy prescriptions will differ for every ecological and social system combination. Coevolutionary arguments will put more emphasis on system interactions, evolution, energy flows, and transaction costs and less emphasis on the returns to individual factors or the effect of a particular institution. But the choice of specifics will depend on which social and ecological characteristics and interactions are deemed most critical, a step that will initially depend on good intuition as much as sound science. The coevolutionary framework allows for the possibility of social progress while acknowledging ecological processes and the difficulties inherent in influencing interactive change. A coevolutionary perspective may only be an entrée to linking economic and ecological thinking; but this entrée and linking can begin to resolve the present incongruity between the descriptions and policy prescriptions of natural scientists and economists.[20]

[. . .]

Notes

1   The concept of coevolution was introduced by Paul R. Ehrlich and Peter H. Raven in "Butterflies and Plants: A Study of Coevolution," *Evolution* 18 (1964): 586–608. In its original context, the concept refers to a mutual interaction in predator-prey, host-parasite, model-mimic, and competitor-competitor systems in which the nature of the relationship becomes more tightly defined in a race that could lead to extinction for one or the other. See also Herbert G. Baker and Paul D. Hurd, Jr., "Intrafloral Ecology," *Annual Review of Entomology* 13 (1968): 385–414.

2   Norgaard, "Sociosystem and Ecosystem Coevolution in the Amazon."

3   Some of the complexities associated with benefits and costs over time in this definition are considered later in this section and the next.

4   For an interesting account of this interaction, see Clifford Geertz, *Agricultural Involution: The Processs of Ecological Change in Indonesia* (Berkeley: University of California Press, 1963).

5   Eugene Odum, "The Strategy of Ecosystem Development," *Science* 164 (April 18, 1969): 262–70. Also, see Kenneth E.F. Watt, *Principles of Environmental Science* (New York: McGraw-Hill Book Co., 1973), chaps. 11 and 12.

6   To the extent that these adjustments occur in the social system and are financed by general tax revenues or the adjustments occur incompletely and social costs remain, private market incentives will encourage too much or incorrect adjustments, and social participation in decisions involving agriculture will be justified in many cases.

7   John Perkins, *Insects, Experts, and the Insecticide Crisis: The Quest for New Pest Management Strategies* (New York: Plenum Publishing Corp., 1981).

8   This statement also suggests how the coevolutionary perspective may be compatible with the empirical evidence of the "declining economic importance of land." Private rents from land may be declining because the services of land are increasingly complements of the knowledge-generating and environmental regulatory institutions of the public sector rather than complements of activities over which the individual "landowner" has control.

9   Many readers are no doubt uncomfortable with my condensing the economic problem at this stage to simple energy terms. Energy is common, if imperfect, currency of the two systems, which at this level of abstraction serves a very useful purpose. This usage is more fully developed in Robert Costanza, "Embodied Energy and Economic Evaluation," *Science* 210 (December 1980): 1219–24.

10   See Georgescu-Roegen, *Entropy Law*. His views have generally found favor among natural scientists because of their appeal to natural law. Attempts by economists to refute his pesimistic conclusions have frequently resulted in statements that defy the Second Law of Thermodynamics. See Nicholas Georgescu-Roegen's review of his critics in "Energy and Economic Myths," *Southern Economic Journal* 41 (January 1975): 347–81. A similar defiance is voiced by Simon and ridiculed by his natural science critics. Stuart Burness, Ronald Cummins, Glenn Morris, and Inja Paik clarify thermodynamic principles and the questions they raise for economic theory in "Thermodynamic and Economic Concepts as related to Resource-Use Policies," *Land Economics* 55 (February 1980): 1–9.

11 See esp. Georgescu-Roegen, *Entropy Law*, chap. 8, "Evolution versus Locomotion." The import-ance of irreversibility should not be slighted. The mechanistic nature of the neoclassical economic model allows for processes to be reversed. This is a key complaint of Georgescu-Roegen (chap. 9). Also, see Kenneth J. Arrow and Anthony C. Fisher, "Environmental Preservation, Uncertainty, and Irreversibility," *Quarterly Journal of Economics* 88 (May 1974): 312–19, and the issues raised in the subsequent discussion of this and a related article in *American Economic Review* 64 (December 1974): 1021–39.

12 See Harold F. Blum, *Time's Arrow and Evolution* (Princeton, N.J.: Princeton University Press, 1968). The idea that the earth was unusually well-suited for life to evolve was first explored by Lawrence J. Henderson in *The Fitness of the Environment* (New York: Macmillan and Co., 1913).

13 Alternatively, if our favored position to date is due to a supreme being, then we must be careful to not let this good fortune lapse into a false sense that we control our destiny through good science.

14 The studies cited in n. 8 generally conclude that there is little or no evidence of resource scarcity, for the amount of capital and labor needed to produce a unit of output in the extractive industries has declined dramatically over the past century. This indicator, however, has never impresed natural scientists, because it says nothing about the quantity and quality of resources remaining or the difficulty of developing new technologies. From this perspec-tive, the indicator does not contradict Georgescu-Roegen's hypothesis. From a coevolutionary perspective, the indicator completely ignores the increasing organizational complexity neces-sary for the social and environmental regulation of new technologies. Purchased agricultural inputs, fuel, electricity, water, fertilizers, and pesticides – the inputs associated with modern agricultural technologies and whose share of expenditures now rivals that of labor – are not included in the indicator. The production and distribution of these inputs now link American agriculture with every significant sector of the economy and the far corners of the earth. For all extractive industries, the index ignores the more than proportional growth in the public sector for the provision of education, research and development, transportation and other physical infrastructure, environmental management, and, to some extent, even defense that makes modern resource exploitation possible.

15 Related views are elaborated in Daly.

16 With respect to the possibilities of and our preparedness for climatic change, see Stephen H. Schneider and L. Mesirow, *The Genesis Strategy* (New York: Plenum Publishing Corp., 1976).

17 Ruttan and Binswanger, "Induced Innovation and the Green Revolution."

18 R.J. Buresh, M.E. Casselman, and W.H. Patrick, Jr., "Nitrogen Fixation in Flooded Soil Systems: A Review," *Advances in Agronomy* 33 (1980): 149–92.

19 This paragraph and the subsequent one draw on Norgaard, "Sociosystem and Ecosystem Coevolution in the Amazon."

20 Economists in both national and international development agencies now find their authority attenuated, albeit only moderately, by separate environmental planning and project review staffs. This is documented in International Institute for Environment and Development, *Banking on the Biosphere, Multilateral Aid and the Environment: The Environmental Policies and Practices of Nine Multilateral Aid Institutions* (Washington, D.C.: International Institute for Environment and Development, 1978).

READING 12.2   FOUNDERS IN ENVIRONMENTAL EDUCATION

A. Greenall Gough

Source: Deakin University Press, Geelong, 1993: 38–43

Exploring the instrumental roots of environmental education

The story of environmental education in which the founders are inextricably entwined has its roots in an environmentalism of the rational scientific variety, where the earth is conceived of as an object of instrumental value, there only to meet human needs. Carolyn Merchant quotes the natural philosopher of the Enlightenment era Francis Bacon (1561–1626) to support this notion, arguing that "man" (the term used by Bacon) operates on nature 'to create something new and artificial. Here "nature takes orders from man and works under his authority" ... "By art and the hand of man" nature can then be "forced out of her natural state and squeezed and molded". In this way, "human knowledge and human power meet as one"' (Merchant 1980: 171). She also argues that Bacon reduced "female nature to a resource for economic production" (Merchant 1980: 165). Several hundred years later, a similarly instrumental approach remains in the report of the World Commission on Environment and Development which states that:

> Humanity has the ability to make development sustainable – to ensure that it meets the needs of the present without compromising the ability of future generations to meet their own needs ... technology and social organisation can both be managed and improved to make way for a new era of economic growth.
>
> (World Commission on Environment and Development 1987: 8)

Accompanying this rational scientific approach to the environment is a vision of a socially reconstructed, environmentally responsible society which can be achieved through education. Education is seen as an instrument for achieving the scientists', or environmentalists', goals. As scientist Otto Frankel argued at the 1970 Australian Academy of Science Conference, "what is needed is not only a fuller understanding of the biosphere, but a new sense of values, a new perception of our own role and responsibilities in and for the biosphere ... Our only hope is that this new understanding may develop through the education of old and young" (Frankel 1970: 8). More recently, the World Commission on Environment and Development (1987: 46) has asked: "How are individuals in the real world to be persuaded or made to act in the common interest? The answer lies partly in education, institutional development, and law enforcement." In both instances (and many more could be cited) education is perceived as a tool, an instrument, for achieving a particular goal which may or may not be a generally accepted function of education.

The scientific environmentalist roots of environmental education are easy to trace through the literature of the 1960s and 1970s, in, for example, the writings of Rachel Carson and Paul Ehrlich, and the reports of conferences such as the 'Education and the Environmental Crisis' conference held by the Australian Academy of Science in April 1970 (see Evans and Boyden 1970) which, as we have seen, gave the first formal recognition to environmental education in Australia. It was the scientists who were calling for environmental education as an essential response to the perceived environmental crisis at this time. As Russell Linke comments, "many scientists in the early 1970s were quite prepared to talk about environmental science and believed that they could do it in a value free way" (Linke, interview transcript, 15 December 1991).

The educational aspects of environmental education can just as easily be traced through the literature of the same period. It refers to environmental education as inter-disciplinary and concerned with values – it is education *for* the environment not just *in* or *about* the environment (see Lucas 1979). Environmental education was described in UNESCO documents of this time in terms reflecting this larger view, that is: "it should adopt a critical approach to encourage careful analysis and awareness of the various factors involved in the situation" (UNESCO 1980: 26).

It was soon recognised that the implementation of environmental education within the formal curriculum was not a simple task, as it did not fit the traditional social reproduction (or transmission) curriculum. Its content was seen as interdisciplinary, which was difficult enough, but it was also concerned with values – "to help social groups and individuals acquire a set of values and feelings of concern for the environment" was an objective of environmental education contained in the Tbilisi Declaration (UNESCO 1978: 27). It was also "to provide social groups and individuals with an opportunity to be actively involved at all levels in working towards resolution of environmental problems" (UNESCO 1978: 27), an area which science (and many other) teachers did not feel confident in handling. Many people persisted in trying to make it fit by leaving out the difficult bits of values, participation and decision making but retaining the relatively uncontroversial ecological content. Robottom (1987: 95) postulated that "if the conventional curriculum is a jigsaw puzzle made up of subject 'pieces', then environmental education may be a piece of a different puzzle altogether". It may be that environmental education is more than just part of a different jigsaw puzzle. As Fensham (1987: 22) notes with respect to the characteristics of environmental education as he saw them in 1977, "we were not to see ourselves as apart from but integrally part of the Australian environment(s)" and "action and learning were seen as being symbiotic aspects of EE in all its stages – a very different pedagogical view from that which prevails in much of substantial learning". Thus not only does environmental education imply a non-conventional curriculum, it also implies a different pedagogical view, and different world views.

The rational scientific or instrumentalist approach to environmentalism is associated with major planning, research, management and educational strategies primarily aimed at merging economic development with the conservation of natural resources. The objective is to create a better environment but without changing anything quickly or fundamentally (Hart 1990: 58). In Australia this instrumentalist approach to environmental education can be traced from the Academy of Science conference through the National Conservation Strategy for Australia (DHAE 1984) to the more recent Department of Prime Minister and Cabinet (DPMC) discussion paper on ecologically sustainable development (DPMC 1990). Each of these constructions of environmental education "produce and reproduce the kinds of metaphors and myths that support the positivist 'scientific detachment' from nature rather than 'intractable involvement' in it" (Gough 1991: 34), and with protecting or restoring the land's instrumental value. For example, one of the purposes of the Academy of Science conference was:

> To enquire into the extent to which educational authorities, especially in Australia, have responded to the present environmental situation by introducing educational programs designed to create an awareness of the nature of this situation and to

stimulate thinking about the ways and means by which society might overcome the threats inherent in it.

(Evans and Boyden 1970: 5)

In the National Conservation Strategy for Australia (NCSA) one of the "strategic principles" was to "educate the community about the interdependence of sustainable development and conservation" (DHAE 1984: 16) and the first priority national action to achieve the objectives of the NCSA, under the heading of "Improving the capacity to manage", was to:

Develop and support informal education and information programs ... which promote throughout the community an awareness of the interrelationships between the elements of the life support systems and which encourage the practice of living resource conservation for sustainable development.

(DHAE 1984: 17)

It would be difficult to find a more instrumental statement for the task of environmental education, unless that mantle could be assumed by the Commonwealth discussion paper on ecologically sustainable development which states, in one of its few references to education, that "public education campaigns can help in modifying behaviour to reduce demand for products with adverse environmental consequences and encourage the use of less damaging alternatives. The emergence of green consumerism attests to the ability of public education to modify consumption patterns" (DPMC 1990: 19).

It is within this instrumentalist culture that the environmental education movement arose.

From its earliest conceptions environmental education advocated not only concern for the environment as a philosophy but also participatory democracies. The Tbilisi goal of providing "social groups and individuals with an opportunity to be actively involved at all levels in working towards resolution of environmental problems" (UNESCO 1978: 27) has already been noted. The intention of the goal was to change people's world views as well as to encourage them to take part in making decisions about, and participating in the resolving of, the environmental problems that surround them. The 1970 International Union for the Conservation of Nature and Natural Resources (IUCN) definition of environmental education, quoted earlier in the Introduction to this monograph (CDC 1975: 2; Linke 1980: 26–7) intimated this. It reflected a perceived need to increase the environmental content of educational programs *and* to change how educational programs were being offered.

IUCN continued the association of environmental education with concern for the environment as a philosophy in the World Conservation Strategy (IUCN 1980, sect. 13) where it stated that the "long term task for environmental education is to foster or reinforce attitudes and behaviour compatible with [a] new ethic where human societies live in harmony with the natural world". However, when the World Conservation Strategy was translated and adapted into the National Conservation Strategy for Australia, the education component was expressed only in instrumental terms.

Most of the statements noted above are consistent with the language and assumptions of modernism and the belief that scientific and technological progress together with the public's possession of information will provide the solutions to our environmental problems.[1] As Giroux states:

For many educators, modernism is synonymous with 'the continual progress of the sciences and of techniques, the rational division of industrial work [and the] intensification of human labour and of human domination over nature'. A faith in rationality, science and technology buttresses the modernist belief in permanent change, and in the continual and progressive unfolding of history.

(Giroux 1990: 7)

While it is not unexpected that much of the rhetoric of environmental education is consistent with a modernist view of the world, given its origins in science and its support by scientists, it can be seen that this view of "human domination over nature" is, nevertheless, under threat. As Michael and Anderson state:

> The social construction of reality that once provided a certain coherence to Western society has been unravelling for decades. It was a world view that valued progress, economic efficiency, science and technology – and saw a world composed of separate entities such as atoms, individuals, academic departments, corporations, cities and nations . . .
>
> The most striking feature of the postmodern world is its systemic character, its astounding proliferation of linkages among once-separate cultures, governments, economies and ecosystems . . .
>
> In the postmodern world everything is connected to everything so that cause and effect, present and future, we and they are utterly ensnarled . . .
>
> (Michael and Anderson 1986: 114–15)

The rhetoric of environmental education is becoming increasingly consistent with the view "that everything is connected to everything". And environmental education has often been written of as interdisciplinary, as taking a holistic approach and as considering the environment in its totality.

Currently, the modernist world view is being questioned from within the profession by scientists themselves – by people such as Birch, Capra, Prigogine and the whole "chaos" movement – and by people outside science. As Gleick argues:

> Where Chaos begins, classical science stops. For as long as the world has had physicists inquiring into the laws of nature, it has suffered a special ignorance about disorder – Now that science is looking, chaos seems to be everywhere . . . Chaos breaks across the lines that separate scientific disciplines. Because it is a science of the global nature of systems, it has brought together thinkers from fields that had been widely separated . . . Believers in chaos . . . feel that they are turning back a trend in science toward reductionism . . . They believe that they are looking for the whole . . . chaos cuts away at the tenets of Newton's physics . . . chaos eliminates the Laplacian fantasy of deterministic predictability.
>
> (Gleick 1988: 3–6)

In a similar vein Birch (1990: 127–8) argues that "the errors of the modern world view are that it is mechanistic, dualistic, substantialist, anthropocentric, simplistic and disciplinary" and that we need a new vision, a postmodern ecological world view.[2] For Birch (1990: 77), such a world view entails an emphasis on relationships between events not substances, on entities as subjects and on entities "as dependent in their constitution upon their environment". He calls this new world view postmodern "because it is destined to supersede the dominant model of today" (Birch 1990: 73).

According to Birch (1990: xvi–xvii), "The reformation of modernism into postmodernism involves a radical transformation of science, religion and culture that constitutes a revolution even greater than the Scientific Revolution and the Enlightenment". He goes on to envisage the results of such a transformation in the following terms:

As contrasted with the modern world view which is sustained more by habit than conviction and which has promoted ecological despoilation, militarism, antifeminism and disciplinary fragmentation, the postmodern world view is postmechanistic and ecological in its view of nature, postreductionist in its view of science, postanthropocentric in its view of ethics and economics, postdiscipline in relation to knowledge and postpatriarchal and postsexist in relation to society.

Postmodernism is not a call back to the premodern but a creative synthesis of the best of the modern, premodern and new concepts in the forefront of holistic thinking ... The word 'ecological' is added because of the emphasis on relationships in the development of postmodern thought that has been influenced by process philosophy.

(Birch 1990: xvi)

Notes

1 Modernism within the history of science has its roots in the early stages of the period of the Enlightenment in the sixteenth and seventeenth centuries. It has acted as the dominant model of the universe, or dominant world view, since its inception and offers a particularly mechanistic interpretation of nature's use and value.

2 Given founder Peter Fensham's friendship with Charles Birch, noted earlier in Part 1 of this monograph, it is interesting to ponder the extent to which Fensham's holistic thinking with respect to science, the environment and environmental education has been influenced through interacting with Birch.

[...]

VIGNETTE 12.1 FRAMEWORKS AND METAPHORS FOR SUSTAINABILITY: THE TENSIONS BETWEEN CULTURAL CHANGE AND EDUCATIONAL PRACTICE

H. Haste, University of Bath

It seems that no-one questions the need for 'environmental education'. All agree that 'new ways of thinking' are needed; the differences lie in what these are. As Harré *et al.* (1999) spell out, 'Greenspeak' challenges huge swathes of Western thought. The first task is to acknowledge how metaphor and grand narrative frame our relations with the natural world. The second is to change those metaphors and narratives.

Greenall Gough and Norgaard reflect two options. For Norgaard, the primary issue is how we think about *systems*. He challenges the rationalist economic mechanistic worldview with a biological metaphor. Mechanistic models search for laws and predictability; once those laws are understood, control is possible. In contrast, biological models emphasise cyclicity, interdependence, and most particularly, the importance of recursivity and feedback. For a system to be sustainable, these recursive processes must enhance, not degrade.

Greenall Gough's concerns are twofold; first that modernist metaphors privilege a view of education as the transmission of facts, and second, that education can be harnessed purely instrumentally to achieve narrow ecological goals. Confronting people with the 'facts' about environmental damage, to make them alter their behaviour appropriately, misses the point about the need to rethink the underlying metaphors, not only of our relationship with the world, but of our relationships within educational practice. The danger is that we may be replacing one kind of technological fix with another – replacing a blind belief in technology, with an equally blinkered optimism about changing micro behaviour patterns.

Greenall Gough's post-modern critique requires that we get away from positioning the human individual as an agent at the centre of the system. We must instead position the human in the larger bio-system. To tackle the problems of materialism and our mechanistic and instrumental attitude to the environment, we must challenge the metaphors of progress that legitimate exploitation, and ultimately challenge our anthropocentric worldview.

Norgaard's systemic model, drawing on biological metaphors, alerts us to the nature of systems themselves – including that inappropriate intervention in parts of the system can cause the whole to degrade. His example of the Brazilian rain forest economy is striking. Norgaard's story is consistent with the message that we must change the metaphor. However, to what extent might we see Norgaard as 'instrumental' in Greenall Gough's terms? Implicit in his description can be read the idea that if we have a better model of the system, we can 'work' it better, to overcome the problems of ecological imbalances. This does not, as such, remove the anthropocentric bias.

Both Greenall Gough and Norgaard address the need to reconstruct our worldview. But what are the implications for education? Why are we educating young people about the environment? And how can we do so effectively? What effect on the larger ecological problems will changes in educational practice and content have? These questions go beyond the issues of instrumentalism. They concern educational theory and assumptions about the role of education in social change.

Let us consider some key questions which reflect the dilemmas of environmental education (Stables and Scott 2001b).

If we change behaviour, is that purely 'instrumental', in Greenall Gough's terms?

People who become aware of the consequences of their own waste disposal and squandering of resources can be strongly motivated to be more responsible about them. This has been, in places, remarkably successful. Similarly, the pressure for 'green' products has altered the behaviour of many producers of goods of all types.

However, value change *per se* is not enough to undermine the modernist worldview. The metaphor of harmony, and 'everything connected to everything', is crucial to seeing and being engaged with the larger picture. Understanding this requires more than just appreciating that demands for more and newer products will diminish natural resources and create more waste and therefore pollution. Educating for recycling is not necessarily enough to educate for the metaphor of cyclicity. For that, one must challenge the whole notion of progress and indeed, the notion that 'technology can fix it'.

If we create active and responsible citizens, will this challenge worldviews?

If we assume that mass grassroots action is an effective force for cultural and social change, then education would be a force for moral and political agency, to create consumer-citizens who will put pressure on industry and government to act more 'responsibly'. To effect this, we must inculcate a *sense of responsibility* in young people, so that they regard it as part of their brief as citizens to exercise that social pressure, and also have a *sense of personal efficacy* – that they can have an effect. These are the established roots of active citizenship (Haste 2001a; Kahn 1999).

One route is through awareness of the direct and visible effect of their own, or other people's irresponsible behaviour. Another is the appeal to altruism and empathy. Children need to engage with a specific aspect of the issues, in order to feel personally efficacious. To be part of a 'global' world is meaningless to a concrete operational thinker; to care about baby tigers or litter in the streets is much more useful. To recognise that CFCs damage the ozone layer, and to stop using hairsprays, engages the teenager, through the act over which she has personal control – her shopping. A small step, but a crucial one for efficacy.

Can we transform a worldview through educational practices?

What skills are necessary for a worldview of global responsibility and environmental awareness that challenges the modernist perspective as described by Greenall Gough and others (e.g. Bowers 1995)? This perspective subscribes to a model of closed, convergent and unitary solutions, and in consequence, educates for linear analytic thinking and the single 'right' answer. It also conveys the message that focusing on only one facet of the issue, excluding the larger picture, is both the best way to reach a solution and the ideal model of 'rationality'. The consequence of such training is to create cultural anxiety about ambiguity and diversity (Haste 2001b).

A first step in developing a less restrictive outlook is to privilege and foster the capacity to manage ambiguity and diversity fruitfully. In a world of rapidly developing technology and philosophical and scientific change, children need to learn to be able to manage ambiguity and diversity in order to be effective members of their culture (Haste 2001b). Support for this comes not only from a philosophical position but also from the extensive work in the natural sciences and mathematics on chaos and complexity. It would – hopefully – prevent the flight into unreasoned searches for certainty, whether scientistic or theological. It is also of inestimable value for those trying to understand and resolve the ecological crisis to have a mindset that can take account of the multiplicity of factors, feedback processes and potential ways to arrive at solutions.

But would this automatically generate eco-centric values, or even moral responsibility and agency? Critics of the 'instrumental' approach to environmental education like Greenall Gough are right that focusing on narrow and reassuringly achievable outcomes does not erode those assumptions about technological fixes, and/or triumphalism in the face of adversity, which are consistent with the traditional model of the autonomous human who can master the world. The analysis of the problem requires a major shift in how we position ourselves in relation to our planet – and in relation to our cultural context. Rejecting an ethic of individualism is a necessary part of recognising our cultural and linguistic interdependence (Haste 1996). Educating our young in ways that take these ideas on board will change how we manage their experience of social and intellectual interaction. It will also change how we manage the classroom and sensitise our young people to their own embeddedness in community and culture.

These are eminently desirable educational goals. They are consistent with contemporary understanding of human development, and will make us more effective educators. But of themselves they do not guarantee the planet's sustainable development.

In the burgeoning eco-literature we see an emergent concept of an embedded, contextualised, and systemic eco-system, which provides a far more satisfactory basis for tackling ecological problems (Bowers 1995; Harré *et al.* 1999; Stables 2001a). This is happening concurrently with a shift to thinking about educational practices in the context of culture and language (Cole 1995). This concurrence is probably not coincidental; both are part of the current philosophical climate. However, they are not causally related and we must not be tempted to conflate them.

VIGNETTE 12.2 ECONOMIC BEHAVIOUR: VALUE AND VALUES

A. Dobson, Open University, UK

Sustainability is not just a matter of getting the science right. Science might be able to tell us what the carbon dioxide tolerances of certain animal and plant species are, but it cannot tell us which species we should be concerned about. Deciding 'what matters' in the context of sustainability involves value judgements that can be informed by science, but not conclusively determined by it.

If this makes sense, then environmental education cannot be simply a question of transmitting a series of 'facts' about the environment to students. It must also be about the negotiation of values. Annette Greenall Gough (1993) argues that values have been present in environmental education practically since its inception, but she is critical of the kind of values that have been implicitly and explicitly transmitted. She writes that, 'The story of environmental education . . . has its roots in an environmentalism of the rational scientific variety, where the earth is conceived of as an object of instrumental value, there only to meet human needs' (p. 38). The idea that nature only has value as a resource for human beings is, in turn, a feature of 'anthropocentrism' (p. 42), according to which human beings are not only the source but also the measure of all value.

An alternative view holds that nature has 'intrinsic' as well as instrumental value – that it has value in itself, as well as a means to human ends. The framework here is 'ecocentric' rather than anthropocentric. At the very least, then, environmental education should confront students with these two alternative ways of valuing nature, and illustrate the different meanings of sustainability that can be built upon them.

There is a third alternative, too, not mentioned by Greenall Gough, but which has made considerable inroads recently in the values debate. Deciding what we want to sustain depends in large measure upon whose interest perspective we adopt when we decide. It might be in the interest of the present generation of anthropocentric human beings to binge on nature's bounty. Ecocentrics will object, though, that this does not take nature's interests into account. These two camps are usually regarded as being at loggerheads, but there is a third value perspective that has the potential to unite them – that of future generations of human beings.

Greenall Gough represents future generation thinking as a simple anthropocentric instrumentalism, and she quotes the famous World Commission on Environment and Development (WCED) definition of sustainable development to prove it: development that 'meets the needs of the present without compromising the ability of future generations to meet their own needs' (p. 39). But in characterising this as a simple anthropocentrism Greenall Gough forgets that we cannot definitively know what the needs of future generations are. Even if we say that they will have a need for food and for beauty, we cannot know how they will want to satisfy those needs. We cannot, in other words, predict what future generations will value.

Assuming that we have the kind of obligation towards future generations to which the WCED refers, then, how can we discharge it? Given that we cannot predict the needs and wants – the 'plans for life' – of future generations, the best (and the most) we can do is to provide them with the wherewithal to make their own choices. This amounts to enjoining us (the present generation) to pass on the broadest 'bequest package' we can. In terms of the natural environment, we should pass on as much diversity as we can, since diversity is the precondition for choice.

Note that this conclusion is exactly the one ecocentrics would probably want us to reach, but we have reached it without recourse to the contested idea of the 'intrinsic value of nature'. Once we see that we cannot definitively determine what the future will regard as valuable, the way is open to a form of 'enlightened anthropocentrism' that defends natural diversity just about as effectively as ecocentrism. As well as instrumental and intrinsic value, then, programmes for environmental education could profitably include reflections on value that derive from taking the interests of future generations into account.

Note, also, that we have moved – almost insensibly – from the question of what we should *value* (ethics), to the question of what we can *know* (epistemology). More precisely, we are in the territory of what we cannot know, and so the ironic challenge for environmental education is to teach us what to do in conditions of constitutive ignorance. This is the area in which the objective of sustainability is in most significant tension to the methods and aspirations of the 'modernity' criticised by the postmodernists cited by Greenall Gough towards the end of her extract. But they miss the point by referring instead to that other grand area of philosophical enquiry, ontology – 'being', or 'what there is'. The modernist project is, as Francis Bacon said, to control nature, and a precondition for control is knowledge. Thus, if our knowledge of nature is constitutively imperfect, so will our control be imperfect. This epistemological point is much more important, to my mind, than the ontological ones expressed by Greenall Gough's postmodernists.

In this context, Norgaard is very much in the modernists' camp. His theory of coevolution is a fascinating attempt to show how we have vastly underestimated the difficulties associated with understanding the relationship between human beings and their environment, but nowhere does he question that, given the right tools (i.e. the ones he provides us with), we *can* understand it. His model, according to which what he calls the 'sociosystem' evolves in response to changes in the ecosystem, which in turn have been produced by the sociosystem, and so on reciprocally in a dialectic dance, is a massive improvement on more simplistic 'action and reaction' models. He is in no doubt that the application of such a model would help us to avoid 'many of the difficulties in western agricultural, resource, and environmental policies today' (p. 530). While he recognises that 'coevolutionary feedback need not benefit man' (p. 528), he is convinced that we can 'learn how to influence the process' (p. 531) and thereby avoid the mistakes that have led to the failure of plans to develop the Brazilian Amazon, for example.

But what if our failure to model human–environment relations is not merely contingent but is, rather, constitutive of that relationship? The modernist would characterise this as fatalism, but ignorance does not imply inaction. Interestingly, Norgaard reaches the same conclusion regarding 'broad bequest packages' as does the enlightened anthropocentric we introduced earlier. He worries that 'high-yielding cultivars that are nearly dependent on the energy-intensive approach may be extinguishing significant future options through the extermination of diverse traditional strains' (p. 532). This amounts to depriving future generations of the opportunity to grow different food in a different way. So a sophisticated model rooted in the drive to know produces the same conclusion as a pragmatic attachment to ignorance. Does this mean that all roads really do lead to Rome? Perhaps. The common factor – common also to the enlightened anthropocentrism that apparently steers a path between simple anthropocentrism and ecocentrism – is the framework provided by thinking about the future. These reflections on Greenall Gough and Norgaard have taken us from ethics to epistemology and from the present to the future; it may be that our non-knowledge of the future, rather than our ethical ruminations in the present, is the foundation on which to build a lasting sustainability.

CHAPTER 13

GLOBALIZATION AND FRAGMENTATION: SCIENCE AND SELF

READING 13.1 CAPITALISM AND SOCIAL PROGRESS: THE FUTURE OF SOCIETY IN A GLOBAL ECONOMY

P. Brown and H. Lauder

Source: Palgrave, Basingstoke, 2001: 218–226

[. . .]

The redefinition of intelligence is a key part of the struggle for collective intelligence. But it is inadequate because of its limited focus on individuals. There are many private troubles felt by people that require public solutions, such as raising productivity, knowledge production, reducing poverty and crime, or improving education or the quality of employment opportunities, which cannot be resolved without collaboration with family, friends, neighbours, co-workers or fellow citizens.[1] In post-industrial societies it is the collective intelligence of families, communities, companies and society at large, which will determine the quality of life as well as economic competitiveness. Despite the obsession of some who still believe that we can find ways of controlling human beings – if not by turning them into machines, which was popular for much of the twentieth century, then by rendering them redundant through the development of artificial intelligence – for the first time in human history we confront the task of developing and pooling the intelligence of *all* of the population of post-industrial societies.

Collective intelligence can be defined as empowerment through the *development and pooling of intelligence* to attain common goals or resolve common problems.[2] It is inspired by a spirit of co-operation rather a Darwinian survival of the fittest. In a society that eulogizes the virtues of competition, self-interest and acquisitiveness, rather than co-operation, common interest and the quality of life, it is difficult to maximize human potential or to co-ordinate opportunities for intelligent action in an efficient manner. The struggle for collective intelligence therefore involves more than a democratization of intelligence, it involves making a virtue of our mutual dependence and sociability which we will need to make a dominant feature of post-industrial society based on information, knowledge and lifelong learning.[3]

To develop our understanding of the social foundations of collective intelligence at any given historical moment, a distinction can be made between the *capacity for intelligence* and *relations of trust*. The capacity for intelligence describes the raw materials on which the development of intelligence depends. It refers to the state of knowledge, scientific discovery, technology and learning techniques, on which societies can draw. It includes the knowledge and technological resources amassed in society in the form of books, journals, databases, computers and computer programmes, universities, research institutes, museums, laboratories, and super-highways to name but a few.

In many respects the capacity for intelligence has become global in scope as new ideas, fashions, technologies and sources of productivity traverse the globe in real time through the media, Internet and MNCs. The Human Genome Program launched by the US Department of Energy and the National Institutes of Health in 1990 is an example. One of its major aims was to identify all of the approximate 100,000 genes in human DNA and combined universities and research centres in the US, the UK, Australia, Canada, Germany, France, Japan, Denmark, Israel and Italy. At a societal level the capacity for intelligence would also include the scale of investment in the knowledge, learning and research infrastructure in the form of schools, colleges, universities, libraries, museums, training centres, research institutes and information superhighways.

Conventional economic approaches have limited our horizons to trying to measure certain facets of the capacity for intelligence, such as attempts to measure the national stock of human capital. Obvious problems with this approach are the crude measures, such as years of formal education, which are used to calculate the quality of a nation's human resources, and the way that human intelligence and learning are reduced to a question of earning a living. If these are serious problems, the death knell of human capital models is the failure to acknowledge intelligence as a social gift. How intelligence is defined; whether its cultivation is restricted to a few or extended to all; the extent of 'our' knowledge, including scientific discoveries, art, literature and music; whether we have the opportunity to use our brains at work; and the quality of the culture which furnishes the definition of intelligence and human nature, are shaped by individuals as members of society. We make our own history but in co-operation with others, and not always in ways that we choose or intend. The nature and distribution of intelligence will be shaped by the social groups to which an individual belongs and the cultural, economic and political fabric of society more generally. In low trust societies, for instance, education, knowledge and learning are treated as part of a zero-sum game, where extending opportunities to less privileged groups and the pooling of intelligence is seen as a threat to the posit ional advantage of social elites.[4] Therefore, the development and pooling of intelligence is severely restricted for less-advantaged social groups and hence for society as a whole.

As human capital ideas have come to dominate government policies there has been a considerable emphasis on increasing post-compulsory access to tertiary education, adult training and wiring-up schools to the Internet. This kind of capacity building is important but inadequate as such policies fail to take account of how the raw materials of postindustrial economies are weaved into the social fabric. The inter-relationship between *capacities* and *relations* is vital because it addresses the extent to which people are institutionally encouraged to pool their intelligence.

To aid our understanding of relations of 'trust' we need to distinguish it from its everyday meaning of whether we think someone is honest. Trust is used here to refer to whether the development and pooling of intelligence is reflected in the relationships between individuals, groups, and social classes that are embedded in classrooms, offices, shopfloors, households, neighbourhoods, welfare policies and taxation systems. This emphasis on institutionally embedded trust does not ignore the importance of national cultures or political ideologies. Confucianism as exhibited in some Asian countries is, for example, usually seen to encourage social harmony, whereas the tenets of Western individualism as applied in the last twenty years or so, has made it virtually impossible for people (even within the same family) to think in terms of co-operation and mutual dependence. The cultural context will clearly have a powerful impact on social values and attitudes: as R.H. Tawney reminded us in our introductory chapter, it is impossible to achieve significant social change without changing the 'scale of moral values which rules the minds of individuals', because it is these values which have shaped social history.[5] But we have to do more than look at the principles which guide how people treat each other. Allan Fox correctly highlights the need to focus on the way social relationships are embedded 'in the institutions, patterns, and processes themselves which are operated by people who are capable of choosing differently'.[6]

At a societal level, the taxation paid by different income groups, the generosity of welfare provision for those who do not have access to waged work, or the provision of lifelong learning to all sections of society whether rich or poor, act as important signals which are easily decoded by people into 'this is a society which is pulling together in the interests of all' or 'this a society based on looking after number one'. The more inclusive the society the more people from all walks of life are likely to feel that they have a stake in the system as Richard Wilkinson has demonstrated in his international study of *Unhealthy Societies*, mentioned above. He found that the social polarization in the 1980s led to a growth in the number of poor people dying prematurely, committing suicide, getting divorced, and whose children were underachieving at school. He is able to show that these social pathologies were less a direct consequence of material deprivation, than a symptom of a collapse in trust as those in poverty saw fellow Americans or Britons as indifferent to their suffering and felt that they were no longer bona fide members of society.

This research not only shows that poverty leads to low trust relations between the haves and have nots but that it undermines the capacity of disadvantaged neighbourhoods for informal 'social learning' because of their social exclusion. Social learning is central to building social capital at the grass-roots. James Coleman thought that social capital inheres in the relationships between individuals in a community which is characterized by high trust relations and shared responsibilities.[7] An example would be a network of the mothers of kindergarten and primary school children, who share the duties of ferrying kids to and from school, and who share the responsibility of looking after other children when the need arises. The reason why this leads to the creation of social capital is that these activities also involve communicating to children a shared set of expectations about appropriate standards of behaviour, the value of education, and the benefits of sharing resources including cars and time. This form of informal learning may not be overt or even oral, but is achieved by prompting such as 'have you got homework today?', or by parental interest in what the children did at school that day. It is the messages of the community in sum that is significant in the creation of social capital. The relative wealth of communities in this respect is reflected in the performance of their children in school as Coleman and Hoffer have demonstrated.[8]

The impact of inequality on the development of informal learning is not difficult to understand, although it often operates in subtle and complex ways. Communities or networks which are rich in social capital, for instance, take time, energy and resources to build. They also depend on a high degree of stability in the family and neighbour context. This is highlighted in Coleman and Hoffer's research as they found that the most significant impact on educational failure was the amount of times a child moves school. But this kind of instability is most frequently found in poor school districts.[9] This is not the only malign effect of poverty in the creation of social capital. The impact of the ghettoization of American inner cities on the decline in social capital is graphically portrayed in the work of William Julius Wilson which was noted earlier and is worth reiterating here.[10] Wilson shows how a perceptive ghetto youngster in a neighbourhood where some people have been able to keep good jobs, even in a context of increasing joblessness and idleness, can continue to see a meaningful connection between education and employment. The problem is that these neighbourhoods show signs of becoming even more polarized when those who are able to find decent jobs leave. As a consequence, the more social groups become isolated from one another the fewer opportunities exist for the kind of informal learning which contributes to collective intelligence.

Building high trust relations is at the heart of the struggle for collective intelligence, in that it is a way of moving towards a form of associated living which involves making experience more communicable by removing the social distance which makes individuals impervious to the interests of others.[11] This conforms to John Dewey's notion of democracy which is more than a system of government as it defines the way people live together and pool their intelligence.[12] Collective intelligence is exercised through the development of the art of conversation and by giving an authentic voice to all constituencies of society. This in turn depends upon the breakdown of social divisions which inhibit the free communication and interaction between people and groups. This applies equally at the level of society where social barriers are constructed around class, race or religion, as it does to the workplace or home, when sharp distinctions are imposed between management and workers or breadwinners and home-makers. Such barriers serve to undermine the potential for collective intelligence. But it is not only the powerless who lose out in these circumstances, its consequences for social elites may be less material and less obvious, but remain insidious as, 'their culture tends to be sterile, to be turned back to feed on itself; their art becomes a showy display and artificial; their wealth luxurious; their knowledge over-specialized; their manners fastidious rather than humane'.[13]

In such a society the development of intelligence is severely constrained by inequality, poverty and cultural elitism. As a result all social groups lack the trust upon which conversation is possible. It denies a society of novel and challenging ideas which frequently stem from diversity in situations and social and cultural experiences. Collective intelligence involves a 'widening of the circle of shared concerns and the liberation of a greater diversity of personal capacity'.[14] A trivial instance was given recently by a friend whose favourite radio programme was *Desert Island Discs*, produced by the British Broadcasting Corporation. The programme involves someone, usually a celebrity or prominent public figure, talking about their life and selecting pieces of music which they would take with them to listen to on their deserted island. Our friend commented that two of the recent castaways were people she had disliked on the basis of their media image. On both occasions she observed how listening to their life stories, anxieties and concerns, had led her to cast these individuals in a more positive light (of course, greater understanding can also lead to the opposite response) because she had had the, albeit brief, opportunity to recognize common points of contact and concern. To share what amounts to a common humanity. In a pluralistic society of different life styles, patterns of behaviour, language and customs, it is basic to the establishment of collective intelligence to recognize aspects of common humanity and for these to be institutionally encouraged.

The development of high trust relations therefore offers the best chance of making a positive feature of cultural pluralism and of meeting post-modern calls for a politics of difference. What is recognized in the struggle for collective intelligence is that different voices which reflect the rich diversity of cultural identity and social experience are the lifeblood which fuels the collective effort to resolve common problems in an attempt to improve the quality of life for all. Equally, this involves recognizing that there are different ways to live a life. But in polarized and divided societies people come to feel isolated and fearsome of groups with which they share little in common and with whom they rarely come into contact. This situation fuels the ideology and practice of self-interest which neutralize ethical decisions, and despite the fact that the struggle for money, power and status leaves most people unfulfilled, it robs people of the opportunity to engage in 'conversations' about the nature of society, working life and personal relationships.

Relations of trust also have profound implications for the organization of economic life in the early decades of the twenty-first century. This is because they shape the nature of co-operation between economic actors, whether as employers, employees, trade union representatives, government policy-makers or consumers. The nature of this cooperation has been historically transformed. Co-operation in pre-industrial societies involved acting for purposes of economic production or distribution on established routines and 'mechanical' solidarity. Cooperation involved little scope for human freedom, as Marx suggested, 'the individual has as little torn himself free from the umbilical cord of his tribe or community as a bee has from his hive'.[15] Marx noted that there were few examples in ancient times of co-operation on a large scale and where this did occur is was founded on slavery. With the rise of industrial capitalism new forms of economic co-operation developed based on the 'free' wage-labourer who sells his or her labour-power to employers and the development of the factory model of production. The factory system involved a fundamental change, in that workers had to be disciplined to co-ordinate their working day and work activities, which greatly increased productivity, as Marx observed, 'the socially productive power of labour develops as a free gift to capital' whenever workers are organized in this way.[16]

Marx saw this form of social co-operation as a valuable source of capital (although he did not use the term social capital). He also believed it to be exploitative as the owner and controllers of production appropriated the fruits of this collective activity, but as workers came to understand the injustice of capitalism production he believed that they would seek to overthrow the system as they had 'nothing to lose but their chains'. History has proved Marx wrong. The development of mass production in the twentieth century not only enhanced corporate efficiency and profitability, but it also gave workers the chance to collectively mobilize to claim an increasing share of the fruits of productive co-operation as we have described in this book.[17] However, the low-trust relations inherent in the factory model inhibited the patterns of commitment and communication which made it difficult to compete with Japan and the Asian Tiger economies in the 1970s and 1980s.

Low-trust relations led to worker resistance, minimum levels of commitment, high rates of absenteeism, and wild cat strikes. These responses have traditionally been interpreted by management as a manifestation of the feckless and irresponsible nature of most workers. Indeed, managers have typically used these responses to justify the introduction of intensive surveillance and the threat of sanctions in the control of the workforce. A more plausible interpretation is that they are a rational response to working conditions where little is expected of workers and little is given in return.[18] Again, we do not subscribe to the view that American and North European workers are innately more lazy, selfish or incapable of assuming responsibility than those in Japan or Singapore. The higher rates of productivity achieved by Japanese manufacturing companies is not simply due to having more robots than their competitors, or having more efficient inventory systems such as JIT, but it also results from having a human relations regime which encourages workers to think rather than leave their brains at the factory gate, to participate in work teams and to feel empowered in the work setting, rather than as a moron who is so distrusted by management that they are forced to pay a deposit if they want to use a knife and fork in order to eat their lunch.[19]

Today the economic imperatives of capitalism in its post-industrial phase represents an historically unprecedented opportunity to redefine co-operation and the foundations of trust relations. The declining significance of mass employment organizations; the decline of the factory model of efficiency and with it the demise of bureaucratic careers and jobs for life, are transforming the model worker-citizen. Co-operation in high-performance companies depends on the collective intelligence of economic actors, as intellectual and emotional intelligence have become a key feature of the learning, innovation and productivity chain. In a knowledge-driven economy characterized by rapid change, adequate job performance cannot easily rely on external controls, as people need to be proactive, solve problems and work in teams. It is no longer enough to bring people together to generate the 'socially productive power of labour'; co-operation which is value added depends on the development of collective intelligence.

There is a growing body of literature which suggests that in circumstances where employees are given room for individual discretion and see some point in what they are doing, they will show a strong tendency towards co-operation and competence rather than resistance and resentment. The reason? It conforms to a basic human trait – the desire for individual and collective growth. Daniel Goleman has noted that the single most important element in what he calls group intelligence is not the average IQ in the academic sense but social harmony, 'it is this ability to harmonize that, all other things being equal, will make one group especially talented, productive, and successful, and another – with members whose talent and skills are equal in other regards – do poorly'.[20] Equally, Nahapiet and Ghoshal build on these insights to argue that the development of high trust can improve the productivity of knowledge workers and the organizational capacity for innovation.

This works best when all social actors have a stake in the economy and society; when they have a sense of security; when there are open networks of communication and interaction; when people have a wide degree of discretion and freedom about the way they work and live their lives; and when mistakes and failures are seen to be part of a learning process of experimentation and innovation rather than as negligence or ineptitude. Then people will be institutionally encouraged to pool their intelligence.

Collective intelligence, therefore, depends upon a new disposition of mind which rejects the absurd excesses of Western individualism and sensitizes us to what binds people together in co-operative human activities, as well as our interdependence and responsibilities to ourselves and others. A.H. Halsey, who has been a keen observer of the nature of social change in the twentieth century, would no doubt remind us that 'Exhortation alone is futile, whether to altruism or to tolerance or to recognition of the equal claim of others to share in the bounty afforded by society. The problem is to discover, to establish, and to strengthen those social institutions that will encourage and foster the kinds of relations between people that are desired'.[21] The task is one of both re-socializing the mind and of embedding the principles of collective intelligence in the social structure. The difficulties involved in this enterprise should not be underestimated. We can not start from scratch nor can we stand still. We may not, as Giddens depicts contemporary social life, be riding the juggernaut of modernity careering out of control, but there is little doubt that any concerted attempt to build a society based on the struggle for collective intelligence will, as Karl Mannheim recognized, be rather like trying to change a wheel on a train in motion.[22] Despite the enormity of the task, the remaining chapters will show how a society based on the principles of collective intelligence would transform the nation state, economy, education, welfare and the foundations of social justice.

Notes

[...]

1   The classic statement of the difference between private troubles and public issues is in C. Wright Mills, 1959 *The Sociological Imagination*, New York: Oxford University Press.

2 This emphasis on problem solving may appear to some readers as too instrumental, leaving insufficient space for forms of collective activities which are analogous to 'art for art sake', but it is better to see our approach as experimental rather than instrumental, because it involves entering into a dialogue with others which is likely to involve differences in political beliefs or interests about what should be seen as the problem to be solved and also different views about the best solutions.

3 Our definition also highlights the fact that the acquisition of intelligence and the ability to use it depends on the learning potential of individuals (and institutions) in all spheres of life and is not restricted to the formal learning which goes on in our schools, offices or factories.

4 See Phillip Brown, 'The globalization of positional competition', *Sociology*, Spring, 2001.

[. . .]

5 Hence, in speaking about these embedded relations of trust we are referring to the perception people have of the trust reposed in their behaviour as it is expressed and embodied in the rules and relations which others seek to impose on them, or they seek to impose on others. See Alan Fox, *Beyond Contract: Work, Power and Trust Relations*, London: Faber & Faber, 1974, p. 15; pp. 67–9.

6 James S. Coleman, 'Social capital in the creation of human capital', *American Journal of Sociology*, 94, Supplement, 1988, S95–S120.

7 James Coleman and Thomas Hoffer, *Public and Private Schools: The Impact of Communities*, New York: Basic Books, 1987.

8 US General Accounting Office, *Elementary School Children: Many Change School Frequently, Harming Their Education*, Report to the Hon. Marcy Kaptur, House of Representatives, Washington, DC, 1994.

9 William Julius Wilson, *The Truly Disadvantaged: The Inner City, The Underclass and Public Policy*, Chicago: Chicago University Press, 1987.

10 Dewey, *Democracy and Education*, New York: Free Press, 1916, p. 141.

11 ibid., p. 101.

12 ibid., p. 98.

13 ibid., p. 87.

14 See the discussion on Emile Durkheim in the previous chapter.

[. . .]

15 Karl Marx, *Capital Volume 1*, Harmondsworth: Penguin, 1976, p. 452.

16 ibid., p. 451. For a classic study of the development of industrial time, see E.P. Thompson, 'Time, work-discipline, and industrial capitalism', *Past and Present*, vol. 38, 1967.

17 For an interesting and controversial account see Peter F. Drucker's account of the 'productivity revolution', in his *Post-Capitalist Society*, London: Butterworth-Heinemann, 1993.

18 For an excellent study of postwar industrial relations, see Alan Fox, *Beyond Contract: Work, Power and Trust Relations*, London: Faber & Faber, 1974.

19 This was certainly the practice at the British Leyland plant at Cowley, Oxford in England during the mid-1970s. The Cowley plant has since lost over half its workforce and British Leyland was taken-over by the Rover Group which became part of the German car company BMW, before it was then sold on for £10.00.

20 [Daniel Goleman, *Emotional Intelligence*, London: Bloomsbury, 1996, p. 160.]

21 A.H. Halsey, *Change in British Society*, 3rd edn, Oxford: Oxford University Press, 1986, p. 173; See also A.H. Halsey with Josephine Webb, (eds) *British Social Trends: The Twentieth Century*, Basingstoke: Macmillan, 2000.

22 What is equally clear is the need for an holistic approach to social change. It must reject the tendency, for instance, to treat questions of productivity and redistribution as separate realms of policy. This may be administratively convenient but it encourages segmental thinking which downplays their interrelationship in the desire to improve the quality of life for all. Zsuzsa Ferge has made the useful distinction between societal policy and social policy in her study of Hungarian society in the post-war period: 'The concept of societal policy . . . is used in a special sense. It encompasses the sphere of social policy (the organisation of social services or the redistribution of income), but also includes systematic social intervention at all points of the cycle of the reproduction of social life, with the aim of changing the structure of society'. See T.H. Marshall and Tom Bottomore, *Citizenship and Social Class*, London: Pluto Press, 1992, pp. 60–3.

READING 13.2   EDUCATING BEYOND VIOLENT FUTURES

F. Hutchinson

Source: Routledge, London, 1996: 143–149

[. . .]

The new cornucopians and globalisation

By the late twentieth century, the major heirs to eighteenth- and nineteenth-century absolutised confidence in Western civilisation's progress are transnational corporate and economic rationalist narratives. Whatever failings there may have been in the past, capitalist technoscience is said to offer the best way to redemption. Propagated as axiomatic are assumptions of unitary laws of development to a hi-tech, post-industrial future, in which people will be provided with the trickle-down benefits of a consumerist cornucopia. 'Imperatives' are stated for the long wave of transition from pre-industrial to industrial and, finally, post-industrial society.

Whilst there is acknowledged a considerable loss of confidence in recent times in late-industrial economies, *L'Époque de Malaise* is interpreted as a temporary phenom-enon. Here, for example, schools are seen as one way of easing this pain of transition through 'renewal' programmes in computer literacy and enhanced school–business links. In these narratives, the decentring of hope and loss of moral certitudes among many leftists is condemned as contributing to the contemporary, short-term malaise. There is strong affirmation that neo-conservatism and technocraticism have the necessary vision and direction for the twenty-first century (Sakaiya 1991; Oldmeadow 1992).

Whereas all societies were pre-industrial before the Industrial Revolution in the late eighteenth and early nineteenth centuries, the process of Western modernisation of planetary culture will mean, it is predicted in these narratives, that by the late twen-tieth century, 'almost everywhere' post-industrial economies will be the norm. There is in Figure 9 a diagrammatic representation of these kinds of assumptions about glob-alised development.

The guiding images of freedom in this changeview are a truncated freedom to competitively adapt either sooner or later, through macro- and micro-level economic reform, to the projected post-industrial future of transnational capitalism. Within the selective traditions of this *Weltanschauung*, images of what might constitute this post-industrial future tend to be tightly closed in their ideological assumptions. This is especially so in matters of distributive justice, eco-peace and more holistic notions of democratic participation. Already, it is argued in these narratives, Pacific Rim coun-tries, such as Japan, Taiwan, South Korea and Singapore, have embraced 'the idea of progress, as previously conceived and nurtured in the West'. They have done so, it is suggested, 'more enthusiastically than is currently the case in most Western economies' (Kahn and Pepper 1980: 166).

The lessons to be learned by countries such as Australia, according to this changeview, are that they cannot afford either the language of business-as-usual or to pander to 'deep-green extremism' and 'welfare-state bludgers'. In such thinking there is no equiv-alent indignation over tax evasion and avoidance schemes by some wealthy members of society. There is myopia towards 'tax bludging'. Meanwhile, what is said to be needed is 'balanced development' and a minimal welfare safety net. To competitively adapt to the post-industrial future and not be retarded excessively in *L'Époque de Malaise*, there must be the rigorous application of the carrot-and-stick principle. Cornucopian

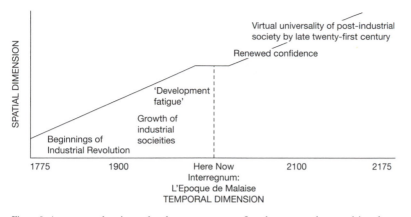

Figure 9 An assumed unitary development pattern for planetary culture: a hi-tech cornucopian perspective.

images of a high-tech, post-industrial future must be combined with 'necessary sacrifices' in making 'a clever country'. High levels of structural unemployment, increased belt-tightening in 'the national interest' and more efficient, often deunionised or deregulated work practices are 'musts' in the transitional phase before the new age of 'abundance of goods and services with a minimum of labour'. Figure 10 presents in simplified form the underlying epistemological assumptions of technocratic dreaming in the late twentieth century (Kahn and Pepper 1980; Toffler 1990).

Economic rationalism is said to dictate major structural adjustments in work practice. In equipping people for the future, a reform agenda is advanced that leaves hidden whose interests might be actually best served by 'the necessary changes'. The reform agenda is defined in terms of a commonality of interests and not sectional interests. Competitive adaptation is said to demand an end to 'union feather-bedding'; moves to 'privatisation'; curbs on 'welfare-state cheats'; greater 'accountability', 'managerial efficiency' and 'school–business links' in the formal education industry sector; more industry 're-skilling' and 'computer literacy' programmes, and, in general, 'a reaffirmation of the idea that market forces are the best method of assuring the efficient allocation of society's resources'. Such perceived developmental requirements have been the subject of a major Film Australia series, titled *Overseas and Undersold* (1991), and a succession of recent educational reports [. . .].

Backed by the formidable intellectual armoury of neo-conservative futurological think-tanks, such as the Hudson Institute in the United States and the Institute of Public Affairs in Australia, there are now powerful efforts to restore flagging confidence in machine culture and a monocultural development paradigm. Previously, largely unproblematised ontology concerning 'natural' development and capitalist technoscience as saviour now receive busy attempts at further legitimation. In this context, there has been a recent tendency to argue the need to acquire competency skills in 'learned optimism'. Seligman (1992) and others, for example, make the valid point that catastrophist thinking should be disputed. However, the proffered forms of disputation generally leave structural violence invisible. Systemic problems are psychologised rather than demystified. There is the promise of personal remedies, such as 'stress management' and 'cognitive behavioural therapies', for meeting life's crises. In the words of the theme tune for the first election campaign by US President, George Bush, 'don't worry, be happy'.

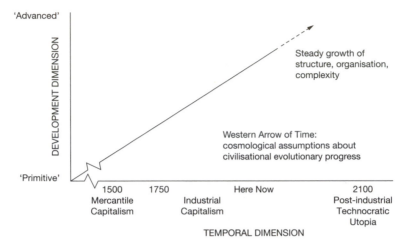

Figure 10 The twenty-first century and beyond: an existential, optimistic perspective on the
Arrow of Time.

The new cornucopians reject Fordism and the modernist 'scientific management'
model but embrace post-Fordism and 'postmodern organisations'. There is a burgeoning business organisational literature on gaining a competitive edge in a time of globalisation and transnational capital. The mechanistic metaphors of the factory production
line of industrial capitalism are acknowledged to be still powerful images but are said to
be now severely limited. Among the new buzz phrases are 'learning organisations',
'cybernetic thinking', 'cyberspace corporations', 'electronic frontiers', 'surfing the Internet', 'infrastructure for the global village', 'imaginisation', 'shared vision', 'interactive
computerised world', 'virtual communities' and 'adaptive cultures' (Morgan 1989; Senge
1992; Peters 1993; Florida 1995; Malone 1995).

In such literature, there is a lack of a critical edge, sociologically speaking, in terms
of power relations, gendered violence and an international division of labour.
Epistemologically speaking, there is a poverty of imagination in that the older metaphors
of clockwork mechanisms, cogs, crankshafts and conveyor belts may be actually in the
process of being replaced by more complex, higher-order machine metaphors of com-
puterisation, cybernetic feedback loops and interactive, multimedia virtual reality:

> Cybernetic thinking, and more generally holistic thinking, does not automatically
> get you out of the world of Descartes and Newton, as many holistic theoreticians
> claim. The cybernetic mechanism may be a more sophisticated model of reality
> than the clockwork model of the seventeenth century but it is still, in the last
> analysis, a mechanism.
>
> (Berman 1990: 24)

Attenuated visions of 'postmodernity' and of transition to the 'postindustrial world'
are being powerfully promoted in late-industrial societies on the eve of the twenty-first
century. Large sums of money are presently expended in communicating images of
progress through state-of-the-art technology, information superhighways and the
freemarket mechanisms of neo-classical economics. The collapse of highly authoritarian
regimes in Eastern Europe in the late 1980s and early 1990s, through popular and
largely non-violent revolutions, has been quite widely interpreted in terms of winning

the Cold War. In neo-conservative narratives, it has been argued as demonstrating the proven rationality of nuclear deterrence strategies and the common sense of peace-through-strength in ensuring future security. It has been appraised, moreover, as a triumph for the Western capitalist model of development (Fukuyama 1989, 1992).

In these narratives, all the hallmarks of uncritical myth-making are in evidence. There is in these strongly culturally edited versions of contemporary history little, if any, critical attempt to look at the underlying causes for the break-up in Eastern Europe of a command economy. The old Soviet model of development is regarded as aberrant rather than being in any way part of a broader, systemic problem of militarism, machine culture and ecologically unsustainable development. Scant attention is given, for example, to the distortions of *both* the Soviet and American economies with the post-World War II arms race, and the consequent diversion in both cases of scarce resources away from peaceful construction. Instead, there is a colonising tendency to posit a *fixum* or an inherent set of priorities in the world's contents in *potentia* for the twenty-first century.

Beyond 'rock logic'

This chapter has explored some dimensions of cultural editing. Powerful cultural myths in late-industrial societies associated with times past, times present and times future have been explored. Such myths may have important implications as to the constructions we place on reality and potential reality and, in turn, may rebound on what we do or do not do in the present. Whether as teachers, parents, students or other members of society, crucial questions have been raised about structure and human agency.

What lessons may be drawn? Edward de Bono (1990) has likened dogmatic closure in our ways of knowing to 'rock logic'. The complexly dialectical nature of the relationships among schools, social change movements and society tends to be obscured in dominant narratives on the future. Metaphorically speaking, rock logic is normalised. There are taken-for-granted views or ingrained habits of thought about things to come. The cluster of emergent values, reconceptualisations, networking initiatives and other potentials associated with 'water logic' is neglected. If the Taoist parodox 'Nothing in the world is as soft and yielding as water; yet for attacking the hard and strong none can triumph so easily' (*Tao Te Ching*) makes some good sense from the perspective of the theory and practice of non-violent action, it makes scarcely any sense from the perspective of machine-culture, linear-mode reasoning.

Those selective traditions of leftist critique that are laden with images of victimology and cosmological assumptions of a Western civilisational arrow of decay and destruction are, if accepted uncritically, likely to be disabling. They abandon the possibility of applied foresight by our teachers, our children, our schools and our societies. They abandon the hope that we may be able to do something practical ourselves about building better futures. As warned by Fromm (1975: 108), radical imagery such as this of the world to come is unlikely to be the cause of quality responses. Rather it is likely to be a cause of 'moral nihilism' and a 'rationalisation of cynicism'. It may even be unwittingly a fertile ground for nihilistic violence and fundamentalism.

If such leftist selective traditions are so lacking in confidence about human agency, the contemporary resurgence of Malthusianism in traditional rightist politics and beyond also displays a strong negativity about the future. However, with the latter, environmental problems are not attributed mainly to rich-world overconsumption but to poor-world overpopulation. As a Western-centric and racist form of demographic reductionism, neo-Malthusianism is very one-eyed in its analysis of systemic environmental problems. It involves scapegoating the poor or the two-thirds world for most of the planetary ills, whilst ignoring the disproportionate environmental impact of the one-third world or the rich. Women in low-income societies are especially blamed. What 'solutions' there may be to local or global environmental problems are likely to be couched in the language of technocentrism, Western-male expert knowledge or even the language of eco-fascism. Kropotkin's perceptive critique in the late nineteenth century of epistemological reductionism in Malthusian thought as giving 'the rich a kind of scientific argument against the ideas of equality' is, in many ways, just as valid now as then (1985: 77). In classrooms where this selective tradition is accepted uncritically, children are presented with an undifferentiated picture of the world in which structural violence is ignored and the poor of the world have their humanity devalued by seeing them negatively through a mechanistic lens as 'the population bomb'.

Contemporary attempts to revive heroic images of Western science and technology and to embrace globalisation are also indicative of cultural editing. Such editing may have important implications, for how and what we teach, what we regard as significant or insignificant knowledge, and what we value as important skills and competencies. Corporate think-tank futurology, technological cornucopianism, the marketing of reductionist forms of information technology in schools 'to fit children for the twenty-first century', school–business links and university–business links are interlinking themes in this uncritical brave new world of cyberspace, 'computer consciousness' and cybernetic learning organisations.

Facilitating futures teaching

Our teachers and schools may become part of self-fulfilling prophecies. Yet, arguably, through encouraging foresight and creative imagination, they may achieve a good deal in facilitating quality responses to feared, violent futures. Instead of self-fulfilling prophecies there may be self-refuting prophecies. Within the constraints and potentialities of site-specific contexts, practical contributions may be made to developing broad rather than narrow literacies on social futures.

There may be encouragement of creative thought and social-living skills for reducing violence against people and planet. In each particular educational context, opportunities for choice and engagement will vary and will be, at times, markedly restrictive, but rarely will the future be a *fait accompli* and individual efforts by teachers and schools entirely unimportant. Collectively, such efforts may be quite significant in their contribution to resisting colonising agendas about the future. The negotiations may be protracted but it is a strict determinist fallacy, as discussed further in the next chapter, to dismiss efforts of this kind by teachers or their students as doomed to ineffectualness.

VIGNETTE 13.1 LIVING IN A MATERIAL WORLD

N. Gough, Deakin University, Australia

The editors of this volume refer to the extracts from *Capitalism and Social Progress* (Phillip Brown and Hugh Lauder 2001) and *Educating Beyond Violent Futures* (Francis Hutchinson 1996) presented elsewhere in this chapter as 'key readings' from the existing literature on globalisation as a central issue in lifelong learning and sustainability. Although I sympathise with the political standpoints from which these authors write, I do not find their propositions and reasoning altogether convincing and, more importantly, I do not believe that these extracts are particularly useful or generative for improving the educational practices in which I participate. In part this is because the respective excerpts consist very largely of exhortations to privilege some abstractions and representations (e.g. 'collective intelligence', 'holistic notions of democratic participation') and diminish others (e.g. 'Western individualism', 'technological cornucopianism').

Brown and Lauder (2001) remind readers of A.H. Halsey's assertion that 'Exhortation alone is futile' (p. 226) but seem not to have taken his advice. Their abstract generalisations and recommendations rarely extend to concrete examples of how such a task might be enacted and embodied. For example, they assert that 'The task is one of both re-socializing the mind and of embedding the principles of collective intelligence in the social structure' (p. 226). But *whose* task is this? In *which* elements of *which* 'social structure' (or *structures*) are these principles to be embedded? Through *what* curriculum and learning technologies might this task be achieved? Concepts such as 'social structure' do not in themselves provide material questions, problems or issues upon which educational decision-makers can deliberate. Like Bruno Latour (1992), I suspect that there are no purely 'social' relations but, rather, 'socio-technical' relations embedded in and performed by a wide variety of different human, technical, 'natural'[1] and textual materials. Also, when writers such as Brown and Lauder (2001) and Hutchinson (1996) choose to discuss a complex and contested concept like globalisation chiefly by reference to other equally complex and contested abstractions, I recall the wise words of the late Lawrence Stenhouse (1980: 14):

> All educational ideas must find expression in curricula before we can tell whether they are day dreams or contributions to practice. Many educational ideas are not found wanting, because they cannot be found at all.
>
> (p. 14)

To be fair, Brown and Lauder (2001) go some way towards expressing the idea of collective intelligence in material terms by providing an example of what they understand by one of its dimensions, namely, *capacity for intelligence*. Moreover, they choose an example of the capacity for intelligence that they regard as 'global in scope', which is particularly significant for this chapter and thus warrants closer scrutiny. Brown and Lauder (2001) describe the capacity for intelligence as 'the raw materials on which the development of intelligence depends' and 'the state of knowledge, scientific discovery, technology and learning techniques, on which societies can draw' (p. 219). This capacity, they write, 'includes the knowledge and technological resources amassed in society in the form of books, journals, databases, computers and computer programmes, universities, research institutes, museums, laboratories, and super-highways to name but a few', and they note that in many respects 'the capacity for intelligence has become global in scope as new ideas, fashions, technologies and sources of productivity traverse the global in real time through the media, Internet and MNCs [multinational corporations]' (p. 219). Brown and Lauder (2001: 219) continue:

> The Human Genome Project launched by the US Department of Energy and the National Institutes of Health in 1990 is an example. One of its major aims was to identify all of the approximate 100,000 genes in human DNA and combined research centres in the US, the UK, Australia, Canada, Germany, France, Japan, Denmark, Israel and Italy.

I have no difficulty in understanding the Human Genome Project as a *product* of what Latour (1986) calls 'powers of association', as a performative *effect* of associating together entities such as those described by Brown and Lauder (2001) – books, journals, databases, computers, universities, research institutes, laboratories etc. But I have great difficulty in accepting that the Human Genome Project might be an example of the *capacity for intelligence on a global scale*, a quality that is possessed by the actors and actants in this Project's network of sociotechnical relations.

The Human Genome Project exemplifies Latour's (1991) proposition that 'technology is society made durable'. Technologies embody social relations and I interpret the Human Genome Project as translating the dominance of biological determinists in technoscientific communities into the durable materials of human gene technologies. If the ascendance of such determinism is an example of 'collective intelligence' then I can see good reason to resist its development. Although mapping the human genome is likely to be very useful in the diagnosis and treatment of illnesses with a unitary genetic cause, such as Huntington's chorea and cystic fibrosis, many scientists seem to expect (or want others to expect) much more of the project. For example, the molecular biologist Christopher Wills (1991) writes that 'the outstanding problems in human biology . . . will *all* be illuminated' (p. 2, my emphasis) by the Human Genome Project. Similarly, Jack Cohen and Ian Stewart (1994) quote from the program of the British Institute of Biology's 1993 symposium on Recent Advances in Human Genetics the assertion that mapping the human genome will provide 'the prime reference material for *all* biological and medical science' (p. 463; emphasis in source). Cohen and Stewart (1994) comment: 'Biologists will tell you that they don't say such naive things. They do' (p. 463).

However, I suspect that such exaggerations are more a matter of the 'cultural editing' to which Hutchinson (1996: 147) refers than individual naïveté. R.C. Lewontin (1994: 120) summarises some of the sociotechnical relations through which the Human Genome Project promotes a deterministic ideology:

> The study of DNA is an industry with high visibility, a claim on the public purse, the legitimacy of a science, and the appeal that it will alleviate individual and social suffering. So its basic ontological claim, of the dominance of the Master Molecule over the body physical and the body politic, becomes part of the general consciousness.

Evelyn Fox Keller (1992) traces the circulation of this consciousness through the social milieus of the state, universities, biotechnology corporations, and the media, producing a largely unquestioned consensus that 'the model of cystic fibrosis is a model of the world' (p. 290). In a disturbing example of how a medical model that begins with a genetic explanation for cystic fibrosis is translated into an explanation of all social and individual variation, Keller (1992) quotes Daniel Koshland, then editor of *Science*, who was asked why the Human Genome Project funds should not be given instead to the homeless; he replied: 'What these people don't realize is that the homeless are impaired . . . Indeed, no group will benefit more from the application of human genetics' (p. 282).[2] If, as Brown and Lauder (2001) infer, the Human Genome Project embodies social relations arising from 'collective intelligence', I think it is equally plausible to suggest that it provides ample evidence of collective stupidity.

I want to emphasise that my criticism of the Human Genome Project is not in itself an endorsement of Hutchinson's (1996) antagonism to 'the language of technocentrism, Western-male expert knowledge' and 'heroic images of Western science and technology' (p. 148). Although these descriptions often are fair characterisations of many Western technoscience projects, they also lend themselves too readily to being deployed as caricatures. Used indiscriminately, they contribute to the very teaching and learning practices that Hutchinson (1996) rightly rejects, such as 'uncritical myth-making'

(p. 147) and presenting learners with 'an undifferentiated picture of the world' (p. 148). My antipathy to the excesses of the Human Genome Project is not only because I find its technocentric (and hubristic) language distasteful but also because I abhor its monumental waste of human, technical, 'natural' and textual material resources.

In conclusion, I would like to suggest that understanding globalisation in relation to lifelong learning and sustainability might well be advanced by accepting the poststructuralist proposition that there is no 'outside' of the text – no nondiscursive reality *and no immaterial discourse*. Science and environmental educators often misunderstand this proposition and so I will emphasise here that poststructuralist scepticism about the narratives and metanarratives of Western science is not an antirealist position. What is at issue here is not *belief* in the real but confidence in its representation. As Richard Rorty (1979) puts it, 'to deny the power to "describe" reality is not to deny reality' (p. 375) and 'the world is out there, but descriptions of the world are not' (Rorty 1989: 5). Dissolving the analytic boundary between world and text (and, indeed, between 'nature' and culture) is strategically useful because it multiplies the possibilities for analyses, critiques, and interventions. Ernesto Laclau and Chantal Mouffe (1985: 110) put it this way:

> The main consequence of a break with the discursive/extra-discursive dichotomy is the abandonment of the thought/reality opposition, and hence a major enlargement of the field of those categories which can account for social relations.

This works both ways, by emphasising not only the materiality of discourse but also the agency of nature and other objects of the world 'out there'. In pointing out that 'discourse is a material practice', Donna Haraway (1989: 111) observes that 'No one can constitute meanings by wishing them into existence; . . . meanings . . . include *particular* structurings of objects of knowledge', where knowledge is understood as 'that which can be known in a particular time and place' (emphasis in original). Notions of particularity, location, and positioning, are central to the 'strong objectivity' of Sandra Harding's (1993) 'standpoint epistemology' and the 'embodied objectivity' of Haraway's (1991: 198) 'situated knowledges', which entail an acceptance of the agency of the objects of inquiry:

> Situated knowledges require that the object of knowledge be pictured as an actor or agent, not a screen or a ground or a resource . . . A corollary of the insistence that ethics and politics covertly or overtly provide the bases for objectivity in the sciences as a heterogeneous whole, and not just in the social sciences, is granting the status of agent/actor to the 'objects' of the world. Actors come in many and wonderful forms. Accounts of a 'real' world do not, then, depend on a logic of 'discovery', but on a power-charged social relation of 'conversation'. The world neither speaks itself nor disappears in favour of a master decoder. The codes of the world are not still, waiting only to be read.

Similarly, globalisation as an object of inquiry does not seem to me to be well-served by being 'coded' as an element of new cornucopian mythology, or as a manifestation of collective intelligence (or the lack thereof). We live in a material world and, like Haraway and Latour, I see globalisation in terms of power-invested sociotechnical relations made durable by their materialisation in texts, technologies and 'natural' environments (the hole in the ozone layer is neither more nor less 'natural' or artefactual as global military spending or international monetary speculation). Working with such materialisations helps us, I believe, to dissolve distinctions between science and politics and to focus on negotiating and sustaining the sociotechnical relations between what is, what is good, and who/what can live together.

Notes

1   The 'scare' quotes here signify that I read terms such as 'natural' and 'nature' *sous rature* (under erasure), following Jacques Derrida's approach to reading deconstructed signifiers as if their meanings were clear and undeconstructable, but with the understanding that this is only a strategy (see, for example, Derrida 1985).

2   For an elaboration of the implications of this analysis for science education see Gough, N. (2001).

VIGNETTE 13.2   COLLECTIVE KNOWLEDGE AND THE CREATIVE IMAGINATION IN A GLOBALISED WORLD

D.E. Clover, University of Victoria

From their diverse platforms of formal and non-formal adult education or social learning, Hutchinson (1996) and Brown and Lauder (2001) focus on creativity and knowledge. They examine various factors in society which determine how knowledge is created, shared or undermined, who has the right to create knowledge, to learn and to be involved in the development of society. Hutchinson, from a school-sector perspective, examines the problematic ideological package of neo-conservative globalisation, the left's debilitating victimology approach, and the negative impact both have on teachers and schools. He expresses concern that schools are ignored and calls on educators to stimulate teachers' creative imaginations as a means to resist "colonising agendas about the future" (p. 149). Brown and Lauder venture into the realm of life-long learning and challenge the limiting strategies of neo-conservatism which attempt to stream-line knowledge away from the general public and into the hands of those who will uphold its ideals. They call for the stimulation of much needed collective intelligence through critical adult and social-learning processes that use the "art of conversation ... [to] fuel the collective effort to resolve common problems in an attempt to improve the quality of life for all" (pp. 222–223). It is interesting to note that, somewhat ambiguously, the authors draw a very negative picture of the left and its ability to uphold what Brown and Lauder refer to as the "the foundations of social justice" (p. 226).

The authors' calls to stimulate collective knowledge and creative imagination are potentially exciting goals for education. However, in order to accomplish these goals, we need to focus on two key areas. The first is to come out of our own malaise and realise that in spite of the so-called all powerful vision of neo-conservatism, many people world-wide simply do not buy into it. Reaching them would mean broadening our capacity to understand where and how learning and change take place. It is also imperative that we re-link educational work to the political process by basing it in/on critical adult education. Secondly, and linked to the first, is the need to re-politicise teacher training programmes and connect them to the broader community by recognising that, as Paulo Freire (1970) argued, so-called neutrality is a political bias in itself, and one which has its own negative impact on teachers' efforts for change.

Both Hutchison, and Brown and Lauder, describe schools solely as creators of "self-fulfilling prophesies" of doom and gloom (Hutchinson 1996: 149), and citizens as mere cogs in the capitalist wheel who "leave their brains at the factory gate" (Brown and Lauder 2001: 225) rather than as agents of change and visionaries of the future. This raises two important points about right and left discourses and their negative impacts on teachers, schools, workers and citizens. The first focuses on the so-called positive power of capitalism/globalisation, a doctrine with a clear vision and plan that has overcome all other frameworks such as communism, socialism, and First Nations governmental structures with their rightness. The vision is one of freedom, affluence and the good life, rugged individualism, efficiency and profitability, the cruel to be kind welfare-less approach through the reduction of needless public spending, and more recently, the terrifying "crusade for democracy" (Macedo 2000: 139). Among other things, the capitalist plan includes vigorously promoting increased knowledge, "a by-product of the constant rapid exchange of information made possible by computer-mediated technologies" (Stromquist and Monkman 2000: viii). Although this "new type of knowledge . . . generates winners and losers . . . the current discourse of globalisation glosses over this possibility" with remarkable agility (ibid.: viii). Secondly, both authors lament the lack of a substantive vision by the left that could capture the imaginations of people around the world. Hutchinson does this by arguing that the main problem is that the left is mired in a perpetual state of critique, victimology and cosmology, while Brown and Lauder take Marxist discourse on collectivity to task and highlight Japanese-style management as a positive beacon.

And yet, in spite of the broad-base of capitalism and its strangle-hold on the media that tells us what to think, feel and believe with mesmerising speed and efficiency, imaginative ideas continue to flow from a discontented populous. In spite of cultural and social homogenising or the "cultural editing" project as it is referred to by Hutchinson (p. 147), there is resistance. In spite of Marx's under-estimation of our ability to enslave ourselves and the co-option of the collective by corporations, people come together in their thousands to challenge. In spite of an attempt to rob citizens "of the opportunity to engage in conversations about the nature of society" (Brown and Lauder 2001: 223) and although the mainstream media only shows negative images of young people breaking glass on the streets of Quebec City, Seattle and Genoa, and the rest of the world as merely victims of war and perpetual poverty in need of Western assistance, truer images and dialogues continue to emerge. For example, in spite of the attempts to totally depoliticise education, kindergarten teachers are now seen to join their unions in protest against the reformist education policies of measurable outcomes and economic efficiency (Stromquist and Monkman 2000).

Hutchinson's call for the stimulation of the creative imagination is fundamental. The imagination is not simply a matter of individual genius, escapism from ordinary life, or a simple dimension of aesthetics. It is a faculty that informs our daily lives in myriad ways. It is the imagination that allows us to challenge and resist state and corporate violence, seek social and environmental redress, and design new forms of civic engagement and collaboration (Appadurai 2001). It is the imagination, more than any other capacity, that breaks through the inertia of habit, enables the crossing of spaces between ourselves and others "and permit us to give credence to alternative realities" (Greene 1995: 3).

Although I too tire of the catch-up politics of the left, to argue that the left perpetuates a vision of hopelessness as Hutchinson does, is to fall victim to the images created by the right. For two important reasons, I see our role as educators as re-politicising the educational system, making links between social change and political policy, and encouraging voice and action. The first is that the political arena is still where the power lies. Although corporations may rule the world, they do so with the blessing and support of national governments, and without that, they would not be where they are today (Korten 2001). The second is that current educational policies are being informed more and more by financially driven agendas and there is growing governmental interest in reducing public spending on education (Stromquist and Monkman 2001). Because it is supposed that teachers should be neutral and de-linked from the political process when they finally come to realise the negative effects of neo-conservative policies such as larger class sizes, less money for supplies, and unhealthy competitions amongst schools for funds, their legitimate protests which truly have the well-being of children in mind are ignored at best and at worst, characterised as expressions of self-interest.

Based within what can be called a framework of critical adult education, Brown and Lauder argue for the development of collective intelligence through dialogic processes which create new knowledges and challenge the "positional advantage of social elites" (p. 220). The essential strategy of the type of critical teaching/learning practice they call for is dialogue, critique, and visioning. It is a process based on understanding "how ideological systems and societal structures hinder or impede the fullest development of humankind's collective potential" (Welton 1995: 14). The role of educators is to create learning settings in which students are able to reflect on their own social, historical, and cultural realities, instil hope and imagine, as Brown and Lauder argue, "a society which is pulling together in the interest of all" (p. 221). But, as feminists have argued for a number of years, the processes behind the development of collective intelligence – the creation of new knowledge and relationships – must be based on the study of power and go beyond simply a class-based analysis (Walters and Manicom 1996; Tisdess 1993; Weiler 1988). The "low trust relations" the authors discuss are not simply between the economic "haves and have nots" (Brown and Lauder 2001: 221). Educational practices and theories, while appearing to be universal in their application, have failed to adequately address gendered and racial differences in experiences. The relationship "between teaching and learning requires not only a discourse of practice . . . but also the social visions they support as they teach" (Scott *et al.* 1998: 103). I will add a cautionary note here about the way in which Brown and Lauder hold Japanese corporations' ways of doing business as an example to the West. It is few corporations on any side of the globe who put their employees before profits, and even fewer who would support the creation of collective knowledge if it were to challenge the fundamentals of capitalism.

Within our pedagogical institutions, let us as educators and researchers collectively imagine and create teacher training programmes that are linked to the activities of social movements and society as whole. For it is in this connection that there is more "political space to develop alternatives than the ideologies of capitalism allow" (Stromquist and Monkman 2000: ix). It is within spaces of social movements, through theatre, poetry, activism and critical adult education practices of dialogue and debate, where the world we want is being imagined. Let us encourage teachers to link themselves to the political process, and see themselves as important players in the process of social change. But let us also heed the point made by Brown and Lauder, that knowledge creation and learning take place outside the walls of pedagogical institutions – in church basements, community centres, the workplace, forests, libraries and museums. And although the neo-conservative agenda attempts to sets limits and deny us "the novel and challenging ideas which frequently stem from diversity in situations and social and cultural experiences" (p. 223), active learning and challenge are all around us. Let us collectively and imaginatively join in.

CHAPTER 14

WHAT HAPPENS NEXT?

READING 14.1 JOHANNESBURG SUMMIT 2002: KEY COMMITMENTS, TARGETS AND TIMETABLES FROM THE JOHANNESBURG PLAN OF IMPLEMENTATION

United Nations

Source: United Nations, New York, 2002

Key outcomes of the Summit

- The Summit reaffirmed sustainable development as a central element of the international agenda and gave new impetus to global action to fight poverty and protect the environment.
- The understanding of sustainable development was broadened and strengthened as a result of the Summit, particularly the important linkages between poverty, the environment and the use of natural resources.
- Governments agreed to and reaffirmed a wide range of concrete commitments and targets for action to achieve more effective implementation of sustainable development objectives.
- Energy and sanitation issues were critical elements of the negotiations and outcomes to a greater degree than in previous international meetings on sustainable development.
- Support for the establishment of a world solidarity fund for the eradication of poverty was a positive step forward.
- Africa and NEPAD were identified for special attention and support by the international community to better focus efforts to address the development needs of Africa.
- The views of civil society were given prominence at the Summit in recognition of the key role of civil society in implementing the outcomes and in promoting partnership initiatives. Over 8,000 civil society participants attended the Summit, reinforced by parallel events which included major groups, such as NGOs, women, indigenous people, youth, farmers, trade unions, business leaders, the scientific and technological community and local authorities, as well as Chief Justices from various countries.
- The concept of partnerships between governments, business and civil society was given a large boost by the Summit and the Plan of Implementation. Over 220 partnerships (with $235 million in resources) were identified in advance of the Summit and around 60 partnerships were announced during the Summit by a variety of countries.

Key commitments targets and timetables from the Johannesburg Plan of Implementation[1]

Poverty eradication

Halve, by the year 2015, the proportion of the world's people whose income is less than $1 a day and the proportion of people who suffer from hunger (*reaffirmation of Millennium Development Goals*).

By 2020, achieve a significant improvement in the lives of at least 100 million slum dwellers, as proposed in the "Cities without slums" initiative (*reaffirmation of Millennium Development Goal*).

Establish a world solidarity fund to eradicate poverty and to promote social and human development in the developing countries.

Water and sanitation

Halve, by the year 2015, the proportion of people without access to safe drinking water (*reaffirmation of Millennium Development Goal*).

Halve, by the year 2015, the proportion of people who do not have access to basic sanitation.

Sustainable production and consumption

Encourage and promote the development of a 10-year framework of programmes to accelerate the shift towards sustainable consumption and production.

Energy

Renewable energy

Diversify energy supply and substantially increase the global share of renewable energy sources in order to increase its contribution to total energy supply.

Access to energy

Improve access to reliable, affordable, economically viable, socially acceptable and environmentally sound energy services and resources, sufficient to achieve the Millenium Development Goals, including the goal of halving the proportion of people in poverty by 2015.

Energy markets

Remove market distortions including the restructuring of taxes and the phasing out of harmful subsidies. Support efforts to improve the functioning, transparency and information about energy markets with respect to both supply and demand, with the aim of achieving greater stability and to ensure consumer access to energy services.

Energy efficiency

Establish domestic programmes for energy efficiency with the support of the international community. Accelerate the development and dissemination of energy efficiency and energy conservation technologies, including the promotion of research and development.

Chemicals

Aim, by 2020, to use and produce chemicals in ways that do not lead to significant adverse effects on human health and the environment.

Renew the commitment to the sound management of chemicals and of hazardous wastes throughout their life cycle.

Promote the ratification and implementation of relevant international instruments on chemicals and hazardous waste, including the Rotterdam Convention so that it can enter into force by 2003 and the Stockholm Convention so that it can enter into force by 2004.

Further develop a strategic approach to international chemicals management, based on the Bahia Declaration and Priorities for Action beyond 2000, by 2005.

Encourage countries to implement the new globally harmonized system for the classification and labeling of chemicals as soon as possible, with a view to having the system fully operational by 2008.

Management of the natural resource base

Water

Develop integrated water resources management and water efficiency plans by 2005.

Oceans and fisheries

Encourage the application by 2010 of the ecosystem approach for the sustainable development of the oceans.

On an urgent basis and where possible by 2015, maintain or restore depleted fish stocks to levels that can produce the maximum sustainable yield.

Put into effect the FAO international plans of action by the agreed dates:

- for the management of fishing capacity by 2005; and
- to prevent, deter and eliminate illegal, unreported and unregulated fishing by 2004.

Develop and facilitate the use of diverse approaches and tools, including the ecosystem approach, the elimination of destructive fishing practices, the establishment of marine protected areas consistent with international law and based on scientific information, including representative networks by 2012.

Establish by 2004 a regular process under the United Nations for global reporting and assessment of the state of the marine environment.

Eliminate subsidies that contribute to illegal, unreported and unregulated fishing and to overcapacity.

Atmosphere

Facilitate implementation of the Montreal Protocol on Substances that Deplete the Ozone Layer by ensuring adequate replenishment of its fund by 2003/2005.

Improve access by developing countries to alternatives to ozone-depleting substances by 2010, and assist them in complying with the phase-out schedule under the Montreal Protocol.

Biodiversity

Achieve by 2010 a significant reduction in the current rate of loss of biological diversity.

Forests

Accelerate implementation of the IPF/IFF proposals for action by countries and by the Collaborative Partnership on Forests, and intensify efforts on reporting to the United Nations Forum on Forests, to contribute to an assessment of progress in 2005.

Corporate responsibility

Actively promote corporate responsibility and accountability, including through the full development and effective implementation of intergovernmental agreements and measures, international initiatives and public-private partnerships, and appropriate national regulations.

Health

Enhance health education with the objective of achieving improved health literacy on a global basis by 2010.

Reduce, by 2015, mortality rates for infants and children under 5 by two thirds, and maternal mortality rates by three quarters, of the prevailing rate in 2000 (*reaffirmation of Millennium Development Goal*).

Reduce HIV prevalence among young men and women aged 15–24 by 25 per cent in the most affected countries by 2005 and globally by 2010, as well as combat malaria, tuberculosis and other diseases (*reaffirmation of General Assembly resolution*).

Sustainable development of small island developing States

Undertake initiatives by 2004 aimed at implementing the Global Programme of Action for the Protection of the Marine Environment from Land-based Activities to reduce, prevent and control waste and pollution and their health-related impacts.

Develop community-based initiatives on sustainable tourism by 2004.

Support the availability of adequate, affordable and environmentally sound energy services for the sustainable development of small island developing States, including through strengthening efforts on energy supply and services by 2004.

Review implementation of the Barbados Programme of Action for the Sustainable Development of Small Island Developing States in 2004.

Sustainable development for Africa

Improve sustainable agricultural productivity and food security in accordance with the Millennium Development Goals, in particular to halve by 2015 the proportion of people who suffer from hunger.

Support African countries in developing and implementing food security strategies by 2005.

Support Africa's efforts to implement NEPAD objectives on energy, which seek to secure access for at least 35 per cent of the African population within 20 years, especially in rural areas.

Means of implementation

Ensure that, by 2015, all children will be able to complete a full course of primary schooling and that girls and boys will have equal access to all levels of education relevant to national needs (*reaffirmation of Millennium Development Goal*).

Eliminate gender disparity in primary and secondary education by 2005 (*reaffirmation of Dakar Framework for Action on Education for All*).

Recommend to the UN General Assembly that it consider adopting a decade of education for sustainable development, starting in 2005.

Institutional framework for sustainable development

Adopt new measures to strengthen institutional arrangements for sustainable development at international, regional and national levels.

Enhance the role of the Commission on Sustainable Development, including through reviewing and monitoring progress in the implementation of *Agenda 21* and fostering coherence of implementation, initiatives and partnerships.

Facilitate and promote the integration of the environmental, social and economic dimensions of sustainable development into the work programs' UN regional commissions.

Establish an effective, transparent and regular inter-agency coordination mechanism on ocean and coastal issues within the United Nations system.

Take immediate steps to make progress in the formulation and elaboration of national strategies for sustainable development and begin their implementation by 2005.

Key initiatives and announcements from the Johannesburg Summit[2]

Water and sanitation

- The United States announced $970 million in investments over the next three years on water and sanitation projects.
- The European Union announced the "Water for Life" initiative that seeks to engage partners to meet goals for water and sanitation, primarily in Africa and Central Asia.
- The Asia Development Bank provided a $5 million grant to UN Habitat and $500 million in fast-track credit for the Water for Asian Cities Programme.
- The UN has received 21 other water and sanitation initiatives with at least $20 million in extra resources.

Energy

- The nine major electricity companies of the E7 signed a range of agreements with the UN to facilitate technical cooperation for sustainable energy projects in developing countries.
- The European Union announced a $700 million partnership initiative on energy and the United States announced that it would invest up to $43 million in 2003.
- DESA, UNEP and the US EPA announced a partnership on Cleaner Fuels and Vehicles with broad support from confirmed partners from the private sector, the NGO community, developed and developing countries.
- The South African energy utility Eskom announced a partnership to extend modern energy services to neighboring countries.

- The United Nations Environment Programme launched a new initiative called the Global Network on Energy for Sustainable Development to promote the research, transfer and deployment of green and cleaner energy technologies to the developing world.
- The UN has received 32 partnership submissions for energy projects with at least $26 million in resources.

Health

- The United States announced a commitment to spend $2.3 billion through 2003 on health, some of which was earmarked earlier for the Global Fund.
- The UN has received 16 partnership submissions for health projects with $3 million in resources.

Agriculture

- The United States will invest $90 million in 2003 for sustainable agriculture programmes.
- The UN has received 17 partnership submissions with at least $2 million in additional resources.

Biodiversity and ecosystem management

- Canada and Russia announced they intended to ratify the Kyoto protocol.
- The United States announced $53 million for forests in 2002–2005.
- The UN has received 32 partnership initiatives with $100 million in resources.

Cross-cutting issues

- Agreement to the replenishment of the Global Environment Facility, with a total of $3 billion ($2.92 billion announced pre-Summit and $80 million added by EU in Johannesburg).
- Norway pledged an additional $50 million towards following up the Johannesburg commitments.
- The United Kingdom announced it was doubling its assistance to Africa to £1 billion a year and raising its overall assistance for all countries by 50 per cent.
- The EU announced that it will increase its development assistance with more than 22 billion euros in the years to 2006 and by more than 9 billion euros annually from 2006 onwards.
- Germany announced a contribution of 500 million euros over the next five years to promote cooperation on renewable energy.
- Canada announced that, as of 1 January 2003, it will eliminate tariffs and quotas on almost all products from the least developed countries, and that by 2010, it would double development assistance.
- Japan announced that it will provide at least 250 billion yen in education assistance over a five-year period and that it would extend emergency food aid amounting to $30 million dollars to save children in southern Africa from famine.
- Japan also announced it would provide cooperation in environment-related capacity building by training 5,000 people from overseas over a five-year period.
- Ireland announced that it has allocated almost 8 million euros in emergency funding in response to the humanitarian needs of the African region.

Notes

1   This list is not exhaustive but provides information on the key commitments set out in the Johannesburg Plan of Implementation. For the full text, including the exact terms in which these commitments were made, visit the official website: www.johannesburgsummit.org.
2   The following list is not exhaustive, but reflects some key initiatives announced during the Johannesburg Summit.

READING 14.2 SUSTAINING THE POOR'S DEVELOPMENT

The Economist
Source: *The Economist*, London, 2002: 11

The biggest environmental gathering in a decade could do some good – but only if it does not overreach

Just what is the UN's "World Summit on Sustainable Development" for? This giant jamboree, which opened in Johannesburg this week and will culminate on September 4th with a meeting of over 100 heads of government, risks being about everything and therefore, in the end, about nothing. No one in their right mind is against "sustainable development". Everyone thinks it would be terrific if there were less poverty, less pollution, less disease, less war, less corruption. Not quite everyone, alas, favours more democracy, especially in the poorer parts of the world; in the richer world, too, not quite everyone, alas, favours more economic growth. But the world did not need tens of thousands of people to travel to South Africa in order to learn all of that.

Such a gathering is bound to do some good, simply through the contacts made and ideas exchanged, in myriad small but useful ways. But there are also big dangers in summits such as these. Grand meetings, like the "Earth Summit" in Rio de Janeiro in 1992 to which this was originally meant to be a follow-up, can breed confusion and cynicism. Confusion, because of the cacophony of different voices and objectives, to which this broader summit looks especially prone. Cynicism, because the bold promises made are so rarely met. How many countries have actually hit (or are really on their way to hitting) the targets set at Rio, or in Kyoto in 1998, for cutting greenhouse-gas emissions? Precious few.

Keep the real agenda simple

George Bush has responded to these dangers by staying away, sending his secretary of state, Colin Powell, instead. That was a mistake, offering carte blanche for criticism of America for almost any environmental or economic ill, some justified, most not. That is a pity, for America has actually played a more constructive role at the summit than most think [. . .]. Other rich-country leaders can, however, learn from that public-relations blunder. But only if they focus on what really matters, and on what can really be achieved.

The first thing they should do is to tell the truth about poverty, growth and the environment. Thabo Mbeki, South Africa's president, delighted the anti-growth lobby with his opening speech, but did a huge disservice to the facts. "Sadly", he said, "we have not made much progress in realising the grand vision . . . the tragic result of this is the avoidable increase in human misery and ecological degradation, including the growing gap between North and South. It is as though we are determined to regress to the most primitive condition of existence in the animal world, of the survival of the fittest."

In contrast, what responsible heads of government should say is that the ten years since the Rio summit (home of that "grand vision") have seen lots of progress in enhancing human welfare, especially in the most populous countries of the world, China and India, thanks to those countries' decisions to liberalise their economies and to open their borders to more trade and investment. Such globalisation has already narrowed the overall gap between North and South. But some countries, notably in Africa and the Middle East, have chosen not to take part in that process, and misery there has increased. Others, particularly in southern Africa, have been so beset by disease that they have been unable to take part. Much more can, and should, be done to help them do so. And measures can and should be taken to ensure that the future economic growth of the poor world, if that happy outcome occurs, does not unduly exacerbate the problem of global warming.

The second thing that western leaders can do is to state clearly what they can, and cannot, do for their poorer counterparts. They cannot "share assets more equitably", as some claim; making the rich poorer will not make the poor richer. Virtually everything needed to help countries grow and reduce poverty depends chiefly on domestic policies – ask South Korea, China and even India. Western leaders can still, however, be helpful, in two powerful ways. They can open their country's markets to the goods that many poor countries are best suited to produce, namely food and textiles. And they can focus their overseas aid on the issue that is most difficult for poor countries to deal with themselves: disease.

There are signs that the summit could achieve something on both fronts. Farm subsidies are properly the domain of the new round of world trade talks launched in Doha last November, but are also a source of much hypocrisy. It is outrageous that rich countries preach free trade to the poor while lavishing over $300 billion a year on their own farmers. Despite its recent increase in production subsidies (to levels still below Europe's), the United States recently put forward a welcome long-term proposal for reducing subsidies for agriculture, much pooh-poohed in Europe. The Johannesburg summit offers a fresh opportunity to embarrass the Europeans into taking the proposal seriously, and to get all sides committed to a broader dismantling of subsidies in the Doha round.

On disease, too, progress could be made. The scourge of AIDS is debilitating African economies, as are other diseases such as malaria and tuberculosis. More broadly, dirty water and air, and poor sanitation, are the biggest preventable causes of death. Faster economic growth would help poor countries solve those problems. But disease itself thwarts that growth. There has been much useful talk at the summit of agreements between businesses, aid organisations and governments to try to fight against disease, in ways both big and small. The anti-business lobbyists may not like it, but the UN has been right to encourage such agreements, and rich-country leaders should welcome them too. Better still, they should make further increases in their official aid budgets to take on these diseases, both bilaterally and through global funds.

But what of the environment? Isn't that what this summit was supposed to be about? Yes, but enabling poor countries to grow and be healthier will go a long way towards protecting it. If they want to make one big green gesture, though, leaders could most usefully agree to phase out the subsidies they pay for the dirtiest fuels, particularly coal. That way, both rich and poor can work together to avoid global warming.

EDITORS' VIGNETTE: LAST WORD

W.A.H. Scott and S.R. Gough, University of Bath

Just what did the 2002 UN Summit on Sustainable Development mean for learning and its relation to sustainable development?

Media coverage of the event was notable for just how little education or learning was mentioned. Rather, the substantive emphases were on: land, biodiversity, climate change, agriculture and trade, good governance, aid, chemical pollution, water and sewage, health, energy, poverty and the desirability, or not, of development. Of course, solving all these problems would be a fine thing to do, and any advocacy of learning, for example, as occurs throughout the companion volume to this book (*Key Issues in Sustainable Development and Learning: A Critical Review*) is not intended to elevate its importance relative to them. Rather, and as we have argued in more detail in Chapter 6 of that volume, our case is that because environmental problems are *caused* by the interaction of environmental and social processes, our search for solutions should include consideration of all relevant social processes. Among these, learning is crucially important because of its power to influence all the others, for better or worse.

A second focus of media coverage of the Summit was on the political (and micropolitical) interactions between the major Summiteers (UN, governments, World Trade Organization, World Bank, International Monetary Fund etc.), business, NGOs, and the gathering of landless people. Also in Chapter 6 of the companion volume, we set out a framework for thinking about the institutional loyalties people have, and how these affect their thinking and their arguments. Suffice it here to restate that *all* institutions must compete for real resources, status and influence. Accordingly, they form oppositions and alliances, and espouse particular practices and ways of looking at problems. This is not to argue that institutions (and therefore the individuals who belong to them) are *not* concerned with the quality of argument and pursuit of a mission: it is, rather, to suggest that they do not assess quality or pursue a mission in a vacuum, but in an institutional context. If we wish to understand why it was that, out of the sometimes confused debates of the Summit, there emerged strongly two particular references to learning, we should seek the answer as much in these institutional interactions as in the strength of particular arguments. These two references were: firstly, a re-affirmation of the internationally-agreed Millennium Development Goals of universal primary education by 2015 and the elimination of gender disparities in primary and secondary education by 2005; and, secondly, confirmation of the crucial role to be played in sustainable development by civil society – and the need for the public to be (at least) aware of this.

The substantive outcomes of the Summit are, in fact, represented rather well by this media coverage. If we go back only as far as 1998 it is possible to discern quite easily a focus on learning in UN documents. In that year the 6th session of the UN Commission on Sustainable Development (UNCSD) agreed seven priority areas for action and identified tasks associated with each of these. They were all confirmed by the 2002 Summit. The priorities focus on:

- clarifying and communicating sustainable development concepts and key messages;
- reviewing national education policies and reorienting practices, including teacher education and higher education teaching and research;
- incorporating education within national sustainable development strategies and planning processes;

- promoting sustainable consumption and production through education;
- promoting investment in education;
- identifying and sharing innovative practices;
- raising public awareness.

The need for learning seems implicit throughout. Added to this is that 2005–14 has been accepted by the UN General Assembly as the 'decade of education for sustainable development'.

Coming forward to the present, and so to Reading 14.1, the UN's "Johannesburg Summit 2002", we may say that the notion of learning hardly dominates the document (any more than it dominated the media coverage of the Summit). However, it is hard to see the UN's ambitious goals being achieved without a great deal of learning happening across all sectors – arising from education, training, professional development and other programmes.

To summarise, the outcome of the Johannesburg Summit is that learning is cast in a supporting role in relation to a wide range of important issues relating to development, health, good governance, trade and environment which have collectively come to define 'sustainable development'. This is partly a result of genuine debate about what sustainable development should mean, and partly a result of the related, but substantially independent manoeuvrings of a whole range of institutions and interest groups seeking to foreground the issues of most concern to themselves. These range from: at one extreme, the smallest and most tightly-focused environmental NGOs, to, at the other extreme, the US government which, according to the reported views of Jan Pronk (*The Economist*, 31 August 2002: 65), a leading organiser of the Summit, saw an opportunity to establish at Johannesburg a constructive dimension in counterpoint to its 'war on terrorism'. It is surely no coincidence, therefore, that the two principal references to learning to emerge from the Summit (see above) were essentially uncontroversial. In the abstract (almost) no one is against small children going to school, and (almost) everyone claims democratic intent.

Is this supporting role for learning satisfactory? We would argue that, though it is much better than nothing, the answer must in the end be 'no'. This is because the approach taken is overwhelmingly one for which learning enters the equation only *after* it has been decided what – in terms of development, health, good governance, trade, environment and so on – should be done. This is unsatisfactory for three reasons. First, the attempt to achieve sustainable development takes place under conditions of complexity and uncertainty, and in the context of people's perceptions of risk and necessity, it is often *not possible*, at least within any practicable time scale, to establish what should be done. Further, even where it is possible to say what needs to happen from a particular perspective (that of development say, or environment) and/or a particular discipline (economics, say, or conservation biology), such perspectives and disciplines do not necessarily give us the same answers. Under these circumstances, seeking to promote learning seems the only way forward that is very much better, rationally speaking, than guessing.

Second, learning professionals of all kinds – in schools, colleges, universities, training institutes and elsewhere – are likely to point out that their core business is *learning* by their students, and not the promotion of a contested, and quite possibly transitory, policy notion like 'sustainable development'. They are quite likely to resent being told what they ought to be teaching, and what their professional priorities should be, since these are things for them to know and for others to enquire after. Hence, if sustainable development requires learning, then *educational* goals must be *core* to sustainable development. Environmental, developmental and other goals to be achieved through learning at someone else's behest will not do by themselves, either in principle or in practice. This is something that has yet to be appreciated by many in the mainstream.

Third, we should consider afresh the implications of the following divisions, which we routinely make: of knowledge into a particular set of disciplines; of policy-making into areas of ministerial responsibility; of the natural environment itself into political jurisdictions; and of sustainable development into economic, environmental, social and sometimes other components. These divisions are useful, practical, and in principle entirely necessary ways by which extremely complex entities are rendered manageable. They are also simplifications. For example, and as we discuss in detail in Chapter 11 of the companion volume, the economy, the environment and society are *not* in fact separable. Each of them cannot comprise a coherent entity without the others. Hence, sustainable development cannot arise from the independent insights of economists, environmental scientists and social scientists, each working with different assumptions and methodologies. Learning is required across and between them and the constituencies they serve.

Readers will recognise these issues from the readings and vignettes in this volume. In the companion volume we have drawn on those readings, on other extracts from published work in a range of disciplines, and on practical examples from around the world, to develop a case which, we believe, offers a way forward. This case is summarised here:

- The human relationship with nature is coevolutionary: society adapts to its environment; the environment responds to human activity and both shift over time.
- Society's adaptations are influenced by, and assessed in terms of, human values and knowledge. Values can change. Knowledge can be gained or lost, but it cannot be *complete* in any imaginable time-frame. Of course, more knowledge is better than less: but nevertheless uncertainty and complexity are often inherent and inescapable – indeed, this is one of the most potentially useful things we *know*.
- However, in order to live (well or otherwise), humans cannot escape the necessity both to face up to this uncertainty and complexity, *and* to deal with risk which derives from it. Learning is integral in such processes.
- Both social and environmental processes are continuous, though each may be more or less rapid and dramatic at different times and places. This means that human learning, managed or unmanaged, is a centrally constituent part of the process.
- Sustainable development cannot possibly mean an 'end state' to be achieved because there *are no* 'end states': if sustainable development means anything it can only be a way of describing an adaptive approach to managing human-environment coevolution.
- However, when faced with uncertainty, people typically try to resolve it through the application of a particular rationality, a way of making sense of things. There appears to be convincing evidence that at least four of these rationalities can co-exist in relation to a problem: the *individualistic*; the *egalitarian*; the *hierarchical*; and the *fatalistic*.
- The particular rationalities which particular individuals apply vary from problem to problem, context to context, and over time.
- The rationality employed depends on the person's institutional affiliations (that is, their attachments to organisational institutions, cultural institutions, literacies and practices) in relation to that problem and context. This results in completing *problem definitions*, each of which, in turn, suggests a particular type of solution.

- Advocates of these preferred 'solutions' often propose educational or other means by which such solutions may be implemented. However, the proper role of educators (teachers/trainers/facilitators/curriculum designers/policy experts/etc.) in these circumstances has to be to help learners confront the generic underlying uncertainty and complexity through engagement with multiple credible problem definitions, and hence *learn* – though what they learn will not necessarily be what others might wish.
- Finally, important though the foregoing is, it is also crucial not to forget that there will be many occasions where uncertainty and complexity are absent or manageable, and determining what is to be learned will therefore be more or less straightforward and uncontroversial (see particularly Chapter 4 of the companion volume and Figure 11).

Sen (1999: 74) has written of the importance of the development of: "The substantive freedoms – the capabilities – to choose a life one has reason to value". Learning is a poor tool for implementing the policy prescriptions of others, and such implementation is, in turn, a very questionable route to sustainable development. Rather, learning will contribute to sustainable development to the extent that it enhances the things emphasised by Sen – freedom, capability, choice, reason and personal value – and to the extent that it informs society's discussions with itself about how best these may be promoted.

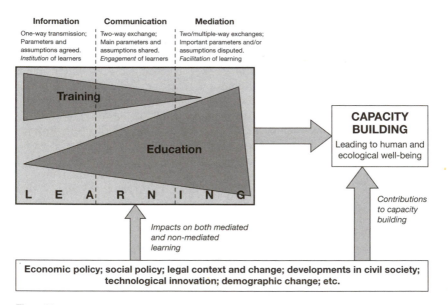

Figure 11

Note: Information, communication and pedagogy do not contribute to learning or capacity building if they are false, useless to the recipient, domineering or exploitative. Some learning occurs without any deliberate third party intervention.

REFERENCES

Note: some references contained in the notes sections at the end of readings and vignettes are not repeated here.

Adams, E. and Ward, C. (1982) *Art and the Built Environment*, Harlow: Longman for the Schools Council.
Adams, John (1995) *Risk*, London: UCL Press.
Angel Maya, A. (1995) *La fragilidad ambiental de la cultura*, Bogotá: Editorial Universidad Nacional.
Apffel-Marglin, Frederique (ed.) (1998) *The Spirit of Regeneration: Andean Culture Against Western Notions of Development*, London: Zed Books.
Appadurai, A. (ed.) (2001) *Globalization*, Durham and London: Duke University Press.
Argyris, C. and Schön D.A. (1996) *Organizational Learning II: Theory, Method and Practice*, Reading, MA: Addison Wesley.
Armstrong, A. (1979) *Planning and Environmental Education*, Occasional Paper No. 7, London: Centre for Environmental Studies.
Bakhtin, M. (1981) *The Dialogic Imagination: Four Essays*, trans. Caryl Emerson and Michael Holquist, Austin, TX: University of Texas Press.
Banco Mundial (1999) *Informe sobre el desarrollo mundial. El conocimiento al servicio del desarrollo*, Madrid: Mundi Prensa.
Barrow, R. and Woods, R.G. (1988) *An Introduction to the Philosophy of Education* (3rd edn), London: Routledge.
Bartlett, V.L. (1989) 'Look into My Mind: Qualitative Enquiry in Teaching Geography', in Fien, J., Gerber, R. and Wilson, P. (eds) *The Geography Teacher's Guide to the Classroom*, 2nd edn, Melbourne: Macmillan.
Bate, J. (1991) *Romantic Ecology: Wordsworth and the Environmental Tradition*, London: Routledge.
Bateson, G. (1972) *Steps Towards an Ecology of Mind: Collected Essays in Anthropology, Psychiatry, Evolution and Epistemology*, London: Granada.
Bauman, Z. (1998) *Globalization: The Human Consequences*, Cambridge: Polity Press.
Beck, U. (1992) *Risk Society: Towards a New Modernity*, London: Sage.
Beck, U. (1999) *World Risk Society*, Cambridge: Polity Press.
Beck, U., Giddens, A. and Lash, S. (1994) *Reflexive Modernisation*, Cambridge: Polity Press.
Bell, D. (1973) *The Coming of Post-industrial Society: A Venture in Social Forecasting*, New York: Basic Books.
Berman, H. (1990) 'The Cybernetic Dream of the 21st Century', in Clark, J. (ed.) *Renewing the Earth*, London: Green Print.
Berryman, T. (2000) 'Relieving Modern Day Atlas of an Illusory Burden: Abandoning the Hypermodern Fantasy of an Education to Manage the Globe', in Jarnet, A., Jickling, B., Sauvé, L., Wals, A. and Clarkin, P. *The Future of Environmental Education in a Postmodern World?* Whitehorse: Yukon College, pp. 88–97.
Bérubé, M. (1998) *The Employment of English*, New York and London: New York University Press.
Birch, C. (1990) *On Purpose – A New Way of Thinking For the New Millenium*, Kensington, NSW: University of NSW Press.
Bishop, K.N., Reid, A.D., Stables, A.W.G., Lencastre, M., Stoer, S. and Soetaert, S. (2000) 'Developing Environmental Awareness through Literature and Media Education: Curriculum Development in the Context of Teachers' Practice', *Canadian Journal of Environmental Education*, 5, pp. 268–286, available at http://www.edu.uleth.ca/ciccte/cjee/volume_5/contents.html.
Bizzell, P. (1994) '"Contact Zones" and English Studies', *College English*, 56(2), pp. 163–169.

Blanchard, K. (1995) 'Seabird Conservation on the North Shore of the Gulf of St Lawrence, Canada', in Palmer, J., Goldstein, W. and Curnow, A. (eds) *Planning Education to Care for the Earth*, Gland: IUCN, p. 47.

Bloom, A. (1987) *The Closing of the American Mind*, New York: Simon & Schuster.

Bly, Robert (1990) *Iron John: A Book About Men*, Reading, MA: Addison-Wesley.

Boff, L. (1996) *Ecologia, mundializacão espiritualidade. A emergência de un novo paradigma* (Série Religião e cidadania), São Paulo: Atica.

Bookchin, M. (1995) *Re-enchanting Humanity. A Defense of Human Spirit against Anti-humanism, Mysanthropy, Mysticism and Primitivism*, London: Cassell.

Bourne, D. (2002) 'Global Perspectives in Lifelong Learning', *Research in Post-Compulsory Education*, 6(3), pp. 325–338.

Bowers, C.A. (1995) *Educating for and Ecologically Sustainable Culture*, Albany, NY: SUNY Press.

Bowers, C.A. (2001) *Educating for Eco-justice and Community*, Athens, GA: University of Georgia Press.

Bown, L. (2000) 'Lifelong Learning: Ideas and Achievements at the Threshold of the Twenty-first Century', *Compare*, 30(3), pp. 341–351.

Braudel, F. (1981) 'Structures of Everyday Life: The Limits of the Possible', in Reynolds, S. (ed.) *Civilisation and Capitalism, 15th–18th Century*, Part 1, London: Collins.

Bray, M. (1999) *The Shadow Education System: Private Tutoring and its Implications for Planners*, Paris: UNESCO International Institute for Educational Planning.

Broadfoot, P. (2002) 'Editorial. Assessment for Lifelong Learning: Challenges and Choices', *Assessment in Education*, 9(1), pp. 5–7.

Brown, L. (2001) *Eco-economy – Building an Economy for the Earth*, Earth Policy Institute, London: Earthscan.

Brown, P. and Lauder, H. (2001) *Capitalism and Social Progress: The Future of Society in a Global Economy*, Basingstoke: Palgrave.

Brundtland Commission (1987) *Our Common Future*, The World Commission on Environment and Development, Oxford: Oxford University Press.

Bruner, J. (1966) *Toward a Theory of Instruction*, Cambridge, MA: Harvard University Press.

Bruner, J. (1986) *Actual Minds, Possible Worlds*, Cambridge, MA: Harvard University Press.

Bruner, J. (1990) *Acts of Meaning*, Cambridge, MA: Harvard University Press.

Buell, L. (1995) *The Environmental Imagination: Thoreau, Nature Writing and the Formation of American Culture*, Cambridge, MA: Harvard University Press.

Bull, David (1986) *Environment Liaison Centre*, World Commission on Environment Development Public Hearing, Nairobi, 23 September.

Carlsen, M.B. (1988) *Meaning-making: Therapeutic Processes in Adult Development*, New York: W.W. Norton.

Carr, M. and Claxton, G. (2002) 'Tracking the Development of Learning Dispositions', *Assessment in Education*, 9(1), pp. 9–37.

Casella, R. (1998) *The Theoretical Foundations of Cultural Studies in Education*, http://www.ed.uiuc.edu/EPS/PES-Yearbook/1998/casella.html.

Castells, M. (1996) *The Rise of the Network Society*, Oxford: Blackwell.

CEE (Council for Environmental Education), Field Studies Council, SEEC (Scottish Environmental Education Council), Shell Education Service and WWF–UK (World Wide Fund for Nature) (1999) *Lessons in Life: Sustainable Development Education*, London: Shell Education.

Christensen, C.U. and Schnack, K. (1992) 'Environment and Nature', in *School-improvement, Development and Innovation*, Copenhagen: The Royal Danish School of Educational Studies.

Clover, D., Follen, S. and Hall, B. (2000) *The Nature of Transformation: Environmental Adult Education*, 2nd edn, Toronto: University of Toronto Press.

Cohen, Jack and Stewart, Ian (1994) *The Collapse of Chaos: Discovering Simplicity in a Complex World*, New York: Viking.

Cole, M. (1995) *Cultural Psychology; a Once and Future Discipline*, Cambridge, MA: Harvard University Press.

Coote, A. and Lenaghan, J. (1997) *Citizens Juries: Theory into Practice*, London: Institute for Public Policy Research.

Corson, D. (1988) 'Making the Language of Education Policies More User-friendly', *Journal of Education Policy*, 3(3), pp. 249–260.

Council of the Earth (1992) *Environmental Education for Sustainable Societies and Global Responsibility*, NGO Treaty as part of the Global Forum, Rio de Janeiro, June 1992.

CDC (Curriculum Development Centre) – Environmental Education Committee (1975) 'A Proposal for the Support of Environmental Education in Australia', Interim Report, August, Canberra: Curriculum Development Centre.

Dake, K. and Thompson, M. (1993) 'The Meanings of Sustainable Development: Household Strategies for Managing Needs and Resources', in Wright, S.D., Dietz, T., Borden, R., Young,

G. and Guagnano, G. (eds) *Human Ecology: Crossing Boundaries*, Fort Collins, CO: The Society for Human Ecology.

Da Silva, T.T. (1999) 'The Poetics and Politics of Curriculum as Representation', *Pedagogy, Culture & Society*, 7(1), pp. 7–33.

de Bono, E. (1990) *I am Right – You are Wrong*, London: Viking.

de Geus, A. (1997) *The Living Company*, Boston, MA: Harvard Business School Press.

De Haan, G. and Harenberg, D. (1999) *Expertise 'Förderprogramme Bildungfür nachhaltige Entwicklung'*, MS. Berlin: Freie Universität.

Delruelle, E. (1993) *Le consensus impossible – Le différend éthique et politique chez H. Arendt et J. Habermas*, Brussels: Éditions OUSIA S.C.

Department of Home Affairs and Environment (DHAE) (1984) *A National Conservation Strategy for Australia*, Canberra: AGPS.

Department of Prime Minister and Cabinet (DPMC) (1990) *Ecologically Sustainable Development*, Canberra: AGPS.

Derrida, Jacques (1985) 'Letter to a Japanese Friend', in Wood, David and Bernasconi, Robert (eds) *Derrida and Différance*, Warwick: Parousia Press, pp. 1–5.

Devall, B. (1988) *Simple in Means, Rich in Ends*, Salt Lake City, UT: Peregrine Smith Books.

Devall, B. and Sessions, G. (1985) *Deep Ecology: Living as if Nature Mattered*, Salt Lake City, UT: Peregrine Smith Books.

DfID (2000a) 'Environmental Sustainability and Eliminating Poverty', Consultation document, London: Department for International Development.

DfID (2000b) 'Education for All – the Challenge of Universal Primary Education', Consultation document, London: Department for International Development.

Di Chiro, G. (1987) 'Environmental Education and the Question of Gender: A Feminist Critique', in Robottom, I. (ed.) *Environmental Education: Practice and Possibility*, ECT339 Environmental Education, Geelong: Deakin University.

Disinger, J.F. (1987a) *Environmental Education in K-12 Curricula*. ERIC/SMEAC Environmental Information Bulletin No. 2., Columbus: SMEAC Information Reference Center.

Disinger, J.F. (ed.) (1987b) *Trends and Issues in Environmental Education: EE in School Curricula. Reports of a Symposium and a Survey*. Environmental Education Information Reports, Columbus: SMEAC Information Reference Center.

Disinger, J.F. (1990) 'Environmental Education for Sustainable Development?', *Journal of Environmental Education*, 21(4), pp. 3–6.

Douglas, M. (1978) *Cultural Bias*, Occasional Paper No. 35, London: Royal Anthropological Institute of Great Britain and Ireland.

Douglas, M. (1982) *Essays in the Sociology of Perception*, London: Routledge and Kegan Paul.

Douglas, M. (1986) *How Institutions Think*, Syracuse, NY: Syracuse University Press.

Douglas, M., Gasper, D., Ney, S.T. and Thompson, M. (1998) 'Human Needs and Wants', in Rayner, S. and Malone, E. (eds) *Human Choice and Climate Change Volume One, The Societal Framework*, Columbus, OH: Battelle Press.

Drengson, A.R. (1991) 'Introduction: Environmental Crisis, Education and Deep Ecology', *The Trumpeter*, 3(3), pp. 97–98

Dreyfus, S.E. (1981) *Formal Models v Human Situational Understanding: Inherent Limitations in the Modelling of Busines Expertise*, mimeo, Schloss Laxenburg, Austria: International Institute for Applied Systems.

Economist, The (2002) 'Sustaining the Poor's Development', London: *The Economist*, 31 August 2002, p. 11.

Elias, N. (2000) *The Civilizing Process*, revised edn, Oxford: Blackwell.

Elliott, J. (1993) 'Professional Education and the Idea of a Practical Educational Science', in Elliott, J. (ed.) *Reconstructing Teacher Education*, London: Falmer Press.

Elliott, J. (1998) *The Curriculum Experiment: Meeting the Challenge of Social Change*, Buckingham: Open University Press.

Engleson, D.C. and Yocker, D.H. (1994) *Environmental Education: A Guide to Curriculum Planning*, 2nd edn, Bulletin Number 94371, Milwaukee, WI: Wisconsin Department of Public Instruction.

Escobar, A. (1995) *Encountering Development: The Making and Unmaking of the Third World*, Princeton, NJ: Princeton University Press.

Escobar, A. (1998) 'Whose Knowledge, Whose Nature? Biodiversity Conservation and Social Movements Political Ecology', *Journal of Political Ecology* (electronic journal), available at http://cbik.org/Sources/Whose%20Knowledge,%20whose%20Nature-Escobar.htm.

Esteva, G. and Prakash, M. (1998) *Grassroots Postmodernism*, London: Zed Books.

Esteva, J. (1997) 'Ambientalismo y educación. Hacia una educación popular ambiental en América Latina', in *Centro de Estudios Sociales y Ecológicos. Contribuciones educativas para sociedades sustentables*, Pátzcuaro, Michoacán, México: CESE, pp. 42–56.

Esteva, J. and Reyes, J. (1996) 'La perspectiva ambiental de las personas adulta', *La Piragua. Revista Latinoamericana de Educación y Política. Consejo de Educación de Adultos de América Latina*, 12–13, pp. 104–115.

Evans, J. and Boyden, S. (eds) (1970) *Education and the Environmental Crisis*, Canberra: Australian Academy of Science.

Fairclough, N. (1995) *Critical Discourse Analysis*, London: Longman.

Fensham, P.J. (1978) 'Stockholm to Tbilisi – The Evolution of Environmental Education', *Prospects*, 8(4), pp. 446–455.

Fensham, P.J. (1987) 'Environmental Education – a Tbilisi Benchmark', in Department of Arts, Heritage and Environmental (ed.) *Environmental Education – Past, Present and Future*, Proceedings of the Third National Environmental Education Seminar and Workshops, Canberra, 11–13 February, Canberra: AGPS.

Field, J. (2000) *Lifelong Learning and the New Educational Order*, Stoke-on-Trent: Trentham Books.

Fien, J. (1983) 'Humanistic Geography', in Huckle, J. (ed.) *Geographical Education: Reflection and Action*, Oxford: Oxford University Press.

Fien, J. (1993) *Education for the Environment: Critical Curriculum Theorising and Environmental Education*, Geelong: Deakin University Press.

Florida, R. (1995) 'Toward the Learning Region', *Futures*, 27(5), pp. 527–536.

Flyvberg, B. (1998) *Rationality and Power*, Chicago: University of Chicago Press.

Foster, J. (1999) 'What Price Interdisciplinarity? Crossing the Curriculum in Environmental Higher Education', *Journal of Geography in Higher Education*, 23(3), pp. 358–366.

Foster, J. (2001) 'Education *as* sustainability', *Environmental Education Research*, 7(2), pp. 153–165.

Foster-Turley, P. (1996) *Making Biodiversity Conservation Happen: The Role of Environmental Education and Communication*, Washington, DC: GreenCOM.

Fox, Warwick (1990) *Toward a Transpersonal Ecology: Developing New Foundations for Environmentalism*, Boston, MA: Shambhala.

Frankel, O. (1970) 'Chairman's Remarks', in Evans, J. and Boyden, S. (eds) *Education and the Environmental Crisis*, Canberra: Australian Academy of Science.

Freire, P. (1970) *Pedagogy of the Oppressed*, London: Penguin Books.

Fromm, E. (1975) *The Art of Loving*, London: Unwin.

Fukuyama, F. (1989) 'The End of History', *The National Interest*, 16(summer), pp. 3–18.

Fukuyama, F. (1992) *The End of History and the Last Man*, London: Penguin.

Gadamer, H.-G. (1975) *Truth and Method*, London: Sheed and Ward.

Gage, N.L. (1989) 'The Paradigm Wars and their Aftermath: A "Historical" Sketch of Research on Teaching since 1989', *Educational Researcher*, 18(7), pp. 4–10.

Geertz, C. (1973) *The Interpretation of Cultures*, New York: Basic Books.

Giroux, H.A. (1990) *Curriculum Discourse as Postmodernist Critical Practice*, ECS802 Curriculum Theory, Geelong: Deakin University.

Gleick, J. (1988) *Chaos*, London: Cardinal.

Gonzáles-Gaudiano, E. (1998) *Centro y periferia de la educación ambiental. Un enfoque anti-esencialista*, México: Mundi Prensa, 89 pp.

González-Gaudiano, E. (1999) 'Otra lectura a la historia de la educación ambiental en América Latina y el Caribe', *Tópicos en Educación Ambiental*, 1(1), pp. 9–26.

Gonzáles-Gaudiano, E. (2001) 'Complexity in Environmental Education', *Educational Philosophy and Theory*, 33(2), pp. 153–166.

Goodson, I. (1994) *Studying Curriculum*, Buckingham: Open University Press.

Gorz, A. (1999) *Reclaiming Work: Beyond the Wage-based Society*, Cambridge: Polity Press.

Gough, N. (1987a) 'Greening Education', in Hutton, D. (ed.) *Green Politics in Australia*, Sydney: Angus & Robertson.

Gough, N. (1987b) 'Learning with Environments: Towards an Ecological Paradigm for Education', in Robottom, I. (ed.) *Environmental Education: Practice and Possibility*, ECT339 Environmental Education, Geelong: Deakin University.

Gough, N. (1991) 'Narrative and Nature: Unsustainable Fictions in Environmental Education', *Australian Journal of Environmental Education*, 7, pp. 31–42.

Gough, N. (1999) 'Rethinking the Subject: (De)constructing Human Agency in Environmental Education Research', *Environmental Education Research*, 5(1), pp. 35–48.

Gough, N. (2001) 'Teaching in the *(Crash)* Zone: Manifesting Cultural Studies in Science Education', in Weaver, John A., Morris, Marla and Appelbaum, Peter (eds) *(Post) Modern Science (Education): Propositions and Alternative Paths*, New York: Peter Lang, pp. 249–273.

Gough, S.R. (2001) 'Editorial to the Special Issue of EER on the Language of Sustainability', *Environmental Education Research*, 7(2), pp. 117–120.

Gough, S.R. and Scott, W.A.H. (2001) 'Curriculum Development and Sustainable Development: Practices, Institutions and Literacies', *Educational Philosophy and Theory*, 33(2), pp. 137–152.

Graff, G. (1988) 'What Should We Be Teaching – When There is no "We"?', *The Yale Journal of Criticism*, 1(2), pp. 189–211.

Gray, J. (1998) *False Dawn*, London: Granta Books.

Green, A. (1994) 'Postmodernism and State Education', *Journal of Education Policy*, 9(1), pp. 67–83.

Greenall Gough, A. (1993) *Founders in Environmental Education*, Geelong: Deakin University Press.

Greenall Gough, A. and Robottom, I. (1993) 'Towards a Socially Critically Environmental Education: Water Quality Studies in a Coastal School', *Journal of Curriculum Studies*, 25(4), pp. 301–316.

Greene, M. (1995) *Releasing the Imagination, Essays on Education, the Arts and Social Change*, San Francisco: Jossey-Bass Publishers.

Gross, J. and Rayner, S. (1985) *Measuring Culture*, New York: Columbia University Press.

Guattari, F. (1997) *As três ecologias*, São Paulo: Papirus.

Gudynas, E. (1992) 'Los múltiples verdes del ambientalismo latinoamericano', *Neuva Sociedad, Caracas*, p. 122.

Habermas, J. (1971) *Knowledge and Human Interest*, Boston, MA: Beacon.

Habermas, J. (1981) *New Social Movements*, London: Telos.

Hall, R. (1989) 'Developing Environmental Awareness and Appreciation', in Fien, J., Gerber, R. and Wilson, P. (eds), *The Geography Teacher's Guide to the Classroom*, 2nd edn, Melbourne: Macmillan.

Hall, S. (ed.) (1997) *Representation: Cultural Representations and Signifying Practices*, London: Sage/Open University.

Hamm, B. and Muttagi, P.K. (1998) *Sustainable Development and the Future of Cities*, London: Intermediate Technology Publications, p. 2.

Handy, C. (1995a) *The Empty Raincoat*, London: Random House.

Handy, C. (1995b) *Beyond Certainty*, London: Random House.

Haraway, Donna J. (1989) *Primate Visions: Gender, Race, and Nature in the World of Modern Science*, New York: Routledge.

Haraway, Donna J. (1991) *Simians, Cyborgs, and Women: The Reinvention of Nature*, New York: Routledge.

Harding, C, (ed.) (1992) *Wingspan: Inside the Men's Movement*, New York: St. Martin's Press.

Harding, S. (1993) 'Rethinking Standpoint Epistemology: "What is Strong Objectivity?",' in Alcoff, Linda and Potter, Elizabeth (eds) *Feminist Epistemologies*, New York: Routledge, pp. 49–82.

Hargreaves, A. (ed.) (1997) *Rethinking Educational Change with Heart and Mind: 1997 ASCD Yearbook*, Alexandria, VA: Association for Supervision and Curriculum Development.

Harré, R., Brockmeier, J. and Mühlhausler, P. (1999) *Greenspeak; a Study of Environmental Discourse*, Thousand Oaks, CA: Sage.

Hart, P. (1979) 'Environmental Education: Identification of Key Characteristics and a Design for Curriculum Organization', unpublished doctoral dissertation, Burnaby, Canada: Simon Fraser University.

Hart, P. (1987) *Science for Saskatchewan Schools: A Review of Research Literature, Analysis and Recommendations*, Regina, Canada: Saskatchewan Instructional Development and Research Unit.

Hart, P. (1990) 'Environmental Education in Canada: Contemporary Issues and Future Possibilities', *Australian Journal of Environmental Education*, 6, pp. 45–65.

Hart, P. (1993) 'Alternative Perspectives in Environmental Education Research: Paradigm of Critical Reflective Inquiry', in Mrazek, R. (ed.) *Alternative Paradigms in Environmental Education Research*, Troy, OH: North American Association for Environmental Education, available at http://www.edu. uleth.ca/ciccte/naceer.pgs/pubpro.pgs/alternate/pubfiles/09.Hart.rev.htm.

Hart, P., Taylor, M. and Robottom, I. (1994) 'Dilemmas of Participatory Enquiry: A Case Study of Method-in-action', *Assessment & Evaluation in Higher Education*, (19)3, pp. 201–214.

Haste, H.E. (1996) 'Communitarianism and the Social Construction of Morality', *Journal of Moral Education*, 25(1), pp. 47–55.

Haste, H.E. (2001a) 'The New Citizenship of Youth in Rapidly Changing Nations', *Human Development*, 44(6), pp. 375–381.

Haste, H.E. (2001b) 'Ambiguity, Autonomy and Agency; Psychological Challenges to New Competence', in Rychen, D.S. and Salganik, L.H. (eds) *Defining and Selecting Key Competencies*, Seattle: Hogrefe & Huber, pp. 93–120.

Held, D. (1996) *Models of Democracy*, Cambridge: Polity Press.

Hendriks-Jansen, H. (1966) *Catching Ourselves in the Act: Situated Activity, Interactive Emergence, Evolution, and Human Thought*, Cambridge, MA: MIT Press, A Bradford Book.

Hesselink, F., Van Kempen, P.P. and Wals, A. (2000) *ESDebate – International Debate on Education for Sustainable Development*, Gland, Switzerland: The World Conservation Union.

Hirst, P.H. (1974) *Knowledge and the Curriculum*, London: Routledge and Kegan Paul.

Hlebowitsh, P. (1999a) 'The Burdens of the New Curricularist, *Curriculum Inquiry*, 29(3), pp. 343–354.

Hlebowitsh, P. (1999b) 'More on "the Burdens of the New Curricularist"', *Curriculum Inquiry*, 29(3), pp. 369–373.

Holling, C.S. (1979) 'Myths of Ecological Stability', in Smart, G. and Stansbury, W. (eds) *Studies in Crisis Management*, Montreal: Butterworth.

Holling, C.S. (1986) 'The Resilience of Terrestrial Ecosystems', in Clark, W. and Munn, R. (eds) *Sustainable Development of the Biosphere*, Cambridge: Cambridge University Press.

Holt, J.G. (1988) 'A Study of the Effects of Issue Investigation and Action Training on Characteristics Associated with Environmetnal Behavior in Non-gifted eighth Grade Students', unpublished research paper, southern Illinois University at Carbondale.

Hopkins, C. (1998) 'The Content of Education for Sustainable Development', in Scoullos, M.J. (ed.) *Environment and Society: Education for Public Awareness for Sustainability*, Proceedings of the Thessaloniki International Conference organised by the UNESCO and the Government of Greece, 8–12 December, 1997, Athens: University of Athens, MIOECSDE and Ministry for the Environment, Ministry of Education, pp. 169–172.

Hopkins, C., Damlamian, J. and López Ospina, G. (1996) 'Evolving towards Education for Sustainable Development: An International Perspective', *Nature and Resources*, 32(3), pp. 2–11.

Huckle, J. (1983) 'Environmental Education', in Huckle, J. (ed.) *Geographical Education: Reflection and Action*, Oxford: Oxford University Press.

Huckle, J. (1985) 'Geography and Schooling', in Johnston, R.J. (ed.) *The Future of Geography*, London: Methuen.

Huckle, J. (1986) 'Ten Red Questions to Ask Green Teachers', *Green Teacher*, 2, pp. 11–15.

Huckle, J. (1991) 'Education for Sustainability: Assessing Pathways to the Future', *Australian Journal of Environmental Education*, 7, pp. 43–62.

Hungerford, H.R. (1996) 'The Development of Responsible Environmental Citizenship: A Critical Challenge', *Journal of Interpretation Research*, 1(1), pp. 25–37.

Hungerford, H.R., Peyton, R.B. and Wilke, R.J. (1983) 'Yes, EE does have definition and structure', *Journal of Environmental Education*, 14(3), pp. 1–2.

Hungerford, H.R. and Volk, T. (1990) 'Changing Learner Behavior through Environmental Education', *Journal of Environmental Education*, 21(3), pp. 8–17.

Hungerford, H.R., Volk, T.L., Dixon, B.G., Marcinkowski, T.J. and Sia, A.P. (1988) *An Environmental Education Approach t the Training of Elementary Teachers: A Teachers Education Programme*, Paris: UNESCO/UNEP

Hungerford, H.R., Volk, T.L. and Ramsey, J.M. (1990) *A Prototype Environmental Education Curriculum for the Middle School*, Paris: UNESCO/UNEP.

Hutchinson, F.P. (1996) *Educating Beyond Violent Futures*, London and New York: Routledge.

Hyland, T. (1994) *Competences, Education and NVQs*, London: Cassell.

IAEA (1991) *International Advisory Committee, The International Chernobyl Project: Technical Report, Assessment of Radiological Consequences and Evaluation of Protective Measures, Part F: Health Impact, Section 3.11.3*, Vienna: IAEA, p. 389.

ICSIR (1985) *Report on Scientific Studies on the Release Factors Related to Bhopal Toxic Gas Leakage*, New Delhi: Indian Council of Scientific and Industrial Research, December.

International Union for the Conservation of Nature and Natural Resources (IUCN) (1980) *World Conservation Strategy*, Gland, Switzerland: IUCN.

Ison, R. and Russell, D. (2000) *Agricultural Extension and Rural Development – Breaking out of Traditions, a Second-order Systems Perspective*, Cambridge: Cambridge University Press.

Jacobs, M. (1993) *The Green Economy: Environment, Sustainable Development, and the Politics of the Future*, Vancouver: University of British Columbia Press.

Jänicke, M. (1979) *Wie das Industriesystem von seinen Mißständen profitiert*, Cologne.

Jensen, B.B. (1998) 'Handling, sundhed og undervisning – erfaringer fra Den Sundhedsfremmende Skole (Action, Health and Education – Experiences from the Health Promoting School)', *Research Journal of The Royal Danish School of Education*, 2, pp. 61–80.

Jensen, B.B. and Schnack, K. (1997) 'The Action Competence Approach in Environmental Education', *Environmental Education Research*, 3(2), pp. 163–178.

Jickling, B. (1991) 'Environmental Education, Problem Solving, and some Humility Please', *Trumpeter*, 8(3), pp. 153–155.

Jickling, B. (1992) 'Why I Don't Want my Children Educated for Sustainable Development', *Journal of Environmental Education*, 23(4), pp. 5–8.

Jickling, B. (1997) 'If Environmental Education is to Make Sense for Teachers, We Had Better Rethink How to Define it!', *Canadian Journal of Environmental Education*, 2, pp. 86–103.

Jickling, B. (1999) 'Beyond Sustainability: Should We Expect More from Education?', *Southern African Journal of Environmental Education*, 19, pp. 60–67.

Jickling, B. (2000) 'Education for Sustainability: A Seductive Idea, But is it Enough for My Grandchildren?', in Blanken H. (ed.) *NME met een duurzaam perspectief, essaybundel bij de slotconferentie NME Extra Impuls 1996–1999 (EE in a Sustainable Perspective: A Collection of Essays in the Context of the Final Conference of the Programme Extra Impulse EE 1996–1999)*, Amsterdam: NCDO, pp. 34–38.

Jörissen, J., Kopfmüller, J., Brandl, V. and Paetau, M. (1999) *Em integratives Konzept nachhaltiger Entwicklung*, Wissenschaftliche Berichte, Karlsruhe: Forschungszentrum Karlsruhe.

Kahn, H. and Pepper, T. (1980) *Will She Be Right? The Future of Australia*, St Lucia: University of Queensland Press.

Kahn, P. (1999) *The Human Relationship with Nature; Development and Culture*, Cambridge, MA: MIT Press.

Kant, I. (1787/1956), *Kritik der reinen Vernunft*, Hamburg: Felix Meiner Verlag.

Keddie, N. (1971) 'Classroom Knowledge', in Young, M. (ed.) *Knowledge and Control*, London: Collier-Macmillan.

Keen, Sam (1991) *Fire in the Belly: On Being a Man*, New York: Bantam.

Keller, Evelyn Fox (1992) 'Nature, Nurture, and the Human Genome Project', in Kevles, Daniel J. and Hood, Leroy (eds) *The Code of Codes: Scientific and Social Issues in the Human Genome Project*, Cambridge, MA: Harvard University Press, pp. 281–299.

Kemmis, S. and Fitzclarence, L. (1986) *Curriculum Theorising – beyond Reproduction Theory (ECS802: Curriculum Theory)*, Geelong: Deakin University Press.

Kemmis, S. and McTaggart, R. (1988) *The Action Research Planner*, 3rd edn, Geelong: Deakin University Press.

Kemmis, S. and Stake, R. (1988) *Evaluating Curriculum*, Geelong: Deakin University Press.

Klinger, G. (1980) ' The Effect of an Instructional Sequence on the Environmental Action Skills of a Sample of Southern Illinois Eighth Graders', unpublished masters thesis, southern Illinois University at Carbondale.

Knowles, M.N. (1980) *The Modern Practice of Adult Education: From Pedagogy to Andragogy*, revised and updated, Chicago: Follett.

Korten, D. (2001) *When Corporations Rule the World*, 2nd edn, San Francisco: Berrett-Koheler Publications Krimsky.

Krimsky, S. (1991) *Biotechnics: The Rise of Industrial Genetics*, New York: Praeger.

Kropotkin, P. (1985) [1899] *Fields, Factories and Workshops Tomorrow*, London: Freedom Press (with introduction by C. Ward).

Kuhn, T.S. (1996) *The Structure of Scientific Revolutions*, 3rd edn, Chicago: University of Chicago Press.

Laclau, Ernesto and Mouffe, Chantal (1985) *Hegemony and Socialist Strategy: Towards a Radical Democratic Politics*, London: Verso.

Laclau, E. (1990) *New Reflections on the Revolution of Our Time*, London: Verso.

Laclau, E. (1998) 'Política y los límites de la modernidad', in Buenfil, R.N. (ed.) *Debates políticos contemporáneos. En los márgenes de la modernidad*, México: Plaza y Valdés, pp. 55–73.

Lansing, Stephen J. (1991) *Priests and Programmers: Technologies of Power in the Engineered Landscape of Bali*, Princeton, NJ: Princeton University Press.

Latour, Bruno (1986) 'The Powers of Association', in Law, John (ed.) *Power, Action and Belief a New Sociology of Knowledge?*, London: Routledge and Kegan Paul, pp. 264–280.

Latour, Bruno (1991) 'Technology is Society Made Durable', in Law, John (ed.) *A Sociology of Monsters? Essays on Power, Technology and Domination*, London: Routledge, pp. 103–131.

Latour, Bruno (1992) 'Where Are the Missing Masses? Sociology of a few Mundane Artefacts', in Bijker, Wiebe E. and Law, John (eds) *Shaping Technology, Building Society: Studies in Sociotechnical Change*, Cambridge MA: The MIT Press, pp. 225–258.

Laurillard, D. (2002) *Rethinking University Teaching: A Conversational Framework for the Effective Use of Learning Technologies*, 2nd edn, London: RoutledgeFalmer.

Layton, D. (1973) *Science for the People*, London: Allen and Unwin.

Lefebre-Pinard, M. (1983) 'Understanding and Auto-control of Cognitive Functions: Implications for the Relationship between Cognition and Behavior', *International Journal of Behavioral Development*, 6(1), pp. 15–35.

Lewontin, R.C. (1991) *Biology as Ideology: The Doctrine of DNA*, New York: HarperCollins.

Lewontin, R.C. (1994) 'The Dream of the Human Genome', in Bender, Gretchen and Druckrey, Timothy (eds) *Culture on the Brink: Ideologies of Technology*, Seattle: Bay Press, pp. 106–127.

Lindblom, C.E. (1977) *Politics and Markets*, New York: Basic Books.

Lindblom, C.E. (1992) *Inquiry and Change: The Troubled Attempt to Understand and Shape Society*, New Haven, CT: Yale University Press.

Linke, R.D. (1980) *Environmental Education in Australia*, Sydney: Allen & Unwin.

Lomborg, B. (2001) *The Sceptical Environmentalist*, Cambridge: Cambridge University Press.

Lucas, A.M. (1979) *Environment and Environmental Education: Conceptual Issues and Curriculum Implications*, Melbourne: Australian International Press and Publications.

Luke, T. (1997) *Ecocritique. Contesting the Politics of Nature, Economy, and Culture*, Minneapolis, MN: University of Minnesota Press.

Lundgren, U.P. (1991) *Between Education and Schooling: Outlines of a Diachronic Curriculum Theory*, Geelong: Deakin University Press.

Lynch, G. (1974) 'Ideology and the Social Organisation of Educational Knowledge in England and Scotland 1840–1920', MA dissertation, Institute of Education, University of London.

Macbeth, D. (2001) 'On "Reflexivity" in Qualitative Research: Two Readings, and a Third', *Qualitative Inquiry*, 7(1), pp. 35–68.

MacDonald, M., Stem, C. and Snelson, D. (2002) *Report of the WWF-US Population and Gender Review*, Washington DC: WWF-US.

McClaren, M. (1987) 'The Problem of Curriculum Infusion in Environmental Education', in Disinger, J. (ed.) *Trends and Issues in Environmental Education: Environmental Education in School Curricula*, Colombus, OH: ERIC/NAEE.

Macedo, D. (ed.) (2000) *Chomsky on MisEducation*, Lanham, MD: Rowman and Littlefield.

Maher, M. (1988), 'The Powers that Be: Political Education through an Environmental Study', *Australian Journal of Environmental Education*, 4(3), pp. 1–8.

Makgoba, M. (ed.) (1999) *African Renaissance*, Mafube: Tafelberg.

Malone, T. (1995) 'Computers, Networks and the Corporation', *Scientific American*, special edition, *The Computer in the Twenty-first Century*, pp. 140–147.

Manes, Christopher (1990) *Green Rage: Radical Environmentalism and the Unmaking of Civilization*, Boston, MA: Little Brown.

March, J. (1988) *Decisions and Organizations*, New York: Blackwell.

Marcinkowski, T. (1990–1991) 'The New National Environment Education Act: A Renewal of Commitment', *Journal of Environmental Education*, 22(2), pp. 7–10.

Marcinkowski, T.J., Volk, T.L. and Hungerford, H.R. (1990) *An Environmental Education Approach to the Training of Middle Level Teachers: A Teacher Education Programme Specialization*, Paris: UNESCO/UNEP.

Merchant, C. (1980) *The Death of Nature: Women, Ecology and the Scientific Revolution*, New York: Harper & Row.

Merriam, S.B. and Caffarella, R.S. (1991) *Learning in Adulthood: A Comprehensive Guide*, San Francisco: Jossey-Bass.

Merriam, S.B. and Clark, M.C. (1993) 'Learning from Life Experience: What Makes it Significant?', *International Journal of Lifelong Education*, 12(2), pp. 129–138.

Mezirow, J. (1991) *Transformative Dimensions of Adult Learning*, San Francisco: Jossey-Bass.

Michael, D.N. and Anderson, W.T. (1986) 'Norms in Conflict and Confusion', in Didsbury, H. (ed.) *Challenges and Opportunities: From Now to 2001*, Washington, DC: World Future Society.

Minsch, J. (2000) *Nachhaltige Entwicklung I. Grundlagen nachhaltigen Wirtschaftens*, MS. Wien: Universität für Bodenkultur.

Mires, F. (1990) *El discurso de la naturaleza: Ecologia y política en América Latina*, San José, Costa Rica: Departmento Eduménico de Investigaciones.

Mires, F., George, S., Galeano, E., Munoz, F., Tamames, R. and Boff, L. (1996) *Ecología Solidaria*, Barcelona: Fundación Alfonso Comín-Trotta (Colección Estructuras y Procesos).

Morgan, G. (1989) *Creative Organisation Theory*, Newbury Park: Sage.

Mrazek, R. (ed.) (1993) *Alternative Paradigms in Environmental Education Research*, Troy, OH: NAAEE.

NACSO (2002) *Namibia's Community-based Natural Resource Management Programme*, Namibia: NACSO.

Naess, A. (1989) *Ecology, Community, and Lifestyle: Outline of an Ecosophy*, trans. and ed. David Rothenberg, Cambridge: Cambridge University Press.

Nagy, Imre V. (1981) *National Environment Protection Committee of the Patriotic People's Front, Hungary*, WCED Public Hearing, Moscow, 8 December.

National Science Board Commission on Precollege Education in Mathematics, Science and Technology (1983) *Cognition and Behavior Relevant to Education in Mathematics, Science, and Technology*, Federation of Behavioral, Psychological, and Cognitive Sciences and Technology. Washington, DC: National Science Foundation.

Norberg-Hodge, H. (1992) *Ancient Futures: Learning from Ladakh*, San Francisco: Sierra Club Books.

Norgaard, R.B. (1984) 'Coevolutionary Agricultural Development', *Economic Development and Cultural Change*, 32(2), pp. 528–535.

OECD (1996) *Lifelong Learning for All*, Paris: Organisation for Economic Co-operation and Development, pp. 94–97.

OECD (1997) *Desarrollo sustentable. Estrategias de la OCDE para el Siglo XXI*, Paris: OECD.

O'Hear, A. (1981) *Education, Society and Human Nature* London: Routledge and Kegan Paul.

Oldmeadow, H. (1992) 'The Past Disowned: The Political and Postmodernist Assault on the Humanities', *Quadrant*, 36(284), pp. 60–64.

Orellana, I. and Fauteux, S. (2000) 'Environmental Education: Tracing the Highpoint of its History', in Jarnet, A., Jickling, B., Sauvé, L., Wals, A. and Clarkin, P. (eds) *The Future of Environmental Education in a Postmodern World*, Whitehorse: Yukon College, pp. 2–12.

O'Riordan, T. (1989) 'The Challenge for Environmentalism', in Peet, R. and Thrift, N. (eds) *New Models in Geography*, Vol. 1, London: Unwin Hyman, pp. 77–102.

Palmer, J. (1998) *Environmental Education in the 21st Century: Theory, Practice, Progress and Promise*, London: Routledge.

Pamphilon, B. (1999) 'The Zoom Model: A Dynamic Framework for the Analysis of Life Histories', *Qualitative Inquiry*, 5(3), pp. 393–410.

Payne, P. (1999) 'Postmodern Challenges and Modern Horizons: Education "for Being for the Environment"', *Environmental Education Research*, 5(1), pp. 5–34.

Peters, M. (1996) *Poststructuralism, Politics and Education*, Westport, CT: Bergin & Garvey.

Peters, M. and Roberts, P. (eds) (1998) *Virtual Technologies and Tertiary Education*, Palmerston North, New Zealand: The Dunmore Press.

Peters, M.A. (2001) *Poststructuralism, Marxism and Neoliberalism: Between Theory and Politics*, Boulder, CA: Rowman & Littlefield.

Peters, M.A. (2002) (ed.) *Heidegger, Education and Modernity*, Boulder, CA: Rowman & Littlefield.

Peters, M.A. and Marshall, J.D. (1999) *Wittgenstein: Philosophy, Postmodernism, Pedagogy*, Westport, CT and London: Bergin & Garvey.

Peters, M.A., Marshall, J.D. and Smeyers, P. (2001) (eds) *Nietzsche's Legacy for Education: Past and Present Values*, Westport, CT and London: Bergin & Garvey.

Peters, T. (1993) *Liberation Management*, London: Pan Macmillan.

Peters-Grant, V.M. (1987) 'The Influence of Life Experiences in the Vocational Interests of Volunteer Environmental Workers', *Dissertation Abstracts International*, 47(10).

Peterson, N.J. (1982) 'Developmental Variables Affecting Environmental Sensitivity in Professional Environmental Educators', unpublished master's thesis, Southern Illinois University at Carbondale.

Plant, M. (2001) *Developing and Evaluating a Socially Critical Approach to Environmental Education at Philosophical and Methodological Levels in Higher Education*, Nottingham: Nottingham Trent University.

Posch, P. (1988) 'The Project "Environment and School Initiatives"', in OECD/CERI, *Environment and School Initiatives. Report of the International Conference on the Teaching and Learning of Environmental Issues in Primary and Secondary Schools*, Linz, Austria: Organization for Economic Cooperation and Development, Centre for Educational Research and Innovation.

Posch, P. (1991) 'Environment and Schools Initiatives: Background and Basic Premises of the Project', in Centre or Educational Research and Innovation, *Environment, Schools and Active Learning*, Paris: OECD, pp. 13–18.

Posch, P. (1999) 'The Ecologisation of Schools and its Implications for Educational Policy', *Cambridge Journal of Education*, 29(3), pp. 340–348.

Prakash, M. and Esteva, G. (1998) *Escaping Education*, New York: Peter Lang.

Pratt M.L. (1991) 'Arts of the Contact Zone', *Profession*, 91, pp. 33–40.

Prigogine, I. (1996) *El fin de las certidumbres*, Santiago, Chile: Andrés Bello.

Puiggrós, A. (1996) 'Refundamentación político pedagógica de la educación popular en la transición al Siglo XXI', *La Piragua. Revista Latinoamericana de Educación y Política. Consejo de Educación de Adultos de América Latina*, 12–13, pp. 10–18.

Putnam, R.D. (2001) *Bowling Alone*, New York: Simon & Schuster.

Quicke, J. (1999) *A Curriculum for Life: Schools for a Democratic Learning Society*, Buckingham: Open University Press.

Quicke, J. (2000) 'A New Professionalism for a Collaborative Culture of Organizational Learning in Contemporary Society', *Educational Management and Administration*, 28(3), pp. 299–316.

Radnofsky, M. (1996) 'Qualitative Models: Visually Representing Complex Data in an Image/Text Balance', *Qualitative Inquiry*, 2(4), pp. 385–410.

Rainbird, H. (2000) 'Skilling the Unskilled: Access to Work-based Learning and the Lifelong Learning Agenda', *Journal of Education and Work*, 13(2), pp. 183–197.

Ramsey, J. *et al.* (1981) 'The Effects of Environmental Action and Environmental Case Study Instruction on the Oven Environmental Behavior of Eigth-grade Student', *Journal of Environmental Education*, 13(1), pp. 24–30.

Ramsey, J.M. (1989) 'A Study of the Effects of Issue Investigation and Action Training on Characteristics Associated with Environmental Behavior in Seventh Grade Students', *Dissertation Abstracts International*, 49(7) p. 1754–A.

Rauch, F. (2000a) 'Schools – A Place of Ecological Learning', *Environmental Education Research* 6(3), pp. 245–258.

Rauch, F. (2000b) *Schulentwicklung im Spiegel von Umweltbildung, externer Unterstützung und Schulleitung*, MS. Klagenfurt: IFF.

Rauch, F. (2002) 'The Potential of Education for Sustainable Development for Reform in Schools', *Environmental Education Research*, 8(1), pp. 43–51.

Rawls, J. (1971) *A Theory of Justice*, Oxford: Oxford University Press.

Rees, G., Gorard, S., Fevre, J. and Furlong, J. (2000) 'Participating in the Learning Society', in Coffield, F. (ed.) *Differing Visions of a Learning Society*, Research Findings Volume 2, Bristol: Policy Press, pp. 171–192.

Rees, W. (1989) *Defining Sustainable Development* (CHS Research Bulletin), Vancouver, British Columbia: UBC Centre for Human Settlements.

Reid, W.A. (1999) *Curriculum as Institution and Practice: Essays in the Deliberative Tradition*, Mahwah, NJ: Lawrence Erlbaum.

Reisch, L.A. (2001) 'Time and Wealth: The Role of Time and Temporalities for Sustainable Patterns of Consumption', *Time and Society*, 10(2/3), pp. 367–385.

Rescher, N. (1993) *Pluralism – Against the Demand for Consensus*, New York and Oxford: Clarendon Press.

Rickinson, M. (2001) 'Learners and Learning in Environmental Education: A Critical Review of the Evidence', *Environmental Education Research*, 7(3), special issue, pp. 208–320.

Rist, G. (1996) *Le développement – Histoire d'une croyance occidentale*, Paris: Sciences Po.

Robottom, I. (1983) 'Science: A Limited Whole for Environmental Education?', *The Australian Science Teachers' Journal*, 29(1), pp. 27–31.

Robottom, I. (1987) 'Towards Enquiry-based Professional Development in Environmental Education', in Robottom, I. (ed.) *Environmental Education: Practice and Possibility*, ECT339 Environmental Education, Geelong: Deakin University.

Robottom, I. and Hart, P. (1993) *Research in Environmental Education: Engaging the Debate*, Geelong: Deakin University Press.

Rorty, Richard (1979) *Philosophy and the Mirror of Nature*, Princeton, NJ: Princeton University Press.

Rorty, Richard (1989) *Contingency, Irony, and Solidarity*, Cambridge and New York: Cambridge University Press.

Rosa, E.A. (2000) '*Modern Theories of Society and the Environment: The Risk Society*', in Spaargaren, G. Mol, A. and Buttel, F. (eds) *Environment and Global Modernity*, London: Sage.

Ross, A. (1994) *The Chicago Gangster Theory of Life: Nature's Debt to Society*, New York: Verso.

Rosue, J. (1987) *Knowledge and Power: Toward a Political Philosophy of Science*, Ithaca, NY: Cornell University Press.

RSA (1997) *White Paper on Environmental Management Policy for South Africa*. Pretoria: Government Printer.

Runnals, David (1986) *International Institute for Environment and Development*, WCED Public Hearing, Ottawa, 26–27 May.

Rushkoff, D. (1997) *Children of Chaos. Surviving the End of the World as We Know it*, London: Harper-Collins.

Sachs, W. (1991) 'Environment and Development: The Story of a Dangerous Liaison', *The Ecologist*, 21(6), pp. 253–257.

SAIRR (1995) *Race Relations Survey 1994/1995*, Johannesburg: SAIRR.

Sakaiya, T. (1991) *The Knowledge – Value Revolution or a History of the Future*, Tokyo: Kodansha International.

Sale, K. (1991) *Dwellers in the Land: The Bioregional Vision*, Philadelphia, PA: New Society Publishers.

Sanera, M. (1998) 'Environmental Education: Promise and Performance', *Canadian Journal of Environmental Education*, 3, pp. 9–26.

Sauvé, L. (1999) 'Environmental Education, between Modernity and Postmodernity – Searching for an Integrative Framework', *Canadian Journal of Environmental Education*, 4, pp. 9–35.

Sauvé, L. and Berryman, T. (2001) 'Contre de nouvelles aliénations', *Politis – Hors-Série*, 34, décembre 2001–janvier 2002, Paris: Éditions SA, p. 18.

Sauvé, L., Berryman, T. and Brunelle, R. (2000) 'International Proposals for Environmental Education: Analysing a Ruling Discourse', *Actes de la conférence internationale sur l'éducation relative à l'environnement (Environmental Education in the Context of Education for the 21st Century: Prospects and Possibilities)*, Larisa: Grèce, 6–8 octobre 2000, pp. 42–63.

Schama, S. (1995) *Landscape and Memory*, London: HarperCollins.

Schnack, K. (2000) 'Action Competence as a Curriculum Perspective', in Jensen, B.B., Schnack, K. and Simovska, V. (eds) *Critical Environmental and Health Education*, Copenhagen: The Danish University of Education, pp. 107–126.

Scholl, M. (1983) 'A Survey of Significant Childhood Learning Experiences of Suburban/Urban Environmentalists', paper presented at the 12th Annual Conference of the North American Association for Environmental Education, Ypsilanti, Michigan.

Schön, Donald A. (1967) *Technology and Change: The New Heraclitus*, New York: Delacorte Press.

Schuller, T. and Field, J. (1998) 'Social Capital, Human Capital and the Learning Society', *International Journal of Lifelong Education*, 17(4), pp. 226–235.

Schwab, J.J. (1969) 'The Practical: A Language for Curriculum', *School Review*, 78, pp. 1–24.

Schwab, J.J. (1978) 'The "Impossible" Role of the Teacher in Progressive Education', in Westbury, I., and Wilkof, N.J. (eds) *Science, Curriculum and Liberal Education*, Chicago: University of Chicago Press, pp. 170–171.

Schwandt, T. (1999) 'On Understanding Understanding', *Qualitative Inquiry*, 5(4), pp. 451–464.

Schwarz, M. and Thompson, M. (1990) *Divided We Stand: Redefining Politics, Technology and Social Choice*, Philadelphia, PA: University of Pennsylvania Press.

Scott, S., Spenser, B. and Thomas, A. (eds) (1998) *Learning for Life: Canadian Readings in Adult Education*, Toronto: Thompson Educational Publishing Inc.

Scott, W.A.H. and Oulton, C.R. (1999) 'Environmental Education: Arguing the Case for Multiple Approaches', *Educational Studies*, 25(1), pp. 117–125.

Scott, W.A.H. (1995) 'Diversity and Opportunity – Reflections on Environmental Education within Initial Teacher Education Programmes across the European Union', in Brinkman, F.G. and Scott, W.A.H. (eds) *ATEE Cahier No.8: Environmental Education into Initial Teacher Education: 'The State of the Art'*, Brussels: Association of Teacher Education in Europe.

Scott, W.A.H. (2002) *Sustainability and Learning: What Role for the Curriculum?*, Inaugural Professorial Lecture, University of Bath.

Scott, W.A.H. and Reid, A.D. (2001) 'Exploring Our Responsibilities: A Critical Commentary on Education, Sustainability and Learning', *Environmental Education*, 66, pp. 23–24.

SDEP (Sustainable Development Education Program) (1992) *The Rationale for a Sustainable Development Education Program: April, 1992*, unpublished paper.

Segnestam, Mats (1985) *Swedish Society for the Conservation of Nature*, WCED Public Hearing, Oslo, 24–25 June.

Seligman, M. (1992) *Learned Optimism*, Simon & Schuster.

Sen, A. (1999) *Development as Freedom*, Oxford: Oxford University Press.

Senge, P. (1990) *The Fifth Discipline*, New York: Doubleday/Currency.

Senge, P. (1992) *The Fifth Discipline: The Art and Practice of the Learning Organisation*, Sydney: Random House.

Sessions, G. (1995) *Deep Ecology for the 21st Century: Readings on the Philosophy and Practice of the New Environmentalism*, Boston, MA: Shambhala.

Simpson, P.R. (1989) *The Effects of an Extended Case Study on Citizenship Behavior and Associated Variables in Fifth and Sixth Grade Students*, unpublished doctoral dissertation, Southern Illinois University at Carbondale.

Slater, F. and Fien, J. (1983) 'Behavioural Geography', in Huckle, J. (ed.) *Geographical Education: Reflection and Action*, Oxford: Oxford University Press.

Slocombe, D.S. and Van Bers, C. (1991) 'Seeking Substance in Sustainable Development', *Journal of Environmental Education*, 23(1), pp. 11–18.

Soetaert, R., Top, L. and Eeckhout, B. (1996) 'Art and Literature in Environmental Education: Two Research Projects', *Environmental Educational Research*, 2(1), pp. 63–70.

Stables, A.W.G. (1993) 'English and Environmental Education: The Living Nation in Macbeth', *The Use of English*, 44(3), pp. 218–225.

Stables, A.W.G. (1996) 'Paradox in Compound Educational Policy Slogans: Evaluating Equal Opportunities in Subject Choice', *British Journal of Educational Studies*, 44(2), pp. 159–167.

Stables, A.W.G. (1998) 'Environment Literacy: Functional, Cultural, Critical. The Case of the SCAA Guidelines', *Environmental Education Research*, 4(2), pp. 155–164.

Stables, A.W.G. (2001a) 'Who Drew the Sky? Conflicting Assumptions in Environmental Education', *Educational Philosophy & Theory*, 33(2), pp. 245–256.

Stables, A.W.G. (2001b) 'Language and Meaning in Environmental Education: An Overview', *Environmental Education Research*, 7(2), pp. 121–128.

Stables, A.W.G. and Scott, W.A.H. (1999) 'Environmental Education and the Discourses of Humanist Modernity: Redefining Critical Environmental Literacy', *Educational Philosophy and Theory*, 31(2), pp. 145–155.

Stables, A.W.G. and Scott, W.A.H. (2001a) 'Post-humanist Liberal Pragmatism? Environmental Education out of Modernity', *Journal of Philosophy of Education*, 35(2), pp. 269–279.

Stables, A.W.G. and Scott, W.A.H. (2001b) 'Editorial' (special edition 'Education and the Environment'), *Educational Philosophy and Theory*, 33(2), pp. 133–135.

Stavrakakis, Y. (1997) 'Green Ideology: A Discursive Reading', *Journal of Political Ideologies*, 2(3), pp. 259–278.

Stavrakakis, Y. (1999) 'Fantasía verde y lo Real de la naturaleza: elementos de una crítica lacaniana del discurso ideológico verde', *Tópicos en Educación Ambiental*, 1(1), pp. 47–58.

Stenhouse, L. (1967) *Culture and Education*, London: Nelson Books.

Stenhouse, L. (1975) *An Introduction to Curriculum Research and Development*, London: Heinemann.

Stenhouse, L. (1980) 'Curriculum Research and the Art of the Teacher', *Study of Society*, 11(1), pp. 14–15.

Sterling, S. (1990a) 'Environment, Development, Education: Towards an Holistic View', in Lacey, C. and Williams, R. *Deception, Demonstration and Debate: Towards a Critical Environment and Development Education*, London: World Wide Fund for Nature (UK) and Kogan Page.

Sterling, S. (1990b) 'Environmental Education and the Green Debate – Relationships and Response', paper presented at the 'Ideas into Action' European Environmental Education Conference, Glasgow.

Sterling, S. (2001) *Sustainable Education – Re-visioning Learning and Change*, Schumacher Society Briefing No. 6, Dartington: Green Books.

Stevenson, R. (1987) 'Schooling and Environmental Education: Contradictions in Purpose and Practice', in Robottom, I. (ed.) *Environmental Education: Practice and Possibility*, Victoria, Australia: Deakin University Press.

Stokking, H., van Aert, L., Meijberg, W. and Kaskens, A. (1999) *Evaluating Environmental Education*, Gland/Cambridge: IUCN.

Strain, M. (2000a) 'Editorial', *Educational Management and Administration*, 28(3), pp. 243–246.

Strain, M. (2000b) 'Schools in a Learning Society: New Purposes and Modalities of Learning in Late Modern Society', *Educational Management and Administration*, 28(3), pp. 281–298.

Stromquist, N. and Monkman, K. (eds) (2000) *Globalization and Education*, Lanham, MD: Rowman and Littlefield.

Tanner, T. (1980) 'Significant Life Experience: A New Research Area in Environmental Education', *Journal of Environmental Education*, 11(4), pp. 20–24.

Tesh, S.N. (1988) *Hidden Arguments: Political Ideology and Disease Prevention Policy*, New Brunswick, NY: Rutgers University Press.

Tharp, R. and Gallimore, R. (1988) *Rousing Minds to Life*, Cambridge: Cambridge University Press.

Tharp, R. and Gallimore, R. (1991) 'Theories of Teaching as Assisted Performance', in Light, P., Sheldon, P. and Woodhead, M. (eds) *Learning to Think*, London: Routledge, pp. 42–59.

Thompson, M. (1983a) 'Postscript: A Cultural Basis for Comparison', in Kunreuther, H.C. *et al.*, *Risk Analysis and Decision Processes*, Berlin: Springer.

Thompson, M. (1983b) 'The Aesthetics of Risk: Culture or Context?', in Schwing, R. and Albers, W. (eds) *Societal Risk Assessment*, New York: Plenum.

Thompson, M. (1997) 'Security and Solidarity: An Anti-reductionist Framework for Thinking about the Relationship between Us and the Rest of Nature', *The Geographical Journal*, 163(2), pp. 141–149.

Thrift, N. (1996) *Spatial Formations*, London: Sage.

Tilbury, D. and Walford, R. (1996) 'Grounded Theory: Defying the Dominant Paradigm in Environmental Education Research', in Williams, M. (ed.) *Understanding Geographic and Environmental Education: The Role of Research*, London: Cassell, pp. 51–64.

Timmerman, P. (1986) 'Myths and Paradigms of Interactions between Development and Environment', in Clark, W.C. and Munn, R.E. (eds) *Sustainable Development of the Biosphere*, Cambridge: Cambridge University Press.

Tisdess, J.E. (1993) 'Feminism and Adult Learning: Power, Pedagogy and Practice', *New Directions for Adult and Continuing Education*, 57, pp. 10–15.

Toffler, A. (1990) *Powershift: Knowledge, Wealth and Violence at the Edge of the 21st Century*, New York: Bantam.

UK Department for Education and Skills (DfES) (1999) *The Learning Age*, London: DfES.

UN Development Programme (1999) *Human Development Reports*, Oxford: Oxford University Press.

UN Environment Programme (2000) *Global Environmental Outlook*, Nairobi: UN Environment Programme.

UNESCO (1978) *Intergovernmental Conference on Environmental Education, Tbilisi, USSR, 14–26 October 1977: Final Report*. Paris: UNESCO.

UNESCO (1980) *Environmental Education in the Light of the Tbilisi Conference*, Paris: UNESCO.

UNESCO (with UNEP) (1988) *International Strategy for Action in the Field of Environmental Education and Training for the 1990s*, Paris and Nairobi: UNESCO/UNEP.

UNESCO (1997) *Éduquer pour un avenir viable: Une vision transdisciplinaire pour l'action concertée*, International Conference on Environment and Society, Thessaloniki, Greece, December 8–12, 1997.

United Nations (1992) *Agenda 21: Chapter 36*, New York: United Nations, pp. 221–227

United Nations (2002) *Johannesburg Summit 2002: Key Commitments, Targets and Timetables from the Johannesburg Plan of Implementation*, New York: United Nations.

United States Global Change Research Information Office (1997) *Education for Sustainability: An Agenda for Action*, Washington, DC: Global Change Research Information Office.

Vaillancourt, J.G. (1992) 'Le développement durable ou le "compromis" de la Commission Brundtland', in *Collectif, L'avenir d'un monde fini – Cahiers de la Recherche éthique*, Montréal: Fides, pp. 17–44.

Van Slyck, P. (1997) 'Repositioning Ourselves in the Contact Zone', *College English*, 59(2), February, pp. 149–170.

Vygotsky, L.S. (1962) *Thought and Language*, Cambridge, MA: MIT Press.

Wals, A.E.J. (1993) 'What You Can't Measure Still Exists!', in Mrazek, R. (ed.) *Alternative Paradigms in Environmental Education Research*, Troy, OH: NAAEE, pp. 297–298.

Wals, A.E.J. and Jickling, B. (2000) 'Process-based Environmental Education: Setting Standards without Standardizing', in Jensen, B.B., Schnack, K. and V. Simovska (eds) *Critical Environmental and Health Education*, Copenhagen: Royal School of Educational Studies.

Wals, A.E.J. and van der Leij, T. (1997) 'Alternatives to National Standards for Environmental Education: Process-based Quality Assessment', *Canadian Journal of Environmental Education*, 2, pp. 7–28.

Walters, S. and Manicom, L. (1996) 'Introduction', in Walters, S. and Manicom, L. (eds) *Gender in Popular Education*, London: Zed Books.

WCED (World Commission on Environment and Development) (1987) *Our Common Future*, London: Oxford University Press.

WCED (World Commission on Environment and Development) (1993) *Agenda 21 – Sustainable Development Action Program – Rio Declaration on Environment and Development*, United Nations Conference on Environment and Development, June 1992, Rio de Janeiro, Brazil. New York: United Nations.

Weber, M. (1958) *The Protestant Ethic and the Spirit of Capitalism*, New York: Free Press.

Weiler, K. (1988) *Women Teaching for Change: Gender, Class and Power*, South Hadley, MA: Begin & Garvey.

Welton, M. (ed.) (1995) *In Defense of the Lifeworld; Critical Perspectives on Adult Learning*, Albany, NY: State University of New York Press.

Westbury, I. (1999) 'The Burdens and the Excitement of the "New" Curriculum Research: A Response to Hlebowitsh's "The Burdens of the New Curriculuarist"', *Curriculum Inquiry*, 29(3), pp. 355–364.

Wildemeersch, D., Finger, M. and Jansen, T. (eds) (1998) *Education and Social Responsibility*, Frankfurt, Germany: Peter Lang Verlag.

Wilkins, R. (2000) 'Leading the Learning Society: The Role of Local Education Authorities', *Educational Management and Administration*, 28(3), pp. 339–352.

Williamson, O. (1975) *Markets and Hierarchies*, New York: Free Press.

Wills, Christopher (1991) *Exons, Introns, and Talking Genes: The Science Behind the Human Genome Project*, New York: Basic Books.

Wilson, E.O. (1998) *Consilience: The Unity of Knowledge*, New York: Alfred A. Knopf.

Wilson, J. (1969) *Thinking with Concepts*, Cambridge: Cambridge University Press.

World Resources Institute (2000) *The Fraying Web of Life*, Washington, DC: World Resources Institute.

WWF (1999) *Education and Conservation: An Evaluation of the Contributions of Education Programmes to Conservation within the WWF Network* [Final Report], Gland/Washington: WWF International and WWF-US.

WWF (2002) 'Field Staff Comment', *WWF Population, Gender and Environment Forum*, Washington DC: WWF-US.

Young, M. (1976) 'The Schooling of Science', in Whitty, G. and Young, M. (eds) *Explorations in the Politics of School Knowledge*, Driffield: Nafferton Books.

Young, M.D.F. (1998) *The Curriculum of the Future: From the 'New Sociology of Education' to a Critical Theory of Learning*, London: Falmer.

Zais, R. (1976) *Curriculum: Principles and Foundations*, New York: Harper & Row.

INDEX

Note: **Bold** page references indicates authorship of a reading or vignette.